Role of Leadership in Facilitating Healing and Renewal in Times of Organizational Trauma and Change

Lynda Byrd-Poller
Thomas Nelson Community College, USA

Jennifer L. Farmer
Renewed Mindset LLC, USA

Valerie Ford
ISP Global Communications LLC, USA

A volume in the Advances in Human Resources Management and Organizational Development (AHRMOD) Book Series

IGI Global
PUBLISHER of TIMELY KNOWLEDGE

Published in the United States of America by
IGI Global
Business Science Reference (an imprint of IGI Global)
701 E. Chocolate Avenue
Hershey PA, USA 17033
Tel: 717-533-8845
Fax: 717-533-8661
E-mail: cust@igi-global.com
Web site: http://www.igi-global.com

Library of Congress Cataloging-in-Publication Data

Names: Byrd-Poller, Lynda, 1967- editor. | Farmer, Jennifer, 1976- editor. | Ford, Valerie, 1961- editor.
Title: Role of leadership in facilitating healing and renewal in times of organizational trauma and change / Lynda Byrd-Poller, Jennifer Farmer, and Valerie Ford, editor.
Description: Hershey, PA : Business Science Reference, [2022] | Includes bibliographical references and index. | Summary: "This book will highlight global perspectives and present new and significant information and observations about organizational trauma and offer insights derived from a solidly and sufficiently broad knowledge base of theory, research and/or practice"-- Provided by publisher.
Identifiers: LCCN 2021024025 (print) | LCCN 2021024026 (ebook) | ISBN 9781799870166 (hardcover) | ISBN 9781799870173 (paperback) | ISBN 9781799870180 (ebook)
Subjects: LCSH: Quality of work life. | Psychology, Industrial. | Psychic trauma. | Organizational sociology. | Leadership.
Classification: LCC HD6955 .R64 2022 (print) | LCC HD6955 (ebook) | DDC 331.25/6--dc23
LC record available at https://lccn.loc.gov/2021024025
LC ebook record available at https://lccn.loc.gov/2021024026

This book is published in the IGI Global book series Advances in Human Resources Management and Organizational Development (AHRMOD) (ISSN: 2327-3372; eISSN: 2327-3380)

British Cataloguing in Publication Data
A Cataloguing in Publication record for this book is available from the British Library.

All work contributed to this book is new, previously-unpublished material. The views expressed in this book are those of the authors, but not necessarily of the publisher.

For electronic access to this publication, please contact: eresources@igi-global.com.

Advances in Human Resources Management and Organizational Development (AHRMOD) Book Series

Patricia Ordóñez de Pablos
Universidad de Oviedo, Spain

ISSN:2327-3372
EISSN:2327-3380

Mission

A solid foundation is essential to the development and success of any organization and can be accomplished through the effective and careful management of an organization's human capital. Research in human resources management and organizational development is necessary in providing business leaders with the tools and methodologies which will assist in the development and maintenance of their organizational structure.

The **Advances in Human Resources Management and Organizational Development (AHRMOD) Book Series** aims to publish the latest research on all aspects of human resources as well as the latest methodologies, tools, and theories regarding organizational development and sustainability. The **AHRMOD Book Series** intends to provide business professionals, managers, researchers, and students with the necessary resources to effectively develop and implement organizational strategies.

Coverage

- Employee Evaluation
- Coaching and Mentoring
- Human Resources Development
- Employee Benefits
- Collaborative Method
- Disputes Resolution
- Organizational Learning
- Upward Feedback
- Personnel Retention
- Outsourcing HR

IGI Global is currently accepting manuscripts for publication within this series. To submit a proposal for a volume in this series, please contact our Acquisition Editors at Acquisitions@igi-global.com or visit: http://www.igi-global.com/publish/.

The Advances in Human Resources Management and Organizational Development (AHRMOD) Book Series (ISSN 2327-3372) is published by IGI Global, 701 E. Chocolate Avenue, Hershey, PA 17033-1240, USA, www.igi-global.com. This series is composed of titles available for purchase individually; each title is edited to be contextually exclusive from any other title within the series. For pricing and ordering information please visit http://www.igi-global.com/book-series/advances-human-resources-management-organizational/73670. Postmaster: Send all address changes to above address.

Titles in this Series

For a list of additional titles in this series, please visit:
http://www.igi-global.com/book-series/advances-human-resources-management-organizational/73670

Effective Strategies for Communicating Insights in Business
Ross Jackson (Wittenberg University, USA) and Amanda Reboulet (Jacoulet, USA)
Business Science Reference • ©2021 • 261pp • H/C (ISBN: 9781799839644) • US $195.00

Handbook of Research on Remote Work and Worker Well-Being in the Post-COVID-19 Era
Daniel Wheatley (University of Birmingham, UK) Irene Hardill (Northumbria University, UK) and Sarah Buglass (Nottingham Trent University, UK)
Business Science Reference • ©2021 • 420pp • H/C (ISBN: 9781799867548) • US $265.00

Cases on Critical Practices for Modern and Future Human Resources Management
Devi Akella (Albany State University, USA) Niveen Eid (Birzeit University, Palestine) and Anton Sabella (Birzeit University, Palestine)
Business Science Reference • ©2021 • 322pp • H/C (ISBN: 9781799858201) • US $195.00

Asian Women in Corporate America Emerging Research and Opportunities
Sambhavi Lakshminarayanan (Medgar Evers College, City University of New York, USA)
Business Science Reference • ©2021 • 263pp • H/C (ISBN: 9781799843849) • US $185.00

Critical Issues on Changing Dynamics in Employee Relations and Workforce Diversity
Radha Yadav (Dayananda Sagar University, India) Priyanka Panday (Doon Business School, India) and Naman Sharma (Indian Institute of Foreign Trade, India)
Business Science Reference • ©2021 • 326pp • H/C (ISBN: 9781799835158) • US $215.00

Handbook of Research on Autopoiesis and Self-Sustaining Processes for Organizational Success
Małgorzata Pańkowska (University of Economics in Katowice, Poland)
Business Science Reference • ©2021 • 432pp • H/C (ISBN: 9781799867135) • US $275.00

Designing and Implementing HR Management Systems in Family Businesses
Luca Gnan (University of Rome "Tor Vergata", Italy) and Giulia Flamini (University of Rome "Tor Vergata", Italy)
Business Science Reference • ©2021 • 368pp • H/C (ISBN: 9781799848141) • US $195.00

Transforming Human Resource Functions With Automation
Anchal Pathak (Bule Hora University, Ethiopia) and Shikha Rana (IMS Unison University, India)
Business Science Reference • ©2021 • 192pp • H/C (ISBN: 9781799841807) • US $195.00

IGI Global
PUBLISHER of TIMELY KNOWLEDGE

701 East Chocolate Avenue, Hershey, PA 17033, USA
Tel: 717-533-8845 x100 • Fax: 717-533-8661
E-Mail: cust@igi-global.com • www.igi-global.com

Editorial Advisory Board

List of Reviewers

Table of Contents

Detailed Table of Contents

studies by offering leaders a framework and specific ways to understand and consequently embrace and harness uncertainty. With the turmoil of 2020 as backdrop, effective leaders will need to master 3 tasks: 1) to pace the changes to which their teams are exposed, 2) to shape how changes are perceived by their team, and 3) to manage the team's emotional reactions to change. As leaders envision the future, guide choices, tame apprehension, regulate expectations, experiment nimbly, and collaborate frequently, they will be able to channel the pressures of change to create positive outcomes for their teams and organizations. More importantly, organizations that create routines and processes that encourage, develop, and enable these behaviors internally will lead in a world where customer needs, employee demands, and shareholder expectations are continuously evolving.

This chapter provides the reader with background and discussion regarding the transformational leadership model developed by James MacGregor Burns in 1978. The theory was further refined by Bernard Bass through the 1980s and 1990s and has become a hallmark for leaders who wish to embrace change and improve their organization's performance. Collaboration, empathy, trust, and a genuine concern for all employees or followers in the organization are vital to the success of the transformational leader. A comparison of the theory of instructional leadership to transformational leadership provides the reader with an understanding of the differences between these leadership models. Discussion shifts to focus on how trauma negatively affects employees and organizations and how the elements and practices of transformational leadership can work to bring healing and wholeness to school communities and weather the potentially negative effects that change has on a learning community.

Significant changes in organizational leadership are often accompanied by organizational members suffering from trauma. This situation is not for the faint of heart; however, it is an opportunity to employ a leadership style that enables an inviting and safe environment. This "culture of care" maintains efficiency and clearly articulates the vision of the organization, while addressing its mission and goals. Leading during a time of turmoil, trauma, and drastic change requires a leader to be intentional. The leader must know who they are, what they believe, and what they value. They must establish a clear path for the organization, and plan for the unexpected. The leader's compassion, consistency, empathy, fairness, honesty, professionalism, and transparency will serve as the standard by which all others follow.

This chapter will embody a day in the life of a licensed therapist and four individuals (who are leaders from various professional backgrounds) with a universal trauma response to the COVID-19 pandemic. On any given day, their jobs are not for the faint of heart; they are accustomed to seeing people at their nadir. However, this pandemic has made them question their resiliency, tapped into their reserves, and exhausted their previous effective coping mechanisms. In an effort to seek refuge and respite, their answers lie in their last resort: self-care (something none of them make time for, but something all of them require). Through their collaborative work with a therapist, these leaders were able to prioritize safety within their organizations, facilitate accountability among staff, and encourage social support within their departments.

A vicarious 15-hike executive leadership resilience incubator in Mann Gulch, Montana, permits readers to upgrade their resilience leadership skills. Monday's hikes focus on sense-receiving, skills such as the leveraging of received national cosmologies, received community cosmologies, and received organizational cosmologies. Tuesday's hikes focus on sense-losing skills, moving from initial retentive sense-losing through a vicious cycle of selective sense-losing to the brutally honest audits of enactive sense-losing. Wednesday's hikes focus on sense-improvising skills by differentiating among temporality sense-improvising, identity sense-improvising, and social sense-improvising. Thursday's hikes focus on sense-remaking skills, moving from the enactive sense-remaking period through the virtuous cycle of selective sense-remaking to the retentive sense-remaking hinge between the catastrophe and the post-catastrophe. Friday's hikes focus on sense-transmitting skills, leveraging transmitted organizational cosmologies, transmitted community cosmologies, and transmitted national cosmologies. This chapter explores these five resilience leadership skills.

The chapters in this section explore the concepts of resilience, trauma, and healing in educational and business settings. In addition, the discussion focuses on why healing and resilience matters, why trauma is problematic, and what to do about it. Some of the chapters also provide practical recommendations to strengthen organizations and to help organizations heal from organizational trauma.

"Job pressure" is the number one cause of stress according to The American Psychological Association. However, there has been no systematic transformation in business practice to intentionally establish stress-reducing psychosocial work environments and to stop the "churn and burn" of employment. Such stress is compounded and becomes a sort of combat stress for employees in high-risk, high-emotion professions. Healing Comes First is an analysis of the critical impact of work stress on the individual employee and organizational productivity. Using the Jobs Demand-Resource Model as a foundational framework, this chapter provides leaders a pathway forward from identifying symptoms of a "stressed out" work environment to enacting mitigating strategies to reduce work stress consequences. Furthermore, the chapter recommends the incorporation of trauma-sensitive practices and the creation of a positive psychosocial work environment to help mitigate the effects of work stress on productivity.

The authors of this chapter contextualize terms such as individual trauma, collective trauma, and toxic stress; discuss how trauma impacts school environments; and propose steps to triage traumatic effects among faculty, staff, and students. Based on existing research and studies conducted by the authors of this chapter, strategies are introduced to help school leaders and teachers to overcome the effects of trauma and create a safe culture of healing during and after a traumatic event. While the context surrounding immediate trauma responses may default to macro-level discussions like violence, school shooting incidents, and school closures due to the COVID-19 pandemic, it is noteworthy to underscore less-publicized traumatic events such as adverse childhood experiences, adult workplace trauma, and collective organizational trauma. The authors provide case studies to help practitioners process organizational trauma scenarios.

Effective communication and resilience are integral components in an organization's structure, particularly during and after situations of trauma. Trauma includes both internal factors (i.e., layoffs, mergers, unexpected changes in management, lack of positive social support) and external factors (natural disasters, economic insecurity, social violence). An organization's level of resilience to these factors is determined by the event's type, timing, location, rate of recurrence, and duration. In addition, proactive planning impacts organizational resilience. This chapter will focus on the importance of resilience during times of trauma, how resilience relates to leadership, and mental health experiences by employees.

Organizational trauma, which results from a singular event or the sum of multiple experiences that occur over time, has an impact on the individuals and the collective that constitute the organization. For an organization to overcome its challenges and function in a new normal, leadership must play an integral role in engaging its individuals in a way that is explicit and intentional. The efforts of the leadership must first effectively describe the culture, as well as define leadership and its role. Undiagnosed and/or unresolved trauma (both crisis and systemic organizational trauma) within an institution may have exponential implications for both the person and the organization as a whole. To restore the organization to a state of wholeness, there must be an acknowledgement of organizational trauma as well as a committed approach to organizational healing. These efforts shift the organization from one that is experiencing organizational trauma to one that is considered to be a restorative community.

Foreword

As an organizational trauma researcher and consultant, I am humbled when academics and scholar-practitioners appreciate my work. I was pleasantly surprised when the co-editors of this book asked me to write the foreword. I said yes without hesitation. I am thrilled that the trauma conversation continues to grow beyond what I could have imagined. This new research gives me hope that every reader will have a newfound understanding and passion for recognizing organizational trauma and strengthening resilience. Trauma has been at the heart of my work for more than 40 years.

In 1999 Seattle Rape Relief closed its doors. The 30-year nonprofit organization imploded when leadership transition slammed into unhealed organizational trauma. Leadership did not have the knowledge or capacity to navigate turbulence and grief within the organizational culture caused by trauma. Board members were exhausted, connections to the community were fragile, and staff were suffering from the nature of their work. My colleague, Pat Vivian, and I volunteered with Seattle Rape Relief in the 1970s. We researched and wrote about the closing of the rape crisis center, deepening our appreciation for organizational culture and the suffering caused by organizational trauma. Since that time, we have committed to strengthening resilience in highly mission driven organizations through research, writing, and consulting. Our book *Organizational trauma and healing* written in 2013 names the types and sources of organizational trauma and provides information and scenarios to help organizational teams and cultures to be healthy and connected.[1]

Fast forward to the new millennium and to three scholar-practitioners who have conversations about seeing the pervasiveness of organizational trauma across sectors. From their exploration an exciting book emerges that invites us to a larger conversation about organizational trauma and helping people heal, that challenges us to deepen our understanding of trauma in complex systems.

Dive into the stories in these chapters that detail trauma in education, health care, and business. The stories will engage you with thought-provoking perspectives regarding the importance of understanding organizational culture and trauma. The authors illustrate how cultures can facilitate healing or exacerbate trauma.

Leaders and organization members may expect leadership to have all the answers. However, leadership does not have all the answers when trauma occurs. One defining characteristic of trauma is that systems do not have the knowledge and skills to cope with the tragedy they experience. Resilient systems bounce back over time; however, at least in the short term, systems are wounded and suffer. The authors express understanding that organizational trauma is new territory for many in leadership and that new learning is needed. Being open to learning requires us to be vulnerable, to hold ourselves and others with grace as we learn, stumble, fall, and learn more. May you who are in leadership allow yourselves to be vulnerable, to learn, and to ask for help as needed. As Maya Angelou said, "Do the best you can until you know better. Then when you know better, do better."

Shana Hormann
Antioch University, USA

Shana Hormann *has been a consultant and professor for over 30 years (University of Alaska Southeast, University of Washington, Muckleshoot Tribal College, Antioch University). She holds a Bachelor's degree in Sociology and Master's in Social Work from the University of Washington and a Ph.D. in Leadership and Change from Antioch University. Shana consults and teaches on leadership, group process and facilitation, organizational trauma, organizational culture, resilience, interpersonal violence, and spirit at work. She has undertaken a variety of consulting assignments for organizations in the nonprofit, public, tribal, and private sectors in the United States and abroad. Her co-authored book with colleague Pat Vivian, Organizational Trauma and Healing (2013), focuses on organizational trauma in non-profit organizations. Shana has worked, trained, and consulted with advocates, therapists and counselors, law enforcement officials, social service professionals, clergy and lay people, attorneys, judges, school personnel, and parents.*

ENDNOTE

1 We are grateful to the hundreds of organizations with whom we have worked, and to the individuals and organizations whose work informs ours.

Preface

The start of this new decade represented the opportunity to make progress in our lives and our work in new and novel ways. However, that optimism came to an abrupt end when the World Health Organization announced that COVID-19 was a global pandemic. A call for racial justice followed shortly thereafter as millions of people around the world watched the murder of an African-American man in real-time on TV and social media. Experiencing these crises while being locked down in our homes was especially tough. As practitioners and researchers, the co-editors of this book began to have regular discussions to try to make sense of their experiences. During one of the discussions, the co-editors started talking about their organizational trauma chapter that was co-authored a few years ago and how these current experiences felt a lot like the trauma they wrote about. The editors eventually came to the conclusion that the best way to work through this trauma was to write about it and encourage others to write about it too—that is how the seed for this book was planted.

This book was also motivated by the desire to contribute to the body of work regarding organizational trauma, healing, renewal, resilience and leadership. For the co-editors, the editing of this book was therapeutic. Although the topics in this book focus on leadership, organizational trauma, healing, resilience and renewal, the book at its core is about surviving and thriving after trauma. And this new decade has certainly brought trauma front and center to everyday life. To extend the metaphor of 20/20 vision to the year 2020 is to talk about having clear vision. The social justice and global issues of 2020 did not necessarily provide clear vision as much as it brought these issues into clear focus.

Thus, the starting point for this new book is to advance understanding by reviewing the most current research and literature on organizational trauma, leadership and change and then drawing new or enhanced conclusions based on the findings. Finally, the authors in this book share their views on what new research is necessary to advance perceptions regarding organizational trauma, leadership and change in the 21st century.

WHY THIS RESEARCH MATTERS

The broad perspective of this book represents the deep appreciation and insight into the ambiguity, dilemmas and contradictions associated with leadership. The fact is, it is a critical time to be studying and practicing leadership. Societies, states and markets around the globe are in a period of profound, transformative change (Benington, 2011), and there are many different leadership approaches to those challenges (Crosby & Bryson, 2018). Further, globalization has had both very positive and also deeply negative effects on societies, with growing economic and social inequality and a darkening sense of resentment and injustice (Hartley, 2018). At the same time, technological developments bring both opportunity and threat to employment, social relations, democracy, public discourse, knowledge, income distribution, surveillance and crime, in ways which leave many people feeling unsettled and distrustful (Hartley, 2018). Further, distressing problems such as climate change, international trade relations, migration and immigration, an aging population, the rise of illiberal democracies provide a powerful mix for leadership to try to grapple with (Hartley, 2018). In an increasingly volatile, uncertain world, leadership matters more than ever.

Traumatic experiences have significant impacts on wellbeing and increase the risk of many adverse outcomes—including physical and mental health problems (Vivian & Hormann, 2013). Similar to the trauma that individuals experience, organizational trauma is emotionally and cognitively devastating (Vivian & Hormann, 2013). Organizational trauma theory examines the psychological and physical effects of trauma on individuals and groups within an organization. In general, organizational trauma is a result of stress (both physical and emotional) in the workplace (Kahn, 2003). Organizational trauma is currently playing out in our organizations today and organizational scholars, leaders and managers are looking for ways to mitigate this trauma without having explicit knowledge or understanding of how to deal with it. Despite the increasing need to better understand organizational trauma and how to address it, this body of research has not played a prominent role in mainstream organization and management theory.

ORGANIZATIONAL TRAUMA

Trauma can affect organizations just as it affects individuals, families and communities (Vivian & Hormann, 2013). Sometimes, the disruptions are external and caused by societal, economic or political changes. Recent traumatic events such as the COVID-19 pandemic and racial tensions stemming from social injustices, present even greater challenges for leaders. Individual trauma—the individual mental and emotional disruptions that affect the well-being of self, often contribute to organizational trauma (Vivian & Hormann, 2013).

The organizational trauma knowledge domain is part of the organizational development field and intersects with the clinical discipline of trauma (Hormann, 2007). In the clinical realm, trauma is defined as an individual's emotional response to a terrible event like an accident or natural disaster (Hormann, 2007). A key point is that the individual remains the focus in the clinical domain (Vivian & Hormann, 2013). However, trauma can affect organizations just as it affects individuals, families, and communities. In organizations, trauma is identified at the collective and/or systems level and is described as a dysfunctional change in the behavioral patterns that exist at the organizational level (Hopper, 2012; Hormann, 2007; Kahn, 2003). Systems can become traumatized through natural disasters or human behaviors, through single events or over time (Kahn, 2003). Moreover, unresolved emotional trauma is a significant barrier to employee performance and wellbeing within organizations (De Klerk, 2007).

Studying the behavior of individuals in work environments has long been of interest to researchers in the management sciences (Galavandi & Ashrafi-Salimkandi, 2018). Furthermore, today's uncertain environment means that organizations must increasingly strive to adapt to the changes taking place in their surroundings, and as a result, focus a large part of their efforts on trying to ensure that their organizations are healthy and that their people are healthy too (Galavandi & Ashrafi-Salimkandi, 2018). An important aim of this book is to provide insights into the key concepts and issues regarding leadership, trauma and change in a complex, globally interconnected world as well as suggest practical recommendations on how to deal with the consequences of trauma and change.

LEADERSHIP IN THE 21ST CENTURY

Leadership in the 21st century will require individuals with certain adaptive skills in leadership to help their organizations deal with the continuous challenges and trauma that come with the persistent changes felt at the individual, group, organizational and societal levels. Within the first six months of 2020 the speed of change had disrupted and permanently altered everything individuals do – from education to simply going to work. Leadership is needed now more than ever because leadership is the Sherpa that guides people, groups and organizations from states of disorder and ambiguity to reimagined states of order with new standards, new rules, and new paths to unimagined outcomes. Leadership in the 21st century will take dynamic groups of people who understand and work together to help their organizations through the trauma of change.

After reading this book, the hope is that it will inspire readers to look at leadership more holistically and move away from the top-down bureaucratic view to a more heterarchical view in which all members of the organization participate. Leadership as a dynamic emergent process means that a person who has the title and authority of the leader role is leading today, but someone else can and will lead tomorrow or the next day. That is the meaning of emergent leadership. Individuals lead when they have to no matter where they are in the organization. This emergent, dynamic leadership-as-a-process approach is by default building on the idea of wellbeing because it empowers people to be their whole self and come to work and be a leader, follower, friend, ally and so on.

WHO SHOULD READ THIS BOOK?

This book covers a variety of topics and has a primary objective to provide information and insights regarding 21st century leadership, organizational trauma, healing, resilience and wellbeing. Therefore, this book is meant for academics, practitioners, organizational leaders or anyone who is interested in learning about trauma in organizations and how leadership can help or harm when trauma is present. More specifically, this book covers the following topics:

- Conceptions and Issues of Leadership and Leaders
- Healing and Resilience from Organizational Trauma
- Dysfunctional Leadership and Organizational Trauma
- Healing Organizational Trauma in the Education Context

HOW THIS BOOK IS ORGANIZED

A brief description of each of the chapters in this book is provided below:

Chapter 1: This chapter explores 21st century leadership practices in the theories of complexity and adaptive leadership as a path to addressing uncertainty, volatility and complexity in an increasingly interconnected global world. In this exploratory chapter, the authors, discuss the notion of leaders versus leadership and argue that leadership is a process that people do and not a role. The authors assert that complexity and adaptability are key in addressing trauma that results from change that occurs inside and outside the organization.

Chapter 2: This chapter offers insight into how change and uncertainty challenges effective leadership practices and offers guidance on how leaders can successfully lead in uncertain times. It adds to the existing field of studies by offering leaders a framework and specific ways to understand and consequently embrace and harness uncertainty. With the turmoil of 2020 as backdrop, effective leaders will need to master three tasks: (1) pace the changes to which their teams are exposed, 2) shape how changes are perceived by their team, and 3) manage the team's emotional reactions to change. As leaders envision the future, guide choices, tame apprehension, regulate expectations, experiment nimbly, and collaborate frequently, they will be able to channel the pressures of change to create positive outcomes for their teams and organizations.

Chapter 3: This chapter discusses the Transformational Leadership Model, developed by James MacGregor Burns in 1978. The theory has since become a hallmark for leaders who wish to embrace change and improve their organization's performance. Collaboration, empathy, trust and a genuine concern for all employees or followers in the organization are vital to the success of the transformational leader. A comparison of the theory of Instructional Leadership to Transformational Leadership is also discussed and provides an understanding of the differences between these leadership models. The discussion shifts to focus on how trauma negatively affects employees and organizations and how the elements and practices of Transformational Leadership can work to bring healing and wholeness to school communities that weather the potentially negative effects that change has on a learning community.

Chapter 4: Significant changes in organizational leadership are often accompanied by organizational members suffering from trauma. This situation is not for the faint of heart; however, it is an opportunity to employ a leadership style that enables an inviting and safe environment. This "culture of care" maintains efficiency and clearly articulates the vision of the organization, while addressing its mission and goals. Leading during a time of turmoil, trauma, and drastic change requires a leader to be intentional. The leader must know who they are, what they believe, and what they value. They must establish a clear path for the organization, and plan for the unexpected. The leader's compassion, consistency, empathy, fairness, honesty, professionalism, and transparency will serve as the standard by which all others follow.

Chapter 5: The content of this chapter discusses a day in the life of a licensed mental health clinician and four individuals (who are leaders from various professional backgrounds) with a universal trauma response to the COVID-19 pandemic. On any given day, their jobs are not for the faint of heart; they are accustomed to seeing people at their worst. However, this pandemic has made them question their own resiliency, tapped into their reserves and exhausted their previous effective coping mechanisms. In an effort to seek refuge and respite, their answers lie in their last resort- self-care (something none of them make time for, but something all of them require). Through their collaborative work with a therapist, these leaders were able to prioritize safety within their organizations, facilitate accountability among staff and encourage social support within their Departments.

Chapter 6: A vicarious fifteen-hike executive leadership resilience incubator taking place over five days in Mann Gulch, Montana, is discussed in this chapter as a way to upgrade resilience leadership skills. Monday's hikes focused attention on sense-receiving skills such as the leveraging of received national cosmologies, received industrial cosmologies, and received environmental cosmologies. Tuesday's hikes elaborated upon sense-losing skills, moving from initial retentive sense-losing, through a vicious cycle of selective sense-losing, to the brutally honest audits of enactive sense-losing. Wednesday's hikes explored sense-improvising skills by differentiating among temporal sense-improvising, identity sense-improvising, and social sense-improvising. Thursday's hikes elaborated upon sense-remaking skills, moving from the generative sense-remaking period, through the virtuous cycle of selective sense-remaking, to the retentive sense-remaking hinge between the catastrophe and the post-catastrophe. Friday's hikes elaborated upon sense-transmitting skills, leveraging transmitted organizational cosmologies, transmitted industrial cosmologies, and transmitted national cosmologies. The chapter is thus a pilot elaborative meta-analysis of Weick's 1993 Mann Gulch cosmology episode study.

Chapter 7: Job pressure is the number one cause of stress according to The American Psychological Association. However there has been no systematic transformation in business practice to intentionally establish stress-reducing psychosocial work environments and to stop the "churn and burn" of employment. Such stress is compounded and becomes a sort of combat stress for employees in high-risk, high emotion professions. Healing Comes First is an analysis of the critical impact of work stress on the individual employee and organizational productivity. Using the Jobs Demand-Resource model as a foundational framework (Bakker & Demerouti, 2007), this chapter provides leaders a pathway forward from identifying symptoms of a "stressed out" work environment to enacting mitigating strategies to reduce work stress consequences. Furthermore, the chapter recommends the incorporation of trauma sensitive practices and the creation of a positive psychosocial work environment to help mitigate the effects of work stress on productivity.

Chapter 8: This chapter contextualizes terms such as individual trauma, collective trauma, and toxic stress; discusses how trauma impacts school environments; and proposes steps to triage traumatic effects among faculty, staff, and students. Based on existing research and studies conducted by the authors of this chapter, strategies are introduced to help school leaders and teachers to overcome the effects of trauma and create a safe culture of healing during and after a traumatic event. While the context surrounding immediate trauma responses may default to macro-level discussions like violence, school shooting incidents, and school closures due to the COVID-19 pandemic, it is noteworthy to underscore less-publicized traumatic events such as adverse childhood experiences, adult workplace trauma, and collective organizational trauma.

Chapter 9: Effective communication and resilience are integral components in an organization's structure, particularly during and after situations of trauma. Trauma includes both internal factors (i.e., layoffs, mergers, unexpected changes in management, lack of positive social support) and external factors (natural disasters, economic insecurity, social violence). An organization's level of resilience to these factors is determined by the event's type, timing, location, rate of recurrence, duration. In addition, proactive planning impacts organizational resilience. This chapter focuses on the importance of resilience during times of trauma, how resilience relates to leadership, and mental health experiences by employees.

Chapter 10: Organizational trauma, which results from a singular event or the sum of multiple experiences that occur over time, has an impact on the individuals and the collective that constitute the organization. For an organization to overcome its challenges and function in a new normal, leadership must play an integral role in engaging its individuals in a way that is explicit and intentional. The efforts of the leadership must first effectively describe the culture, as well as define leadership and its role. Undiagnosed and/or unresolved trauma (both crisis and systemic organizational trauma) within an institution may have exponential implications for both the person and the organization as a whole. To restore the organization to a state of wholeness, there must be an acknowledgement of organizational trauma as well as a committed approach to organizational healing. These efforts shift the organization from one that is experiencing organizational trauma to one that is considered to be a restorative community.

Chapter 11: This chapter discusses a qualitative case study design to examine whether the leadership theory of Proposition Modelling, Respect and Motivation (MRM), could be used as a framework to guide a primary school through and out of trauma it was experiencing. The research findings demonstrated that by focusing on building trust, pursuing community engagements, managing conflicts, and building capacity, the principal was able to help the school community overcome its trauma. The chapter concludes that an essential ingredient in effective management of organizational trauma is building and maintaining trust and this strategy is aided by engagement of stakeholders, respecting the collective wisdom, and meaningful power-sharing.

LIMITATIONS OF THIS BOOK

Several constraints exist for this book. First, the primarily exploratory, qualitative approach for much of the content provides an initial examination of complex constructs and does not allow for a comprehensive understanding of leadership, organizational trauma and change that quantitative methods might address. Understanding research bias is important because bias exists in all research, across research designs and is difficult to eliminate (Sica, 2006). Cultural and personal bias may be another limitation for the contents of this book. In this book, the editors describe cultural bias as a tendency to interpret a word or action and derive meaning assigned to it according to their country of origin's culture (Sica, 2006). A personal bias is a tendency to interpret a word or action in terms of a personal significance assigned to it. Personal bias can derive from culturally defined interpretations but can also originate from other sources grounded in personal experience (Sica, 2006). It is important to note that cultural and personal biases can influence the way a person views the behaviors and actions of others—specifically those in leadership roles. Further research is required to examine whether cultural or personal bias plays a role in how trauma is viewed and perspectives on acceptable leadership practices.

CONCLUSION

The current decade has certainly presented the world with challenges and opportunities. That is what makes this a very interesting time for organizations and the people who work in them. The global pandemic, the call for racial and social justice have demonstrated that the boundary between work and life is flexible and permeable. And this realization requires new ways of thinking about leadership in organizations and how to identify new approaches to healing, renewal and resilience after trauma has occurred. It is the hope that the chapters in this book provide additional insights and understanding regarding the topics of organizational trauma, leadership and change.

Organizational trauma is currently playing out in our organizations today and organizational scholars, leaders and managers are looking for ways to mitigate this trauma without having explicit knowledge or understanding of how to deal with it. An important aim of the book is to provide insights into the key concepts and issues regarding leadership, trauma and change in a complex, globally interconnected world as well as suggest practical recommendations on how to deal with the consequences of trauma and change.

Although, this book focuses primarily on responding to trauma, it is important to see that there may be a bright side. Perhaps, trauma is an opportunity for growth on many different fronts. First, on a personal level, it provides the chance for reflection and introspection about how this challenging time has brought out the best and worst parts in people and how individuals can choose to respond and grow in a positive way. Second, for organizations, maybe this is an opportunity to think about the boundary permeability between the organization and how the outside world impacts individuals on the inside. How should organizations and their leaders rethink their actions with the realization of the interconnectedness of just about everything in the world?

The broad perspective of this book also represents the deep appreciation and insight into the ambiguity, dilemmas and contradictions associated with leadership. The fact is, it is a critical time to study and practice leadership. Because traumatic experiences have significant impacts on wellbeing and increase the risk of many adverse outcomes—including physical and mental health problems (Vivian & Hormann, 2013). The time is now for organizations to reinvent themselves if they want to survive and thrive.

REFERENCES

Benington, J. (2011). From Private Choice to Public Value? In J. Benington & M. Moore (Eds.), *Public Value: Theory and Practice* (pp. 31–51). Palgrave Macmillan. doi:10.1007/978-0-230-36431-8_2

Crosby, B. C., & Bryson, J. M. (2018). Why leadership of public leadership research matters: And what to do about it. *Public Management Review*, *20*(9), 1265–1286. doi:10.1080/14719037.2017.1348731

De Klerk, J. (2007). Healing emotional trauma in organizations. *Organization Development Journal*, *25*(2), 35–41.

Galavandi, H., & Ashrafi-Salimkandi, F. (2018). The Relationship of Organizational Trauma with Reducing Organizational Ethics. *International Journal of Ethics & Society*, *1*(1), 1–10.

Hartley, J. (2018). Ten propositions about public leadership. *International Journal of Public Leadership*, *14*(4), 202–217. doi:10.1108/IJPL-09-2018-0048

Hopper, E. (2012). *Trauma and Organizations*. Routledge.

Hormann, S. (2007). Organizational Trauma: A phenomenological study of leaders in traumatized organizations. Academic Press.

Kahn, W. A. (2003). The Revelation of Organizational Trauma. *The Journal of Applied Behavioral Science*, *39*(4), 364–381. doi:10.1177/0021886303261954

Sica, G. T. (2006). Bias in research studies. *Radiology*, *238*(3), 780–789. doi:10.1148/radiol.2383041109 PMID:16505391

Vivian, P., & Hormann, S. (2013). *Organizational Trauma and Healing*. CreateSpace.

Acknowledgment

Editing this book has been more challenging than we thought and more rewarding than we could have ever imagined. The editors would like to acknowledge and express their sincere gratitude to all of the people involved in this project. Specifically, we owe an enormous debt of gratitude to the authors and reviewers that took part in the review process. Without their support, this book would not have been possible.

First, the editors would like to thank each one of the authors for their contributions. Our sincere gratitude goes to the chapter's authors who contributed their time and expertise to this book.

Second, the editors wish to acknowledge the valuable contributions of the editorial advisory board members and reviewers for their input regarding the improvement of quality, coherence, and content presentation of the chapters.

Third, the editors would like to express their gratitude to the publication team at IGI Global for their support and guidance throughout this process.

And finally, we are sincerely grateful to you, the reader for choosing this book. May it bring you a wealth of insights and learning.

Valerie Ford
ISP Global Communications LLC, USA

Lynda Byrd-Poller
Thomas Nelson Community College, USA

Jennifer L. Farmer
Renewed Mindset LLC, USA

Section 1

Conceptions and Issues of Leadership and Leaders

Leadership is one of the most complex and multidimensional theories to which organizational and psychological research has been applied. Further, the disparate ways in which leadership has been defined have resulted in different approaches to conceptualizing, measuring, investigating, and critiquing leadership. To that end, this first section discusses leadership and its many forms. Topics such as transformational, complex and adaptive leadership, and leader self-care are discussed. There is also a discussion of what leadership should look like in organizations of the future.

Chapter 1
21st Century Leadership in Times of Global Change and Organizational Trauma

Valerie Ford
ISP Global Communications LLC, USA

Jennifer Farmer
Renewed Mindset LLC, USA

Lynda Byrd-Poller
Thomas Nelson Community College, USA

ABSTRACT

This chapter explores 21st century leadership practices found in the theories of complexity and adaptive leadership as a path to addressing uncertainty, volatility, and complexity in an increasingly interconnected global world. In this exploratory chapter, the authors discuss the notion of leaders versus leadership and argue that leadership is a process that people do and not a role. The authors also assert that complexity and adaptability are key in addressing trauma that results from change that occurs inside and outside the organization.

INTRODUCTION

A few short years ago, Byrd-Poller, Farmer and Ford (2017) the authors of *The role of leaders in facilitating healing after organizational trauma*, published a chapter on how leaders can facilitate healing and restore wellbeing after trauma in an organization has occurred. In that chapter, the authors examined the conceptual relationship between organizational trauma, organizational change, transformational leadership behaviors and their influence on engagement, wellbeing and professional identity. With the desire to continue and advance their exploration, the authors started with a simple question: What has changed since the publication of the previous chapter? The answer—everything. The world is in the midst of a

DOI: 10.4018/978-1-7998-7016-6.ch001

global pandemic, there is social and political unrest and a global reckoning with racial inequity. What is unique about these changes? They are all external forces—changes over which no one in the organization or the world had any control. Furthermore, these aforementioned external forces have likely caused trauma in the lives of individuals and in organizations.

In this chapter, the authors revisit their assumptions about leadership, trauma and change. Previously, the authors argued that transformational leadership behaviors were required to promote wellbeing and healing when trauma resulted from a planned organizational change (Byrd-Poller et al., 2017). However, the connectedness of the world and organizations has created a complex environment in which individuals must work and thrive. In this new organizational context, what kind of leadership is needed? Further, what kinds of leadership foster healing and resilience from trauma in this new, complex world of work? The authors also expand on the notion of organizational change by broadening their perspective to include the effect that external forces in the form of unplanned environmental changes have on employees within organizations. They also explore how complexity and adaptive leadership may be a path to responding to organizational trauma and change that promotes healing and resilience and enhances the wellbeing of both individuals and organizations.

How This Chapter Is Organized

This chapter is organized as follows:

- *Conceptual Framework* describes the relevant variables discussed in this chapter and the relationship between them. This section discusses the authors' previous framework as well as the revised conceptual framework.
- *Background* provides an overview of the key concepts and theories explored in this chapter.
- *Overview of Complexity and Adaptive Leadership* provides a high-level review of the literature on complexity and adaptive leadership theories.
- *How External Forces Create Organizational Change* focuses on how planned and unplanned changes can cause trauma in organizations.
- *How External Forces Create Organizational Trauma* discusses how external factors, such as pandemics, social unrest, natural disasters and mass shootings can cause trauma in organizations.
- *Why it Matters: Discussion and Implications for Practice* argues that the right forms of leadership can help organizations to heal after a trauma has occurred.
- *Conclusion* summarizes the concepts, theories, insights and recommendations for the variables in this chapter.

The next section discusses the conceptual framework and sets the foundation for the discussion in this chapter.

CONCEPTUAL FRAMEWORK

Figure 1 depicts the authors' original conceptual framework. In this framework, the authors focused on planned organizational change as a cause of trauma to employees in organizations. Further, specific

Figure 1. Conceptual Framework (2017)

leader behaviors were necessary to alleviate trauma and promote healing through restoring professional identity, increasing engagement and wellbeing.

The updated conceptual framework is shown in Figure 2 and expands on the authors' notions about organizational change and leadership.

The previous framework focused solely on internal, planned change as a potential cause of organizational trauma and how transformational leadership can restore healing and wellbeing. However, this new framework introduces the idea of change imposed by external forces and what type of leadership is required to deal with this complexity. In today's environment, the organization is no longer insulated from the outside world and the external forces that can cause trauma, hurt and harm. As a result, orga-

Figure 2. Updated Conceptual Framework

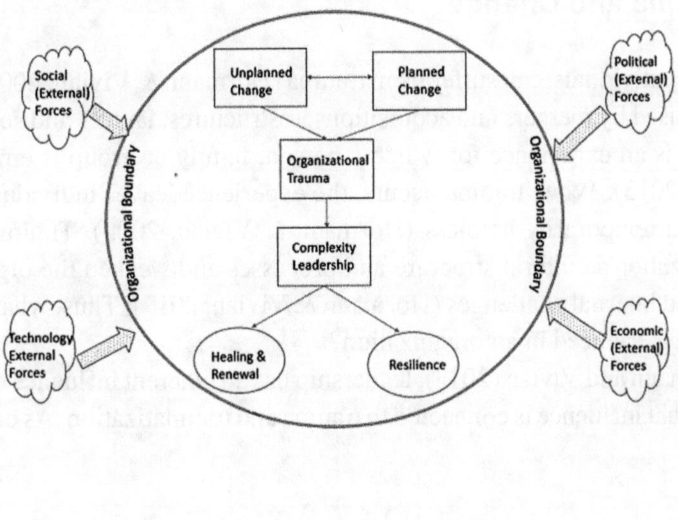

Table 1. Description of External Forces Affecting Organizations

External Force	Description / Definition
Political	Political forces impact organizations to the extent to which a government may make decisions or influence laws. This includes government policy, political stability or instability, and other government policies.
Social	Social forces are the result of the racial and other social inequities that exist.
Economic	Economic forces are related to how economic conditions impact organizations.
Technological	The technological forces refer to how innovation and developments in technology has changed how humans interact and how the world operates.

nizations must be able to respond to all types of change, whether it be internal or external forces that continue to impact organizations in trauma-inducing ways.

External forces in this context are those influences, circumstances or situations that an organization cannot control that affect the decisions that are made and impacts the wellbeing of individuals (Descza et al., 2019). There are many external forces that can have a direct impact on the ability of organizations to achieve their goals. However, this conceptual framework considers the four that the authors deem most important to this discussion. These external forces are described in Table 1.

Further, the authors view leadership very differently in this new conceptualization. The authors maintain that organizations are made up of many leaders—not just those that have been assigned a formal role in the organization. The more complex the world becomes the more complex organizations get. This shift requires more complex forms of leadership. In the future, organizations will have to explore ways to ensure that everyone in the organization is prepared to lead when or if the time comes. This new complexity has prompted the authors to explore a different perspective on leadership and how leadership might help to promote healing and resilience when a trauma has occurred.

Whether leading a family, an organization or a country, leadership in today's volatile, complex, and ever-changing world is a challenging issue. The problems that are facing the planet are more complex and interconnected and require new ways of thinking to resolve and manage them.

BACKGROUND

Leadership, Trauma and Change

Organizations, just as individuals, can suffer from trauma (Hormann & Vivian, 2005). Trauma in organizations is typically caused by mergers and acquisitions, restructures, layoffs and so on (Jacobsen, 2012). Trauma by definition is an experience for which a person, family or group is emotionally unprepared (Hormann & Vivian, 2013). When trauma occurs, the experience leaves individuals and organizations feeling vulnerable and temporarily helpless (Hormann & Vivian, 2005). Trauma and traumatization overpower the organization's cultural structure and processes and weaken the organization's ability to respond to external and internal challenges (Hormann & Vivian, 2017). Thus, what role does leadership play when trauma is experienced in an organization?

According to Hormann and Vivian (2013), leadership has an inherent influence on organizational patterns and culture and that influence is connected to trauma and traumatization. As organizations continue to adjust to changing social, cultural, economic, political, and demographic influences, knowledge of how leaders should act in these transformed organizations is extremely important (Austin, 1997; Rank & Hutchison, 2000; Tafvelin et al., 2014). Kotter and Heskett (1992) argued that organizational cultures that are adaptive, where the culture encourages continuous change, or those with cultures that are strategically appropriate for the current conditions are the best performing organizations (Frontiera, 2010).

There is no question that leadership in today's complex and ambiguous environment is an urgent and challenging issue (Iordanoglou, 2018). Organizations around the world are trying to figure out how to lead as they face new challenges, embrace change, deal with crises, solve real-world problems, and at the same time, have a positive impact on not only their organizations but on society as a whole (Iordanoglou, 2018). Finding new ways of conceptualizing leadership and developing future leaders are an organizational imperative as organizations continue forward into an uncertain future. Over the last three decades, transformational leadership has become one of the most prominent theories of organizational behavior (Wright et al., 2012). Transformational leadership is focused on the development of the fullest potential of individuals and their motivation toward the greater good versus their own self-interests, within a value-based framework (Avolio, 2007). In this chapter, the authors argue that in times of trauma, organizations should explore additional leadership approaches and theories to help their organizations heal. Two thought-provoking theories are complexity and adaptive leadership. The remainder of this chapter discusses these leadership theories and how they might have a positive impact on organizational trauma and resilience.

OVERVIEW OF COMPLEXITY AND ADAPTIVE LEADERSHIP

Complexity leadership theory may be one of the best ways to understand how organizations adapt to the profound environmental changes on the horizon. According to Drucker (2012), organizations of the 21st century face a complex, competitive environment called "the threshold of chaos" that is largely led by globalization and technological revolution. As a result, organizations need to adopt strategies to improve and change their traditional organizational structure into modern models by focusing on flexible leadership styles if they intend to survive (Adams & Stewart, 2015; Byrne & Callaghan, 2014). Moving beyond the traditionally accepted management perspectives on leadership can lead to dramatic, radical changes in the classical-bureaucratic management perspective (Edmonstone, 2016). One such flexible approach is complexity leadership.

Over the past 50 years, most leadership paradigms have been based on classical management perspectives that include mostly static models of a top-down hierarchical style (Edmonstone, 2016). These models for the most part do not account for the changes in the way organizations and the world are changing. Research on complexity leadership has challenged traditional ideas about leadership by shifting attention away from the attributes of leaders and the actions of individuals towards the relational, dynamic and distributed nature of leadership processes (Uhl-Bien et al., 2007). Drawing from complexity science (Marion, 1999), complexity leadership theory offers a new perspective on leadership within the framework of the idea of a complex adaptive system (CAS). Complexity science is associated with the intricate intertwining or interconnectivity of elements within a system and between a system and its environment (Uhl-Bien et al., 2007). In such systems, relationships are not typically defined hierarchically, as they are in bureaucratic systems, but rather by interactions among heterogeneous agents and across agent networks (Uhl-Bien et al., 2007).

Complexity Leadership Theory

Complexity leadership theory is grounded in a paradigm that frames leadership as a complex interactive dynamic from which adaptive outcomes, such as learning and innovation emerge (Uhl-Bien et al., 2007). Complexity leadership views leadership not only as a position and authority but also as an emergent, interactive dynamic where agents within a system interact in ways that produce new patterns or new ways of operating (Plowman et al., 2007; Uhl-Bien et al., 2007). When coupled with adaptive leadership, which is the practice of accepting the disequilibrium of a system, these two forms of leadership can be a powerful way to respond to complex problems (Andenoro et al., 2017).

The administrative, adaptive and enabling functions of complexity leadership are described in Table 2 (Mendes et al., 2016).

Table 2. Complexity Leadership Functions

Function	Description
Administrative	This function is managerial and formal and involves planning and coordination. This is similar to the typical organizational hierarchical leadership roles and functions (Mendes et al., 2016).
Enabling	This function is in between administrative and adaptive and creates the conditions for complex interactions and dynamics (Mendes et al., 2016).
Adaptive	This function is more informal, emergent, complex and dynamic and develops from interactions that result from conflicts, ideas or preferences and adaptive, creative learning actions that emerge from the interactions within a system (Mendes et al., 2016). In the adaptive leadership function, leadership is shared and emerges from a given context. In a volatile world, no one person can lead at all times and in all situations (Torres & Reeves, 2011).

These leadership functions create an interwoven process called "entanglement" (Schneider & Somers, 2006). Entanglement is a dynamic relationship between the top-down formal administrative structures (bureaucracy) and the informal, resonant structures of the social system (Uhl-Bien, 2006; Uhl-Bien et al., 2007). Interaction between administrative and adaptive leadership in organizations shapes complexity leadership. In this context, administrative leadership can work with adaptive leadership to prevent the formation of overly authoritarian, bureaucratic control mechanisms that can deprive the organization of its adaptive capacity (Uhl-Bien et al., 2007). It is important to note that in formal organizations, there will be times and conditions in which the formal, hierarchical authority should be emphasized, such as during periods when the environment is stable (Uhl-Bien et al., 2007). At other times, organizations may need to emphasize complexity when the environment is unstable and uncertain. The important point is for organizations to be vigilant and responsive enough to know the difference and to be adaptive enough to pivot when necessary.

Leaders in organizations have the opportunity to redesign their relationships to encourage self-organizing tools and systems, and to allow for change to emerge (Uhl-Bien, 2006). Complexity theory is well suited to today's interconnected organizations (Uhl-Bien et al., 2007). The definitive aspect of complex adaptive systems that challenges the traditional focus of leadership is a shift of control from a central guiding intelligence to the collective possibility of the network (Uhl-Bien, 2006). Complexity leadership theory embraces environmental change and leverages it by creating systems and tools that are self-organizing and self-correcting, allowing for emergence to occur (Uhl-Bien et al., 2007). Again, leadership is not about designated people in positions of authority, it is about the collaborative processes that unfold as institutions and groups adapt to changes in their environments (Uhl-Bien & Arena, 2018).

Adaptive Leadership

Adaptive leadership (AL) is an important complement to complexity leadership. First, adaptive leadership maintains that both organizations and human beings are self-organizing complex adaptive systems (CAS), nested within a hierarchy of complex adaptive systems (Heifetz et al., 2009). Second, both theories see leadership as a practice, an activity that people do at different times depending on the situation. In adaptive leadership, leadership is shared and emerges from the given context (Torres & Reeves, 2011). According to Heifetz et al. (2009), people have long confused the idea of leadership with authority, power and influence. Authority and power are important tools, but they do not define leadership (Heifetz et al., 2009). Third, adaptive leadership is about embracing uncertainty and adopting new approaches to find a path in the midst of turbulent conditions. With adaptive leadership, the role of leader should be taken by the person or group best positioned to guide a specific decision (Torres & Reeves, 2011).

Adaptive leadership has its roots in leadership theory but also has significant ties to scientific theory (Thygeson et al., 2010). The focus on adaptation comes from biology and evolution, with an emphasis on how new adaptations have the potential to significantly displace, re-regulate, and rearrange old structures (Heifetz et al., 2009). Adaptive leadership recognizes that there are two kinds of problems: technical and adaptive. With technical problems, a reasonable pre-determined response is already available and experts who possess the skills and abilities are sought out to address the issue (Heifetz et al., 2009). Overall, technical problems are mechanical and can be solved by professionals. On the other hand, with adaptive challenges, there are absolutely no trained experts to deal with the problems. No established rules or procedures exist to address the issue. In most cases, the definition of the problem is unclear and there are not any technical solutions (Heifetz et al., 2009).

Adaptive challenges differ from technical challenges in three basic ways: First, recognizing the problem, and figuring out how to solve it both require learning by everyone in the organization (Thygeson et al., 2010). Second, implementing a solution requires fundamental behavior change. Those in authority roles cannot do this work for the employees (Thygeson et al., 2010). And third, the behavior change required to respond to adaptive challenges involves trade-offs and losses and this creates fear and resistance to change and sometimes avoidance of adaptive work (Thygeson et al., 2010).

Resistance to change is tied to another key attribute of adaptive leadership. And that is it helps people navigate through periods of disturbance called disequilibrium (Heifetz et al., 2009). This disequilibrium can foster everything from conflict, frustration, and panic to confusion, disorientation and fear of losing something important (Thygeson et al., 2010). Adaptive challenges usually arise when substantial change in a person's internal state or environment causes performance deterioration, or creates a gap between the way things are and the way things should be (Thygeson et al., 2010). To survive and thrive in the face of an adaptive challenge, people have to adapt. This requires that they recognize the need to change, learn new behaviors and abandon old behaviors, beliefs and attitudes that no longer serve them. Respecting the idea that adaptive processes will be accompanied by distress or disequilibrium means having compassion for the pain that comes with profound change (Heifetz et al., 2009; Thygeson et al., 2010).

In summary, adaptive leadership is about change that enables the capacity to thrive. Adaptive leadership relies on diversity and values diverse views. Also, it is in such situations that the expertise of an adaptive leader becomes useful. An adaptive leader first helps to define the problem and then mobilizes colleagues to come up with possible solutions.

Leaders vs. Leadership

Complexity leadership (CLT) and adaptive leadership theory (ALT) distinguish between leadership and leaders. Both theories view leadership as an emergent, interactive dynamic that produces adaptive outcomes (Heifetz et al., 2009; Uhl-Bien et al., 2007). Leadership functions are not restricted to one person, such as the CEO, or a group, like the senior management team. Instead, the theories emphasize creating conditions that enable effective, adaptive states. This means that formal leaders are not always in full control of organizational dynamics, and colleagues are empowered to collectively learn and implement new solutions (Heifetz et al., 2009; Lichtenstein et al., 2006; Russ & Uhl-Bien, 2001; Uhl-Bien et al., 2007). In other words, leadership is a team sport.

In CLT and ALT, leaders are seen as individuals who act in ways that influence the interactive dynamic and outcomes, while leadership is viewed as an emergent, interactive dynamic (Heifetz et al., 2009; Uhl-Bien et al., 2007). This is not to say that there is no room for administrative leadership. But instead, it emphasizes the idea that the administrative leaders work to create a culture around an emergent process that says leadership means lead when you have to no matter where you are in the organization. Although the complexity and adaptive leadership approaches re-direct emphasis away from the individual as leader, they in no way diminish the importance of leadership as an organizational phenomenon; rather, they recognize that leadership transcends the individual by being fundamentally a system phenomenon (Hazy, 2006; Russ & Uhl-Bien, 2001).

One of the biggest challenges facing leaders today is the need to position and enable organizations and people for adaptability in the face of increasingly dynamic and demanding environments (Uhl-Bien & Arena, 2018). Leaders are typically thought of as strong personalities that impose their will on compliant organizations (Torres & Reeves, 2011). However, organizations are beginning to realize that there is something missing in this view of the leader as hero. The role of leaders is becoming more challenging, as they are now expected to manage their responsibilities in environments characterized by globalization, changing technologies, diminishing resources, and increased costs (Kinicki et al., 1996; Murphy, 2002; Uhl-Bien & Arena, 2018).

In response to these demands, it has become a practical imperative for leaders to engage in empowering initiatives that involve their employees, as it is neither feasible nor realistic for leaders "to have all the answers" or "make all the decisions" (Lovelace et al., 2007, p. 375). In addition, both scholarly (Stewart et al., 2012) and practical (Wirthman, 2014) evidence indicates that organizations and teams that use empowering initiatives outperform their counterparts that rely mainly on traditional hierarchical structures. In summary, shifts in today's global environment require new thinking about the nature of leaders and leadership. There is a critical need for empowering leadership in contemporary work settings.

Complexity leadership scholars maintain that "traditional, hierarchical views of leadership are less and less useful given the complexities of our modern world" (Lichtenstein et al., 2006, p. 2). Therefore, it is becoming increasingly important to explore ways that organizations can work through trauma and other issues without simply focusing on the role of a person or persons to resolve them. Moreover, complexity and adaptive leadership approaches create a dual response to addressing complex problems (Andenoro et al., 2017). Leadership is not solely performed by an individual or group of individuals at the top of the organization. Leadership is a dynamic process which is an adaptive, complex and seemingly chaotic dynamic involving everyone in the organization (Uhl-Bien & Arena, 2018).

EXTERNAL FORCES CREATE ORGANIZATIONAL CHANGE

Change is said to be a constant in life and in organizations. Additionally, change is seen as an important factor in the strategic success and survival of many organizations (Cameron & Quinn, 2011; Kotter & Schlesinger, 2008). Change is also a key competence for organizations to adequately predict, adapt to and maximize the opportunity of market changes, technology disruptions, technological evaluation, and economic and social transformations (Kotter & Heskett, 1992). This section provides a brief overview and history of change management theory and suggests a new application of The Bridges Transition Model to respond to traumatic change or changes that cause organizational trauma.

Overview of Organizational Change Theory

Change management models and research are still relevant for the 21st century. Today's change management strategies and techniques derive from the theoretical work of a number of early researchers. The seminal research regarding change management started with the Lewin studies in 1947 (Burnes, 2020; Lewin, 1947). Lewin's theory proposes that individuals and groups of individuals are influenced by restraining forces, or obstacles that counter driving forces aimed at keeping the status quo (Lewin, 1947). He also argued that changing the status quo requires organizations to execute planned change activities using a three-step model for change (Burnes, 2020; Lewin, 1947). The three steps in Lewin's Change Model are as follows:

- Unfreezing, or creating problem awareness, making it possible for people to let go of old ways/patterns and undoing the current equilibrium.
- Changing/moving, which is seeking alternatives, demonstrating benefits of change, and decreasing forces that affect change negatively (e.g., brainstorming, role modeling new ways, coaching, training).
- Refreezing, which is integrating and stabilizing a new equilibrium into the system so it becomes habit and resists further change.

Since Lewin's seminal work, there have been many theories for organizational change. Some of the theories include: Schein's Extension of Lewin's Change Model (Schein, 1980); Kotter's Eight Step Change Model (Kotter, 1996); Jick's Ten-Step Model (Kanter et al., 1992); and Bridges' Transition Model (Bridges, 2016). A defining element in each of these organizational change models is the absence of mutual exclusivity between them, such that overlap occurs at intersections such as type, origin, and so on. The point is, that no matter which change management theory that is espoused, organizations that are able to adapt and change in today's highly competitive environment will differentiate the winners from the losers. In essence, many organizations will disappear because they do not know how to adapt.

Major organizational changes typically involve many different types and levels of personal loss. For this reason, changes can be stressful events, met in many instances with resistance and often resulting

Table 3. Bridges' Transition Model Phases

Transition Phase	Description
Ending, Losing, Letting Go	Letting go of the old ways and the old identity people had. This first phase of transition is an ending, and the time when you need to help people to deal with their losses.
The Neutral Zone	Going through an in-between time when the old is gone but the new isn't fully operational. We call this time the "neutral zone"; it's when the critical psychological realignments and re-patternings take place.
The New Beginning	Coming out of the transition and making a new beginning. This is when people develop the new identity.

(Bridges, 2016)

in sabotaging actions (Bridges, 2016; Kotter & Schlesinger, 2008). The authors argue that unplanned changes require a different perspective on managing change, such as the one proposed by the Bridges' Transition Model (Bridges, 2016). The Bridges' Transition Model does not focus on the change itself (which is situational and happens to individuals) or purport to manage the change. Instead, it focuses on the transition, which is the psychological process of internalizing change (Bridges, 2016, p. 3). Table 3 describes the three phases of the Bridges transition phases.

Bridges' Transition Model and Change in Organizations

Typically, when a planned organizational change happens, employees are given advance notice of the upcoming change. And if the organization buys in to a change methodology, it provides employees with resources to help them on their change journey. However, when unexpected things happen in life or in the organization, it is as if a loss occurs (Bridges, 2016). In these situations, the authors suggest that the Bridges' Transition Model could be employed, along with other organizational change methodologies because it emphasizes the psychological transitioning process, which is most likely what happens when things occur that are not expected (Bridges, 2016). Transition is the state that change puts people into (Bridges, 2016). The change itself is external and could be a different policy, practice, or structure that the organization is trying to bring about, while transition is internal—a psychological reorientation that people have to go through before the change can take place (Bridges, 2016). The Bridges' Transition Model also complements complexity and adaptive leadership. In adaptive leadership, the behavior change required to respond to adaptive challenges involves trade-offs and losses and this creates fear and sometimes resistance to change (Thygeson et al., 2010). Additionally, complexity leadership attempts to create conditions that enable effective, adaptive states. The authors believe that the enabling conditions and adaptive states that are created provide individuals with the space to deal with their loss and to create and define their own new adaptive outcomes.

In the Bridges Transition Model, the first requirement is that people have to let go of the way that things used to be (Bridges, 2016). Individuals have to let go of their experience, their sense of identity, and even reality itself. In some cases, even after people have let go of their old ways, they find themselves unable to start over. When this happens, individuals enter the second phase of transition. This phase is called the neutral zone, and that in-between state is full of uncertainty and confusion that simply coping with it takes most of people's energy (Bridges, 2016). Successful transition, however, requires that an organization and its people spend some time in the neutral zone. This time in the neutral zone is where the creativity and energy of transition are found and the real transformation takes place (Bridges, 2016).

The third phase is called Moving Forward or New Beginnings (Bridges, 2016). Some people fail to get through transition and the neutral zone. But for those that are able to get through the first two phases, then the new beginning occurs. This new beginning means people have to begin behaving in a new way, and that can be distressing because it puts one's sense of competence and value at risk (Bridges, 2016). The authors also maintain that change itself, whether internal or external can cause trauma in the organization and to individuals. For example, the past year has brought tremendous social and political disruption that most employees may not have ever experienced. As a result, many employees brought their fear, anxiety and anger to work. When many individuals bring their trauma to work, there is collective trauma in the organization.

The next section focuses on the impact of what the authors call 21st century leadership practices (in the form of complexity and adaptive leadership) on organizational trauma and organizational change.

EXTERNAL FORCES CREATE ORGANIZATIONAL TRAUMA

Events like the global pandemic of COVID-19, as well as the global reckoning with racial inequity have had massive socio-political and economic consequences that continue to cause disturbances, pain and upset around the world and in the workplace. Individuals who are also employees experience these events and although they are happening outside the organization, these events have a severe impact on them and shake them to their core. These events shake them so profoundly that they can only be described as traumatic. Individual trauma happens when a person experiences an event outside of the usual human experience that would be markedly distressing because it is a threat to his or her life, family, or community or even if they watch it happen to someone else (American Psychiatric Association, 1994).

Interestingly, organizations can experience traumas just as individuals and families can (Stein, 2009). Organizational trauma has its origins in the clinical discipline and is generally defined as dysfunctional behavioral patterns at the organizational level (Hopper, 2012; Hormann, 2007; Kahn, 2003). These dysfunctional patterns negatively affect the organizations' longer-term development (Kahn et al., 2013), adversely impact their identity (Hopper, 2012) and threaten their existence (Hormann, 2007). In recent years, several researchers have suggested that trauma theory is extremely important when it comes to understanding the burnout experience of people working within a confined unit, such as an organization (Horwitz, 1998; Kahn, 2003). This has also led to a number of theories that speculate that the emotional impact of traumatic conditions in the workplace can be contagious and easily spread through empathic processes (Venugopal, 2016). Additionally, organizational trauma is believed to typically be the result of downsizing, outsourcing, mergers, restructuring and continual changes (De Klerk, 2007; Hopper, 2012; Hormann, 2007; Kahn, 2003). But what about other traumatic events that occur outside the organization—external forces, like pandemics and social injustices that cause trauma to individuals?

The authors argue that when employees bring the trauma that they have experienced outside into the organization, the trauma can be spread to others or shared and become collective trauma and start to impact organizational and individual performance. Although organizational trauma is not frequently associated with life-or-death situations, how should organizations respond when those traumatic situations their employees experience outside of work are now being felt in the workplace? How can organizations be more resilient to help people cope and heal from trauma? The Bridges Transition Model is one way to help individuals that experience a loss due to a traumatic experience. The Bridges Transition Model is similar to the Kubler-Ross Five Stages of Grief (Corr, 2018) and allows individuals to grieve their traumatic loss in their own time in a safe space. Complexity and adaptive leadership create the spaces that enable healing.

Why It Matters: How Leadership Can Facilitate Healing and Resilience After Trauma

Why do some organizations thrive and grow more resourceful and able to tackle future challenges, while others fail in the face of environmental disruptions? The authors maintain that answering these questions is important given that organizations exist in an increasingly interconnected and complex world. In fact, organizations are constantly searching for new approaches to address their biggest concern for the future—their health (Brown, 1997). The concept of organizational resilience may help to answer these questions. Resilience is the maintenance of positive adjustment when dealing with internal and external changes, risks or disruptions such that an organization emerges from those conditions stronger (Vogus & Sutcliffe, 2007). Organizational resilience is the ability to cope with and learn from the unexpected (Vogus & Sutcliffe, 2007). One group of researchers describe resilience as a function of three capabilities: adaptive capacity, situational awareness and the management of root-cause vulnerabilities (McManus et al., 2008). Defining resilience as a function of attributes, demonstrates that resilience is a complex concept (Vogus & Sutcliffe, 2007). Resilience as a complex idea aligns well with complexity and adaptive theories that consider organizations as complex adaptive systems (CAS).

Complexity and adaptive leadership theory can provide valuable pieces of the puzzle to help employees heal after a trauma has occurred. CLT and ALT as a theoretical perspective is well suited to organizational trauma and healing as they manage to focus on the collective, interactional generative emergence process and yet does not lose sight of individual agency (Lichtenstein et al., 2006). Another challenge facing organizations and their leaders is the need to position and enable their organizations and people for adaptability (Uhl-Bien & Arena, 2018). More specifically, resilient organizations promote competence, restore efficacy, and encourage growth through the behavioral process of self-organization by employees (Vogus & Sutcliffe, 2007). CLT and ALT create the enabling conditions that allow these patterns of growth, efficacy and competence to emerge.

The following are some adaptive and complexity leadership principles that may help organizations and the people within them to navigate uncertainty, heal from trauma and become more resilient.

Principle 1: Embrace uncertainty and adopt new approaches that allow the organization and its people to pivot quickly in a turbulent environment. Adaptive leaders forego rigid rules and instead set goals and objectives and hold organization members accountable (Torres & Reeves, 2011).

Principle 2: Cultivate an environment where diverse perspectives are encouraged. Adaptive leadership styles de-emphasize hierarchy and take into account the perspectives of front line employees, who are responsible for delivering products and services and are most likely to raise critical questions about external realities (Torres & Reeves, 2011).

Principle 3: Allow leadership to be shared and to emerge from the given context. In a volatile world, no single person can lead at all times and in all situations (Andenoro et al., 2017; Uhl-Bien & Arena, 2018; Uhl-Bien et al., 2007). The role of the leader should be assumed by the person that is in the best position to guide or make decisions (Uhl-Bien et al., 2007). This type of model promotes consistency and allows for changes to become fully realized because results are not dependent on formal leaders as it is with traditional leadership models (Torres & Reeves, 2011).

Principle 4: Maintain a sense of curiosity about the external environment. Adaptive leaders are always looking outward and realigning their organizations with the changing environment. These leaders read between the lines, intuitively grasp patterns that may be masked by complexity, and test their own assumptions by running through "what if" scenarios (Torres & Reeves, 2011).

Principle 5: Lead with empathy by seeing the world through the eyes of others and creating a shared sense of purpose (Torres & Reeves, 2011). In this scenario, adaptive leaders identify the shared purpose and work out how to harness it and empower employees to deliver results (Torres & Reeves, 2011).

CONCLUSION AND RECOMMENDATIONS

The focus of this chapter is on examining complexity and adaptive leadership and their influence on trauma, change and resilience. Based on the literature, resilience is an important concept because of its focus on how being adaptable and resilient helps organizations survive and thrive. Further, complexity and adaptive leadership have attributes that are well suited to foster resilience in their enabling and adaptive conditions. And practicing these types of leadership mobilizes people to tackle tough challenges and thrive (Heifetz et al., 2009). A resilient organization is a hopeful system because hope is a confidence grounded in a realistic appraisal of the challenges in the environment (Vogus & Sutcliffe, 2007). As organizations continue to face uncertainty, focusing on complex, adaptive, emergent leadership may help to strengthen the organization overall and facilitate healing and resilience for individuals. Complexity and adaptive leadership are poised to help organizations make sense of advanced technology, globalization, intricate markets, cultural change, and much more. In short, the science of complexity and adaptation can help to address the challenges and opportunities in this new era of human history (Turner & Baker, 2019).

This chapter's review of the literature also shows that some areas of research have matured, but other domains deserve more exploration. Although complexity and adaptive leadership are discussed in this chapter, there is still a lot to learn about these constructs. According to Uhl-Bien and Arenas (2018), leadership for organizational adaptability is different from traditional leadership or leading change. It involves enabling the adaptive process by creating space for ideas advanced by entrepreneurial leaders to engage in tension with the operational system and generate innovations that scale into the system to meet the adaptive needs of the organization and its environment. Leadership for organizational adaptability calls for scholars and practitioners to recognize organizational adaptability as an important organizational outcome, and enabling leadership (i.e., enabling the adaptive process through adaptive space) as a critical form of leadership for adaptive organizations (Uhl-Bien & Arena, 2018).

Implications for Research and Practice

There is a plethora of research and study on individual trauma and trauma therapy with its different schools of psychotherapy (Hirschberger, 2018). Also, there has been much research conducted on company crisis analysis and management as well as risk management (Hirschberger, 2018). There are also several research studies on effectively managing changes, such as massive downsizing and restructuring of companies and how to keep them going (Hirschberger, 2018). However, the missing piece is how to facilitate healing and resilience from organizational trauma regardless of how the trauma got to the workplace.

Given that there is not a lot of research on the interaction of trauma, complexity and adaptive leadership and change, the authors' goal was to explore the existing research on leadership trauma, change and resilience. The authors also wanted to develop a conceptual framework for describing and explaining the process of how complexity and adaptive leadership may be an important approach necessary to build resilient organizations and facilitate healing from trauma. Understanding how organizations positively adjust under conditions of adversity and emerge more resilient will help to answer the most pressing questions facing modern organizations. Thus, more research is needed to explore these leadership approaches and their impact on trauma and resilience.

There is also a strong ethical case for focusing on resilience and its impact on employee wellbeing (Muchiri et al., 2011; Samad et al., 2015). Resilience is the maintenance of positive adjustment under challenging conditions such that an organization emerges from those conditions stronger (Vogus & Sutcliffe, 2007). Challenging conditions include scandals, crises, disruptions and so on. To be resilient is to be vitally prepared for adversity. The world needs resilient individuals to build resilient organizations (Biggs et al., 2012). The concept of organizational resilience is also important because of its potential impact and influence on not just organizations, but on other areas of life. Organizational resilience influences community resilience, societal resilience, economic resilience, city or urban resilience and socio-ecological resilience (Ruiz-Martin et al., 2018). Exploring resilience in all of these contexts is important for future research. Although grounded in prior research, the assertions made throughout this chapter should be treated as suggestive until they are examined empirically.

Recommendations

An important focus of this chapter was on complexity and adaptive leadership. These flexible leadership approaches provide some important implications for practice. In the 21st century, it is time to explore other leadership theories like complexity and adaptive leadership, as necessary to respond to the complex and globally interconnected challenges that plague individuals and organizations. The implementation of new technological innovations in the workplace and globalization are two indicators of the future of organizations and signal the intensification of complexity in the workplace due to an increasing rate of unpredictable change, information overload, globalization, and geopolitical unrest (Turner & Baker, 2019). As organizations become increasingly interdependent ecosystems and organizational boundaries are blurred, who is leading whom? With complexity and adaptive leadership, the answer is—it depends on the situation, the circumstances or the problem.

Agents, individuals as well as groups of individuals, who "resonate" through sharing common interests, knowledge and/or goals due to their history of interaction and sharing of worldviews is a hallmark of complexity leadership. A complex systems perspective, introduces a new leadership "logic" to leadership theory and research by understanding leadership in terms of an emergent event rather than a person. A complexity view suggests a form of "distributed" leadership that does not lie in a person but rather in an interactive dynamic, within which any particular person will participate as leader or a follower at different times and for different purposes (Brown & Gioia, 2002; Gronn, 2002). So, these leadership approaches may have significance when addressing diversity, equity and inclusion in the workplace when it comes to key decisions and roles.

Although organizations espouse that they welcome diverse ideas and people, the makeup and cultures of organizations tell a different story. However, adaptive leadership along with complexity leadership can facilitate social change with the creation of adaptive space. The adaptive space does not refer to the action of any one person, but is an emergent, interactive, dynamic that produces adaptive outcomes, such as learning, adaptiveness and creativity (Heifetz et al., 2009; Uhl-Bien & Arena, 2018). What these outcomes suggest is a certain high quality of interactions, reflecting a shared context of mutual respect, trust, and psychological safety (Lichtenstein, 2014). This emergence eliminates the social issue of exclusivity as in traditional leadership models. In traditional leadership models, leaders are appointed to an exclusive club by exclusive club members. However, with leadership as an emergent and dynamic process, employees are empowered to step up and take charge.

The science of trauma has opened new pathways for understanding and addressing some specific organizational problems as well as social problems (Carter & Blanch, 2019). Trauma science intersects with the research on resilience (Carter & Blanch, 2019). In the vernacular of prevention, traumatic experiences are risk factors for a variety of negative outcomes, while resilience is attributed to internal strengths and external supports that buffer the impact of adversity (Carter & Blanch, 2019). Although the term trauma-informed organizations is primarily used to refer to social services organizations, it provides the context needed to respond effectively to the signs and symptoms of trauma in traditional organizations. The authors recommend exploring the research on trauma-informed organizations and looking for ways to apply that research in traditional organizations. As organizations become more globally interconnected and demands on employees increase, having an awareness and understanding of what trauma is and what trauma looks like in the organization is key to preventing or alleviating it through healing. While leaders cannot always protect organizations from trauma, leaders can strengthen resilience, recognize when trauma occurs, address the trauma effectively, and protect the system from spiraling into traumatization (Vivian & Hormann, 2002).

Although this chapter was written in the context of the unprecedented events of 2020, the authors want to end on an optimistic note. If resilience is the maintenance of positive adjustment under challenging conditions such that the organization emerges stronger, then organizations have a big opportunity in front of them and should take advantage of this adaptive space (Vogus & Sutcliffe, 2007). For individuals, resilience is built on the underlying assumption that the individual has undergone a situation of significant adversity and has adapted positively, then quickly returns to or increases in performance and psychological wellbeing (Hormann, 2018; Riolli & Savicki, 2003). It is the hope of the authors that anyone who has managed to survive this past year, walk confidently into their future and thrive—become the embodiment of resilience.

REFERENCES

Adams, T., & Stewart, L. (2015). Chaos Theory and Organizational Crisis: A Theoretical Analysis of the Challenges Faced by the New Orleans Police Department During Hurricane Katrina. *Public Organization Review, 15*(3), 415–431. doi:10.100711115-014-0284-9

Andenoro, A. C., Sowcik, M. J., & Balser, T. C. (2017). Addressing Complex Problems: Using Authentic Audiences and Challenges to Develop Adaptive Leadership and Socially Responsible Agency in Leadership Learners. *Journal of Leadership Education, 16*(4), 1–19. doi:10.12806/V16/I4/R1

Austin, D. (1997). The profession of social work: In the second century. In M. Reisch & E. Gambrill (Eds.), *Social work in the 21st century* (pp. 396–401). Pine Forge. doi:10.4135/9781483326405.n36

Avolio, B. J. (2007). Promoting more integrative strategies for leadership theory-building. *The American Psychologist*, *62*(1), 25–33. doi:10.1037/0003-066X.62.1.25 PMID:17209677

Biggs, D., Hall, C. M., & Stoeckl, N. (2012). The Resilience of Formal and Informal Tourism Enterprises to Disasters: Reef Tourism in Phuket, Thailand. *Journal of Sustainable Tourism*, *20*(5), 645–665. doi:10.1080/09669582.2011.630080

Bridges, W. (2016). *Managing Transitions: Making the Most of Change* (4th ed.). De Capo Lifelong Books.

Brown, E. H. (1997). Improving organizational health by addressing organizational trauma. *Journal of Organizational Change Management*, *10*(2), 175–178. doi:10.1108/09534819710160835

Brown, M. E., & Gioia, D. A. (2002). Making things click: Distributive leadership in an online division of an offline organization. *The Leadership Quarterly*, *13*(4), 397–419. doi:10.1016/S1048-9843(02)00123-6

Burnes, B. (2020). The Origins of Lewin's Three-Step Model of Change. *The Journal of Applied Behavioral Science*, *56*(1), 32–59. doi:10.1177/0021886319892685

Byrd-Poller, L., Farmer, J., & Ford, V. (2017). In R. B.-T. S. Háša (Ed.), *Impact of Organizational Trauma on Workplace Behavior and Performance* (pp. 318–340). IGI Global. doi:10.4018/978-1-5225-2021-4.ch014

Byrne, D., & Callaghan, G. (2014). *Complexity Theory and the Social Sciences: The State of the Art*. Routledge.

Cameron, K. S., & Quinn, R. E. (2011). *Diagnosing and Changing Organizational Culture*. Jossey-Bass.

Carter, P., & Blanch, A. (2019, Summer). A Trauma Lens for Systems Change. *Stanford Social Innovation Review*, 49–54.

Corr, C. A. (2018). Elisabeth Kübler-Ross and the "Five Stages" Model in a Sampling of Recent American Textbooks. *Omega*, *82*(2), 294–322. doi:10.1177/0030222818809766 PMID:30439302

De Klerk, J. (2007). Healing emotional trauma in organizations. *Organization Development Journal*, *25*(2), 35–41.

Descza, G., Ingols, C., & Cawsey, T. F. (2019). *Organizational Change: An Action-Oriented Toolkit*. Sage Publications, Inc.

Drucker, P. (2012). *Managing in the Next Society*. Routledge.

Edmonstone, J. (2016). Complex adaptive leadership: Embracing paradox and uncertainty. *Action Learning Research and Practice*, *13*(1), 86–89. doi:10.1080/14767333.2015.1130353

Frontiera, J. (2010). Leadership and organizational culture transformation in professional sport. *Journal of Leadership & Organizational Studies*, *17*(1), 71–86. doi:10.1177/1548051809345253

Gronn, P. (2002). Distributed leadership as a unit of analysis. *The Leadership Quarterly*, *13*(4), 423–451. doi:10.1016/S1048-9843(02)00120-0

Hazy, J. K. (2006). Measuring leadership effectiveness in complex socio-technical systems. *Emergence, 8*(3), 58–77.

Heifetz, R., Grashow, A., & Linsky, M. (2009). *The Practice of Adaptive Leadership: Tools and Tactics for Changing Your Organization and the World*. Harvard Business Press.

Hirschberger, G. (2018). Collective Trauma and the Social Construction of Meaning. *Frontiers in Psychology, 9*, 9. doi:10.3389/fpsyg.2018.01441 PMID:30147669

Hopper, E. (2012). *Trauma and Organizations*. Routledge.

Hormann, S. (2007). *Organizational trauma: A phenomenological study of leaders in traumatized organizations* [Doctoral Thesis, Antioch University]. https://aura.antioch.edu/etds/184

Hormann, S. (2018). Exploring Resilience: In the Face of Trauma. *Humanist Management Journal, 3*(3), 91–104. doi:10.100741463-018-0035-0

Hormann, S., & Vivian, P. (2005). Toward An Understanding of Traumatized Organizations and How to Intervene in Them. *Traumatology, 11*(3), 159–169. doi:10.1177/153476560501100302

Hormann, S., & Vivian, P. (2013). *Organizational Trauma and Healing*. Academic Press.

Hormann, S., & Vivian, P. (2017). Intervening in Organizational Trauma: A Tale of Three Organizations. In S. A. Tirmizi & J. D. Vogelsang (Eds.), *Leading and Managing in the Social Sector: Strategies for Advancing Human Dignity and Social Justice* (pp. 175–189). Springer International Publishing. doi:10.1007/978-3-319-47045-0_11

Horwitz, M. (1998). Social worker trauma: Building resilience in child protection social workers. *Smith College Studies in Social Work, 68*(3), 363–377. doi:10.1080/00377319809517536

Iordanoglou, D. (2018). Future Trends in Leadership Development Practices and the Crucial Leadership Skills. *Journal of Leadership, Accountability and Ethics, 15*(2).

Jacobsen, D. (2021). Protecting Employees from Organizational Trauma. *Workhuman*.

Kahn, W. A. (2003). The Revelation of Organizational Trauma. *The Journal of Applied Behavioral Science, 39*(4), 364–381. doi:10.1177/0021886303261954

Kahn, W. A., Barton, M. A., & Fellows, S. (2013). Organizational Crises and the Disturbance of Relational Systems. *Academy of Management Review, 38*(3), 38. doi:10.5465/amr.2011.0363

Kanter, R. M., Stein, B. A., & Jick, T. D. (1992). *The Challenge of Organisational Change*. Free Press.

Kinicki, A. J., McKee, F. M., & Wade, K. J. (1996). Annual Review, 1991–1995: Occupational Health. *Journal of Vocational Behavior, 49*(2), 190–220. doi:10.1006/jvbe.1996.0040

Kotter, J. P. (1996). *Leading Change*. Harvard Business School Press.

Kotter, J. P., & Heskett, J. L. (1992). *Corporate culture and performance*. The Free Press.

Kotter, J. P., & Schlesinger, L. A. (2008). Choosing Strategies for Change. *Harvard Business Review*, 1–11. PMID:10240501

Lewin, K. (1947). *Field Theory in Social Science*. Harper & Row.

Lichtenstein, B. B. (2014). *Generative emergence*. Oxford University Press. doi:10.1093/acprof:oso/9780199933594.001.0001

Lichtenstein, B. B., Uhl-Bien, M., Russ, M., Seers, A., Orton, J. D., & Schreiber, C. (2006). Complexity leadership theory: An interactive perspective on leading in complex adaptive systems. *Emergence*, *8*(4), 2–12.

Lovelace, K. J., Manz, C. C., & Alves, J. C. (2007). Work stress and leadership development: The role of self-leadership, shared leadership, physical fitness and flow in managing demands and increasing job control. *Human Resource Management Review*, *17*(4), 374–387. doi:10.1016/j.hrmr.2007.08.001

Marion, R. (1999). *The edge of organization: Chaos and complexity theories of formal social organizations*. Sage Publications.

McManus, S., Seville, E., Vargo, J., & Brunsdon, D. (2008). Facilitated Process for Improving Organizational Resilience. *Natural Hazards Review*, *9*(2), 81–90. doi:10.1061/(ASCE)1527-6988(2008)9:2(81)

Mendes, M., Gomes, C., Marques-Quintiero, P., Lind, P., & Curral, L. (2016). Promoting learning and innovation in organizations through complexity leadership theory. *Team Performance Management*, *22*(5/6), 301–309. doi:10.1108/TPM-02-2016-0004

Muchiri, P., Pintelon, L., Gelders, L., & Martin, H. (2011). Development of maintenance function performance measurement framework and indicators. *International Journal of Production Economics*, *131*(1), 295–302. doi:10.1016/j.ijpe.2010.04.039

Murphy, J. (2002). Reculturing the Profession of Educational Leadership: New Blueprints. *Educational Administration Quarterly*, *38*(2), 176–191. doi:10.1177/0013161X02382004

Plowman, D. A., Baker, L. T., Beck, T. E., Kulkarni, M., Solansky, S. T., & Travis, D. V. (2007). Radical change accidentally: The emergence and amplification of small change. *Academy of Management Journal*, *50*(3), 513–541. doi:10.5465/amj.2007.25525647

Rank, M. G., & Hutchison, W. S. (2000). An Analysis of Leadership Within the Social Work Profession. *Journal of Social Work Education*, *36*(3), 487–502. doi:10.1080/10437797.2000.10779024

Riolli, L., & Savicki, V. (2003). Optimism and Coping as Moderators of the Relation Between Work Resources and Burnout in Information Service Workers. *International Journal of Stress Management*, *10*(3), 235–252. doi:10.1037/1072-5245.10.3.235

Ruiz-Martin, C., Lopez-Paredes, A., & Wainer, G. (2018). What we know and do not know about organizational resilience. *International Journal of Production Management and Engineering*, *6*(1), 11–28. doi:10.4995/ijpme.2018.7898

Russ, M., & Uhl-Bien, M. (2001). Leadership in Complex Organizations. Management Department Faculty Publications, 11.

Samad, A., Reaburn, P., Davis, H., & Ahmed, E. (2015). An empirical study on the effect of leadership styles on employee wellbeing and organizational outcomes within an Australian regional university. *Proceedings Of The Australasian Conference On Business And Social Sciences.*

Schein, E. (1980). *Organizational psychology*. Prentice-Hall.

Schneider, M., & Somers, M. (2006). Organizations as complex adaptive systems: Implications of Complexity Theory for leadership research. *The Leadership Quarterly*, *17*(4), 351–365. doi:10.1016/j.leaqua.2006.04.006

Stein, H. F. (2009). Understanding and Consulting with Inconsolable Organizations. *Illness, Crisis & Loss*, *17*(3), 243–259. doi:10.2190/IL.17.3.e

Stewart, G. L., Courtright, S. H., & Barrick, M. M. (2012). Peer-Based Control in Self-Managing Teams: Linking Rational and Normative Influence With Individual and Group Performance. *The Journal of Applied Psychology*, *97*(2), 435–447. doi:10.1037/a0025303 PMID:21895352

Tafvelin, S., Hyvönen, U., & Westerberg, K. (2014). Transformational leadership in the social work context: The importance of leader continuity and co-worker support. *British Journal of Social Work*, *44*(4), 886–904. doi:10.1093/bjsw/bcs174

Thygeson, M., Morrissey, L., & Ulstad, V. (2010). Adaptive leadership and the practice of medicine: A complexity-based approach to reframing the doctor-patient relationship. *Journal of Evaluation in Clinical Practice*, *16*(5), 1009–1015. doi:10.1111/j.1365-2753.2010.01533.x PMID:20846289

Torres, R., & Reeves, M. (2011). Adaptive Leadership: How many of these practices do you employ? *Leadership Excellence*, *28*(7).

Turner, J. R., & Baker, R. M. (2019). Complexity Theory: An Overview with Potential Applications for the Social Sciences. *Systems*, *7*(1), 22. doi:10.3390ystems7010004

Uhl-Bien, M. (2006). Relational Leadership Theory: Exploring the social processes of leadership and organizing. *The Leadership Quarterly Yearly Review of Leadership*, *17*(6), 654–676. doi:10.1016/j.leaqua.2006.10.007

Uhl-Bien, M., & Arena, M. (2018). Leadership for organizational adaptability: A theoretical synthesis and integrative framework. *The Leadership Quarterly*, *29*(1), 89–104. doi:10.1016/j.leaqua.2017.12.009

Uhl-Bien, M., Marion, R., & McKelvey, B. (2007). Complexity Leadership Theory: Shifting leadership from the industrial age to the knowledge era. *The Leadership Quarterly*, *18*(4), 298–318. doi:10.1016/j.leaqua.2007.04.002

Venugopal, V. (2016). Understanding Organizational Trauma: A Background Review of Types and Causes. *IOSR Journal of Business and Management*, *18*(10), 65–69.

Vivian, P., & Hormann, S. (2002). Trauma and Healing in Organizations. *OD Practitioner*, *34*(4), 37–42.

Vogus, T. J., & Sutcliffe, K. M. (2007). Organizational resilience: Towards a theory and research agenda. In *2007 IEEE International Conference on Systems, Man and Cybernetics*, Montreal, QC, Canada. 10.1109/ICSMC.2007.4414160

Wirthman, L. (2014). Is flat better? Zappos ditches hierarchy to improve company performance. *Forbes*.

Wright, B. E., Moynihan, D. P., & Pandey, S. K. (2012). Pulling the levers: Transformational leadership, public service motivation, and mission valence. *Public Administration Review*, *72*(2), 206–215. doi:10.1111/j.1540-6210.2011.02496.x

KEY TERMS AND DEFINITIONS

Complex Systems Theory: States that complex systems are composed of many components which may interact with each other. These interactions are unpredictable, dynamic and multi-dimensional.

Complexity Leadership: Frames leadership as a complex interactive dynamic from which adaptive outcomes, such as learning, innovation, and adaptability emerge.

Empathy: The ability to share and see the world through another person's eyes.

Organizational Change: The field of management theory that focuses on the stages that companies go through as they evolve.

Organizational Healing: The work of repairing practices, routines, and structures and strengthening organizational functioning through social relationships as the result of disruptions.

Resilience: The ability of organization and people to anticipate, prepare for, respond, and adapt to incremental change and sudden disruptions in order to survive and prosper.

Wellbeing: The state of employees' mental and physical health that results from interactions inside and outside the workplace.

Chapter 2
Embracing and Harnessing Uncertainty:
Leadership Skills for Uncertain Times

Camilla Ellehave
The RBL Group, Denmark

Erin Wilson Burns
The RBL Group, USA

Dave Ulrich
University of Michigan, USA

ABSTRACT

This chapter offers insight into how change and uncertainty challenges effective leadership practices and offers guidance on how leaders can successfully lead in uncertain times. It adds to the existing field of studies by offering leaders a framework and specific ways to understand and consequently embrace and harness uncertainty. With the turmoil of 2020 as backdrop, effective leaders will need to master 3 tasks: 1) to pace the changes to which their teams are exposed, 2) to shape how changes are perceived by their team, and 3) to manage the team's emotional reactions to change. As leaders envision the future, guide choices, tame apprehension, regulate expectations, experiment nimbly, and collaborate frequently, they will be able to channel the pressures of change to create positive outcomes for their teams and organizations. More importantly, organizations that create routines and processes that encourage, develop, and enable these behaviors internally will lead in a world where customer needs, employee demands, and shareholder expectations are continuously evolving.

DOI: 10.4018/978-1-7998-7016-6.ch002

INTRODUCTION

Think back twelve months. What did you expect then to happen in the ensuing twelve months? How many of the events of the last year have matched your plans and predictions? How have these contextual changes affected your professional and personal life? If you are like most people, the previous twelve months have presented you with some unexpected (and perhaps startling or even devastating) situations that you could never have anticipated. And, in all probability, the next twelve months will bring additional unpredictable events that will shape both how you lead and the context in which you lead.

While everyone may always have been living in uncertain times, society has been able to progressively remove more and more elements of uncertainty from the environment (anything from controlling fire to making air travel possible). This ability to reduce uncertainty in the environment can create an illusion of omnipotence when it comes to humanity's belief in its ability and reach of control. Nevertheless, the element of unpredictability persists and defies accurate simulations or predictions as described within the field of Complex Adaptive Systems (Holland, 1992; Lansing, 2003). This condition has more recently simply been referred to as VUCA – Volatility, Unpredictability, Complexity and Ambiguity (Bennett & Lemoine, 2014; Bolman & Deal, 2015; Mack et al., 2016).

The Covid-pandemic and other radical, global changes have effectively obliterated this illusion of control and predictability. The need for productive responses is now greater than ever. At a simple level, when change happens it introduces uncertainty. How leaders respond to the uncertainty created by change determines their ability to turn the challenges of change into opportunities—or to harness uncertainty. Metaphorically, under pressure some rocks break into pieces and others become diamonds; likewise, under the demands of change, some leaders falter and others excel. In this sense, we concur with Feinstein's (2020) idea that uncertainty cannot and should not be reduced to risk and treated as a negative factor, even if our definition of uncertainty may be ontologically different.

Uncertainty is a multidimensional concept drawing on theory and research from many disciplines as described in Table 1. This chapter is less about the theory of uncertainty, than it is about how unrelenting changes in the current business world require leaders to harness uncertainty differently. The authors want to guide leaders and those who support their development on how to successfully steer their teams and organizations through tumultuous situations. Specifically, the authors address four questions:

1. What is uncertainty? Drawing on concepts in Table 1, the authors review the ways different fields have tried to define and manage uncertainty.
2. When does change become uncertainty? Highlighting the relationship between change and uncertainty, and why this is an important distinction for leaders.
3. What are past approaches to the leadership tasks of "harnessing uncertainty?" Summarizing how previous leadership theories address change and uncertainty?
4. What are leadership practices of successfully embracing and harnessing uncertainty? Offering specific guidance to leaders on how to excel along with concrete, real-world examples from leaders who demonstrated the behaviors needed to excel in times of radical uncertainty.

The authors hope this approach will provide both theoretical context and practical inspiration for how to successfully maneuver teams and organizations through radical changes.

Table 1. Terms and Concepts Related to Uncertainty

Term	Concept
Adaptive systems	Systems all have to adapt to uncertainty
Ambiguity	Lack of clarity about future
Complexity	Things are multi-dimensional
Disorderliness	Lack of regular structure
Incompleteness	Lack of information to fully capture
Incomprehensibility	Things are not easily understood, e.g., a joke
Inconsistency	Divergence, non-conformity, dissimilarity
Indefinition	There are multiple answers, not precise (all opinions count)
Insolubility	Some things can't be solved (unsolvable problem)
Non-transparency	Hidden information, obscurity
Polysemous	Things have multiple meanings or interpretations
Tentativeness	Can't come to a clear decision; resistance to final answer
Unfamiliarity	Things are new, novel, strange
Unpredictability	Randomness of future outcomes
Variation	Diversity, multiplicity, variation, many options

Sources: (Braun, 2007; Brodbeck et al., 2000; Burgess & Burgess, 2011; Cao et al., 2018; DiMaggio & Powell, 1977; Dosi & Marengo, 2007; Gorman, 2003; Martin H. et al., 2009; Scoblic, 2020; Stacey, 2011; Tapscott & Ticoll, 2003; Watson, 2015; Weick & Roberts, 1993)

Despite the fact that uncertainty is not a new phenomenon, the massive, global changes of 2020 and 2021, such as the Covid-pandemic, #metoo, Black Lives Matter, political squabbles, emotional deficits, etc. has still managed to expose another layer of lack of control and inability to forecast accurately. Even in the world of business, where conditions are uncertain, unpredictable, downright chaotic and (sometimes) completely outside of our control, the dramatic and abrupt nature of this change has offered new insights and learning (Einhorn, 2020; Robinson, 2020).

Three aspects of the global changes made the message of unpredictability impossible to miss, perhaps most markedly illustrated by the Covid-pandemic.

1. First, the joint inability as a global community to contain and treat the disease unmasked the illusion of safety and control. While other pandemics or historical events in recent history have certainly been as or even more disruptive, they have been more geographically contained and/or lasted a shorter period of time. The Covid-pandemic exposed not only the individual and collective vulnerability, it also lay bare the global interdependence and interconnectedness.
2. Second, the speed with which the threat of this virus was translated into radical changes of what was formally thought of as die-hard routines and ways of living was shocking to most people. In a matter of hours or days, the ways of working, dating, shopping, travelling, partying, and studying were radically altered or completely put on hold.
3. Third, the inability to predict the duration of these massive changes to everyday lives eliminated any last slivers of the illusion of control. People were not able to conclusively determine if their "during-the-pandemic" ways of life should be considered a *short-term, intermediate, or* indeed was going to be a more *permanent change.*

Table 2. Disciplines Studying Uncertainty

Discipline (reference)	Insights	Harness Uncertainty to...
Military (US Army, 2018)	(VUCA) Establish disciplined processes for quick action; centralize operations, decentralize execution; empower people how to think.	Win the war by empowering troops.
Neurology (David Rock[1])	Pay attention to the brain functioning that sense threat vs. opportunity (SCARF).	Seize opportunity more than threat.
Finance ISO standards on risk (Rock, 2021)	Manage risk of investments by calculating variance and probability of earnings.	Target investments.
Psychology (Dweck, 2007)	Focus on a growth mindset where failure is an opportunity to learn; do honest self-assessment; be calm, curious, and compassionate.	Grow, learn, and have well being
Strategy (Doz and Kosonen, 2008)	Establish strategic agility: explore scenarios, innovate fast, and disrupt industries.	Win in the market.
Health Care (Han, Klein, Arora, 2011)	Remove or reduce "uncertainty" to improve "uncertainty tolerance" for treatments and health care.	Improve patient outcomes.
Physics (Lindley, 2007)	Recognize that two objects cannot occupy the same space at the same time. (Heisenberg principle)	Deal with balancing competing demands.
Information (Ash, 1990)	Attend to reliability, credibility, and adequacy of information for decisions.	Make better decisions.
Religion (Hargood, 1997)	Act on faith without fully knowing the outcome; acquire hope for what can be.	Discover hope—find meaning.

As Table 1 points out, the concept of uncertainty has many dimensions and has always been an integral part of the human experience. Many and diverse academic disciplines have approached uncertainty as a key challenge, offered insights about uncertainty, and suggest positive outcomes from harnessing it as shown in Table 2. Each of these disciplines have focused on particular dimensions of uncertainty. They have also described and prescribed different courses of action to manage, control, limit, etc. the nature, perceptions and emotions related to uncertainty.

Despite the fact that we are all familiar with and use a number of these synonyms interchangeably, there is a need to further elaborate on a couple dimensions of the concept of uncertainty if we aim to assist leaders in turning uncertainty from threat to opportunity.

To assist leaders in embracing and harnessing uncertainty requires that leaders are able to distinguish between change and the reactions to change (of which uncertainty may be one). These distinctions and their relevance to the leader is discussed in more detail below.

WHEN DOES CHANGE BECOME UNCERTAINTY?

There is a subtle, yet important distinction between the phenomena of "change" and that of uncertainty. The term uncertainty is a description of *our emotional reaction* to specific conditions (changing or otherwise), or as Anderson et al. (2019), states: "uncertainty is fundamentally a mental state, a subjective, cognitive experience of human beings rather than a feature of the objective, material world".

To leaders, this is a particularly important distinction. Some of the changes to which their teams are subjected are of their own doing and inside of their control (strategic re-prioritizations, adding people to or letting people go from the team, establishing new project teams, etc.). Some changes are clearly outside of both their and our control. Whereas the first type of change resembles the concept traditionally described as 'planned' or 'deliberate' change, the latter exhibits more features similar to those described as 'emergent', 'unplanned', 'diffusions' or 'unpredictable' changes (Beer & Nohria, 2005; Bennis et al., 1961; Burnes, 2004; Kanter et al., 1992; Rogers et al., 2005).

To our team, however, independent of whether their leader has control or not, all of these changes constitute exactly that: a change.

When an employee is asked by their manager to work from home from tomorrow morning and until further notice, it may matter less to this person if this is because of Covid or because of a cost-reduction policy change in headquarters. Both will produce the exact same changes to the employee's working conditions. How this change is perceived, and whether this change will indeed produce uncertainty for the employee are entirely different matters.

Changes do not in and by themselves necessarily produce a sense of uncertainty. While the feelings of uncertainty may not be completely unrelated to changes, the depth of the feeling is probably more intimately related to an individual's perception of the changes and their individual ability to handle the changes than with the objective changes themselves. This may appear trivial, even bordering on self-explanatory, yet the authors find that there are important insights to be gained by clarifying first what challenges a leader (and their team) are facing as a leader *and* then choosing an intervention (Bridges & Bridges, 2017).

As a consequence, the authors propose for leaders to pay particular attention to three separate phenomena to better grasp the complexity of this challenge:

- The *nature of the change*
- The team's *perception of the change*
- The team's *reactions to the change*.

As mentioned above, there are no direct cause and effect nor proportionality between a team's reaction and the "objective" change that the team has been exposed to or asked to implement. In our view, however, being aware of and able to accurately assess the most critical dimensions of each of these phenomena will enable the leader to successfully lead their team in times of turbulence.

Table 3 provides examples of these three phenomena, how they may differ and what the consequent leadership considerations should be.

Changes

As individuals and teams, we all have different capacities for handling changes and may also perceive and react radically differently to similar changes (Weick, 1993). That being said, particular types of changes are more likely to produce particular perceptions and emotional reactions (Gioia et al., 1994; Gioia & Chittipeddi, 1991; Gioia & Thomas, 1996).

For example, changes which are perceived to be minor and evolutionary are more likely to produce less and weaker feelings of surprise, threat, or uncertainty than fast, radical changes with unknown consequences (Watzlawik et al., 1974). Large, abrupt, unplanned and unforeseeable changes produced by a

Table 3. Change, Perceptions of Change, Team Reactions & Leadership Tasks

Phenomenon	Examples of Relevant Continuums	Dimensions Impacting Leadership Challenge	Related Leadership Tasks
Changes	*From* Self-produced/initiated/ controlled changes *to* Externally initiated, outside own control *From* Minor, incremental *to* Major, revolutionary *From* Concrete *to* Abstract *From* Repetitive, rhythmic *to* Sudden (e.g., Kotter (1996), Lewin (1935), Benjamin & Mabey (1993), Watzlawick, Weakland & Fisch (1974), Weick & Quinn (1999)).	• Size of change • Pace of change • Impact of change • Self-initiated or externally produced	• Assess the size, nature and impact of the existing/ongoing changes affecting the team – and adjust own pace and magnitude of changes accordingly, when possible • Key leadership behaviors: envision the future, guide choices
Perceptions of Changes	*From* Positive, benign *to* Negative, threatening *From* Expected *to* Unexpected *From* Opportunity *to* Threat *From* Minor impact on status quo *to* Major impact on status quo *From* Temporary conditions *to* Permanent conditions (e.g., Bhopal (Shrivastava, 1987), Mann Gulch (Weick 1993), McMaster et al. (2005), Gersick (1991), Kaplan & Orlikowski (2014)).	• Desired to non-desired • Magnitude of impact of change	• Assess and manage the perceptions of the change within team, organization, industry stakeholders • Key leadership behaviors: tame apprehension and regulate expectations
Team Reactions	*From* Positive/opportunistic *to* Negative/fatalistic *From* Controlled, emotionally stable *to* Unhinged, derailing behavior *From* Resistance, cool *to* Ambassador *From* Balanced *to* Disrupted/disruptive (e.g., Dirks, Cummings, and Pierce (1996), Chreim (2006), Kaplan & Orlikowski (2014)).	• Range of emotions • Degree of support	• Assess, assist and/or manage individual and team reactions to perceptions of change by pushing forward into the unknown • Key leadership behaviors: Experiment nimbly and collaborate frequently

global pandemic like Covid are more likely to be perceived as threatening and thus to produce a feeling of uncertainty (Maitlis & Sonenshein, 2010).

Changes that are perceived as minor, tangible and temporary, all other things equal, requires the leader to intervene less in the team's sense-making and change absorption processes to keep the emotional reactions of uncertainty of the team at bay.

Perception of Changes

As illustrated in Table 3, all changes are not created equal. Furthermore, how the authors perceive the exact same changes can differ immensely. While one may find seasonal weather changes to be a negative change; others find them a welcome and rhythmic reminder presenting an opportunity to change their modes of transportation and outdoor activities. The seasonal changes are the same – our perceptions of them are not.

Similar or even the same changes may very well be perceived differently from one person to the next, or even by the same person at different times or in different contexts. While a changed bus route on a tourist destination in the summer may lead to some inconvenience for its passengers, it is more likely to provoke annoyance among commuters in the winter, or in situations where people are already running late. Seemingly similar changes thus may lead to different perceptions.

How we perceive and experience a change and its effects on us will naturally influence how we end up feeling about the change. Again, the perceptions of change can be distributed along a continuum stretching from a minor, incremental and benign change to a major, revolutionary and threatening change. And again, this has less to do with the objective dimension of the change itself than it does with the eyes seeing and minds' sense-making about it (McMaster et al., 2005; Shrivastava, 1987; Weick, 1993).

Reactions to Changes

To make matters even more complicated for the leaders navigating in turmoil, even similar perceptions of similar changes may evoke radically different reactions.

The same message from a leader instructing a team to work from home due to Covid restrictions may have the exact same consequences and be perceived as equally disruptive and outside of one's own control by all members of a team, and yet, they may experience and exhibit radically different reactions.

In general, the emotional reactions within the team are likely to follow the same patterns in so far that large, unpredictable changes are more likely to cause more, deeper and more challenging emotional reactions among the team than smaller, incremental changes are. That being said, individuals on a team are exactly that: individuals. And their patterns of reactions will not follow any linear patterns or necessarily align. The task of the leader, thus, becomes both to assess the types of change, the team's emotional reactions and how to engage to best manage the individual and collective emotional reactions within the team.

With the above distinction between changes, perceptions of changes and reactions to changes and clarification of which dimensions the leader should pay particular attention to, we are left with a question of how this influences the types of leadership tasks required to successfully cope in times of great uncertainty.

In the context of Table 3, it becomes evident that the first tasks are related to leaders' responsibilities for assessing the size, speed, impact, etc. of ongoing changes, and consequently for pacing the changes the leaders themselves want to introduce to match the capacity of the team. The second type of tasks are related to the leaders' active engagement in managing the team's perceptions of ongoing or planned changes. And thirdly, the leaders are required to engage with and ease the reactions of the team to changes and feelings of uncertainty.

What are Past Approaches to the Leadership Tasks of "Harnessing Uncertainty"

Within the field of leadership and change there is now a widespread agreement that leaders have a special role to play in times of changes. There is also widespread agreement that this context may present distinct and particular challenges. Before we venture into how we have seen leaders successfully navigate in unpredictable contexts, we will address some of the ways in which this challenge has been presented and discussed within this field of study.

Clarifying what role leaders have been granted within the field of leadership is challenged by the fact that the researchers within the field have almost all worked by their own particular definition of the concept, and there has consequently not been much agreement about the concept of leadership as such (Bass, 1981).

That being said, traditional leadership theories do very little — if anything at all — to address the context in which the leader is navigating, and the concept of uncertainty is therefore also of limited interest and relevance to most of the traditional leadership approaches (Barnard, 1938; Fayol, 1929; Lewin, 1935; Taylor, 1911).

Traditional leadership approaches barely consider the external contexts in which leaders operate. This is perhaps most evident in Leadership Trait approaches which emphasize the personal characteristics of the leader dating back to Galton's (1869) Hereditary Genius in which he argued that the personal qualities defining effective leadership were naturally endowed, passed from generation to generation.

The exclusion of considering external factors, however, is also present in the Leadership Style approaches (evident in e.g., the Ohio and Michigan State studies), which considers how the leader behaves and exhibits concern for rather than the conditions in which these behaviors are performed (Likert, 1955; Stogdill, 1948).

The turn in leadership research away from trait theory towards behavioral dimensions, often attributed to Stogdill (1948), was succeeded by studies based on the Contingency approaches which included and acknowledged the importance of dimensions outside the individual leader (Fiedler, 1974; Hersey & Blanchard, 1988).

Later leadership studies were born out of a need to understand what denoted leadership role, behavior and performance in business environments that was characterized by crisis and change. These leadership theories were consequently tasked with accounting for and establishing requirements to the leader's ability to cope with radical change, for instance in situations where they had to manage turnarounds of troubled businesses. Empirical findings of what actually made leaders (and made them effective) also supported and further accelerated the need for new leadership theories to grasp, describe and prescribe leadership practices under changing conditions.

In the early 1990's, the field of Change Management arose as a separate discipline within the field of leadership theory and practices. The growing popularity of this field from the 1990s to well into the 2000s both embraced and addressed the growing realization among business leaders of the unpredictability of their contexts and the importance of guiding the emotional reactions of employees for greater success of their enterprises. Building on classical theories such as the "Unfreeze – change – (Re)freeze"-model proposed by Lewin (1947), there were a growth spurt of publications, academic offerings and organizational departments dedicated specifically to managing change. Great leadership theorists have specialized their thinking and contributed greatly to the understand and practicing of managing change. These thinkers in essence captured both how to successfully lead changes and how to successfully lead in contexts that are changing (Drucker, 1995; Handy, 1989, 1996; Kanter, 1997; Kotter, 1996).

In parallel to the more conceptual discussions of change within the field of leadership, there were disruptions happening within managerial practices of operations, which are also relevant to the topic of this chapter.

W. Edwards Deming (1986) published his original thinking, which lay the foundation for Total Quality Management, Just-in-time production as well as a stream of other operational and tactical techniques. Focusing on incremental changes and continuous learning, Deming provided a new type of lens through which to see change and some new tools with which change could be managed. For Deming, change and learning were not just necessary for gaining success; as a leader you had to ensure continuous adaptations and learning for your enterprise to survive. This required the design and implementation of planned changes with the specific intent of improving output and ensuring necessary changes.

Today, the heritage of Deming's thinking can be found in managerial interventions such as the ones referred to as LEAN, Process Excellence and Six Sigma, as well as the more recent invention of Agile and Scaled Agile (SAFE) (Eklund et al., 2014; Rigby et al., 2020).

In the past decade or so, "Agile" has been brought forward as the answer to businesses and leaders' need for leadership practices that will enable them to adapt fast to even faster changes in their surroundings. In the context of "Agile", change is – similarly to the thinking of Deming – a precondition for organizational life and survival, and with markedly more attention to designing and implementing operational improvements than to how those changes are perceived by and might affect employees.

Change, ambiguity and the role of leadership has been addressed within the field of leadership theories and practices in numerous ways and from a wide array of perspectives throughout the past 60 years. After the earliest leadership theories, which were largely devoid of any references to contextual conditions, came a period of time where "change "and theories of change management took center stage and made how to bring about and manage change and uncertainties themselves the central point of leadership attention. Over the past decades, the predominant beliefs seem to be that change is a non-avoidable condition for all people in all industries and geographies. This means organizations will continuously need to anticipate, shape, adapt to and position in changing conditions – not in order to succeed, simply in order for the enterprise to survive (Yeung & Ulrich, 2019). The following section will further elaborate on and exemplify ways in which successful leaders have and could embrace change, perceptions of change and their teams' reactions to better harness uncertainty.

THE LEADERSHIP PRACTICES OF SUCCESSFULLY EMBRACING AND HARNESSING UNCERTAINTY

Harnessing means capturing energy (harness wind and solar energy or harness personal energy), protecting oneself for safety (wearing a harness in dangerous settings), focusing attention (using harnesses to control animals), and driving change (harness racing). *Harnessing uncertainty* means turning the threat of not knowing the future into an opportunity for greater success by becoming more energized, psychologically safe, focused, and agile. Leaders who are able to harness uncertainty are those whose teams and organizations excel when others falter. Leaders who help their teams and organizations prepare for and embrace change are those who are able to consistently meet customer, investor, and community expectations. Leaders who win.

As discussed, the continuum and dimensions of changes, perceptions, and reactions described in Table 3, the authors also identified the leadership tasks and key leadership behaviors. In this section, the authors connect the tasks with behaviors and provide examples of leaders who have demonstrated these behaviors in times of great uncertainty:

- Envision the future
- Guide choices
- Tame apprehension
- Regulate expectations
- Experiment nimbly
- Collaborate frequently

One would be pardoned for responding to this list with the comment that none of these behaviors is unique to leading in times of great uncertainty. Good leaders must always be able to envision the future, guide choices, tame apprehension, etc. However, the particulars of what these behaviors look like does shift in times of uncertainty. More importantly, they become not just one of many important leadership behaviors but instead are pre-requisites for success to a degree that is not the case under less ambiguous circumstances. In other words, weakness in these behaviors can be fatal to individual careers and organization viability during times of uncertainty.

While many of the examples used to illustrate these behaviors are taken from the context of the extreme disruptions of 2020, they are useful and relevant even during more routine times. Awareness and attention to these behaviors can not only be a "cure" for extreme uncertainty, they can be "preventative" during times of more routine changes. Deliberately cultivating and strengthening these behaviors as an individual leader and in leadership development efforts improves day-to-day performance, avoids unexpected disruptions, and builds leadership "muscle" that can be more readily accessed when larger disruptions emerge. As such, these six leadership tips for harnessing uncertainty are not only descriptive of what has happened, but prescriptive in terms of would leaders could do in future uncertain situations.

Step 1: Envision the Future

The concept of envisioning the future is not new but takes on added importance and complexity during times of extended disruption and uncertainty. When major disruptions hit suddenly (pandemics, wars, even sudden changes to historical trade agreements, etc.), things that used to be seen as unknown begin to appear as incremental changes. As early warning signals begin to unfold, exceptional leaders react with purposeful curiosity as the first step to harnessing the potential uncertainty. That purposeful curiosity includes three phases:

- **Phase One**: **Information gathering:** Exceptional leaders reach out to experts of all sorts to begin to imagine what impact the event will have in the short-, medium, and long-term. They look for areas where there may be new opportunities at least as much as they focus on where there are risks or dangers to the business.

- **Phase Two**: **Scenario development**: They sift and sort the expert opinions and use them to develop their own point-of-view about what the future could hold. They include internal and external stakeholders in the process, sharing and testing multiple scenarios for how events could play out and how each scenario will impact their organization as well as which scenario they see as most likely.
- **Phase Three**: **Direction setting**: This last phase is critical and somewhat delicate. As probability moves to reality, leaders must put a stake in the ground. In the midst of so many unknowns, leaders know that even the most likely scenario will probably be off the mark. They must convey confidence in a given direction while maintaining humility about what they do not know. They must inspire urgent, purposeful action while acknowledging that they will likely have to shift the direction of that action even after the work is underway.

In essence, envisioning the future is a leadership practice focused on addressing and molding the team's perceptions of what a change could become or lead to.

Several examples from the current pandemic stand out:

Khaldoon al-Mubarak, Managing Director and Group CEO of Mubadala, a $230B sovereign wealth fund for Abu Dhabi, spent mornings on the phone with Asia, afternoons with Europe, and evenings with North America. He tapped experts in business, investment, and health leaders around the world before concluding that the world had the resources to beat the pandemic and that it offered huge opportunity to diversify his country's resources away from oil. Instead of minimizing risk by reducing investments in 2020 as many other sovereign wealth firms did during this period, his willingness to embrace risk has allowed the fund to diversify faster than during a standard economy (Jones & Gottfried, 2020).

Facing huge demand and public pressure to increase production, leaders of paper product manufacturers went through a similar process in March. As they evaluated actual usage (v. demand), potential additional capacity, costs of warehousing extra product, and health risks to their workforce, most increased production only modestly if at all (Corkery & Maheshwari, 2020). In this case, there was no need for a change to current production, no opportunities to be gained by increasing it, only higher costs that would erode profits not offer new growth opportunities (Lemieux, April 13, 2020). Looking into the future for paper production revealed that while there may be shifts in where toilet paper was consumed, resisting pressure to increase production was the scenario that would best maintain profitability.

Step 2: Guide Choices

The most-likely scenario developed as a leader envisions the future becomes the public foundation for guiding choices moving forward. Leaders must translate the scenario into clear short-term goals and help each individual identify how their work contributes to the achievement of that short-term goal. The leadership practice of guiding choices aims to influence the reactions of the team to (their perceptions of) a change, and to purposefully widening and qualifying the options. As the leaders focus their teams on the choices within their control and let go of the choices outside their control, employees feel empowered again to act.

At the same time, privately they hold open alternate scenarios and continue to reassess these scenarios. The intensity of the information gathering does not abate just because they have set a direction. They understand that the environment remains fluid and as they have access to additional information in the external world and as they see the results of actions, they have decided to take that different scenarios may emerge as more promising. As they hold these scenarios open and even continue to develop other scenarios, they guide choices in two critical ways. First, they make adjustments to the short-term goals based on new information. Second, they make decisions that keep as many promising future scenarios open as possible. This ability to tolerate ambiguity, continually reassess future scenarios, and guide the organization forward in a fluid, agile way ensures the best possible outcome.

Again, several examples from the current pandemic stand out:

Carol Tome', who became CEO of UPS in the middle of the pandemic, has created focus and direction to guide choices. With surging volumes, critical safety concerns, and existing initiatives, she led the executive team through a process to focus on key priorities and become "Better not bigger." As she explains "the leadership team is at the bottom of the pyramid because we bear the weight for the actions that we take and the decisions that we make. We bear that weight so that we can free up our associates who are at the top of the pyramid, so that they can take care of the customers. If you bear the weight, you can free up people to do the right thing, to give the best experience (Pressman, October 19, 2020)."

Another example comes from Nike, who had already been moving towards more direct-to-consumer digital sales but saw an opportunity in the pandemic to accelerate that move. The initial impact of the pandemic had a significant impact on sales and by mid-summer, retail sales had declined by almost 40%. At the same time, digital sales had grown by 75% and by July, CEO Jon Donahoe was doubling-down on a "Consumer Direct Offense (Thomas, July 22, 2020)." Layoffs announced at the time were connected not to the pandemic but to a stronger pivot towards an existing strategy (Arcieri, July 9, 2020). This clear direction, relatively early in the pandemic, helped guide choices throughout the company. Initiatives to grow digital sales were supported by a growing digital ecosystem that included apps (some offered for free during the pandemic), a creative #playinside #playfortheworld advertising campaign, and opportunities for regular people to interact with Nike sponsored athletes.

More broadly, leading CEOs in many industries without essential workers have actively worked to harness the uncertainty about where to work. When the virus first hit, companies around the world complied with government shutdowns but leading companies took a further step with clear guidance about who could work remotely and for how long. This clear messaging allowed employees to move forward with putting a specific disruptive event (working from home today/this week/this month) into a foreseeable pattern (working from home for six months) that provided stability and context for both work and personal decision-making. These same companies, and many others, used this short-term "experiment" to envision and test future patterns (how we might work in the future).

Step 3: Tame Apprehension

Individual purpose and contribution are just some of the needs employees need met in order to fully engage. Trusting relationships, feeling part of a team, and a stable predictable work experience are also important (Emmett et al., June 29, 2020). In normal times leaders need to inspire and connect with employees. In times of extreme uncertainty, the need for this is greater and the barriers are more numerous. The leadership practice of taming apprehensions is directed at managing the teams' perception of the changes, and also potentially at the teams' reactions. While leaders may need to tame their own apprehensions and at least make preliminary efforts to tame the immediate concerns of the workforce earlier in the process, the substantive work of taming apprehension can only be done once the initial direction through the crisis has been arrived at.

Leaders need to take two key actions to tame apprehension:

- Listen and empathize: in order to tame apprehension, leaders must first understand it. Given a radical new world and/or a new direction that may have adverse impacts on employees or those they work with, what are their biggest concerns. In the current pandemic is it job security, health concerns, finding a space to work, adapting to new technology requirements, etc. Before a leader can tame apprehension, they must understand it.
- Respond in a practical and positive way: Once leaders understand the concerns, they need to provide practical solutions and communicate them in a positive, hopeful way (while being realistic).

Several examples from the current world situation stand out. Marvin Ellison understands the concerns of front-line essential workers in a way that many CEOs don't. As a former retail security guard who worked his way up through various retail chains, he has maintained a closeness to the needs of associates and customers. That empathy has translated into over $750,000,000 in special bonuses to front-line workers, additional paid sick leave for higher-risk associates, and free medical advice for any associate. Lowe's is among hundreds of companies, large and small, who made significant adjustments to reduce fears for their workers. From covering all out-of-pocket medical expenses to reducing work expectations for employees caring for sick or out-of-school family members, from committing to no layoffs or pay cuts to removing limits on sick days, from installing makeshift protective barriers to limited retail hours, leaders around the globe listened and responded to a wide variety of fears to support employees, protect their health, and maintain engagement as much as possible (Gallucci & Seetharaman, April 13, 2020). Some companies, like American Airlines (transporting medical supplies, military mail, and packages instead of passengers) and Ford (producing ventilators, face shields, and disposable respirators instead of cars and trucks) (Rock, 2021). In Germany, McDonalds partnered with Aldi to temporarily "lease" employees so they could continue to work and receive salaries (Neerman, March 20, 2020).

Another example of listening and responding positively and realistically comes out of the United States' Black Lives Matter movement, also in 2020. While many companies' responses were seen as mere lip service, Levi's Straus & Co.'s President and CEO, Chip Bergh, was one of a handful of leaders who listened, empathized, and then took meaningful, positive action. He spoke clearly and directly about the pain employees and customers experienced because of ongoing inequality, made substantive contributions to groups leading cultural change, and published (for the first time in the company's 167-year history) Levi's diversity statistics and a plan to fix them (Beheshti, June 18, 2020).

Step 4: Regulate Expectations

While taming apprehensions is critical to harnessing uncertainty, it must be paired with regulating expectations. There are hard realities of limited resources and unknown futures that cannot be wished away. Great leaders are clear about the limits of what they can influence, and they remind people of the truths they don't want to acknowledge. They deliberately work to fight the instinctive desire others may have to opt only for the most realistic scenarios by sharing objective data for a range of scenarios. They remind people of the uncertainty of the future even while laying out a clear path forward and projecting optimism that collectively, the organization can transcend the challenges it is facing. As they share both the bad news and the good news in an open way, they generate trust with both internal and external stakeholders. The leadership practice of regulating expectations takes the facts of any changes into consideration and then moves its focus to how these changes are perceived. Taming apprehensions includes a leader's ability to alter the perceptions of a change from a threat to an opportunity, and then to engage the team in ceasing this.

Several examples from the current pandemic stand out. At an individual level, managers everywhere are having to manage the expectations of their teams on a regular basis. One leader in hospitality looking to fill a role talks very candidly about the state of the business and the short-term prospects so that candidates come in with a clear understanding about what to expect while also sharing her passion for the company and the reasons she believes the company will survive and grow in the long run. Another leader in a consulting firm regularly shares revenue projections, updates on government subsidies, and the point at which layoffs will have to kick in while also highlighting the pivots the firm is making to adapt.

Managing expectations of external stakeholders is equally important. One firm that navigated that challenge well was Airbnb. Beginning the year by losing half the company's market value is not the typical path to an IPO, but Airbnb just completed a highly successful IPO. Founder and CEO Brian Chesky's has inspired trust by regulating expectations and being clear about the uncertainties ahead. His track record of overcoming obstacles as varied as accusations of racism, increased regulations, and safety concerns directly and transparently—including a personal apology to hosts this spring—contributed to their ability to successfully IPO. Most observers credit a combination of quick action and the ability to tell a compelling story to the investment community about how their recovery is different than others in the industry and how the pandemic actually accelerates their vision of a future where people "live anywhere." (Griffith, December 10, 2020)

Step 5: Experiment Nimbly

Continuous reinvention is the key to any company's long-term viability but during periods of extreme uncertainty, the ability to experiment nimbly—and sometimes radically—can be the key to survival. Extreme uncertainty, as in the current pandemic, can require changes to business models, service delivery, and work conditions. Additionally, it brought a myriad of changes to how we eat, shop, heal, celebrate, learn, mourn, worship, and socialize which offer both risks and opportunities for individuals and organizations. The leadership practice of experimenting nimbly focuses on managing, directing and motivating the team's reactions to (perceptions of) changes. It must incorporate an understanding of the emotional reactions of the team, which may otherwise leave the team in a fight-flight-or-freeze-mode, to foster an environment in which experimentation is the norm and the making of errors are truly accepted as necessary for getting through the uncertainty.

Uncertain settings often give rise to incredible innovation of ideas and solutions as all of the sudden the risks of not experimenting so far outweigh the risks of experimentation. Great leaders are both predisposed to engage in experiments and know how to encourage and guide the experimentation of others. They encourage their teams to experiment by trying things they have not tried before. They encourage others to explore new ways to approach old (or new) problems. They celebrate what works and learn from what does not. They put existing resources to new uses.

The results of these experiments, along with additional data as the situation progresses, feeds back into scenario planning and direction setting, at times shifting the direction of the organization by degrees or pivots.

Several examples from the current pandemic stand out. The old adage "necessity is the mother of invention" certainly played out in the arts as performers around the world began radically experimenting with ways to deliver performances. What began in many cases as free concerts designed to maintain contact with their audiences or honor first responders evolved to a wide variety of virtual experiences: concerts, dance parties, lectures, livestreams, pay-per-view, virtual lessons, personal performances, etc. Late night comedy hosts engaged their families in producing their nightly shows. Artists changed media or posted works in online galleries. Movies went straight to Netflix. Museums produced virtual tours. Groups gathered on Zoom to practice and perform together. But the arts lived on and were important sources of solace to many.

In India, with the world's second largest population, the government's Department of Telecom reached out to the telecom operators for support in getting the message out. In early March, with less than 50 confirmed cases in India, the government asked telecom operators to play a 30-second message on how to stop the spread of the virus instead of the normal ringtone. As the pandemic unfolded, the message was updated and proved a simple and powerful way to disseminate health information in a country where even the country's 26% illiterate population mostly have a phone in their pocket (Pandey, June 16, 2020).

Key to any experimentation is the learning that follows. In Taiwan, the government led by President Tsai Ing-wen is widely seen as leading one of the best government responses globally. A number of factors play into that response, but key among them is lessons learned during the SARS outbreak in 2003. The learnings from having experienced a similar pandemic resulted in early and aggressive monitoring of the outbreak in nearby Wuhan, followed by aggressive contract tracing and isolation that contained the virus that helped the country avoid the large-scale lockdowns that so many other nations experienced. It also anticipated other disruptions, monitoring commodity demand and ensuring adequate availability of medical grade masks. These actions resulted in Taiwan being the only country in the world to post positive economic growth in 2020 (Everington, December 4, 2020).

Step 6: Collaborate Frequently

In a radically new situation, the more partners you have, the more information and alternatives you can explore. Exceptional leaders have broad and deep networks that they use regularly. In times of radical uncertainty, they rely more heavily on those networks to learn and adapt. They learn from and with others by testing ideas, coming together to solve shared problems, and share learnings. They invite their advice and their ideas. They are open to joint solutions. The leadership practice of frequent collaboration addresses the reactions of the team to (perceptions of) changes, and insists on keeping fearful emotional reactions at bay, and engage actively and constructively in - even unproven and potentially frightening - new ways of working together with internal and external stakeholders.

Several examples from the current pandemic stand out:

For hospitality, Covid-19 has been devastating. Given the sudden and complete impact on travel as the world shut down in early 2020, Hyatt executives had to take immediate action to ensure liquidity. Furloughs bought time for a strategic approach to widespread staffing cuts.[2] At the same time, they began preparing for ways to restore confidence and safety for both the workforce and guests. Conversations with medical, other travel industry leaders, and even architects about how to safely resume operations allowed hotels to gradually reopen in various parts of the world.[3]

They helped leaders in these adjacent industries learn from each other's experiments and prepare for emerging developments like rapid tests, air travel bubbles, and plan together to safely resume conferences and other travel as soon as possible.

Perhaps the most highly touted collaboration of the current pandemic has been in medical care as doctors and scientists around the world came together in unprecedented ways to speed up vaccine development and share learnings about treatments as quickly and broadly as possible. From large pharmaceuticals partnering with start-ups and governments to speed up vaccine development to doctors sharing lessons learned on blogs and informal networks to virtual reality videos demonstrating coronavirus treatments, the global medical and scientific community has collaborated in unprecedented ways to try and "flatten the curve."

CONCLUSION

Change is - and probably always has been - an inevitable part of the human experience. And we may be increasingly aware of the fact that this is so. Our contexts, including those in which we operate as leaders, are increasingly difficult to predict, as are the consequences for ourselves, our teams and our organizations.

Our ability to remove uncertainties and to control an increasing number of dimensions of our lives and our context may have lured us into thinking that we were somewhat in the driver's seat. The past year's events (think: anything from the Covid-pandemic to the United States 2020 Presidential election) can turn our understanding of the world upside-down and leave us with a sense of uncertainty. As individuals and teams, we handle changes – even the same ones – differently: we asses our own impact on them differently, we react different emotionally on them and our behavioral reactions differ as well.

Our argument in this chapter is that there are important distinctions to be made about the phenomena of change, perceptions of change and reactions to change, respectively. And that these distinctions carry particular relevance for the leader who will be tasked with 1) understanding, pacing and managing the rate and speed of change to which their teams are exposed, 2) shaping how changes are perceived by their team, to 3) managing the team's individual and collective emotional reactions to those changes.

While previous studies have addressed the idea of managing change or leading in changing conditions, we want to offer leaders a terminology and examples of ways to embrace and harness uncertainty so that change turn from uncertainty or anxiety provoking events to leadership opportunities.

As leaders develop the skills that allow them to envision the future, guide choices, tame apprehension, regulate expectations, experiment nimbly, and collaborate frequently, they will be able to channel the pressures of change to create positive outcomes for their teams and organizations. Even more importantly, organizations who are able to create routines and processes that encourage, develop, and enable these behaviors in their leaders will lead out in meeting evolving customer needs and shareholder expectations.

REFERENCES

Anderson, E. C., Carleton, N. R., Diefenbach, M., & Han, P. K. J. (2019). The Relationship Between Uncertainty and Affect. *Frontiers in Psychology*, 10. PMID:31781003

Arcieri, K. (2020). *Nike levels up digital game in wake of coronavirus hit*. https://www.spglobal.com/marketintelligence/en/news-insights/latest-news-headlines/nike-levels-up-digital-game-in-wake-of-coronavirus-hit-59265634

Barnard, C. I. (1938). *The Functions of the Executive*. Harvard University Press.

Bass, B. M. (1981). *Handbook of Leadership: Theory, Research, and Managerial Applications* (3rd ed.). The Free Press.

Beer, M., & Nohria, N. (2005). Cracking the code of change. *Harvard Business Review*, *78*(3), 133–141. PMID:11183975

Beheshti, N. (2020). End Business as Usual—Leaders Must Boldly and Fearlessly Respond to Black Lives Matter. *Forbes*. https://www.forbes.com/sites/nazbeheshti/2020/06/18/end-business-as-usual-leaders-must-boldly-and-fearlessly-respond-to-black-lives-matter/?sh=33c42de24b6a

Bennett, N., & Lemoine, G. J. (2014). What VUCA Really Means for You. *Harvard Business Review*.

Bennis, W. G., Benne, K. D., & Chin, R. (1961). *The Planning of Change*. Holt, Rinehart & Winston.

Bolman, L. G., & Deal, T. E. (2015). Think—Or sink. Leading in a VUCA world. *Leader to Leader*, *76*, 35–40. doi:10.1002/ltl.20176

Braun, B. (2007). Biopolitics and the molecularization of life. *Cultural Geographies*, *14*(1), 6–28. doi:10.1177/1474474007072817

Bridges, W., & Bridges, S. (2017). *Managing Transitions: Making the most of Change*. Da Capo Lifelong Books.

Brodbeck, F. C., Frese, M., Akerblom, S., Audia, G., Bakacsi, G., Bendova, H., & Castel, P. (2000). Cultural variation of leadership prototypes across 22 European countries. *Journal of Occupational and Organizational Psychology*, *73*(1), 1–29. doi:10.1348/096317900166859

Burgess, A., & Burgess, J. (2011). *Truth*. Princeton University Press. doi:10.23943/princeton/9780691144016.001.0001

Burnes, B. (2004). Emergent change and planned change – competitors or allies? The case of XYZ construction. *International Journal of Operations & Production Management*, *24*(9), 886–902. doi:10.1108/01443570410552108

Cao, Y., Gao, J., Lian, D., Rong, Z., Shi, J., Wang, Q., Wu, Y., Yao, H., & Zhou, T. (2018). Orderliness predicts academic performance: Behavioural analysis on campus lifestyle. *Journal of the Royal Society, Interface*, *15*(146), 20180210. doi:10.1098/rsif.2018.0210 PMID:30232241

Corkery, M., & Maheshwari, S. (2020). Is There Really a Toilet Paper Shortage? *New York Times*.

Deming, W. E. (1986). *Out of the Crisis*. Massachusetts Institute of Technology.

DiMaggio, P. J., & Powell, W. W. (1977). The Iron Cage Revisited: Institutional Isomorphism and Collective Rationality in Organizational Fields. *American Sociological Review*, *48*(2), 147–160. doi:10.2307/2095101

Dosi, G., & Marengo, L. (2007). On the Evolutionary and Behavioral Theories of Organizations: A Tentative Roadmap. *Organization Science*, *18*(3), 491–502. doi:10.1287/orsc.1070.0279

Drucker, P. (1995). *Managing in a Time of the Great Change*. Truman Talley Books.

Einhorn, C. S. (2020, August). How to Make Rational Decisions in the Face of Uncertainty. *Harvard Business Review*.

Eklund, U., Olsson, H., & Strøm, N. (2014). *Industrial challenges of scaling agile in mass-produced embedded systems. Agile Methods. Large-Scale Development, Refactoring, Testing, and Estimation*. Springer International Publishing.

Emmett, J., Schrah, G., Schrimper, M., & Wood, A. (2020). *Covid-19 and the employee experience: How leaders can seize the moment*. https://www.mckinsey.com/business-functions/organization/our-insights/covid-19-and-the-employee-experience-how-leaders-can-seize-the-moment#

Everington, K. (2020). Taiwan president ranked in Bloomberg 50 for crushing Covid. *Taiwan News*. https://www.taiwannews.com.tw/en/news/4069341

Fayol, H. (1929). *Industrial and General Administration*. Management Institute.

Feinstein, O. (2020, May). Development and Radical Uncertainty. *Development in Practice*, *30*(8), 1105–1113. doi:10.1080/09614524.2020.1763258

Fiedler, F. E. (1974). The Contingency Model—New Directions for Leadership Utilization. *Journal of Contemporary Business*, *3*(4), 65–80.

Gallucci, J., & Seetharaman, M. (2020). How Fortune 500 companies are utilizing their resources and expertise during the coronavirus pandemic. *Fortune*. https://fortune.com/2020/04/13/fortune-500-companies-coronavirus-response-covid-19-pandemic/

Galton, F. (1869). *Hereditary Genius*. doi:10.1037/13474-000

Gioia, D., Thomas, J. S. C., & Chittipeddi, K. (1994). Symbolism and Strategic Change in Academia: The Dynamics of Sensemaking and Influence. *Organization Science*, *5*(3), 363–383. doi:10.1287/orsc.5.3.363

Gioia, D. A., & Chittipeddi, K. (1991). Sensemaking and sensegiving in strategic change initiation. *Strategic Management Journal*, *12*(6), 433–448. doi:10.1002mj.4250120604

Gioia, D. A., & Thomas, J. B. (1996). Institutional identity, image, and issue interpretation: Sensemaking during strategic change in academia. *Administrative Science Quarterly*, *41*(3), 370–403. doi:10.2307/2393936

Gorman, J. (2003). *Rights and Reason: An Introduction to the Philosophy of Rights*. Acumen Publishing. doi:10.1017/UPO9781844653461

Griffith, E. (2020). Airbnb Tops $100 Billion on First Day of Trading, Reviving Talk of a Bubble. *New York Times*. https://www.nytimes.com/2020/12/10/technology/airbnb-tops-100-billion-on-first-day-of-trading-reviving-talk-of-a-bubble.html?auth=login-email&login=email

Handy, C. (1989). *The Age of Unreason*. Harvard Business School Press.

Handy, C. (1996). *Beyond Certainty*. Arrow Business Books.

Hersey, P., & Blanchard, K. H. (1988). *Management of organizational behavior* (5th ed.). Prentice Hall.

Holland, J. (1992). Complex Adaptive Systems. *Daedalus*, *121*(1), 17–30.

Jones, R., & Gottfried, M. (2020). Abu Dhabi's $230 Billion Man Bet the World Would Overcome Covid-19. *The Wall Street Journal*.

Kanter, R. M., A., S. B., & Jick, T. D. (1992). How effective leaders achieve success in critical change initiatives, part 2: Why change leadership must transcend project management for complex change initiatives to be successful. *Healthcare Quarterly*, *10*(2), 70–75. PMID:17491570

Kanter, R. M. (1997). *The Change Masters*. International Thomson Press.

Kotter, J. P. (1996). *Leading Change*. Harvard Business School Press.

Lansing, J. S. (2003). Complex Adaptive Systems. *Annual Review of Anthropology*, *32*(1), 183–204. doi:10.1146/annurev.anthro.32.061002.093440

Lemieux, P. (2020). Toilet Paper: Increasing Marginal Cost. *The Library of Economics and Liberty*. https://www.econlib.org/toilet-paper-increasing-marginal-cost/

Lewin, K. (1935). *A Dynamic Theory of Personality*. McGraw-Hill.

Lewin, K. (1947). Frontiers in group dynamics: Concept, method and reality in social science equilibrium and social change. *Human Relations*, *1*(1), 5–41. doi:10.1177/001872674700100103

Likert, R. (1955). *Developing patterns in management*. American Management Association.

Mack, O., Khare, A., Krämer, A., & Burgartz, T. (2016). *Managing in a VUCA world*. Springer. doi:10.1007/978-3-319-16889-0

Maitlis, S., & Sonenshein, S. (2010). Sensemaking in Crisis and Change: Inspiration and Insights from Weick. *Journal of Management Studies*, *47*(3), 551–580. doi:10.1111/j.1467-6486.2010.00908.x

Martin, H. J., de Lope, J., & Maravall, D. (2009). Adaptation, Anticipation and Rationality in Natural and Artificial Systems: Computational Paradigms Mimicking Nature. *Natural Computing*, *8*(4), 757–775. doi:10.100711047-008-9096-6

McMaster, T., Wastell, D., & Henriksen, H. Z. (2005). Fooling Around: The Corporate Jester as an Effective Change Agent for Technological Innovation. In R. Baskerville, L. Mathiasen, J. Pres-Heje, & J. DeGross (Eds.), *Business Agility and Information Technology Diffusion*. Springer. doi:10.1007/0-387-25590-7_8

Neerman, P. (2020). Aldi to employ redundant McDonald's staff. *Food*. https://www.retaildetail.eu/en/news/food/aldi-employ-redundant-mcdonald's-staff

Pandey, G. (2020). Covid-19: The woman who has become India's 'corona voice. *BBC News*. https://www.bbc.com/news/world-asia-india-53047296

Pressman, A. (2020). *The holidays used to be UPS's busiest time. Then came COVID-19*. https://www.google.com/amp/s/fortune.com/longform/ups-ceo-carol-tome-shipping-coronavirus-covid-19-pandemic-home-depot-cfo/amp/

Rigby, D., Berez, S., & Elk, S. (2020). *Doing Agile Right*. Harvard Business Review Press.

Robinson, B. (2020, Nov.). 6 Ways To Cope With More Uncertainty. *Forbes Magazine*.

Rock, D. (2021). *Dr. David Rock*. https://davidrock.net/publications/

Rogers, E. M., Medina, U. E., & Wiley, C. H. (2005). Complex adaptive systems and the diffusion of innovations. *The Innovation Journal, 30*, 1–26.

Scoblic, J. P. (2020). Learning from the future: How to Make Robust Strategy in Times of Deep Uncertainty. *Harvard Business Review, 98*(4), 37–47.

Shrivastava, P. (1987). Bhopal: Anatomy of a Crisis. Ballinger.

Stacey, R. D. (2011). *Strategic Management and Organisational Dynamics: The Challenge of Complexity to Ways of Thinking about Organisations*. Pearson Education.

Stogdill, R. M. (1948). Personal factors associated with leadership: A survey of the literature. *The Journal of Psychology*, (25), 35–71.

Tapscott, D., & Ticoll, D. (2003). *The naked corporation: How the age of transparency will revolutionize business*. Free Press.

Taylor, F. W. (1911). *Shop Management*. Harper & Brothers.

Thomas, L. (2020). Nike shakes up its executive team to bolster its digital business, announces job cuts. *CNBC*. https://www.cnbc.com/2020/07/22/nike-shakes-up-its-executive-team-announces-job-cuts.html

Watson, J. (2015). *Strategy: An Introduction to Game Theory*. WW Norton.

Watzlawik, P., Weakland, J. H., & Fisch, R. (1974). *Change: Principles of problem formation and problem resolution*. Norton.

Weick, K. E. (1993). The collapse of sensemaking: The Mann Gulch disaster. *Administrative Science Quarterly, 38*, 628–652.

Weick, K. E., & Roberts, K. H. (1993). Collective Mind in Organizations: Heedful Interrelating on Flight Decks. *Administrative Science Quarterly, 38*(3), 357–381.

Yeung, A., & Ulrich, D. (2019). *Reinventing the Organization*. Harvard Business Review Press.

Chapter 3
The Transformational Leader:
Managing Organizational Trauma Through Seasons of Change

David W. Gaston
Gaston Educational Consulting LLC, USA

ABSTRACT

This chapter provides the reader with background and discussion regarding the transformational leadership model developed by James MacGregor Burns in 1978. The theory was further refined by Bernard Bass through the 1980s and 1990s and has become a hallmark for leaders who wish to embrace change and improve their organization's performance. Collaboration, empathy, trust, and a genuine concern for all employees or followers in the organization are vital to the success of the transformational leader. A comparison of the theory of instructional leadership to transformational leadership provides the reader with an understanding of the differences between these leadership models. Discussion shifts to focus on how trauma negatively affects employees and organizations and how the elements and practices of transformational leadership can work to bring healing and wholeness to school communities and weather the potentially negative effects that change has on a learning community.

INTRODUCTION

"Everything changes but change" (Israel Zangwill).

Improvement, innovation, and change must be embraced by an organization if it desires to grow, evolve, and maintain relevance. Schools and school divisions as organizations are no exception to these practices as they work to meet the unique and challenging needs and demands of learners and, more importantly, build infrastructures that encourage and support innovative learning practices. Schools and school districts have recently shifted from leadership models that have been almost exclusively focused on instructional leadership to models that closely mirror their counterparts in the business world, blend complex leadership practices with bottom-line accountability standards (Anderson, 2017). Twenty-

DOI: 10.4018/978-1-7998-7016-6.ch003

first-century demands of equity, diversity, and inclusion—highlighted and underscored by the severe disruption to our educational programs brought on by the COVID-19 pandemic—have further stressed these systems. Local schools and districts have been scrambling to establish online learning and hybrid teaching models to meet the learning demands of students, many of whom were already experiencing significant challenges or deficits prior to the pandemic.

Organizations that attempt to redefine what they do or who they are with any degree of success are exceptionally rare (Anthony & Schwartz, 2017). Simply mentioning change within any organization sends shivers down the spines of employees as they struggle to understand why change must take place, what is driving the need for the change, and how these new actions will be implemented. While most employees realize that change, innovation, and improvement must take place to ensure the longevity of their organization, the trauma or fear that oftentimes accompanies this process produces a level of discomfort among employees that can be unsettling. These negative emotions among employees and other stakeholders in the organization discourage and threaten their chances of success. Leaders who understand and embrace change, encourage and involve individuals in this process, and inspire and lead the process of transformation often experience greater success in championing improvement and successfully moving forward.

In the wake of crises that threaten organizations, school leaders need to consider expanding their leadership capacity beyond traditional tasks of instructional leadership, hiring and evaluating teachers, community outreach, developing and managing budgets, and supporting struggling learners to embrace private sector leadership practices like strategic planning and staff support (Anderson, 2017). Preparing educational leaders to go beyond these traditional roles requires increased and continuous training in leadership theory that sets leaders up for success through times of change or trauma, whether change comes from within the organization, as enacted by the leader, or acts on it externally, such as a pandemic or safety crisis. While the negative effects of change and transformation will be felt through all layers of an organization, leaders who subscribe to the practices and behaviors of transformational leadership can mitigate the negative effects of trauma within their schools and across their school districts.

TRANSFORMATIONAL LEADERSHIP

James V. Downton, a sociologist and professor at the University of Colorado at Boulder, first coined the term "transformational leadership" in 1973. The concept of transformational leadership, however, was not fully developed into a modern leadership theory until James MacGregor Burns, a presidential biographer, historian, and leadership researcher at Williams College, expanded on Downton's work in his book *Leadership* (1978). Burns' theory of transformational leadership differed markedly from other leadership concepts, most notably transactional leadership, which was based on the give and take aspects of leaders, or traditional compliance models, where the leader asks their employees to complete a task and expects compliance. Instead, Burns focused on what he termed a "transforming" leader, describing how successful leaders value the beliefs, ideals, and needs of their followers and lead change within their organizations by motivating and inspiring their followers. These leaders work with their followers to identify specific and needed changes within the organization, develop a vision for change to guide the organization through the transformation process, and successfully move through the change process with all members of the group, staying committed to successful outcomes (Burns, 1978).

Burns' transformational leader is not a micromanager; rather, they trust their employees to reflect, innovate, and own their decisions within their specific position in the organization (White, 2018). This encouragement allows employees to grow and develop as change agents, problem solvers, and creative thinkers and to become transformational leaders themselves. The magnanimous empowerment and nature of this type of leader create a virtuous and willing partner in leadership whose aim is to be the rising tide to lift all employee's boats, encouraging morality, positive development, clear values, priorities, and standards to guide them past self-interests to a place in the larger common good (White, 2018).

Bernard Bass, a professor and leadership researcher at Binghamton University, expanded Burns' work in 1985 by measuring the impact that transformational leaders have on their followers and describing the levels of motivation and performance of an organization's employees (Cherry, 2020). Specifically, Bass' transformational leadership theory determined that the extent to which a leader is transformational is directly related to the amount of influence that the leader has on their followers (Bass, 1990). The levels of trust, respect, loyalty, and admiration present in employees were measures that Bass posited would determine the extent to which the leader was truly transformational. This was critical to transformational leadership, for the leader is a motivating force in their role; they move their employees to fully embrace the vision and mission of the organization and provide the organization with their culture or identity. They truly believe in and care deeply about their followers, knowing that they can develop into their best selves and become empowered to do their best work for the organization.

Bass (1985) identified four central components of transformational leadership. The first type is intellectual stimulation (IS). Transformational leaders encourage their employees to be creative and innovative by challenging the status quo and exploring new ways to approach and accomplish tasks and challenges. The leader and their followers are learners and do not shy away from engaging in opportunities to learn new approaches to help them challenge tradition and cultural norms.

The second type is individualized consideration (IC). Followers are provided genuine concern by the transformational leader for their needs and feelings. Personal attention is provided to followers by the leader to build deep and meaningful relationships that allow the leader and follower to be honest with one another. Transformational leaders can work with their followers to provide training and development should they need assistance in their roles. Additionally, followers feel comfortable around the leader and, because of the trust that is built, are more willing to provide input and feedback into decisions, thus increasing buy-in to the decisions that are rendered.

The next type is idealized influence (II). This concept sees the transformational leader walking the walk and talking the talk. The leader is seen by their followers as a role model for the organization because they embody positive characteristics and inspire their followers to practice and develop these traits. Obviously, these characteristics must be the ones that the leader wishes to see embodied through all levels of their organization and its culture. The leader becomes an inspiration to their followers, thus building additional trust.

Finally, the last type is inspirational motivation (IM). Where there is no vision, the people perish. A transformational leader must have a clear vision and be able to clearly articulate and model that vision to their followers. The passion that the leader has for this vision is also clearly articulated to their employees.

Idealized influence and idealized motivation are the two components of Bass's transformational leadership theory that create the leader's charisma (Bass, 1985). Not to be confused with the traditional concept of charismatic leadership, Bass's definition of a leader's charisma was more approachable and attainable than what is normally attributed to historically charismatic leaders such as Dr. Martin Luther King, Jr. or Mohandas Gandhi. According to Lynch (2015), charisma is:

derived from respect and is a visible projection of responsibility... followers will follow other followers. If a leader is able to distribute tasks and have those tasks completed effectively... then others will latch onto that and naturally follow. In effect, a leader can grow their charisma by utilizing their resources effectively. (p.2)

Transformational Leadership in Business

The concepts that Burns and Bass developed and refined over the past 40 years quickly gained traction in the business world (St. Thomas University, 2018). Today, transformational leaders may be found across all sectors and are easily embodied in the leadership styles of Jeff Bezos or Steve Jobs. Often called quiet leaders, their ability to lead by example, develop a rapport with their employees, inspire and engage their followers, and possess the courage and confidence to advance bold ideas to benefit the greater good of everyone in the company are well-known (St. Thomas University, 2018). While these individuals are traditional examples of transformational leaders, their success as executives lies in their ability to innovate and change their businesses to ensure that they remain viable and elastic in their markets. This flexibility is a vital feature and explains why the theory of transformational leadership remains a leading concept.

Transformational vs. Transactional Leadership

Burns' work compared transformational leadership to transactional leadership. Transactional leadership is a more traditional model, where a leader does not attempt to innovate but strives to keep things consistent, routine, and structured to combat inefficiency and disorder (White, 2018). Transactional leaders strive to maintain consistent development, versus a transformational leader, who encourages their employees to remain agile and anticipatory as they assume risk to develop and innovate their products. At the same time, it seems like a strange concept for a leader to assume risk and failure in developing their products; the key to success lies in the leader's ability to encourage, support, and connect with their followers and empower them to find solutions to the challenges of product and business development. The trust that the leader instills in their employees, and the idea of one for all and all for one, set the transformational leader apart from a transactional leader. On the surface, this element of risk and planned change in a traditional corporate environment would be a tremendous stressor on any organization's employees. The transformational leader, however, builds confidence and courage by involving and encouraging followers in the decision-making process and trusting them to innovate and improve product development.

When it comes to transformation in business, many corporations desire to change and evolve; however, few companies really succeed in redefining what they produce or accomplish (Anthony & Schwartz, 2017). While an underlying and interesting quality of transformational leaders is that they are indeed visionary, they often have had very little previous experience in their industry. For example, Jeff Bezos had no direct industry in retail; rather, his prior leadership experience centered around the world of finance. Even so, as the CEO of Amazon, he worked to reinvent the retail industry from the ground up without any predetermined idea of how to approach transforming Amazon from the start (Anthony & Schwartz, 2017).

Transformational leaders who come to their leadership positions with relevant experience, but no actual or direct leadership experience in their corporate sector as a CEO, are known as "Insider-Outsiders" (Anthony & Schwartz, 2017). The interesting and somewhat unnerving aspect of transformational leadership is that there is no specific playbook on how the leader should implement this leadership style. It is an iterative process, and the leader must make a conscious decision to adopt a transformational style (Farnsworth et al., 2019). Their ability to arrive in their organization as an outsider, but with relevant long-term experience prior to assuming their leadership position, allows them to make change happen within their organization. They also maintain an outsider's perspective as they explore opportunities to pivot and change their business model, keeping their company relevant and pointed future-forward. Regardless of their perspective, they must commit to the tenets of a transformational leadership style.

Differentiating Instructional From Transformational Leadership

While transformational leadership theory has been predominant in the business world, the theory that Burns initially developed emerged from his work as a political scientist and historian studying the leadership styles of presidents and political leaders. While this would seem to naturally gravitate to the business world, this theory can also benefit educational leaders who seek to change and transform the business of learning in their schools and promote a culture of innovation and improvement.

Instructional leadership appeared in the 1980s with the effective schools' movement, and its initial arrival in education took a ready-fire-aim approach. Reformers, eager to effect change within schools and increase student achievement and accountability, raced to establish a leadership model that would provide a one-size-fits-all approach in their very noble and magnanimous efforts to improve conditions in all schools. The movement became so pervasive among policymakers that the Federal government established Leadership Academies in every state to lead the charge of preparing leaders who would turn the tide of student achievement. Unfortunately, in their zealousness to establish these academies in every state, they relied on the assumption that there was a credible knowledge base underlying the development of principal leadership (Hallinger, 2010). This was no further from the truth. The framework for instructional leadership was drawn from emerging research that was incorrectly and hastily translated into a model of strong, decisive instructional leadership that placed the principal at the center of all instructional functions and decisions (Hallinger, 2010). The issue was that every school in the United States was its own community or culture of learners that could not simply benefit from the same resources as other schools. They also could not benefit from having a principal leader with the same leadership traits and characteristics as another school leader at a different school.

Despite the quick jump into instructional leadership, further research offered modifications to its framework as it was implemented. Unfortunately, misunderstanding and misconception with the model created an initial view of the principal leader as an individual who would not compromise high standards, who took on enormous responsibility setting and establishing learning and improvement goals for their school, and who became managers, supervisors, coordinators, and guardians of curriculum and instruction in their schools (Hallinger, 2010). As instructional leadership evolved, additional dimensions to this model expanded and defined the leadership roles of the principal. For example, a mission and vision for each school had to be determined, as well as clear, measurable goals and objectives were needed to guide the improvement process for each school community. In developing this aspect of the model, however, it was never specified as to who would be the responsible party in establishing these elements, leaving it up for grabs as to whether the principal would include or involve their faculty and staff in developing a strategic plan (Hallinger, 2010). With accountability and achievement demands looming large and consequences surrounding underperforming schools becoming increasingly punitive, the principal quickly became the individual largely responsible for these expectations.

Research focusing on the relationship of instructional leadership, teaching, and student achievement was not adequately studied, even as the 21st century approached (Blase & Blase, 1999). As studies surrounding these relationships were completed, their findings produced curious results. In cases where principals allowed their teachers the flexibility and freedom to determine their instructional methodologies, standard and rigid teaching approaches were substituted with innovative and more student-centered interactions, including inquiry, reflection, experimentation, and exploration (Blase & Blase, 1999). Additional studies showed that effective instructional leaders encouraged their teachers to critically reflect on their practices, valued and participated in professional learning practices and reflection with their teachers, and provided purposeful, non-threatening, and appropriate feedback to teachers during post-observation conferences (Blase & Blase, 1999). Praise and support for collaborative practice were also found to increase teacher morale, self-esteem, teamwork, and efficacy and led to the establishment of peer observation and sharing of methodologies (Blase & Blase, 1999).

Ironically, as instructional leadership practice evolved, its success depended largely on leadership qualities and characteristics that integrated the conscious practices of a transformational leader. Empowerment, listening, caring, and sensitivity to the professional knowledge of teachers remained genuine practices. Originally found in the theories of Burns and Bass, these qualities enhanced leader efficacy, built trust, loyalty, and admiration among the followers, and allowed for collaborative practice. It also encouraged freedom among teachers to select instructional methodologies for lesson delivery and engage in risk-taking in their classroom. When teachers modeled this behavior each day, it also encouraged students to take risks, lessening their fear of failure and increasing their likelihood of participating in class activities.

Hallinger (2007) compared instructional and transformational leadership methodologies and found that when elements of both models were integrated and implemented with fidelity, a shared sense of purpose in the school, a climate of high expectations with a focus on innovation and invention, reflection on the school's mission and goals as set by and for the faculty and staff, an emphasis on quality staff development and professional growth, and visible leadership that consistently modeled the values of the school's culture resulted. Similarly, Riggio (2009) found that transformational leaders believe that their followers can do their best. Groups led by these leaders have higher levels of performance and job satisfaction than groups who are led by non-transformational leaders (Riggio, 2009).

Repositioning and Creating New Growth

Examples of lesser-known CEOs who transformed their companies in this manner abound in the business literature. A common thread that connects all of them was that as leaders, they produced change by simultaneously engaging two separate tracks or pathways: repositioning their core business while investing and pursuing new growth and innovation in their industry (Anthony & Schwartz, 2017).

Satya Nadella, who signed on as the CEO of Microsoft in 2014, took the company from an insular and risk-averse culture to one that celebrated risk-taking and exploration. Prior to his tenure, Microsoft spent long periods of time focusing on the next version or generation of their programs, such as Windows. An engineer by trade who joined Microsoft in 1992 and specialized in cloud computing, Nadella was different from his counterparts in the tech world. Nadella worked his way up through the company and, when hired by the Board of Directors of Microsoft, established his transformational leadership style by listening, learning, and analyzing the work of his employees and departments.

This quiet leadership style was a far cry from the more public and open forum of leadership practiced by leaders such as Steve Jobs. Moving from a focus on the singular development of the next version of their programs, Nadella created a new world of "infrastructure on-demand," encouraging his employees to vision and develop new features and improvements to these platforms every month, often without any plan as to how these improvements to the product would actually look (Anthony & Schwartz, 2017). His idea of how to motivate his employees was to empower his followers to work on projects for which they had passion. He would also lead a company-wide hackathon to engage employees across the organization.

This shift allowed Microsoft to continue developing its core products and services; however, the CEO also used his knowledge of cloud computing to expand the company into artificial intelligence and cloud services, which by 2017 accounted for upwards of one-third of the company's revenue (Anthony & Schwartz, 2017). While change and transformation were successfully encouraged and generated by the company, the core services of the company also shifted as the transformational leader empowered his employees to lead the push for change and innovation, willingly investing their individual talents, trust, and loyalty as the vision, mission, and culture at Microsoft significantly shifted.

Preparing and Supporting Transformational Leadership in Education

When applied to educational leadership, transformational leadership theory allows the leader to extend beyond the traditional instructional and managerial duties. This empowers teachers and staff to drive organizational change and transition in the school or school district and foster a culture of continuous improvement, growth, and empowerment in the decision-making process. There is an investment in the success and a strengthening of trust in relationships with the common goal of improving student learning outcomes and improving educational quality. The challenge to building, supporting, and encouraging transformational leaders in education lies in how future educational leaders are prepared for their leadership roles and the conscious decision to embrace the concepts of innovation, risk, and change.

Effective school leadership is a critical driver of school success. However, the Thomas B. Fordham Institute (2014) analyzed the recruitment, selection, and placement of school principals and concluded that most principals lacked the capacity to be effective leaders (Anderson, 2017). The study spanned a decade of research in principal preparation and training programs and concluded that these programs failed to provide proper training in the skills that principals needed to promote meaningful school change and meet accountability, student growth, and achievement outcomes. From this research, the conclusion was clear:

Education has become business, and schools have become social organizations conducting daily business. The business nature and complexity of tasks and responsibilities prompt even more concern over whether or not principals and educational leaders are taught the fundamentals of management and practicing good leadership skills. As schools face an environment that has become business-oriented and managerially complex, school leaders may benefit from training and development in leadership styles proven to enhance the success of both business organizations and educational settings. (Anderson, 2017, p. 3)

Leadership in schools today is complex and multifaceted, requiring school leaders to be budget directors, social justice leaders, talent managers, recruiters, strategic planners, marketing and communication experts, and counselors (Van Gronigen et al., 2021). School leadership training programs have historically provided training and preparation in instructional leadership because it focuses on student accountability, curriculum, and instruction as effective practice, especially in teaching children in poor, urban communities (Hallinger, 2007).

Heifetz (1994) saw school leaders working between technical and adaptive challenges. Technical challenges encountered by school leaders are those that are clearly defined, such as the creation of a budget or an after-school transportation schedule. Adaptive challenges are those that are not as simple to solve, such as low teacher morale, trauma, or high rates of student absenteeism. These situations require deeper adaptive capacity, where leaders must coordinate employees and resources to solve more complex issues that cannot be solved by a single leader (Heifetz, 1994).

Leader preparation programs (LPPs) provide a variety of experiences for aspiring educational leaders, predominantly offering online or in-person, university or non-university based, two-year master's programs, or one-semester alternative certification and licensure programs (Van Gronigen et al., 2021). Despite the differences between these programs, the majority of programs offered through a university are relatively stable programs, where faculty and staff focus on five broad areas of leadership: recruitment and selection of aspiring leaders, curriculum, instructional practices, assessment, and clinical experiences (Van Gronigen et al., 2021). Over recent years, however, LPPs have gravitated either toward a technical or adaptive approach to their studies. The technical approach includes the standard five areas, combined with courses in finance, law, or human resources, taught as individual entities, to allow principals to focus on the technical aspects of school leadership (Van Gronigen et al., 2021). Adaptive preparation also focuses on the five core areas; however, it instructs students through the lens of the technical, instructional, and relational aspects of leadership, where aspiring leaders learn how to build collaborative capacity between their followers (Van Gronigen et al., 2021).

While instructional leadership remains a widely accepted model in educational leadership preparatory programs, it certainly was not without its critics. Some individuals felt that the instructional leadership model placed too much emphasis on the principal as the center of expertise, power, and authority in schools and that the centralization of the principal's position as the instructional leader placed too many duties and responsibilities on one position (Cuban, 1984).

During the 1990s, transformational leadership was introduced to principal leadership and preparation programs with a focus on innovating and restructuring schools. As this movement unfolded, it became apparent that school leaders were not just instructional leaders; they were at the head of complex social organizations with intricate managerial tasks, political forces, and strategic demands that closely mirrored those of their business counterparts (Hallinger, 2007). Transformational leadership more strongly supported the restructuring and change demands for schools because it encourages employees to learn new methodologies, builds and strengthens new cultural norms, and fundamentally changes the organizational norms of a school (Anderson, 2017). It also more positively impacts stakeholders, particularly teachers and staff, because school leaders model positive behavior and leadership traits. This, in turn, encourages risk-taking, innovation, new learning, and methodologies in classrooms, increasing student outcomes and achievement.

To affirm and support this shift toward adaptive or transformational leader preparation in LPPs, the standards and expectations for performance for school leaders also needed to reflect this movement. The Interstate School Leaders Licensure Consortium (ISLLC) standards that first appeared in 1996 were revised as recently as 2015 to become the Professional Standards for Educational Leaders (PSEL) that support efforts for school leaders to build and maintain relationships with teachers, students, and community stakeholders (NPBEA, 2015). Clearly, the old ways of managing employees through traditional transactional means are no longer seen as an effective way to build leadership capacity, authentic relationships, and positive student outcomes. Transformational leadership theory, embedded in adaptive preparation practices in university LPP programs, trains school leaders to build teacher skills and integrate successful business management techniques and theory into practical programming (Burrows-McCabe, 2014; Kouzes & Posner, 2012; Van Gronigen et al., 2021). By merging academic and practical knowledge, adaptive preparation programs help aspiring leaders learn how to improve teaching and learning through collaborative and cooperative practices and by building positive, productive relationships (Davis & Darling-Hammond, 2012; Onorato, 2013).

The rise of standards and accountability measures from political bodies, coupled with the global emphasis on performance standards for K-12 education, produced additional pressure for leaders to familiarize themselves with instructional leadership concepts; however, organizational demands for change and innovation in schools did not go away (Hallinger, 2007). The result has been a curious push-pull relationship between the incorporation of concepts from both leadership models to meet the instructional, organizational, and cultural needs of a school and introduce necessary reforms to improve student outcomes.

LEADERSHIP STYLES AND SCHOOL CULTURE

As instructional and transformational leadership continue to be integrated into school leadership training programs, an understanding of the larger effect of each leadership style and the culture that it creates is vital. Each model produces a certain way of doing things—a culture—with the common goal of increasing student achievement. While these systems represent different approaches to leadership, LPPs that offer training in the best features and practices from both models will encourage future leaders to build a culture of continuous improvement and innovation in schools.

A Marathon Versus a Sprint

Instructional and transformational leadership increase the chances of success for reform efforts in schools. The task of changing the culture of any organization, however, is daunting. Most corporations that engage in transformational processes are normally not successful in implementing change. Leaders must be deliberate and intentional in their commitment to change. Their consistent and persistent practices, coupled with modeling desired characteristics with fidelity and evenness across the entire organization, fuel success and change. But this work is by no means a short-term engagement. Typically, transformations can take years (about ten years on average) to complete (Anthony & Schwartz, 2017). In most cases, changes that are initiated cannot be completed by a school leader during their average tenure of four years for principals and six years for district superintendents (AASA, 2010; Levin & Bradley, 2019). While transformational leaders must hit the road with a new pair of track shoes upon assuming their office, the change journey is more of a strategic marathon that must still be seen as a long-term venture, and the leader must pursue a multiphase strategy to reposition traditional practices while finding new areas of growth and development for the school (Anthony & Schwartz, 2017).

EMPLOYEE WELL-BEING AND ORGANIZATIONAL TRAUMA

While discussion and practice typically center on leader behaviors, a larger and more important area of focus is how followers are affected by change and transformative practice. In the ideal setting, a leader's ability to consistently start practices that will draw their followers into a trusting, open, and positive relationship drives success. Research conducted across six German corporations showed that transformational leadership could have a positive influence on employee well-being, as it builds trust and meaningfulness, particularly as the leader individually and personally connects, challenges, and develops their followers (Jacobs et al., 2013). While transformational leadership can promote employee well-being, the bitter fact remains that change is not a comfortable process for most individuals. As new leadership assumes control, there is inevitably a sense of uncertainty, loss, or trauma within an organization as it moves through a season of change. Trauma can be internal to the organization (e.g., restructuring its ranks), or it can be an external threat (e.g., corporate takeover, a downsizing or reduction in force due to declining product sales or student enrollments, or a pandemic that forces difficult decisions to be made to protect and preserve employee health and safety). In each of these scenarios, a transformational leader who consistently holds to their practice can mitigate the negative effects of trauma and change on the organization and its followers.

Change, Trauma, Stress, and Teachers

Teaching remains one of the most stressful and demanding professions, often being compared to public safety positions, such as law enforcement and firefighters (Walker, 2018). Researchers at the University of Missouri found that 93 percent of elementary teachers reported high levels of stress, feeling that they do not have the coping skills necessary to face the daily demands of their classrooms, are demoralized by the changes in their profession, and burned out by the overwhelming amount of duties and demands that are placed on them (Walker, 2018). High levels of stress among a large majority of teachers ostensibly trickles down to students, who become collateral victims of this personal and professional teacher stress and manifest this stress through negative classroom behaviors and declining student achievement (Walker, 2018). This, in turn, perpetuates a cycle of stress and trauma for teachers, as negative student behaviors and poor performance contribute to the stress that teachers feel in their classrooms. Coping skills, stress management techniques, and interventions present options and opportunities for teachers to control stress levels; however, without a consistent commitment by school leaders to create positive, productive, and healthy school environments, education will continue to face the stark reality of increased teacher shortages and high teacher turnover rates driven by stress levels and an inability of leadership to effectively resolve them. The challenges of a pandemic have only served to significantly exacerbate these already alarming rates of teacher attrition, anxiety, and stress.

Coping with change and trauma is difficult. It is the rare individual who does not experience some sense of angst, uncertainty, or anxiety when there is a disturbance or interruption to the normal flow of life events. The already abysmal levels of stress and trauma that exist among faculty and staff in schools have only been exacerbated by the pandemic. More than 45 percent of teachers claim that their morale is lower now than it was prior to the pandemic, and 42 percent state that the pandemic has made them even less motivated at work (Prothero, 2021). Sadly, almost one-third of educators also claim that attempts by their administrators to improve teacher morale had absolutely no effect, with four percent claiming that administrative attempts to improve morale only made their morale worse (Prothero, 2021).

While attempts to improve morale and motivation in the middle of a pandemic might seem to be too little too late or reactive, rather than proactive, the trauma and shock of a pandemic or the ill-effects of sudden and unplanned change cannot be ignored. Teaching is perhaps at its most pivotal and difficult moment in history, with the number of schools across the United States who cannot fill teaching vacancies having tripled between 2011 and 2016 and the number of individuals entering the teaching profession experiencing a decrease of 15.4 percent between 2008 and 2016 (Garcia & Weiss, 2019). While low pay is one consistent factor cited in the research as a major reason for this sharp decrease in individuals entering the teaching profession, working conditions remain one of the largest reasons cited by teachers for low morale and their massive nationwide departure (Garcia & Weiss, 2019). This provides an opportunity for educational leaders to take a harder and more reflective look into their leadership practices to understand how trauma affects their staff and how they can successfully address and heal workplace stress and low morale in schools. Clearly, unresolved stress and trauma in any workplace prevent teachers from realizing their full capacity and potential. Responsive, transformational leadership can bring healing and well-being to learning communities.

Trauma and Stress in Organizational Development

When it comes to the dynamics of any organization, every system is designed to produce the results that it gets (Sparks, 2002). Increasing the levels of professionalism in schools and among school leaders has a positive impact on student achievement. However, this cannot be accomplished when morale is low, when teachers are uncertain about their employment status, or when they feel little to no ownership or investment in school improvement and decision-making processes. Uncertainty, doubt, and fear become the enemies of progress and achievement. Employees will feel emotionally hurt and too traumatized to be able to perform basic tasks or meet expectations when they must struggle with unresolved negative emotions and stress (DeKlerk, 2007). Unlike physical trauma, which can be detected by outward signs of injury, emotional trauma is more difficult to detect. While the physical injuries of trauma can heal with the body's natural abilities to mend, psychological or emotional trauma is not as readily detected and may not outwardly manifest itself. The ability to bring emotional healing to the body involves a more deliberate and planned path and cannot be ignored if the organization and its leaders desire to allow employees to survive, heal, and overcome these occurrences.

There is almost no differentiation between events or incidents that can cause trauma. The pandemic has brought a tremendous sense of loss, isolation, loneliness, economic hardship, and uncertainty to schools across the globe. This trauma only adds to the already mounting pressure that teachers report feeling in their daily work. Job stress was already very real and present prior to the pandemic. Students who might have experienced relatively steady or strong levels of emotional and mental wellness prior to their school closing are increasingly finding it more difficult to maintain positive levels of emotional well-being and mental health. The American Civil Liberties Union of Southern California (2020) found that statewide, 22% of students reported receiving mental health services before the pandemic, and 32% of students who were not receiving services felt that with school closures and interruptions to their learning lives, they may now need services (Walker, 2020).

While increases such as this among students who are directly affected by this trauma are troubling, it must also be recognized that a traumatic event affects those who are indirectly affected by the trauma, such as witnesses, bystanders, or survivors (DeKlerk, 2007). This, coupled with the common misperception that survivors of trauma will be okay once the trauma has ended, if the organization does not take measured and focused steps to address trauma, there is the very real risk that the negative emotions and behaviors associated with trauma will become part of the larger organizational system. This will further weigh down already critical levels of stress, detachment, and morale to compromise productivity and achievement (DeKlerk, 2007).

Groysberg and Abrahams (2020) share fascinating insight into survival psychology and how leaders can manage their organizations through trauma. According to Groysberg and Abrahams (2020), "As CEO's in this crisis, we have no option but to become the wartime CEO, however ill-equipped or prepared we are" (p. 1). This vivid comparison is drawn from the amazing story of Admiral James Stockdale, who survived seven-and-one-half years as a prisoner of war at the infamous Hanoi Hilton during the Vietnam War. When asked how he was able to survive the daily trauma, despair, and physical torture during his captivity, Stockdale's response was that he never lost faith at the end of the story, never doubted that he would get out, and would prevail in the end to turn these events into defining moments in his life that he would not trade (Groysberg & Abraham, 2020). This came as a surprise to many who believed that maintaining a sense of optimism and setting more short-term goals for their release would seem to be the better approach toward survival for these prisoners of war. Unfortunately, as Stockdale pointed out, individuals who felt that they would be released from prison by Christmas would see the holiday come and go and then move to Easter, which would pass, and then on to the next calendar milestone. Eventually, they would give up their will to live and die of broken hearts because they did not have the courage to face the brutal fact that their imprisonment and suffering would be much longer (Leach, 2011).

As the pandemic continues to wage its path of increased infection and mortality rates, the comparison that can be drawn to the Stockdale Theory is stark. According to Groysberg and Abraham (2020):

Your state, industry, organization—or unconscious mind—may be pinning hopes on some other event or date after which some version of "rescue" will come: a vaccine, a cure, a reliable and cheap test, the acquisition of herd immunity. But to review the brutal facts, none of these developments are likely in the foreseeable short term. The possibility remains that there may never be a fully effective vaccine or cure; this virus may be something that we live with and manage for years to come. Doing so will mean changing elements of our social interaction in unprecedented ways that may well lead to irrevocable social changes. (p. 3)

The pandemic has significantly changed the way that people intrinsically perform daily tasks because the normal routine (e.g., tasks as simple as buying a cup of coffee, entering a store, or teaching in the classrooms) has been interrupted. This interruption requires people to consciously think about the new processes involved to complete these tasks, such as wearing masks, maintaining social distancing, and learning new technologies to communicate with other individuals. As the pandemic wears on, the stress of these new thought processes, coupled with the reality that there will be no clear and short-term end to these disturbances in normal life routines, can demotivate, depress, and demoralize school communities. Maintaining optimism in these traumatic situations is akin to pouring lime juice into an already open and raw sore. While it might seem like an appropriate and encouraging response to look for the silver lining in these traumatic situations, such as to "look on the bright side" or "it could always be worse," this phenomenon of "toxic positivity" is something that must be prevented, as it does not promote, nor encourage, resilience (Prothero, 2021).

Interestingly, while intrinsic survival mechanisms common to daily life are interrupted by traumatic long-term instances, such as a pandemic, the negative emotions that accompany these routines force individuals to remain conscious about new routines, such as remembering to wear a mask or regularly washing their hands (Prothero, 2021). Students need to see that their teachers are human beings who are just as stressed and are struggling with trauma as they are in order to understand that it is acceptable to be distressed in these situations. As we continue through this reality, much in the same way that Admiral

Stockdale built his will to survive on the long-term faith that he would get through his ordeal and come out of it stronger, this same attitude must supersede any current toxic directives that prevent teachers from discussing their struggles with parents or posting on social media. According to one teacher, "It would be very helpful if I could hear the words, 'We realize this is really tough, and this sucks right now…It wouldn't change anything, but at least I would feel acknowledged" (Prothero, 2021, p. 3). The Stockdale Paradox (to have faith but to confront reality) is very real and applicable to just about any traumatic experience an organization must weather.

Staying Ahead of the Crisis

No leader can ever anticipate traumatic events that will strain an organization. However, transformational leadership can create structures and opportunities for the leader and their followers to better weather a crisis. Through this leadership modality, differences and diversity are celebrated, and the unique qualities of each individual teacher are honored as significant and contributing factors to the overall success of the organization. Likewise, students benefit from the varied perspectives that are provided through diversity and learn how to appreciate and embrace these differences in their classroom environments and their learning. Encouraging participation in the decision-making process, soliciting input from stakeholders, and basing decisions on these inputs strengthens trust and integrity in the leader. Encouraging and listening to feedback also shows that the leader cares about their community, and their concerns are vital for the process of continuous improvement, the culture, and the outcomes of the organization. It also emphasizes the strong morale and trustworthiness of the leader. Teachers will also feel more secure in their work and careers, have less role ambiguity, and higher task performance and job satisfaction in their work (American University, 2019). Overall, if the culture is taught to embrace and anticipate change and view it as adaptive work rather than a technical directive, it remains purposefully committed to the work and understanding why the change is needed (Wagner, 2006).

While there is certainly no guarantee that an organization can solidly weather change, crisis, or trauma, a transformational leader establishes a framework or model for governance that is dynamic, visionary, genuine, empathetic, and collaborative. Followers understand the leader's vision and can articulate it, as it is consistently reinforced through their actions, words, and character. Trust and confidence are instilled and maintained deep within the organization by the leader, and their followers are encouraged to develop, grow, and, in turn, become leaders themselves. They also are empowered as decision-makers and provide their expertise in their areas of expertise. As information and data are received regarding performance, achievement, and outcomes, the organization pivots to adjust and steer to different course coordinates to ensure that their goals and objectives are achieved.

Transformational leaders will also understand that when a large disaster or event hits their organization, they must assume greater responsibility in ensuring that their character, empathy, trust, and integrity are preserved and consistently communicated. Opportunities for healing, provided over time with understanding and patience, will allow the organization to mend and slowly move forward again, oftentimes with greater strength and resilience. Lessons learned from these situations may also be debriefed and captured in strategies and steps that will be useful in responding to future crises, with critical evaluation and collaborative reflection (Jordan et al., 2020). Transformational leadership establishes structures and practices like this that are natural to the organization and become integrated seamlessly into the culture. Once established and consistently practiced, they become the best strategic defense against a crisis, uncertainty, and the trauma that accompanies change and growth.

LEADING THROUGH THE STORM

The pandemic aside, organizational or work-related trauma is emerging as a major issue that cannot go unnoticed, unrecognized, or unresolved (DeKlerk, 2007). The loss and isolation that is caused by change or uncertainty in schools must be skillfully handled by leaders who are versed in the relational virtues and characteristics of transformational leadership. Managing and leading in a profession that is already navigating some of the most stressful and demanding elements of any career, coupled with the added stressors of a pandemic, places every educator in a position where they are all feeling helpless, lonely, and forgotten. What, then, can leaders do to mitigate these emotions, and how can they raise and restore their schools so that stakeholders can have faith but confront their realities?

According to Mineo (2014), the foundational characteristics of Transformational Leadership cluster around four main areas: 1. The leader building trust through the belief that the greatness of the workplace is built on credibility, respect, and fairness; 2. Open communication, coupled with the assurance that the organization's vision will be acted upon with integrity and competence, that allows a more fair coordination of resources and credibility by leadership; 3. Support for quality professional development, collaboration, and genuine invitation for involvement and contributions by the leader; and 4. Objective decision-making, balanced hiring practices, and the dignified treatment of all employees by the leader, which cultivates respect. As school leaders become conscious and sympathetic to teacher stress, burnout, and the adverse impact of stressors on students and stakeholders, keeping these practices and core values at the center of their leadership practice allow them to take a vital step toward healing and restoration while building a foundation for trust and assurance that will help the school weather the change process.

Intuitive transformational leaders know that symptoms of trauma are natural and necessary for healing to take place. Kubler-Ross (1969) established that individuals move through the classic stages of grief, which include denial, anger, bargaining, depression, and acceptance. This model has been largely misinterpreted by most laymen who believe that an individual will automatically and intrinsically move through each stage to reach acceptance when experiencing trauma or disruption. Experiences such as grief and bereavement are viewed by some as a weakness, but they must be viewed as natural processes that are important to healing and restoration. Many individuals do not move fluidly through each stage and may not always reach acceptance. Leaders must rely on their collaborative and collegial relationships to promote healing among their faculty, staff, and students. Interestingly, it is not the trauma that produces disorders, such as Post-Traumatic Stress Disorder (PTSD), but rather the failure to allow individuals to adequately process the stress or trauma that can lead to dependencies or even pathological behaviors (DeKlerk, 2007).

Healing from organizational trauma in schools must be a deliberate and intentional effort coordinated by the leader with strong support staff and assistance to bring healing, resolution, and restoration. While the larger community may feel the desire to get back to work immediately following a traumatic event or episode, the transformational leader understands that time and effort are needed to ensure that individuals feel nurtured and accepted. Professional intervention that provides individuals with the chance to authentically express their feelings and emotions, both individually and collectively, in an open and non-judgmental environment provides great opportunities for everyone to exorcise the negative effects of trauma and stress and begin the healing process. Interestingly, much like Admiral Stockdale and other survivors of disaster or trauma, research shows that those who survive trauma are able to quickly regain cognitive functioning, adapt to their new environment or reality, and create goals that allow them to survive in the future (Groysberg & Abrahams, 2020).

School has always been the safest and most sacred place for students, especially at-risk students who rely on schools for counseling, hot meals, support, and the basic necessities of acceptance and socialization that they may not receive at home. The pandemic has forced them to remain in this place where they have been trapped for longer-than-anticipated periods of time and deprived of these positive life experiences (Walker, 2020). While educators place a significant focus on learning loss from the pandemic, leaders must realize that before any meaningful, focused, and concentrated learning in schools can take place again, comprehensive trauma screening support for adults and children to confront loss, grief, detachment, and social-emotional support need to be the first step in the re-entry process. School leaders must be prepared to open the emotional wounds that exist and allow everyone to know that a school is a safe place of healing and comfort (Walker, 2020). Finally, schools must collaboratively, purposefully, and strategically focus on creating warm and welcoming environments for students and teachers to return to their classrooms after they have experienced the detached and isolated environments in which they have existed for what will be, in many cases, over a one-year period.

Transformational leaders must maintain their sense of morality, values, meaning, integrity, spirituality, and vision through crisis situations. Studies of survivors have shown that having a value system, a sense of identity, and purpose for existence will increase an individual's chances of survival and resiliency (Groysberg & Abrahams, 2020). Stockdale put it more directly as he reflected on his own experiences while in prison in Vietnam:

If you realize fear and guilt are your enemies and not pain, then you've got a ticket to self-respect and certainly to friendship and support of your fellows. I'm not just telling you now to behave in prison... You've got to start right off by unloading to and confiding in and trusting your fellow officers and your men. (Groysberg & Abrahams, 2020, p. 5)

The most important action that a leader can perform through crisis situations is to consistently articulate and model vision and purpose, connect every task and action to that vision every day to help motivate and encourage everyone past their doubts and steer clear of toxic positivity. They will also need to honor the individuality of each member of their community and understand that not everyone will collectively heal at the same time. Patience and encouragement will need to run long and deep for leaders to ultimately heal every stakeholder in their learning community. By allowing everyone to work through their grief and pain through counseling sessions designed to open their emotional wounds, articulate, share, and represent their feelings and emotions with one another and identify or name the stressors that they are experiencing, leaders will make important strides in providing healing. They can and should listen and validate these feelings to build trust and safety among their stakeholders and provide encouragement that is important to the healing process.

REFERENCES

American Association of School Administrators. (2010). *The American school superintendent decennial study 2010.* https://www.aasa.org/content.aspx?id=458

American University School of Education Online Programs. (2019, December 5). *Transformational leadership in education.* https://soeonline.american.edu/blog/transformational-leadership-in-education

Anderson, M. (2017). Transformational leadership in education: A review of existing literature. *International Social Science Review, 93*(1).

Anthony, S. D., & Schwartz, E. I. (2017, May). What the best transformational leaders do. *Harvard Business Review*. https://hbr.org/2017/05/what-the-best-transformational-leaders-do

Bass, B. M. (1985). *Leadership and performance beyond expectation*. Free Press.

Bass, B. M. (1990). From transactional to transformational leadership: Learning to share the vision. *Organizational Dynamics, 18*(3), 19–31. doi:10.1016/0090-2616(90)90061-S

Blase, J., & Blase, J. (1999). Effective instructional leadership: Teacher's perspectives on how principals promote teaching and learning in schools. *Journal of Educational Administration, 38*(2), 130–141. doi:10.1108/09578230010320082

Bueche, R. A. (2018). *Principal perceptions on transformational leadership in Arizona's preparation program* [Doctoral dissertation]. Grand Canyon University.

Burrows-McCabe, A. (2014). Stepping stones to leadership. *The Learning Forward Journal, 35*(4), 40-43. https://learningforward.org/docs/defaultsource/ jsd-august-2014/stepping-stones-to-leadership.pdf

Cherry, K. (2020). *Transformational leadership: A closer look at the effects of transformational leadership*. Verywell Mind. https://www.verywellmind.com/what-is-transformational-leadership-2795313

Cuban, L. (1984). Transforming the frog into a prince: Effective school research, policy, and practice at the district level. *Harvard Educational Review, 54*(2), 129–151. doi:10.17763/haer.54.2.m07133p087795h38

Davis, S. H., & Darling-Hammond, L. (2012). Innovative principal preparation: What works and how we know. *Planning and Changing, 43*(1-2), 25–45.

DeKlerk, M. (2007). Healing emotional trauma in organizations: An o.d framework and case study. *Organization Development Journal, 25*(2), 35–41.

Farnsworth, D., Clark, J. L., Hall, J., Johnson, S., Wysocki, A., & Kepner, K. (2019). *Transformational leadership: The transformation of managers and associates*. EDIS. https://edis.ifas.ufl.edu

Garcia, E., & Weiss, E. (2019). *U.S. schools struggle to hire and retain teachers*. Economic Policy Institute. https://www.epi.org/publication/u-s-schools-struggle-to-hire-and-retain-teachers-the-second-report-in-the-perfect-storm-in-the-teacher-labor-market-series/

Groysberg, B., & Abrahams, R. (2020, August 17). *What the Stockdale paradox tells us about crisis leadership*. Harvard Business School.

Hallinger, P. (2007). *Research on the practice of instructional and transformational leadership: Retrospect and prospect*. Australian Council for Educational Research. https://research.acer.edu.au/research_conference_2007/7

Hallinger, P. (2010). Developing instructional leadership. Studies in Educational Leadership, 11(10). doi:10.1007/978-90-481-9106-2_5

Heifetz, R. (1994). *Leadership without easy answers*. Belknap Press.

Jacobs, D., Pfaff, H., Lehner, B., Driller, E., Nitzsche, A., Stieler-Lorenz, B., Wasem, J., & Jung, J. (2013). The influence of transformational leadership on employee well-being: Results from a survey of companies in the information and communication technology sector in Germany. *Journal of Occupational and Environmental Medicine*, *55*(7), 772–778. doi:10.1097/JOM.0b013e3182972ee5 PMID:23836019

Jordan, J., Wade, M., & Teracino, E. (2020). Every leader needs to navigate these 7 tensions. *Harvard Business Review*. https://hbrorg.cdn.ampproject.org/c/s/hbr.org/amp/2020/02

Kouzes, J. M., & Posner, B. Z. (2012). *The leadership challenge* (5th ed.). Jossey-Bass.

Kübler-Ross, E. (1969). *On Death and Dying*. Routledge.

Leach, J. (2011). Survival psychology: They won't live. *The British Psychological Society*, *24*, 26–29.

Levin, S., & Bradley, K. (2019, March 19). *Understanding and addressing principal turnover: A review of the research*. Learning Policy Institute. https://learningpolicyinstitute.org/product/nassp-understanding-addressing-principal-turnover-review-research-report

Lynch, M. (2015). *The four attributes of transformational leadership*. The EdVocate. https://www.theedvocate.org/the-4-attributes-of-transformational-leadership/

Mineo, D. L. (2014). The importance of trust in leadership. *Research Management Review*, *20*(1).

National Policy Board for Educational Administration. (2015). *Professional standards for educational leaders 2015*. Author.

Onorato, M. (2013). Transformational leadership theory style in the education sector: An empirical study of corporation managers and educational leaders. *Academy of Educational Leadership Journal*, *17*(1), 33–47.

Riggio, R. (2009, March 24). Are you a transformational leader? *Psychology Today*.

Sparks, D. (2002). *Designing powerful professional development for teachers and principals*. National Staff Development Council.

St. Thomas University. (2018). *What is transformational leadership? How new ideas produce impressive results*. STU Online. https://online.stu.edu/articles/education/what-is-transformational-leadership.aspx

VanGronigen, B. A., Cunningham, K. M. W., Young, M., & Tucker, P. D. (2021). *Exploring Principal Development and Teacher Outcomes*. Routledge.

Wagner, T. (2006). *Change Leadership*. Jossey-Bass.

Walker, T. (2018). *How many teachers are highly stressed? Maybe more than people think*. NEA Today. https://www.nea.org/advocating-for-change/new-from-nea/how-many-teacher-are-highly-stressed-maybe-more-people-think

Walker, T. (2020). *Helping students and educators recover from COVID-19 trauma*. NEA Today. https://www.nea-org/advocating-for-change/new-from-nea/helping-Students-and-educators-recover-covid-19-trauma

White, S. K. (2018). *What is transformational leadership? A model for motivating innovation*. CIO. https://www.cio.com/article/3257184/what-is-transformational-leadership-a-model-for-motivating-innovation.html

Chapter 4
Leading While the Building Is on Fire:
Navigating Changing Leadership, Fractured Departments, External Trauma, and Pandemic Stress

Denelle L. Wallace
Norfolk State University, USA

ABSTRACT

Significant changes in organizational leadership are often accompanied by organizational members suffering from trauma. This situation is not for the faint of heart; however, it is an opportunity to employ a leadership style that enables an inviting and safe environment. This "culture of care" maintains efficiency and clearly articulates the vision of the organization, while addressing its mission and goals. Leading during a time of turmoil, trauma, and drastic change requires a leader to be intentional. The leader must know who they are, what they believe, and what they value. They must establish a clear path for the organization, and plan for the unexpected. The leader's compassion, consistency, empathy, fairness, honesty, professionalism, and transparency will serve as the standard by which all others follow.

INTRODUCTION

How does a leader take the reins of an organization that is in the midst of a raging fire? To answer that question, turn to the brave men and women who serve in the local fire departments to consider their actions in the face of danger. They run into burning buildings when common sense tells them to run in the opposite direction, away from danger. However, even the most seasoned firefighter will not run into a burning building without fundamental ground rules, extensive training, and a plan for a safe exit. In this way, leaders who must lead while the organization is on fire also require ground rules, training, and planning. Success relies upon their positive mindset, relevant knowledge, and a never-ending belief

DOI: 10.4018/978-1-7998-7016-6.ch004

that their leadership will help everyone in the organization come out of the fire not just unharmed, but triumphant.

BACKGROUND

The health, productivity, and success of an organization are often best defined by its leadership. The decisions made by an organization's leaders impact the creativity, confidence, effectiveness, productivity, and well-being of every member of the organization (Ejimabo, 2015). Frequent change in the leadership of an organization for any reason can lead to a sense of fear, distrust, and uncertainty. New leaders can often become frustrated by the need to put out numerous fires created by situations they inherit to keep the organization afloat and maintain efficiency (Craine, 2007). With the addition of a global pandemic to the equation, this can prove overwhelming, even for the most experienced leader. The added layers of fear and uncertainty related to the pandemic increase the anxiety of the members of the organization, particularly those members that were already struggling with personal and professional issues prior to the onset of the pandemic (Walker, 2020).

NAVIGATING LEADERSHIP CHANGE

Issues, Controversies, Problems

Leadership Identity

Changing the organizational climate, reducing tensions among staff, easing feelings of uncertainty, developing trust, and aligning the mission, vision, goals and objectives of an organization is daunting for any leader. This complex work is not easy for a skilled leader, let alone one who might be poorly grounded. Warren G. Bennis (2003) believed that an individual's leadership potential could only be realized if the leader knew themselves, could articulate the vision well, and could garner trust from their colleagues. For each leadership opportunity, there is a new landscape to consider, new goals to attain, and new standards to meet; however, with each new leadership role, the core self of the leader remains constant. The fundamental ground rules by which a leader can bring order out of chaos lie within the foundation of what a leader believes and values in their personal and professional life.

Even in the best of situations, leadership requires that an individual possesses a well-developed understanding of self before attempting to lead others. Organizational change is inevitable and frequent, but leaders must know and recognize their core values and beliefs. At every leader's core should be the attitudes, beliefs, and worldview that drive action, motivation, and decision-making (Baruth & Manning, 2012). In a situation where the organization is experiencing change, particularly if these changes are abrupt, turbulent, and/or unexpected, the approach of the leader provides the example for others to follow in their efforts to adjust to these organizational changes. The research of Niu, Liang, Meng, and Liu (2020) focused on organizations dealing with the aftermath of unethical organizational behavior. These researchers emphasized in their findings that the moral character of a leader had significant influence on the ethical behavior of the organization. A leader who is well grounded can maintain a sense of self, even when the leader experiences fear, fatigue, and frustration as the organization rides the tide of change. Gleeson (2019) emphasized that leading change is difficult, but success is possible with a positive mindset. The establishment of the positive mindset begins with a strong sense of self that is rooted in self-awareness and self-efficacy. A starting point for a leader taking the helm during difficult times is to remember the power of leading by example.

Social learning theory supports the concept that human beings learn from watching the actions and behaviors of the people around them (Kail & Cavanaugh, 2016). Leaders must be keenly aware that when they provide direction, share the vision and mission of an organization, or stand before employees to share information, every gesture they make and word they speak is being analyzed. Much like Schein's definition of organizational culture, what is said and done will be the meter stick by which members of the organization determine their level of commitment to the organization and willingness to trust the leader (Daher, 2016).

When asked to define or describe positive leadership behaviors and characteristics, individuals often refer to a good leader as an individual who can effectively communicate the vision, reach the goals, carry out the mission, and manage the members of an organization (O'Reilly, 2019). A leader's sense of self-efficacy, which Albert Bandura defines as what an individual believes about their own aptitudes, strengths, and talents, is critical in any environment (Kail & Cavanaugh, 2016). For success, particularly in an environment that has experienced traumatic change, a leader must be clear about their core beliefs and values to avoid any loss of the confidence needed to be effective in their leadership role.

Kaplan and Garner (2017) describe a role identity system that accounts for an individual's beliefs about their role, emotions related to the role, and an awareness of the personal and social-emotional characteristics relevant to the role. This role identity system is important, as leaders develop an understanding that decision-making and problem solving are grounded in individual beliefs and role identity. For leaders without such clarity, the waters of a raging storm can be even more treacherous. Competence-environmental press theory relates to a leader's need for an anchor in the midst of chaos. This theory proposes that an individual must be able to adapt their personal and professional aptitudes and skills to the environment in which they assume a leadership role (Kail & Cavanaugh, 2016). Decisions are often made in the heat of the moment as pressure from multiple sides acts upon a leader; however, after the crisis has passed, a leader should be able to reflect upon these decisions and affirm that they were made in the best interest of the organization and in alignment with their core beliefs and professional code of ethics.

The development of beliefs occurs throughout one's lifespan. "Every belief is an interpretation of what has occurred in a person's life" (Jones-Smith, 2019, p. 135). Our beliefs influence our behavior, influence the behaviors of others, and impact our health. Thus, if a leader believes that they are competent, this increases their confidence and allows them to be more willing to seek opportunities that align with their goals and desires. In a nutshell, beliefs strongly encourage one's actions (Breines, 2015). Leaders can develop these beliefs by accepting constructive feedback from supervisors and other respected leaders, developing positive mentor relationships, and engaging in routine reflection and ongoing professional development. Additionally, leaders need to understand that they have the power to control what they believe about themselves. So, when negative self-talk or self-limiting beliefs consume their thoughts, they need to engage in positive affirmations and develop new beliefs to replace the negative ones (Jones-Smith, 2019).

Values are strongly related to our beliefs. Knowing yourself is important in this regard, because personal values in turn align with individual beliefs about yourself, other people, and the larger world. Priest and Middleton (2016) address this concept in their exploration of leader development. According to their findings, if an individual values honesty and transparency, then they will expect others to be honest and transparent, and strive to provide as much honesty and transparency as possible in their capacity as a leader. If one values punctuality, performance, and reliability, it will be reflected in their actions of beginning and ending meetings on time and their expectation that others adhere to and meet established deadlines. In terms of leadership practices, it is vital for a leader to identify their core values and then to reflect upon how these values relate to their personal beliefs, other people, and the world around them. What an individual believes about themselves guides and defines their behavior, decision-making, purpose identification, and future courses of action.

While beliefs and values serve as the foundation of a leader and their practice, extensive change and organizational upheaval place tremendous pressure on this foundation. Whereas a leader's professional behavior and decision-making relies on their values and beliefs, effective leadership is also based upon lessons learned from previous leadership roles (Breines, 2015; Jones-Smith, 2019). Even if organizational trauma has not been a part of previous leadership experience, a leader needs to reflect upon performance feedback and professional growth experiences to continue leadership development in turbulent times (Gibson, Dollarhide, Moss, Aras & Mitchell, 2017).

Research seeks to understand organizational trauma and its impact on the leaders and followers. Venugopal (2016) identified downsizing, workload and job complexity, role definition, relationships, career development, and organizational culture and ethical conflicts as six causes of organizational trauma. For example, due to the COVID-19 global pandemic, numerous companies such as Southwest Airlines Co., Exxon Mobil Corporation, Regal Cinemas, and Danish shipping giant Maersk downsized their workforce, and in extreme cases shuttered doors permanently, which sent thousands of employees to the unemployment line (Borden et al, 2020). Within companies where downsizing has occurred, remaining employees may experience changes in workload and job complexity, role definition, relationships, and career development. Case in point, Walmart Inc. offered other internal positions to employees that experienced the elimination of their previous positions. While Walmart sought to reduce organizational trauma related to organizational culture and ethical conflicts by attempting to meet the needs of its displaced employees, there is no information provided about how the job offers compared to the lost jobs (MacMillan et al., 2020). Therefore, it is quite possible that these Walmart employees experienced one or more of the causes for organization trauma that Venugopal (2016) identified. A leader stepping into these kinds of situations can find them quite difficult, but should also know that they are not impossible. The leader's beliefs and values serve as a foundation for professional behavior around meeting organizational goals and objectives, along with addressing employee needs.

A leader will face countless experiences that will force them to reflect on their beliefs and values. While these encounters will cause an effective leader to pause, reflect, and certainly question their foundational elements, these experiences should not cause the leader to completely abandon or move away from beliefs and core values. Constant reflection and re-evaluation are powerful tools for leadership development, and help leaders understand and identify when change or adaptation is required. It can either cause the leader to find themselves more firmly committed to their core beliefs and values, or to redefine or reframe their understanding of their beliefs and values as they continue to develop their leadership style.

In extreme cases, these experiences may cause leaders to divorce themselves from their leadership role or position, because the role or position conflicts with their values and beliefs. A leader who is honest with themselves and with the individuals whom they lead is a mature individual who knows themselves well. Mature leaders will realize that there may be limitations to the position, duties, or objectives which they cannot overcome, or that there may be tasks they do not have the proper skill set to accomplish (Jones-Smith, 2019).

Entering the Burning Building: The Need for Multiple Leadership Approaches

The dysfunction that results from organizational trauma can resemble a scene from a television show or movie about firefighters. As the flames rage through the building, a scene unfolds where the captains and lieutenants are barking orders to firefighters, trapped victims are screaming, and bystanders are helplessly watching. This situation requires leaders with the ability to maintain composure under pressure, trust previous training and past experience, and make clear, swift, and decisive decisions. This will enable the leader to save lives, bring the fire under control, and maintain order with the crowd that has gathered. It is key to ensuring that the scene has a happy ending.

Every leader undoubtedly has days where they feel helpless, like bystanders, as the enormity of the situation unfolds. Other times, a leader will feel like trapped victims as they attempt to find a clear path to safety. There will be moments when a leader feels like firefighters, as new leadership within the organization barks orders that may contradict directives from previous leaders. Finally, a leader may feel like the captains and the lieutenants as they try to block out the sight of the flames and the sounds of chaos, in order to make the best decisions that will bring everyone out alive. Just as firefighters engage in multiple training exercises that address a variety of scenarios, a leader has to be willing to recognize that the approach to leadership development is ongoing, multifaceted, and vital to their success as an effective leader.

An eclectic approach that infuses multiple leadership development and organizational change theoretical frameworks can serve as the best approach to professional growth.

Strategic Leadership

Strategic leadership provides an opportunity to "focus on choices that enhance the health and well-being of an organization over the long term" (Beatty & Quinn, 2010, p.4). A strategic leadership approach offers a leader the opportunity to foster individual growth while attaining organizational effectiveness and success after organizational trauma. Strategic leadership requires a leader to understand how to formulate and develop long-term goals. An analysis of the strengths, weaknesses, threats and opportunities of the present situation must be recognized. The leader should identify any previous experience and training that best aligns with the analysis, a vision for what could be, goals for bringing that vision to life, the mission of the organization, and the organization's standards and strategic plan must be identified and considered (Beatty & Quinn, 2010).

A general would not charge into battle without first gathering intelligence and data on their adversary, as well as some reconnaissance. In the same way, a strategic leader identifies the external environment and factors that directly and indirectly impact the organization, and utilizes this information to create short- and long-term goals that align with the vision and mission. Strategic leaders take time to understand an organization's history and how potential past conflicts could impede how the organization moves forward. A leader who employs a strategic approach will see the importance of aligning the organization's culture with its systems and structure, while also understanding which critical areas require change (Beatty & Quinn, 2010).

Once a plan is in place, a strategic leader will identify the best approach to execute their plan. This step relies a great deal upon their ability to use their knowledge of the ground rules, key players, and most urgent or pressing needs to create effective teams of individuals with multiple perspectives and diverse backgrounds (Collins, 2001). When a new leader goes into an environment where there is dysfunction resulting from organizational trauma, they will encounter a variety of employees or followers who could be allies or adversaries. These people may be indifferent, disengaged, cautious, optimistic, or pessimistic, especially if there has been significant and frequent change in leadership over a short period of time (Venugopal, 2016). A grounded and informed leader will use their moral compass and ethical code, along with relevant knowledge and a clear plan, to negotiate with these various employees and their differing perspectives toward their organization's leader.

Servant Leadership

A combination of strategic and servant leadership approaches are the best approach for addressing the human beings impacted by organizational trauma. Servant leaders consider the unique set of strengths and skills of each individual and utilize this knowledge to create a positive, long-term impact on the organization that aligns with its vision, mission and goals (Sipe & Frick 2009). A servant leader believes "humans are the catalyst for change in organizations" (Temperley, 2016, p. 14).

In this case, the impact being sought is to calm fears, establish a collegial environment, and maintain organizational effectiveness. According to Larry Spears (2010), the former executive director of the Robert K. Greenleaf Center in Indianapolis, listening, empathy, healing, awareness, persuasion, conceptualization, foresight, stewardship, commitment to individual growth, and community building are the overarching characteristics of a servant leader. In an environment where members of the organization have remained throughout a period of turbulence, a servant leader will utilize these characteristics to bring about calm and healing and reignite optimism and enthusiasm for the future. The servant leader, much like the strategic leader, will quickly identify potential allies and the cautiously optimistic.

The difference between the strategic and servant leader is focus. The strategic leader emphasizes organizational goals while the servant leader places emphasis on the needs of the employees or followers. The leader that merges these foci can experience much success.

Merge Strategic and Servant Leadership to Meet Organizational Goals and Employee Needs

A leader does not enter the burning building without engaging in some reconnaissance. A leader that merges strategic and servant leadership will develop a plan that tackles change in alignment with organizational goals, while simultaneously addressing the needs of the employees. The leader identifies allies, which are individuals in the organization who truly desire positive change and will work to make this change happen if the leader articulates a clear vision and a plan for attaining the end goal. These individuals will want to understand how each decision of the new leader aligns with the vision, mission and goals of the organization as well as have their roles clearly defined. From a strategic vantage point, the needs of the organization are met as these individuals engage in rebranding efforts and professional development offerings to hone their skills. The servant leader will employ stewardship which Bordas (2016) describes as the leader guiding "the locus of control from the leader to the 'We' or people. In this way teamwork, synergy, and group intelligence can surface'' (p. 64).

It would be lovely if everyone in the organization were an ally, but this will not be the case. Change impacts every member of the organization differently. Change due to hostile mergers, corporate or company restructuring, and an untimely death or sudden dismissal of a leader can be traumatic for employees or followers. Some standard reluctant employee types emerge in every organization. Though this concept was initially birthed from an observation of school division faculty, Poller and Wallace (2008) categorized six types of reluctant individuals a leader encounters. The six types of individuals were given the following names:

- Bricks
- Whiners
- Knowledge Royals
- Absentees
- Rebels
- Undercover Sabotage Specialists

From a servant leadership perspective, the focus is on fostering new purpose for the professional lives of these individuals, and nurturing them in a way that best meets the needs of the organization (Greenleaf, 1977). From a strategic leadership perspective, understanding these individuals can help identify potential threats to the organization's goals and objectives, and develop a plan to redirect and minimize negative impact (Beatty & Quinn, 2010).

Bricks are individuals that have probably experienced the greatest amount of upheaval and change in an organization, because they have been in the same position and/or office for a long period of time. They have witnessed their fair share of new techniques, reform measures, initiatives, and innovations that were touted as being "best for the organization," but have not seen any success or change within the organization's climate during this time. Normally, these innovations, initiatives, reform measures, leaders, and approaches that were introduced with such great enthusiasm are thrown aside or fail to become embedded within the organization's culture. For the Bricks, there is an inability to trust the leader's mission, vision, and strategy.

As a leader, the best approach is to *listen*. Ferrari (2012) concluded that a good listener truly wants to understand. Interactions with Bricks require the leader to understand their concerns and identify the aspects of the vision, mission, goals, and related tasks that address their concerns. The leader must be honest and clear about how goals and tasks will be monitored, evaluated, addressed, and changed if necessary. The leader creates opportunities for Bricks to have a seat at the table and provide concrete examples of why and how a proposed approach is best for the organization and how they can assist.

Whiners use complaining to cover up personal and professional insecurities. A leader must employ large doses of empathy with every engagement. According to Beckham and Riedford (2017), "Empathy involves caring, recognition of distress experienced by self and others, and provision of support" (p. 81). Whiners constantly seek reassurance or confirmation from colleagues and supervisors pertaining to how well they are performing, or if they have made correct decisions. When areas in need of improvement are identified by colleagues or supervisors, Whiners shift into "victim mode." If deadlines are not met or projects are unsuccessful, Whiners will register a lack of support from administration, or the absence of team member contributions. Whiners believe they are not the ones that need to be improved upon, but instead the leader, their colleagues, and/or the organization are the problem. Whiners find considerable comfort in complaining. They will garner the sympathy of others who will in return provide them with the attention and affirmation that they crave. These individuals negatively impact the climate of the organization and undermine the efforts of the leader through misplaced blame. If left unchecked, such negativity can spread like wildfire.

Leaders must engage with Whiners, knowing that these individuals are frustrated and fear being exposed as possibly incompetent. Their fear hinders progress toward improvement and their ability to reach out for assistance. One-to-one conversations with these individuals are necessary, where the leader highlights the individual's strengths. Assigned tasks and projects for Whiners must align with their strengths. These individuals need to be paired with colleagues that demonstrate strengths in areas where Whiners need improvement. Whiners need the leader to check in with them periodically through quick emails and phone calls that allow them to share progress and voice concerns.

Of all the groups that get under a leader's skin, **Knowledge Royals** most likely rank as one of the top three. Servant leaders utilize awareness with this group, which Spears (2010) identifies as a leader's ability to understand matters involving ethics, power, and values. Knowledge Royals believe that since they have either earned a degree in leadership, previously led a department within this or another organization, or both, they can do a much better job than the leader. These are the individuals that are looking for every misstep and decision a leader makes that does not yield the intended results. Knowledge Royals will be the first to echo the words, "I told you so."

In many cases, Knowledge Royals often do have a wealth of knowledge, extensive professional experience, and demonstrated success in previous leadership roles. They are often vocal and imply through their words, treatment of colleagues, and mannerisms that neither the present leader nor their colleagues are nearly as intelligent, as well-equipped, or as professional as they are. A strategic leader will identify how their leadership skills can be utilized to advance the goals and objectives of the organization. The leader will take Knowledge Royal's educational and professional experience into consideration and assign them to groups where their leadership can be appreciated, and where they can work toward realizing the vision and mission of the organization. Since these individuals need to be seen and demonstrate their importance, the leader will allow this desire to work for good, and enable the leader to tackle other initiatives and tasks with focus and uninterrupted attention. Like Whiners, the leader needs to check in with Knowledge Royals regularly so that they clearly identify who is in charge. At the same time, leaders should enable Knowledge Royals to share their progress and the outcomes of their initiatives during large meetings, after the leader has reviewed their presentation.

Absentees have essentially checked out as a way to cope with the stress of constant change and their feelings of uneasiness, uncertainty, and frustration. The servant leader will need to employ persuasion with this group. Persuasion involves convincing Absentees to rejoin the organization and support its vision, mission and goals (Spears, 2010). The strategic leader creates opportunities for coaching, mentoring, demonstrated modeling, and other motivational strategies to re-engage Absentees who come to work every day, complete assignments, and even engage in small talk with a few trusted colleagues, but they guard themselves from interactions with the leader.

In speaking with a few individuals that have been Absentees, Poller and Wallace (2018) identified some of the underlying factors contributing to their disconnection. Factors include feeling overwhelmed, time constraints, and a lack of a defined role in addressing the leader's expectations. Venugopal (2016) identified role definition and relationships as causes for trauma. Absentees will often exhibit passive-aggressive behavior in an effort to deal with the trauma caused by abrupt leadership changes, poor leadership, or a lack of departmental success. These individuals avoid engagement and manage their reluctance to buy into a new leader's vision. Absentees need the leader's words to fully align with their actions and vice versa. The leader's expectations for Absentees need to be as clear in written form as they are when spoken. The tasks and time frames for completing these tasks need to be developed with them, and feedback as to how their work moves the organization in the right direction must be provided regularly in oral and written form. This should take place both in whole and small group meetings, and individual consultations. With Absentees, coaching and mentoring opportunities increase trust and garner support for the leader and the organization.

Rebels are the most reluctant of all and are extremely verbal about their reluctance. They make no bones about their displeasure with the leader's initiatives or decisions. Unlike Absentees, Rebels will let everyone know that they are avoiding interaction with the leader and are opposed to their leadership. The leader's first thought may be that annual evaluations and performance reviews will rid them of this headache soon enough, but unfortunately the leader will find that Rebels are often really good at what they do within the organization, even if they are a serious liability when it comes to promoting change and ushering in healing. For the servant leader, healing is the characteristic that works best with members of this group. According to Spears (2010), healing one's self and relationships with others is a great strength of servant leadership. While the leader may not have directly caused the hurt or pain, the leader's very presence is the physical embodiment of their frustration with the organization.

When the Rebel is seen doing his or her own thing, less experienced and less effective members of the organization are influenced to follow the Rebel's lead. This is where the danger of the Rebels comes into play. Like Bricks, they do not trust the leader's plan, vision, or ability to lead. Unlike Bricks, Rebels are not quietly waiting for the leader to go away. Rebels are loud, bold, and routinely successful in taking other employees along with them for the ride that will drive the leader's efforts into the abyss.

The great thing about the Rebel is that at least the leader undoubtedly knows who they are and how they really feel. This enables the leader to employ the servant leader characteristic of awareness (Spears, 2010). The leader uses available information gathered through observations and interactions to help build a relationship. Healing the hurt will come through honesty and clarity. With the Rebel, the leader needs to pick and choose the battles to address while also remembering to research every rule and regulation within the organization related to employee dismissal, performance evaluations, and plans of action. The Rebel will test the leader's patience and ability to remain calm under intense pressure. With some Rebels, the leader's honesty, integrity, and professional ethics coupled with clarity and open communication regarding the vision, mission, and goals will allow healing to take place and a positive relationship built on trust to be formed. However, a leader must be prepared for cases in which the wounds are too deep, and these individuals remain a threat to healing for others in the organization. In these cases, there must be definitive answers that not only have consequences outlined, but identify the correlation between the consequence and the organization's rules and regulations.

Rebels are used to the reality of constant change and getting lost in the shuffle of that change. A leader must bring order through the use of the pen and constant documentation. The leader must look Rebels in the eye without fear, but also with compassion. Like the other reluctant types, they have been wounded as well. The strategic leader understands the importance of consistency in addressing the behaviors that do not benefit the organization, but highlight how the strengths of the individual align with the vision, mission, and goals presented (Beatty & Quinn, 2010).

The **Undercover Sabotage Specialist** brings to mind covert operations in the military, the ways of high paid assassins, or the mysterious worlds of secret societies like knights and ninjas. The Undercover Sabotage Specialist is an interesting breed and probably the most difficult to detect in the beginning. A leader must enter the organization knowing that these individuals may exist even if they have not yet been detected. Undercover Sabotage Specialists often seem to be willing participants in the departmental meetings, can rattle off key points of the leader's vision, mission, and goals, and engage in training or professional development sessions relevant to meeting these goals. These individuals volunteer to assist on projects for which they were not initially assigned and appear motivated to engage with the new leader. However, the leader must beware and proceed with caution.

Undercover Sabotage Specialists are often in partnership with the Rebels and the Knowledge Royals. These groups are in constant companionship in the employee lounge, after departmental meetings, and during the happy hour events away from the office. These individuals admire the direct approach of the Rebel, but do not enjoy the type of confrontation that is involved with the Rebel's vocal approach. Instead the Undercover Sabotage Specialists want to spend their time smiling at the new leader and attempting to appear supportive, but talk with the Rebels about how they really are upset by the approach taken to provide them with yet another vision or directive to follow after the most recent leadership change. Also, the Undercover Sabotage Specialists support Knowledge Royals in the belief that they are knowledgeable enough not to make the same mistakes as the previous leadership, and can foresee the mistakes they are sure the current leader will make. However, they will not share any of these thoughts with the leader. Undercover Sabotage Specialists know how to say just enough to let others know they are aware of the new leader's expectations and goals, but quiet enough so that their true feelings are not easily identified by the new leader, colleagues outside of their trusted circle, or any other supervisors within the organization.

The most damaging effect that Undercover Sabotage Specialists have within an organization is their contribution to a climate of distrust and limited communication. The servant leader characteristic best employed here is conceptualization. Spears (2010) explains that conceptualization allows the servant leader to think beyond the current reality of the organization and to look at problems through a lens that sees patterns, makes meaning of those patterns, and identifies strategies for addressing these problems that align with the vision, mission, and goals of the organization. This approach aligns with the strategic leader. In dealing with the Undercover Sabotage Specialists, the leader seeks to revise faulty, dysfunctional ways of thinking and interacting. They will enable members of the organization to become aware of these existing misconceptions and will work together openly and honestly to address them through collegiality and collaboration.

The Six Types of Reluctant Employees: A Scenario

Often a real-world example is the best tool for understanding abstract concepts such as the aforementioned leadership frameworks and the types of reluctant employees. In this scenario, the principal of a school that has failed to meet state benchmarks over the last three years has been removed from the building and placed in a central office position, while the four assistant principals and the dean of students remain. The new principal has arrived with a clear directive from the superintendent to improve academic achievement. With extensive data in hand, the new principal begins to develop a plan based on organizational goals and objectives, while considering the needs of the stakeholders associated with the school. Although the new principal has identified that a number of the students, parents, and several faculty and staff members are allies, three months of observations and daily interactions with faculty, staff, students, administration, and parents have revealed adversaries that need to be addressed in the plan to raise achievement at this school.

The Bricks are a number of the teachers that have been at the school since before the three years of unsatisfactory performance. They have seen a number of district and building-level initiatives implemented and abandoned over the years, and place little faith in the ability of the new principal to turn things around for the school.

The new principal has identified the assistant principal of instruction as the Whiner. Since the leader has arrived this assistant principal has constantly blamed the current status of the school on limited parental support, poor instructional delivery approaches, inadequate funding and community support, and the previous principal.

One of the other assistant principals is clearly the Knowledge Royal. This individual had hoped to be appointed as the new principal. After nine years at the school as an assistant principal, this individual feels best equipped to move the school in the right direction.

The Absentee is another one of the assistant principals. This individual initially served as the dean of students and was promoted to assistant principal within the last five years. After twelve years under two previous principals, this assistant principal has witnessed the steady decline of the school with regard to academic achievement and climate. As a matter of self-preservation, this assistant principal avoids interaction with the new principal and rarely provides input during meetings.

The department chairs for English and science are the Rebels. These individuals have been members of the faculty for more than 20 years, and have endured three superintendents, four principals and numerous initiatives. They are quite vocal about their distrust of the new leader's plan, vision, or ability to lead.

The Undercover Sabotage Specialist appears to be another one of the assistant principals. This assistant principal constantly volunteers to serve as the lead on special projects and routinely verbally supports the new leader during school meetings and district-wide events. However, unbeknownst to this assistant principal, the new leader overheard a conversation between this individual and the science department chair. The assistant principal expressed their lack of faith in the new principal and how they believed that the school would not see improvement under the new principal's leadership.

Overall, leaders entering a situation where organizational trauma has occurred need to consider how each individual deals with change and trauma in their own way. First Lady Eleanor Roosevelt said, "A mature person is one who does not think in absolutes, who is able to be objective even when deeply stirred emotionally, who has learned that there is both good and bad in all people and in all things, and who walks humbly and deals charitably with the circumstances of life, knowing that in this world no one is all-knowing and therefore all of us need both love and charity." A leader needs to reflect on who they are and what they believe about themselves and other people. They must remember to turn to their moral compass and activate their ethical code, and by all means respect everyone, including themselves.

Preparing for Triage

The onset of the COVID-19 pandemic brought about a level of stress and uncertainty the likes of which most persons in leadership today have never seen in the United States. The shifting of the nature of work came about so rapidly and without warning that everyone was caught off guard. There was no way an organization could have prepared for the aftermath of the initial impact, which saw many being able to telework at home while others were simply out of a job. Masks, hand sanitizer, the hunt for disinfecting wipes and paper goods, and the announcement of the daily death toll on the evening news became the new norm in our lives. The mental toll on individuals within organizations became manifested in their actions during ZOOM, Microsoft Teams, and Business Skype meetings, where some forgot the cameras were rolling as their appearance, level of contribution, and words reflected their fear and frustration as civility and common decency toward one another began to dissipate (Caligiuri, De Cieri, Minbaeva, Verbeke, & Zimmermann, 2020). This is where the leader needs to rely upon a firm understanding of self and a willingness to recognize the impact of trauma on members of their unit. "Trauma refers to an experience that creates a sense of fear, helplessness, or horror, and overwhelms a person's resources for coping" (Hopper, Bassuk, & Olivet, 2010).

Before a leader can assist others in dealing with the trauma associated with the events that have impacted the organization, the leader must be able to demonstrate resilience and order in their own world. A new leader in an environment struggling through numerous leadership changes, and other aspects of trauma prior to the global pandemic, is truly in a difficult position. The members of the organization have yet another layer of trauma with which each one must navigate. Leadership under these circumstances requires laser sharp focus. Dr. Darria Long's triage method serves as an excellent approach to leadership life, particularly in light of organizational trauma. In her 2019 TedTalk, emergency room doctor Darria Long explained how she effectively manages her busy life and the chaotic environment of the emergency room. This TedTalk has golden nuggets of wisdom that can benefit an individual's leadership efforts in the time of COVID and rapid change. Strategic leaders recognize how their daily decisions have a long-term impact on the organization (Beatty & Quinn, 2010). Servant leaders realize the importance of inspiring and supporting the people that they lead, so that the organization can prosper and members of the organization can be empowered in a way that increases their contributions to the organization's mission, vision, and goals (Blanchard & Hodges 2002; Jennings, 2002; Wong & Page, 2003).

In an environment marred by traumatic organizational change, stress levels are high among the organization's members. A leader must serve as a positive example in mitigating this stress and reducing the tensions associated with it. As Dr. Long emphasizes, stress clouds our ability to control our emotions, make sound judgments, and remember important details, while our feelings of anger and anxiety rise. Her suggestion is to engage in a daily activity she terms as *relentless triage*. Leaders must decide what matters require immediate attention, what issues are important but can wait for a short period of time to be addressed, which tasks can use additional research before being implemented, and which approaches, tasks, or matters need to be abandoned because they are no longer relevant to the vision or benefit the organization.

The truth about uncertainty is that if we are not careful, we can allow it to cripple our ability to forge ahead into the unknown. Gabrielle Bernstein said it best when she stated, "Fear is often our immediate response to uncertainty. There's nothing wrong with experiencing fear. The key is not to get stuck in it." During a global pandemic, a leader is going to experience fear, just as followers in the organization will. However, the leader cannot succumb to fear and must work to keep others from focusing on uncertainty. Uncertainty is a barrier to continuing the mission and realizing the vision the leader has conveyed since their arrival at the helm. As Dr. Long said, "you have to get out of your head." In other words, the leader cannot let any negative inner voice deter them from leading with enthusiasm and passion.

One of the characteristics of a servant leader is the ability to lead with enthusiasm and passion (Spears, 2010). The leader demonstrates the steps to take to move beyond fear and into productivity. They model how to keep a global pandemic from dousing creativity and impeding progress. Though the leader may not have been able to predict a global pandemic and does not have a crystal ball to see into the future to determine any pending disaster, a strategic leader plans for derailments, rapid change, and counterproductive moments (Beatty & Quinn, 2010). A true leader helps members of the organization understand the vision and shares the proposed path to bring that vision to life, provides a plan that addresses potential threats and manages likely weaknesses that either already exist or could arise. A good leader, even without the presence of a global pandemic, always has a contingency plan or two in case the first plan or aspects of the initial plan need to change. In other words, leadership requires an expectation of and preparation for the unknown. Effective leaders embrace uncertainty and utilize its presence to fortify their resolve.

SOLUTIONS AND RECOMMENDATIONS

Healing, Resiliency, and Restoration

In the midst of organizational change, leaders need the ability to navigate the ship in the right direction, and adequately address the cares and concerns of the crew. There are some members of your organization that have been traumatized both within and outside of the organization. A leader needs to recognize they are wounded and apply a suitable course of treatment beneficial to the organization and its members. Spears (2010) explains that servant leadership recognizes the strength demonstrated in healing one's self by addressing past hurts, and encourages a leader to help others to heal through relationships. In other words, a servant leader seeks to provide the supports necessary for a relationship of caring and trust that takes into consideration the difficulties that individuals may need to overcome in order to experience success within the organization. A strategic leader recognizes the strengths in members of the organization and creates teams where the strengths of each individual promote growth in the areas needing improvement in another team member (Beatty & Quinn, 2010).

Another characteristic of servant leadership is foresight, which is a servant leader's ability to understand lessons from the past, connect to the realities of present day, and determine the potential long-term impact of decisions made for the future (Spears, 2010). It is this characteristic that enables a servant leader to identify the importance of creating an environment and providing resources that foster healing. The Sanctuary Model is a systems approach developed by Sandra Bloom that focuses on interventions for trauma-informed organizational change. The basic premise is to enable individuals to recover from the impact of interpersonal trauma. The introduction of a worldwide pandemic to an organization that has been weathering abrupt and extensive change adds additional trauma to individuals that have already endured extended exposure to adverse conditions and/or experiences (Esaki, Benamati, & Yanosy, 2018). While all aspects of this model may not apply to the organization, a servant leader will find the model beneficial as a guide for creating a safe space for healing to occur. Key aspects to incorporate and build upon are emotional management and conflict resolution skills, encouraging open communication and shared governance, and establishing healthy relationships between leaders and constituents (Bloom & Sreedhar, 2008).

Organizational leaders can utilize the six principles of the trauma-informed approach endorsed by the Substance Abuse and Mental Health Services Administration (SAMHSA). Once the leader acknowledges the presence of trauma within the organization and identifies that its presence is impacting the productivity and the well-being of organization members for which the leader is responsible, employing this approach can not only benefit the members of the leader's team, but can serve to benefit the organization as a whole and definitely make the leader's job flow more easily.

Step 1: Create safe zones within the organization where members of these teams can openly share their concerns without fear or reprimand or retaliation. The leader must maintain confidentiality and craft approaches to not only align with the leader's beliefs and values, but to also take the needs and values of the individuals into consideration. At all times the leader makes sure that the courses of action are done in a fair and ethical manner, as well as align with the vision and mission.

Step 2: The leader models trustworthiness and transparency. The frequency and depth of the leader's communications with individuals and groups must be consistent and honest.

Step 3: The leader is one person, and cannot do it all. Therefore, leaders create peer support networks. This aspect may require other organizational entities such as human resources and professional counselors that can work with individuals and groups to promote healing, while encouraging forward movement and productivity.

Step 4: The leader models collaboration and mutuality. Within an organization where there is distrust and hurt, silos are present and walls of protection have been built. Therefore, a leader has to demonstrate to everyone how collaboration can be conducted without turmoil.

Step 5: A leader has to have a thick enough skin to endure constructive criticism. A leader cannot provide constructive criticism if that leader is unable to make use of it for the purpose of professional growth. Empower members of the organization to respectfully utilize their voices to promote positive change.

Step 6: Leaders must understand that everyone's experience does not mirror their own. Effective leaders recognize cultural, historical, and gender issues that impact the ability of organizational members to interact with one another and develop trusting relationships. Without cultural competency many an organization has alienated its most promising members and damaged the organization's ability to develop a positive climate and foster diversity (Caligiuri, De Cieri, Minbaeva, Verbeke, & Zimmermann, 2020).

By applying these six principles, leaders position members to heal from previous trauma, prevent new trauma from taking place, and restore trust, collaboration, and a healthy work environment.

FUTURE RESEARCH DIRECTIONS

As the world emerges from a global pandemic, grapples with issues of social injustice, and begins the slow process of economic recovery, research in the areas of resiliency, mental and physical wellness, and leadership roles will be needed. The way in which corporations, schools and other entities conduct themselves will continue to change and evolve from strictly brick and mortar buildings to hybrid operations that involve extensive use of telework options and virtual platforms for collaboration and routine meetings. There are numerous implications for leadership development and the ways in which leaders address efficiency, effectiveness, collegiality, collaboration, and performance evaluations.

CONCLUSION

Whoever said that change is inevitable was correct. Entering a situation in which there has been significant change in organizational leadership, along with organizational members suffering from trauma, is not for the faint of heart. However, there is a wonderful opportunity to employ a leadership style that enables leaders to create an inviting and safe environment. This "culture of care" maintains efficiency in trying times, and clearly articulates the vision of the organization while addressing its mission and goals.

Brenna Yovanoff said, "All great acts are ruled by intention. What you mean is what you get." Leading during a time of turmoil, trauma, and drastic change, requires a leader to be intentional. The leader must know who they are, what they believe, and what they value. They should establish a clear path to take the organization in the best direction, based upon sound research and past experiences. The leader recognizes and understands both allies and adversaries exist, but consideration for both is necessary in bringing the plan together. Speaking of planning, the leader has to plan for the unexpected and the chaos that will occur at various points in time during their leadership role, but cannot allow these moments to deter them from the mission at hand. And of all the requirements and tasks that come with leadership, a leader must remember that they serve as the model for what they would like to see in those they lead.

The leader's compassion, consistency, empathy, fairness, honesty, professionalism, and transparency will serve as the standard by which all others are to follow. The leader's actions and words need to align with their beliefs and values at all times. An individual's leadership approach has the power to enable members of an organization to emerge from the charred remains of the organization's past healed, restored, and triumphant.

REFERENCES

American Psychological Association. (2012). *Building your resilience.* http://www.apa.org/topics/resilience

Baruth, L., & Manning, L. (2012). *Multicultural counseling and psychotherapy: A lifespan approach* (5th ed.). Pearson College Division.

Beatty, K., & Quinn, L. (2010). Strategic command: Taking the long view for organizational success. *Leadership in Action, 30*(1), 3–7. doi:10.1002/lia.1318

Bennis, W. G. (2003). *On Becoming a Leader*. Pegasus Publishing.

Blanchard, K., & Hodges, P. (2002). *The servant leader: Transforming your heart, head, hands, and habits*. J. Countryman.

Bloom, S., & Sreedhar, S. (2008). The sanctuary model of trauma-informed organizational change. *Reclaiming Children and Youth, 17*(3), 48–53.

Bordas, J. (2016). Leadership Lessons from Communities of Color: Stewardship and Collective Action. *New Directions for Student Leadership, 2016*(152), 61–74. doi:10.1002/yd.20209 PMID:27870523

Borden, T., Akhtar, A., Hadden, J., & Bose, D. (2020, October 8). The coronavirus outbreak has triggered unprecedented mass layoffs and furloughs. Here are the major companies that have announced they are downsizing their workforces. *Business Insider*. https://www.businessinsider.com/coronavirus-layoffs-furloughs-hospitality-service-travel-unemployment-2020

Brienes, J. (2015). Three Ways Your Beliefs Can Shape Your Reality. *Psychology Today*.https://www.psychologytoday.com/us/blog/in-love-and-war/201508/3-ways-your-beliefs-can-shape-your-reality

Caligiuri, P., De Cieri, H., Minbaeva, D., Verbeke, A., & Zimmermann, A. (2020). International HRM insights for navigating the COVID-19 pandemic: Implications for future research and practice. *Journal of International Business Studies*, *51*(5), 697–713. doi:10.105741267-020-00335-9 PMID:32836500

Collins, J. (2001). *Good to great: why some companies make the leap and others don't*. Harper Business.

Craine, K. (2008). Managing the cycle of change. *IEEE Engineering Management Review*, *36*(2), 50–54. doi:10.1109/EMR.2008.4534324

Ejimabo, N. (2015). The influence of decision making in organizational leadership and management activities. *Journal of Entrepreneurship & Organization Management*, *04*(02). Advance online publication. doi:10.4172/2169-026X.1000138

Esaki, N., Benamati, J., Yanosy, S., Middleton, J. S., Hopson, L. M., Hummer, V. L., & Bloom, S. L. (2018). The sanctuary model: Theoretical framework. *Families in Society*, *94*(2), 87–95. doi:10.1606/1044-3894.4287

Ferrari, B. T. (2012). *Power listening: Mastering the most critical business skill of all*. Portfolio/Penguin.

Gibson, D., Dollarhide, C., Moss, J., Aras, Y., & Mitchell, T. (2018). Examining leadership with American counseling association presidents: A grounded theory of leadership identity development. *Journal of Counseling and Development*, *96*(4), 361–371. doi:10.1002/jcad.12219

Gleeson, B. (2018). The critical role of leadership development during organizational change. *Forbes*. https://www.forbes.com/

Greenleaf, R. K. (2002). Servant leadership: A journey into the nature of legitimate power and greatness. Paulist Press.

Hopper, E., Bassuk, E., & Olivet, J. (2010). Shelter from the storm: Trauma-informed care in homelessness services settings. *The Open Health Services and Policy Journal*, *3*(2), 80–100. doi:10.2174/1874924001003020080

Jennings, D. B. (2002). Those who would lead must first serve: The praxis of servant leadership by public school principals. *Dissertations Abstracts International*, *63*(04), 1207.

Jones-Smith, E. (2019). *Culturally diverse counseling: theory and practice*. Sage Publications. doi:10.4135/9781071800744

Kail, R., & Cavanaugh, J. (2016). *Human development: a life-span view* (7th ed.). Cengage Learning.

Kaplan, A., & Garner, J. (2017). A complex dynamic systems perspective on identity and its development: The dynamic systems model of role identity. *Developmental Psychology*, *53*(11), 2036–2051. doi:10.1037/dev0000339 PMID:29094968

Kaye, B., Bentley, C., & Rogers, L. (2020). Leveraging pandemic "ahas": Just getting it isn't doing it. *Leadership Excellence*, *37*(11), 16–19.

Long, D. (2019). *An E.R. doctor on triaging your "crazy busy" life*. https://www.ted.com/talks/daria_long_an_er_doctor_on_triaging_your_crazy_busy_life

Macias, O. (2020). Social emotional competence, emotional intelligence, and the prosocial school leader:how the pandemic, school closures and distance learning can guide leaders. *Leadership*, *50*(1), 12–14.

MacMillan, D., Whoriskey, P., & O'Connell, J. (2020, December 16). America's biggest companies are flourishing during the pandemic and putting thousands of people out of work. *The Washington Post*. https://www.washingtonpost.com/graphics/2020/business/50-biggest-companies-coronavirus-layoffs/

Niu, C., Liang, F., Meng, X., & Liu, Y. O. (2020). The inverted U-shaped relationship between authentic leadership and unethical pro-organizational behavior. *Social Behavior and Personality*, *48*(11), 9416. doi:10.2224bp.9416

O'Reilly, N. (2019). *In this together: how successful women support each other in work and life*. Adams Media.

Poller, L., & Wallace, D. (2008, March 15-17). *Types of reluctant educators* [Conference Presentation]. Association for Supervision and Curriculum Development's (ASCD) 63rd Annual Conference and Exhibit Show, New Orleans, LA, United States.

Priest, K., & Middleton, E. (2016). Exploring leader identity and development. *New Directions for Student Leadership*, *49*(149), 37–47. doi:10.1002/yd.20160 PMID:26895262

Sipe, J., & Frick, D. (2009). *Seven pillars of servant leadership: Practicing the wisdom of leading by serving*. Paulist Press.

Spears, L. (2010). Character and servant leadership: Ten characteristics of effective, caring leaders. *The Journal of Virtues & Leadership*, *1*(1), 25–30.

Substance Abuse and Mental Health Services Administration. (2020, September 17). *Infographic: 6 guiding principles to a trauma informed approach*. https://www.cdc.gov/cpr/infographics/6_principles_trauma_info.htm

Temperley, A. J. (2016). *Servant Leadership as Defined by K-12 ACSI Christian School Administrators in Arizona, USA* [Doctoral Dissertation]. Temple University.

Walker, T. (2020). Healing from COVID-19 trauma in our schools. *NEA Today*, *39*(1), 28–31.

Wong, P., & Page, D. (2003). *Servant leadership: An Opponent-Process Model and the Revised Servant Leadership Profile*. Servant Leadership Roundtable.

ADDITIONAL READING

Kuntz, J. (2020). Resilience in times of global pandemic: Steering recovery and thriving trajectories. *Applied Psychology*, *70*(1), 188–215. doi:10.1111/apps.12296 PMID:33362330

Pak, K., & Ravitch, S. M. (2021). *Critical leadership praxis for educational and social change*. Teach College Press.

KEY TERMS AND DEFINITIONS

Leadership Role: A position that requires an individual to manage members of an organization effectively and fairly.

Relentless Triage: An approach taken to prioritize assignments, duties, and tasks in an individual's life with the goal of reducing chaos and/or fostering balance.

Reluctant Employees: Members of an organization that exhibit behaviors that undermine its mission, goals, and objectives.

Resiliency: The ability to successfully overcome adversity, barriers, and setbacks.

Servant Leader: An individual focused on meeting the needs of the followers in order to ensure the goals and objectives of the organization are met.

Social Learning: Theoretical framework built upon the work of Albert Bandura that proposes individuals develop their attitudes, beliefs, values, and worldview through observing and modeling others.

Strategic Leader: An individual focused on aligning the skills of the employees within the organization with the tasks needed to best meet organizational goals and objectives.

Chapter 5
Leaders' Self-Care in Traumatic Times of Change

Tamara Hawkins
Independent Researcher, USA

ABSTRACT

This chapter will embody a day in the life of a licensed therapist and four individuals (who are leaders from various professional backgrounds) with a universal trauma response to the COVID-19 pandemic. On any given day, their jobs are not for the faint of heart; they are accustomed to seeing people at their nadir. However, this pandemic has made them question their resiliency, tapped into their reserves, and exhausted their previous effective coping mechanisms. In an effort to seek refuge and respite, their answers lie in their last resort: self-care (something none of them make time for, but something all of them require). Through their collaborative work with a therapist, these leaders were able to prioritize safety within their organizations, facilitate accountability among staff, and encourage social support within their departments.

INTRODUCTION

What keeps a person up at night? Is it the extra caffeine they have been running on to make it through the day? Is it mindlessly surfing the web? Is it emotional eating? Is it constant worry? This question gives rise to problem-focused thinking. It is externally driven and it has a negative impact on a person's mood and motivation. This author implores the reader to instead ask the question: What gets a person up in the morning? This approach is more solution-focused; it allows someone to discover opportunities about things that could go right instead of ruminating about problems or what could go wrong. Everyone is in this era of rapid, unprecedented change and how they move forward will dramatically depend upon the state of their human psyches. As a licensed therapist, this author is not immune to the problems faced in the everyday lives of others. However, this clinician does ponder the notion that a change in one's perspective is empowering self-determination. The helplessness one feels when problems arise, places a risk to the efficacy of human organisms and organizations. Therefore, the work of true leadership is

DOI: 10.4018/978-1-7998-7016-6.ch005

to foster an environment where employees can tap into their greatest potential. However, the work of a good leader is the ability to foster credibility and maximize their impact among subordinates.

This chapter describes a day in the life of a licensed therapist and four individuals who are leaders from various professional backgrounds. These professionals are a police chief, clergyperson, therapist and healthcare worker. Each of the four individuals has experienced a universal trauma response to the COVID-19 pandemic. These case studies illuminate how those in positions of authority now find themselves powerless to tragic encounters for which they simply cannot prepare. All four individuals who presented to therapy are authorities in their own respective fields, but who do they turn to when the world turns to them for answers? The world, in general, seeks solace in knowing that in the event of a medical emergency, the doctors, nurses, paramedics and other health care workers will use the latest technology to diagnose and treat their ailments. In the event of psychiatric deterioration, it is opined that a mental health clinician would foster an environment conducive to psychological health and well-being. Further, civilians trust that their local law enforcement will protect, serve and defend an individual's life and liberty. In sum, they are the authority figures that society consulted up until this present time. These professions had most or many of the answers to the questions humans sought. Now, everything that these leaders have learned or experienced in life, no longer makes sense to them. How do they now make it make sense to others?

The therapist who has performed countless suicide risk assessments and safety plans with her patients is now contemplating ending her own life. The Police Chief, so disgusted with how his profession handles his own race, struggles with the notion of early retirement. Healthcare workers are experiencing panic attacks and vomiting in the parking lots before starting their shifts because they do not know if they will lose another coworker, patient or succumb to the virus themselves. In addition, they have isolated themselves from their families as a precaution, who previously served as their primary support system. In an effort to get a grip or handle on the shaking of their foundations, they wander down the halls of the hospital corridors and find themselves in the office of the hospital's clinical social worker; a licensed therapist whose job has completely changed to primarily informing families of deceased loved ones (due to COVID-19 precautions, families were restricted from patient visits) and assisting patients and employees with Living Wills/Advanced Directives in the event they contract the virus. By happenstance, this Social Worker receives surprise visits and walk-ins from all walks of life, looking for relief and reprieve from the world crashing-in around them. The therapist now undergoes her own psychotherapy due to the vicarious trauma she has experienced from the collective trauma of the people who enter her office.

Despite the apprehension of these four leaders in their respective professions, they face their fears and look inward to find the strength to overcome this universal trauma-response to the COVID-19 pandemic. They are cognizant of the notion that they have a responsibility to their employers, colleagues, subordinates, patients and stakeholders. These leaders are also aware that their trauma can spill into the workplace and affect all parties involved. On any given day, their jobs are not for the faint of heart; they are accustomed to seeing people at their lowest point. However, this pandemic has made them question their resiliency, tapped into their reserves and exhausted their previous effective coping mechanisms. In an effort to seek refuge and respite, their answers lie in their last resort self-care (something none of them make time for, but something all of them require). Through their collaborative work with a therapist, these leaders were able to prioritize safety within their organizations, facilitate accountability among staff and encourage social support within their departments.

BACKGROUND

Trauma theories in the United States emerged in 1980 when the American Psychiatric Association (1987) designated that Posttraumatic Stress Disorder (PTSD) was a condition of trauma during the Vietnam War Era. Since that time, trauma has been applied to victims of physical and sexual violence and other life-threatening events. As research on trauma became more customary, the designation has been applied more comprehensively to events beyond those originally described, such as abuse, war or natural disaster. Further, contemporary Trauma Theory opines that individuals have undergone events that are unprecedented human experiences, such as the current global pandemic (van der Kolk, 2014).

At the time this chapter was being written, the Centers for Disease Control and Prevention (CDC) reported that there were 92.2 million cases of the 2019 novel Coronavirus (COVID-19; 2019-n-COV) with 2.06 million deaths worldwide. The United States leads in total cases of 24,512,002 with a death toll of 409,072 and counting. Globally, we all have been greatly affected by this virus with a myriad of symptoms ranging from asymptomatic to death. This pandemic has made an impact on the world, especially on healthcare infrastructures and those in the helping professions. One of the occupational hazards of the COVID-19 pandemic for helping professions is vicarious traumatization. In 1990, McCann and Pearlman coined this phrase to delineate "a shift in a helping professional's worldview when they work with individuals who have experienced trauma (p. 1)." In sum, these individuals announce that their core beliefs are altered or impaired due to repeated exposure to traumatic events. This is a universal existential crisis that threatens how organizations run effectively and provide services to their customers. No one is immune to the virus and everyone is increasingly concerned about their own mortality. It is more than just the experience of stress and burnout; helping another person, may, in turn, cause harm to the helper. Vicarious Trauma symptoms can be physical, behavioral, psychological and/or spiritual.

MAIN FOCUS OF THE CHAPTER

The Coronavirus disease (COVID-19) was first recognized in Wuhan City, the Capital of Hubei Province, in the Peoples Republic of China (Shaukat, et. al, 2020). By January 2020, the virus had spread to other countries including France, Germany, Italy, Spain and the USA. As of January 2021 (approximately 1 year later), the virus had engulfed 221 countries, infecting 96.2 million people and causing 2.06 million deaths worldwide. As a consequence, this is viewed as a global pandemic (Dong, Du, Gardner, 2020).

There is scant literature on the growing physical demands and mental health impact this pandemic has made on Healthcare Professionals. The high burden is occurring in real-time, with no precedent to guide leaders on efficacious interventions. As a result of Healthcare Professionals being at greater risk of infection by the Coronavirus Disease, the shortage of staff is further heightened as healthcare facilities and Emergency Rooms are operating at their full capacities. During outbreaks, Healthcare Professionals undergo considerable stress. Which in turn, weakens their immune systems and causes them to be more susceptible to the virus. Healthcare Professionals on the front lines experience a significantly greater risk of infection and death due to the repeated exposure to the Coronavirus Disease (Shaukat, Ali, and Razzak, 2020). The risk factors impacting morbidity and mortality among this population includes working in high-risk Departments, limited Personal Protective Equipment (PPE) access, long contact hours with patients (15+ hour shifts) and diagnosed family members.

The Physical Toll on Healthcare Workers During Disease Epidemics

The Doctor of Medicine (denoted as M.D.) is regarded as one of the most prestigious graduate professional degrees conferred by institutions of higher learning (due to the many years of laborious training required to master the work of a Healer). However, what happens when a physician loses more patients than they save in a day from the same pathogen? Further, what if that same physician now needs the life-saving care from the doctors and nurses at the hospital where they are currently employed because they have now contracted the COVID-19 virus? They have already seen, first-hand, the demise of his patients and colleagues as a result of this deadly virus. In addition, there is a shortage of ventilators and a choice must be made if they receive one. The physical and mental anguish of this physician poses a threat to homeostasis and none of their formal training or expertise bring them closer to the answers they seek.

The author met Dr. Wayne (this surname was used to protect the identity of the patient) after he had been discharged from the same hospital where he worked as an Emergency Room Physician four months prior. He visits this clinician's office on his first day back to work; the time away was a relief, he reported, but survivor's guilt had set in because he had just learned that another fellow physician and two additional nurses in his Department had succumbed to the virus during his four-month convalescence. "It's been four months and I still can't taste anything", he said. He went on further to describe how he does not have an appetite and if he does not purchase the food himself, he would not be able to recognize what he was eating; the possibility of never regaining his sense of taste was daunting to him. Dr. Wayne also had anxiety about re-contracting the virus.

Through experience, he mentioned that those who have contracted the virus once, still had a chance to contract it again. Dr. Wayne recalled, in detail, that he noticed he had difficulty breathing while walking from his car to the hospital doors. He came into this therapist's office with a blank stare on his face as if he did not know where he was at present time. "I didn't realize how ill-equipped I am to return to work today, until I walked through those doors." Although Dr. Wayne had been cleared medically to return to work, the toll of the virus had organically changed him. The long shiftwork and urgency required for ER Physicians to thrive seemed foreign to him. In an effort to ameliorate his nadir, this therapist appealed to his concerns through a biopsychosocial approach and a strengths perspective. The underpinnings of medicine are science. At the core of the job as a physician, is a love of science. As a scientist, Dr. Wayne was intrigued when offered the opportunity to use his experiences as a physician as well as a patient to glean a better understanding of how he could better serve his patients and colleagues during this outbreak. Although Dr. Wayne was not currently capable to meet the physical demands required to return to the ER, he still could be utilized to assist hospital administrators with strategies to reduce the burden of health consequences. These protocols included strict infection control practices, reduced length of shiftwork and provisions for mental health support and services for healthcare workers.

A Behavioral Approach to Policing in Pandemics

One of the most honorable professions has been that of a Police Officer. The goal of the Police Officer is to protect and serve; to promote safety and ensure the peace so that an individual's life and liberty may flourish. Chief Bell (he is called to ensure confidentiality) enters this therapist's office at a crossroads: He has just learned that a fellow African American police chief has died by suicide. He recognizes the urgency for social change and is aware of the increasing escalation in racialized trauma. Nevertheless, he is now feeling unbalanced because the pendulum of justice is swinging too far toward racial inequality.

Law and order are a new kind of Black and White and the waters he now tread are so murky, that his 30 years of expertise in Law Enforcement no longer serves or benefits him as an authority on all things Police.

Chief Bell is dealing with two pandemics: The proliferation of COVID-19 as well as social injustice and racial inequality by the hands of his own brothers in blue. Does he stay in the fight to become a beacon of hope for his race who no longer has faith in the Criminal Justice System? Although surviving a 30-year career in Law Enforcement is a time for celebrating retirement, he still feels he has more to prove. With all the calamity in the world, ending his career at 30 years of service would seem to be perfect timing. He has fought the good fight; he has run his race. He can begin an entirely new chapter in his life with no regrets or judgement from his peers and/or subordinates. Does he retire at his 30-year tenure with full honor and benefits so that his constant exposure to others through individual encounters or super-spreader events/marches/protests no longer increase his chances of getting gunned-down by assailants or contracting COVID-19 (and possibly spreading it to his innocent family at home)? He is in a position of authority and if he stays, he can terminate those police officers who give his profession a bad reputation and employ adequate culturally competent training for those who remain. He could also implement community education about police work and join with the African American community about issues surrounding police brutality.

The Chief has also ruminated about transitioning from public service to civil service and addressing how most essential workers are people of color. He also reported that these front-line workers have a higher risk of exposure to the virus and are primarily employed for organizations that do not offer paid sick leave. As a result, the probability of them continuing to work while they are ill is increased. According to Bates (2020), Law Enforcement officers are directly involved in the pandemic response and are at a higher risk of contracting the virus. In addition, COVID-19 inequalities affect people of color disproportionately. By experiencing and witnessing repeated racism, discrimination and disparity of treatment, this population (including Chief Bell) is skeptical of any newly developed vaccines that their White counterparts suggest they spearhead due to past experiences such as the Tuskegee Syphilis Study (spanning 40 years from 1932 to 1972 by the United States Public Health Service -USPHS).

Chief Bell continued to provide the therapist with what he thought was a history lesson regarding 600 African American men in Macon County, Alabama who were mustered to enter into a scientific experiment on untreated Syphilis. These non-suspecting gentlemen were informed that they were receiving free medical care and treatment for a blood disorder when in actuality, they received no treatment at all. The therapist actively engaged Chief Bell in conversation to form a therapeutic alliance and to demonstrate knowledge of these events. Chief Bell also added that the untreated Syphilis led to damage to major organs such as the brain, heart, liver as well as affected the eyes, bones and joints (Jones, 1993). Chief Bell confided in the author that he was an army veteran, had been deployed during the Persian Gulf War, and was experiencing Behavioral Vicarious Trauma events such as disturbances in sleep, hypervigilance, and negative coping skills like excessive drinking (Pearlman & Mac Ian, 1995). He also reported that due to staff shortages and absenteeism, he has been working extended hours.

As a mental health clinician, the author voiced concerns regarding his difficulty creating a work-life balance and enlightened him on how his past trauma as a combat veteran is a major risk factor for experiencing other traumas. This writer also allowed him the space to brainstorm ways he could assist his officers in obtaining limited equipment and supplies, transporting affected citizens and strengthening the relationship between police officers and public health workers. Chief Bell also decided to alert the police department's staff psychologist in order to provide added mental health support for him and his police officers to address any pandemic fears or anxieties. As a leader, Chief Bell is cognizant that he must possess cultural competence and foster safe environments for employees of color to feel comfortable in relaying their concerns which affect his department and stakeholders collectively.

Therapy for the Therapist

Aa-jes-van Doorn, Bekes, Prout and Hoffman (2020) published an article with the American Psychological Association (APA) to explore how Vicarious Trauma (VT) was experienced by psychotherapists during the COVID-19 pandemic. The authors surveyed 339 mental health clinicians regarding their professional encounters during the pandemic. The subjects were mental health clinicians that were recruited from professional organizations, social media and snowball sampling (individual referrals). The subjects were asked to explain their personal and professional experiences while in-session with patients during the COVID-19 pandemic. Some of the descriptions included empathy (emotional connectedness), therapeutic alliances (strength or closeness of the therapeutic relationship), competence (knowledge/expertise) and tiredness (pandemic fatigue).

These subjects were also evaluated using the Vicarious Trauma Survey (VTS; Vrklevski and Franklin, 2008); a self-report questionnaire that measures distress levels consistent with individuals treating traumatized patients. The Vicarious Trauma Survey is comprised of eight items on a Likert Scale ranging from 1 (strongly disagree) to 7 (strongly agree). The results showed that these clinicians experienced moderate levels of VT on average. Further, fifteen percent of these mental health professionals expressed high levels of VT. Implications for further research suggested several interventions and support for clinicians working amid a global pandemic, such as incorporating mental health support into the workplace, pairing mentors with less experienced clinicians, as well as creating clinical consultation groups to assist with the challenges faced while working with patients undergoing the deleterious effects of the COVID-19 virus.

Mrs. Wylder was a seasoned psychotherapist with a long history of crisis counseling. She had served on various mental health advisory boards, supervised hundreds of interns for licensure and earned an impressive number of certifications. She entered the therapist's office speaking to internal stimuli and exhibiting command auditory hallucinations, telling her to harm herself. Upon mental status examination, her appearance was disheveled with inadequate grooming and she failed personal hygiene as evidenced by foul body odor, and unkempt hair. She was not dressed appropriately for the season or weather. Her clothes appeared worn and she had taken a black marker and drawn an "X" in the center of her shirt (she said it was anti-virus protection). Mrs. Wylder's speech was pressured and rapid, which was the opposite of her usual calm tone. Her attitude toward the author was defensive and her behavior was restless with wringing of the hands and psychomotor agitation. Her mood was labile (fluctuating from bursts of laughter to sobbing uncontrollably).

Her affect was incongruent with her mood and her thoughts were impaired with loose associations; her answers to questions did not make sense. In addition, she had paranoid delusions that she would not contract the virus if she wore the same shirt. She refused to wear a mask (which was mandated by the hospital). She was not oriented to time, place, person or situation. Her insight and judgment were impaired and was positive for suicidal ideation, plan and intent. Mrs. Wylder was escorted to this therapist's office by hospital police because her behavior was not consistent with the poised, professional colleague that everyone knew. Due to her bizarre behavior, this therapist had no other recourse, but to admit her to inpatient psychiatric hospitalization for crisis stabilization. The same ward on which she treated patients for decades is now her fate. The treatment plan for Mrs. Wylder was to refer her to a psychiatrist to address the auditory hallucinations and provide additional support. This was necessary, since Vicarious Tramatization has been linked with psychological deterioration and an adverse impact on treatment efficacy (Pearlman & Mac Ian, 1995). Vicarious Trauma is exceptionally poignant when the helper and helpless are simultaneously facing tragedy and deterioration such as the current global pandemic, the Spanish Flu of 1918, The Great Depression of 1929, The Space Shuttle Challenger Disaster of 1986, Hurricane Katrina in 2005 and the World Trade Center Attacks on September 11, 2001 (Rubel, 2019, Loss, Grief, and Bereavement, p. 285).

The Spiritual Reckoning of Clergy Amid the COVID-19 Outbreak

Another revered profession is that of the Clergy. Be it a Rabbi, Priest, Minister or Chaplain, these individuals are recognized as spiritual or religious guides. Those who experience an existential crisis or believe in a higher power, would find refuge in these leaders through their ability to provide comfort and comprehension to life's most difficult challenges. As a result of the COVID-19 pandemic and resulting deaths, the Clergy has officiated more funerals than ever before and is now seeking guidance of their own while everyone else is searching for meaning amid the chaos. Social distancing has decreased religious gatherings. And many members of congregations, parishioners and their families have died from the COVID-19 virus. One Chaplain in particular, Chaplain Cochran (fictitious name due to anonymity), lamented that this pandemic has been difficult for the Clergy. He further expressed compassion fatigue as he counselled others stricken by sickness, poverty and grief.

As he visits and prays in areas densely populated with COVID-infected patrons, he deals with death on a daily basis. The chaplain asks, "Who counsels the Counselor?" Chaplain Cochran states that the clergy is on the frontlines and do not receive the same recognition as health care workers. And that this recognition should be afforded to clergy without diminishing the work of healthcare professionals and others. The author's approach as a therapist was to validate the selfless work Chaplain Cochran is doing to encourage and instill faith in others during this dark time. The author employed a client-centered approach and incorporated unconditional positive regard in order to foster a therapeutic environment that was a safe space for the chaplain to express his frustrations and experiences. Before the session ended, a psychoeducational approach was provided to explore the spiritual tenants of Vicarious Trauma so that he could recognize the warning signs and triggers associated with pandemic fatigue. Spiritual Vicarious Traumatization warning signs include feelings of hopelessness, decreased sense of purpose, and self-isolation (Cunningham, 2004). The chaplain was encouraged to add the therapist as an additional resource of support, seek consult from peers and mentors, engage in adequate sleep, ensure proper nutrition, increase physical activity and set aside time for prayer and/or meditation to attend to his own self-care and make it easier to provide care for others.

SOLUTIONS AND RECOMMENDATIONS

Self-care is a "multi-dimensional, multi-faceted process of purposeful engagement in strategies that promote healthy functioning and enhance well-being" (Dovociak, Rupert, Bryant and Zahnisen, 2007, p. 325). Self-care is essential for resilience-building when certain life stressors cannot be decreased or eliminated. In sum, when steps are taken to attend to the mind, body and soul, the better equipped they are to live their best lives. However, many leaders, from all walks of life, perceive self-care as a luxury instead of a priority. As a consequence, they are left ill-equipped and too overwhelmed to adequately face the inevitability of life's challenges. For example, the act of meditation is fruitless if someone is not getting adequate sleep. There are people who fall asleep in therapy sessions because they do not attend to their body's need for sleep. Further, sparingly engaging in physical activity will not ameliorate stress if an individual continues to fuel their body with highly processed foods. It is important to evaluate how one cares for themselves in physical, mental, spiritual and social domains to ensure that the mind, body and soul are healthy.

Physical Self-Care

Individuals need to take care of their physical bodies if they want it to operate efficiently. Physical self-care is more than just making time for a monthly massage. It is the continuous invitation of creating space for what is best for each person. Physical self-care includes getting adequate sleep, fueling the body with proper nutrition, engaging in physical activity, attending medical appointments and taking medications as prescribed if needed (American Psychological Association, 2015). People can create the *best* or *worst* version of themselves simply by making these small decisions throughout our day.

Socialization

Social self-care is essential amid the COVID-19 pandemic. Close connections foster positive well-being and time should be prioritized to cultivate and maintain close relationships (Umberson, Montez, 2010). Even though individuals are required to limit their social circles for now, they can create a "COVID bubble" with a few close friends. They could also meet friends outside at a park while wearing a mask and remaining socially distanced. Third, individuals can schedule social time via video conferencing to include activities such as art, exercise, wine tasting and games. The opportunities are endless when unique ideas are formed to stay connected.

Mental Health

Additional support from counselors and therapists amidst this pandemic greatly influences psychological well-being. People should consider engaging in activities that stimulates the mind and practice self-love, radical acceptance, and compassion to maintain a healthier introspection (Pillai, Hall, Dickson, Buschke, Lipton and Verghese, 2011). Positive coping skills are imperative when dealing with uncomfortable feelings. Many emotions such as fear, grief and anxiety are evoked by the coronavirus pandemic. Self-care in this area may involve healthy ways to process these feelings and incorporating activities that help individuals recharge and refuel your emotional tank (Izard, 2009).

Spirituality

Koenig (2015) posited that a life that includes religion and/or spirituality is generally more fulfilling. Nurturing the spirit can allow individuals to create a deeper connection with the world around them. Many people view spiritual self-care as being mindful and more connected to the present through meditation and diaphragmatic breathing. Others are influenced by different ideologies and cultural traditions from their youth. Be it the observance of rituals, attending religious services, or studying philosophies, Spirituality is subjective, with different meanings for different people. The future effects of the CO-

VID-19 pandemic are an unknown. Self-exploration about one's life and experiences will help facilitate purpose and meaning.

FUTURE RESEARCH DIRECTIONS

With the arrival of COVID-19 vaccines, the world will eventually re-open and the impact of the COVID-19 virus on employees' psychological, behavioral, physical and spiritual well-being will be tested again. Employees will continue to feel anxiety about returning to work, sending their children back to school and contracting or re-contracting the virus. Many will also be concerned about new, more aggressive variants of the coronavirus or even second or third waves of the virus if herd immunity is not achieved before sanctions are lifted. The aftermath of the pandemic's effects is still unknown. It would be beneficial for organizations to deal with the long-term effects of the pandemic aftermath by developing and introducing trauma-informed care programs. The efficacy of these interventions can be measured and assessed to determine their validity and reliability. In sum, monitoring whether the programs meet objectives.

CONCLUSION

The Coronavirus pandemic will become a substantial benchmark in the annals of human history. This novel respiratory disease has affected every aspect of humanity: biological, psychological, social, emotional, spiritual, financial and educational. This chapter described the significance of embracing self-care in the forms of spirituality, mental and physical health and socialization as ways to survive and thrive. These self-care techniques enable leaders to recognize the importance of modeling appropriate behaviors and managing workplace trauma and its relationship to organizational continuity. As the world witnesses the next phase of the coronavirus disease response, leaders must think of creative ways to ensure that staff return to work with a sense of safety and support so that they can decide what keeps them up at night or what wakes them up in the morning.

REFERENCES

Aafjes-van Doorn, K., Békés, V., Prout, T. A., & Hoffman, L. (2020). Psychotherapists' vicarious traumatization during the COVID-19 pandemic. *Psychological Trauma: Theory, Research, Practice, and Policy, 12*(S1), S148–S150. doi:10.1037/tra0000868 PMID:32478559

American Psychological Association. (2015). Retrieved January 23, 2021, from https://www.apa.org/news/press/releases/stress/2015/snapshot

Bates, J. (2020). Police Departments, Sheriffs' Offices across the U.S. Grapple with COVID-19's Impact on Public Safety—And Their Own. *TIME*. https://time.com/5812833/coronavirus-police-departments/

Bonkiewicz, L., & Ruback, R. B. (2012). The role of the police in evacuations: Responding to the social impact of a disaster. *Police (Springfield), 15*(2), 137–156. doi:10.1177/1098611112442808

Boscarino, J. A., Figley, C. R., & Adams, R. E. (2004). Compassion fatigue following the September 11 terrorist attacks: A study of secondary trauma among new york city social workers. *International Journal of Emergency Mental Health, 6*, 57–66. PMID:15298076

Culver, L. M., McKinney, B. L., & Paradise, L. V. (2011). Mental health professionals' experiences of vicarious traumatization in post-hurricane katrina new orleans. *Journal of Loss and Trauma, 16*(1), 33–42. doi:10.1080/15325024.2010.519279

Cunningham, M. (2004). Avoiding Vicarious Traumatization: Support, Spirituality, and Self-Care. In N. B. Webb (Ed.), *Social work practice with children and families. Mass trauma and violence: Helping families and children cope* (pp. 327–346). The Guilford Press.

Dong, E., Du, H., & Gardner, L. (2020). An interactive web-based dashboard to track COVID-19 in real time. *The Lancet. Infectious Diseases, 20*(5), 533–534. Advance online publication. doi:10.1016/S1473-3099(20)30120-1 PMID:32087114

Dorociak, K. E., Rupert, P. A., Bryant, F. B., & Zahniser, E. (2017). Development of a Self-Care Assessment for Psychologists. *Journal of Counseling Psychology, 64*(3), 325–334. doi:10.1037/cou0000206 PMID:28277686

Izard, C. E. (2009). Emotion theory and research: Highlights, unanswered questions, and emerging issues. *Annual Review of Psychology, 60*(1), 1–25. doi:10.1146/annurev.psych.60.110707.163539 PMID:18729725

Koenig, H. G. (2015). Religion, spirituality, and health: A review and update. *Advances in Mind-Body Medicine, 29*(3), 19–26. PMID:26026153

Laufs, J., Bowers, K., Birks, D., & Johnson, S. D. (2020). Understanding the concept of 'demand'in policing: A scoping review and resulting implications for demand management. *Policing and Society, 20*, 1–24. doi:10.1080/10439463.2020.1791862

McCann, L., & Pearlman, L. A. (1990). *Constructivist self-development theory as a framework for assessing and treating victims of family violence*. Springer.

Pearlman, L. A., & Saakvitne, K. W. (1995). *Trauma and the therapist: Countertransference and vicarious traumatization in psychotherapy with incest survivors.* New York: W.W. Norton.

Pearlman, L. A., & Mac Ian, P. S. (1995). Vicarious traumatization: An empirical study of the effects of trauma work on trauma therapists. *Professional Psychology, 26*(6), 558–565. doi:10.1037/0735-7028.26.6.558

Pillai, J. A., Hall, C. B., Dickson, D. W., Buschke, H., Lipton, R. B., & Verghese, J. (2011). Association of crossword puzzle participation with memory decline in persons who develop dementia. *Journal of the International Neuropsychological Society, 17*(6), 1006–1013. doi:10.1017/S1355617711001111 PMID:22040899

Rubel, B. (2019). *Loss, grief, and bereavement: Helping individuals cope*. Western Schools.

Shaukat, N., Ali, D. M., & Razzak, J. (2020). Physical and mental health impacts of COVID-19 on healthcare workers: A scoping review. *International Journal of Emergency Medicine*, *13*(1), 40. doi:10.118612245-020-00299-5 PMID:32689925

Stogner, J., Miller, B. L., & McLean, K. (2020). Police stress, mental health, and resiliency during the COVID-19 pandemic. *American Journal of Criminal Justice*, *1*, 1–13. PMID:32837167

Umberson, D., & Montez, J. K. (2010). Social relationships and health: A flashpoint for health policy. *Journal of Health and Social Behavior*, *51*(1_suppl), 54–66. doi:10.1177/0022146510383501 PMID:20943583

Van der Kolk, B. A. (2014). *The body keeps the score: Brain, mind, and body in the healing of trauma.* Penguin Group, LLC.

Vrklevski, L. P., & Franklin, J. (2008). Vicarious trauma: The impact on solicitors of exposure to traumatic material. *Traumatology*, *14*(1), 106–118. doi:10.1177/1534765607309961

Wang, X., Zhang, X., & He, J. (2020). Challenges to the system of reserve medical supplies for public health emergencies: Reflections on the outbreak of the severe acute respiratory syndrome coronavirus 2 (SARS-CoV-2) epidemic in China. *Bioscience Trends*, *14*(1), 3–8. doi:10.5582/bst.2020.01043 PMID:32062645

ADDITIONAL READING

Bergquist, S., Otten, T., & Sarich, N. (2020). COVID-19 pandemic in the United States. *Health Policy and Technology*, *9*(4), 623–638. doi:10.1016/j.hlpt.2020.08.007 PMID:32874854

Czeisler, M. É., Lane, R. I., Petrosky, E., Wiley, J. F., Christensen, A., Njai, R., Weaver, M. D., Robbins, R., Facer-Childs, E. R., Barger, L. K., Czeisler, C. A., Howard, M. E., & Rajaratnam, S. (2020). Mental Health, Substance Use, and Suicidal Ideation During the COVID-19 Pandemic - United States, June 24-30, 2020. *MMWR. Morbidity and Mortality Weekly Report*, *69*(32), 1049–1057. doi:10.15585/mmwr.mm6932a1 PMID:32790653

Daniel, S. J. (2020). Education and the COVID-19 pandemic. *Prospects*, *49*(1-2), 91–96. doi:10.100711125-020-09464-3 PMID:32313309

Gostin, L. O. (2020). The great coronavirus pandemic of 2020: 7 critical lessons. *Journal of the American Medical Association*, *324*(18), 1816–1817. doi:10.1001/jama.2020.18347 PMID:33170229

Hartnett, K. P., Kite-Powell, A., DeVies, J., Coletta, M. A., Boehmer, T. K., Adjemian, J., & Gundlapalli, A. V., & National Syndromic Surveillance Program Community of Practice. (2020). Impact of the COVID-19 Pandemic on Emergency Department Visits - United States, January 1, 2019-May 30, 2020. *MMWR. Morbidity and Mortality Weekly Report*, *69*(23), 699–704. doi:10.15585/mmwr.mm6923e1 PMID:32525856

MacIntyre, C. R. (2020). *Global spread of COVID-19 and pandemic potential. Global Biosecurity, 2(1).* None., doi:10.31646/gbio.55

McDermott, M. M., & Newman, A. B. (2020). Preserving clinical integrity during the coronavirus pandemic. *Journal of the American Medical Association*, *323*(21), 2135–2136. doi:10.1001/jama.2020.4689 PMID:32211830

Tehrani, N. (2004). *Workplace trauma: Concepts, assessment and interventions*. Brunner-Routledge. doi:10.4324/9780203500620

KEY TERMS AND DEFINITIONS

Coronavirus: A respiratory illness first identified in December 2019. It is spread through droplets and virus particles.

Essential Workers: Individuals who provide a myriad of services to maintain critical infrastructure operations.

Leadership: The act of modeling a desired behavior to achieve a collective goal.

Mental Health: Cognitive, behavioral, and emotional preparedness as evidenced by one's ability to cope with various stressors and/or the insight to seek support if warranted.

Pandemic: An infectious disease affecting a substantial number of people globally.

Self-Care: Any human regulatory function designed for the purpose of maintaining health management and overall wellness.

Vicarious Traumatization: A form of countertransference triggered by repeated exposure to traumatic events from persons requiring care.

Chapter 6
Managing the Hell Out of Organizational Trauma:
An Introduction to Five Resilience Leadership Skills

Kari A. O'Grady
Brigham Young University, USA

J. Douglas Orton
https://orcid.org/0000-0002-2529-4565
Center for Trauma Studies and Resilience Leadership, USA

Andrew Moffitt
Brigham Young University, USA

ABSTRACT

A vicarious 15-hike executive leadership resilience incubator in Mann Gulch, Montana, permits readers to upgrade their resilience leadership skills. Monday's hikes focus on sense-receiving, skills such as the leveraging of received national cosmologies, received community cosmologies, and received organizational cosmologies. Tuesday's hikes focus on sense-losing skills, moving from initial retentive sense-losing through a vicious cycle of selective sense-losing to the brutally honest audits of enactive sense-losing. Wednesday's hikes focus on sense-improvising skills by differentiating among temporality sense-improvising, identity sense-improvising, and social sense-improvising. Thursday's hikes focus on sense-remaking skills, moving from the enactive sense-remaking period through the virtuous cycle of selective sense-remaking to the retentive sense-remaking hinge between the catastrophe and the post-catastrophe. Friday's hikes focus on sense-transmitting skills, leveraging transmitted organizational cosmologies, transmitted community cosmologies, and transmitted national cosmologies. This chapter explores these five resilience leadership skills.

DOI: 10.4018/978-1-7998-7016-6.ch006

INTRODUCTION

A striking promise from president-elect Joe Biden on January 19, 2020, was his assertion that the 59th U.S. presidential administration would "manage the hell out of the COVID-19 pandemic." Resilience leadership experts around the world routinely manage the hell out of organizational trauma at all levels of intensity (perturbations, disruptions, crises, disasters, catastrophes) and at all levels of analysis (individuals, teams, organizations, communities, nations) in two ways. The first, most prevalent, meaning of "to manage the hell out of" an organizational trauma is vulgarly, coarsely, and simply to do a good job reducing human suffering. The second meaning—aspired to in this chapter—is spiritually, expertly, and complexly to enact numerous righteous solutions to any given wicked problem through *sense-receiving, sense-losing, sense-improvising, sense-remaking,* and *sense-transmitting* resilience leadership skills.

So how do resilience leadership experts learn to manage the hell out of organizational trauma? Traditional psychological, leadership, and management theories are built for the continuous operation of the world of "known knowns," with occasional deviations into the less easily manageable worlds of "unknown knowns" or "known unknowns." In contrast, resilience psychology, leadership, and management theories are built for the study of the "unknown unknowns" such as the world of organizational trauma (Weick, 1993; O'Grady & Orton, 2016; Orton & O'Grady, 2016). Thus, executives, scholars, professionals, consultants, and students seeking to reduce human suffering must build on their existing mastery of traditional leadership skills by investing significant resources in the development of resilience leadership skills within themselves, their top management teams, their organizations, their communities, and their nations. This chapter is an effort to help readers increase their resilience leadership expertise by summarizing the findings of the 2020 season of one executive leadership resilience incubator.

Among many possible designs to assist executives with their internalization of resilience leadership skills, the 2020 Mann Gulch executive resilience leadership incubator was created as a nature-grounded, evidence-based, internationally embedded, and extreme context-focused expedition. In 2020, the fifteen hikes that constitute the Mann Gulch expedition were divided as follows:

Hikes 1 through 3: exploration of the skill of *sense-receiving*
Expeditions 4 through 6: exploration of the skill of *sense-losing*
Expeditions 7 through 9: exploration of the skill of *sense-improvising*
Expeditions 10 through 12: exploration of the skill of *sense-remaking*
Expeditions 13 through 15: exploration of the skill of *sense-transmitting*

THEORETICAL FOUNDATION

The theoretical foundation for the Yarnell-Mann executive resilience leadership incubator is based on literature professor Norman Maclean's and resilience expert Karl E. Weick's *magnum opus* study of the August 4 through 6, 1949, Mann Gulch cosmology episode (Maclean, 1992; Weick, 1993). Weick wrote an article to reanalyze Maclean's story about a large firefighting disaster in Mann Gulch in which thirteen firefighters died. In his analysis, Weick sought to understand why organizations break down and fail and how they could be more resilient (Weick, 1993). In his article, he perceives the firefighters as an example of a small organization and suggests that the organization disintegrated in the context of the disaster (Weick, 1993). Weick (1993) argued that the organization failure was the result of a simultaneous and interrelated collapse of both "sensemaking" and structure. According to Weick, sensemaking is the process through which people give meaning to experience. Weick (1993) argues that, "the basic idea of sensemaking is that reality is an ongoing accomplishment that emerges from efforts to create order and make retrospective sense of what occurs" (p. 635).

Research Methodology

The research methodology is a series of qualitative meta-analyses of the nearly 6,000 scholarly publications citing Weick's Mann Gulch journal article. This study leverages the most recent 1% of the citations to Weick's Mann Gulch cosmology episode study to elaborate upon sense-receiving, sense-losing, sense-improvising, sense-remaking, and sense-transmitting. Table 1 presents the 60 scholarly publications in the order in which they were made available by Google Scholar through its "sort by date" option. Simplifying modifications were made to project the 60 articles as if they had appeared as one publication per day, Monday through Friday, in the twelve weeks between October 18, 2020, and January 2, 2021. Please note that the week of November 26-December 2, is presented as if it were two weeks because of the large volume of articles. As much as possible, the first pass through the 60 articles was accomplished in near-real-time as the scholarly publications were made available electronically and identified by daily searches of Google Scholar.

Cosmology Episodes Research

Cosmology episode studies is a field of research within the management sub-discipline of organizational resilience that focuses attention on the institutional micro-processes that constitute a cosmology episode. A cosmology episode occurs when individuals suddenly feel that the universe is no longer a rational, orderly system. When a cosmology episode happens, people suffer from the event and, at the same time, lose the means to recover from it (Weick, 1993). The three generations of cosmology episode studies are visible in Weick's books on organizing (1969, 1979), sensemaking (1995), and resilience (Weick & Sutcliffe, 2001, 2007, 2015) and in Weick's five exemplary cosmology episode studies:

- 1949 wildland firefighting catastrophe in Mann Gulch (Weick, 1993)
- 1950s development of the Battered Child Syndrome diagnosis (Weick, 2006)
- 1976 airline disaster in Tenerife, Spain (Weick, 1990)
- 1984 chemical leak in Bhopal, India (Weick, 1988)
- 1999 West Nile Virus outbreak in New York City (Weick, 2005)

Resilience Leadership Expeditions

Although countless executive leadership educators have tried to transmit the lessons of Maclean and Weick's Mann Gulch case study in sterile classrooms, the author believes that a more effective pedagogical method is to internalize the lessons of Mann Gulch through grounded expeditions within the terrain in which the catastrophe took place.

Table 1. Sixty cosmology episode studies published between 10/18/2020-1/2/2021

van Bavel et al. 10/19 Portugal Temporal Models of Disasters	Gaille & Terral 10/20 France Social Sciences and First Wave	Jha 10/21 India National Cosmologies	Secchi et al. 10/22 Sweden Reflections on Disruption	Xu 10/23 Japan Post-earthquake Anime Tourism
Kalkman 10/26 Netherlands Frontline Res-ponder Discretion	Barlette 10/27 France Rapid Failure Strategies	Slade 10/28 Australia Ontological Security	Creed et al. 10/29 IL Embodied/Shared Concern Worlds	Dahlberg et al. 10/30 Denmark Polar Search and Rescue
Sherman & Roberto 11/2 MT Plausible Sensegiving	Hamann 11/3 Sri Lanka 2004 Indian Ocean Tsunami	Rocha et al. 11/4 Canada Re-imagining Capitalism	Carlsson-Wall ... 11/5 Syria Migrant Crisis in Sweden	Ciuchta et al. 11/6 WI Organizational Improvisation
Allen et al. 11/9 FL Emotional Intelligence	Douyon & ... 11/10 France CSR-Aware Sensemaking	LeBoon 11/11 CA Generative Metaphors	Eddy-Spicer ... 11/12 NC Urban Education	Cleary 11/13 CT Change Storytelling in a Merger
Lindén 11/16 Finland Augmented Journalism	Vainio 11/17 Japan Affective Improvisation	Shreeve et al. 11/18 UK Risk Thinking	Flandin et al. 11/19 Switzerland Critical Incident Training	Geiger & ... 11/20 Germany Portfolios of Dy-namic Routines
Mithani & ... 11/23 NJ Fight, Flight, Freeze, etc.	Borjesson 11/24 Sweden Military Risk Balancing	Roulet 11/25 UK Cognitive/Behav-ioral Responding	Mannucci et al. 11/26 Italy Political LARP Improv.	Patriotta 11/27 Czech Rep. JMS Future of the Corporation
Tabesh & Vera 11/28 NY Improvisational Decision-making	Tipaldi et al. 11/29 Italy Emerging Economies	Waldschmidt 11/30 Framing of Engagement	Wessels 11/30 So. Africa Child Grant Policy	Parrish et al. 11/30 AZ Streams of Endo-generous Shocks
Sukhov et al. 12/1 Sweden Corporate Idea Screening	Bustamente et al. 12/1 Chile Entrepreneurial Intentions	Kruke 12/2 Norway Polar Search and Rescue	van der Merwe... 12/3 So. Africa Sense of Coherence Teams	Mayfield et al. 12/4 CA Communication Meaning
Yu & Yu 12/7 China Strategic Improvisation	Fernandez 12/8 France Mountain Search and Rescue	Mueller 12/9 Switzerland Theorizing Craft, Art, and Science	Simone et al. 12/10 Italy Urban Management	Williams et al. 12/11 Australia Job-related Diver-sity in HRTeams
Della Lucia et al. 12/14 Italy Humanistic Tourism	Fuller et al. 12/15 CA Fire, Flood, C19 Communications	Madiot 12/16 Canada Event Planner Improvisation	Miller et al. 12/17 FL Secondary Crisis in Education	Valderrama Ven. 12/18 Chile Methodology: History
Hartmann et al. 12/21 Germany Joy, Team Reflex-ivity, Resilience	Risberg 12/22 Sweden Trying Municipal Diversity	Cripe 12/23 IN School Disruption Sensemaking	Schmuhl 12/24 GA Superintendent Leadership	Secchi & Cowley 12/25 Denmark Embodied, Meso Social Organizing
Cheng 12/28 China Cross-cultural Encounters	Gorel 12/29 AZ Sensemaking, 7S, and SWOT	Rocha et al. 12/30 Canada Re-imagined Capitalism	Permatasari et al. 12/31 Indonesia Perceived Anti-corruption Acts	Arif 1/1/21 WA Misinformation, Disinformation

More specifically, experiential executive expeditions are grounded in Mann Gulch in three ways:

1. They are *emplaced*, meaning that executives travel to Mann Gulch to learn about cosmology episode studies.
2. They are *embodied*, meaning that executives try to experience the sights, sounds, touches, tastes, and smells of Mann Gulch.

3. They are *emplotted*, meaning that executives experience the August 4-6, 1949, Mann Gulch catastrophe in a well-documented chronological sequence.

MANN GULCH EXECUTIVE RESILIENCE LEADERSHIP INCUBATOR DISCUSSION

The Mann Gulch cosmology episode is not yet settled social science, but instead provides an opportunity to receive a "handoff" of one of Karl Weick's many contributions and attempt to elaborate on and "surpass" his initial 1993 proposed cosmology episode concepts (Weick, 2020). Weick leveraged Norman Maclean's 1992 book, *Young Men and Fire*, as rich source material for an exploration of five sources of resilience.

This book was later elaborated upon by Weick and Sutcliffe in their *Managing the Unexpected* book series (2001, 2007, 2015). Weick's concept of "[received] attitudes of wisdom" (later elaborated upon by Weick and Sutcliffe as "preoccupation with failure") is updated in this chapter as the resilience leadership skill, "sense-receiving." Weick's concept of "respectful interaction" (later elaborated upon as "deference to expertise") is updated here as part of the resilience leadership skill, "sense-losing." Weick's concept of "bricolage" (later elaborated as "commitment to resilience") is updated as part of the resilience leadership skill, "sense-improvising."

Weick's concept of "virtual role systems" (later elaborated as "reluctance to simplify") is updated as part of the resilience leadership skill, "sense-remaking." Weick's concept of "[transmitted] attitudes of wisdom" (later elaborated as "sensitivity to operations") is explored as part of the resilience leadership skill of "sense-transmitting."

Countless resilience leadership experts around the world have used the Mann Gulch cosmology episode as a starting point for the identification of institutional micro-processes and resilience leadership skills that can be used to reduce human suffering during wicked problems, cosmology episodes, and organizational trauma. This chapter integrates this work into a five-day executive resilience leadership incubator summarized in this chapter.

Sense-Receiving Monday Hikes: National, Community, and Organizational

Sense-receiving Monday is comprised of a short boat ride from Gates of the Mountains Marina, north of Helena, Montana, to the Meriwether picnic area, a hike up to the eastern upper saddle of Mann Gulch (Maclean, 1992, pp. 5-16), an exploration of the landing area (Maclean, 1992, pp. 85-101), and a descent to Willow Creek (Maclean, 1992, pp. 24-65). The hike up to the Mann Gulch saddle from Meriwether facilitates an elaboration of Weick's proposed "attitudes of wisdom" concept and Weick and Sutcliffe's high-reliability organizing principle of "preoccupation with failure" into the evidence-based, updated, and temporally bifurcated concepts of "received attitudes of wisdom" at the beginning of a cosmology episode and "transmitted attitudes of wisdom" at the end of a cosmology episode. The exploration of the upper saddle of Mann Gulch that provided a hard landing to fifteen smokejumpers and their gear permits the continuing differentiation of three types of received attitudes of wisdom: *received national cosmologies*, *received community cosmologies*, and *received organizational cosmologies* (see Table 2). The descent to Willow Creek serves as an introduction to the twelve organizational cosmologies described in the Tuesday and Thursday hikes, starting with the differentiation of twelve enacted environments:

historical, political, global, economic, volatile, unpredictable, complex, ambiguous, interdependent, leverageable, wicked, and extreme.

Table 2. An Introduction to Sense-receiving Skills during Cosmology Episodes

Received National Cosmologies are attitudes of wisdom that maintain a paradoxical balance between belief and doubt (Jha, 2020) -- built up over thousands of years through deductive, abductive, and inductive reasoning in response to cosmology episodes (Mueller, 2020) -- which are leveraged by resilience leadership experts to respond to vicious streams of disruptive shocks (Parrish et al., 2020).		
Jha 10/21 India Outbreaks Cosmologies as Sources of Ambivalent Wisdom	Mueller Switzerland Wrecks Cosmologies as Abductive Reservoirs of Meaning	Parrish, Clark, & Holloway 11/30 AZ Fires Cosmologies as Assets for Vicious Streams of Shocks
Received Community Cosmologies are portfolios of common operating pictures built from fragmented sensemaking in arenas in which cosmology episodes take place (Dahlberg et al., 2020; Kruke, 2020) – such as public shootings, naval capsizings or structure collapses (Bustamente et al., 2020) – embedded in social structures facilitating the development of resilience leadership skills (Mannucci et al., 2020).		
Dahlberg, Vendelø, … 10/30 Denmark Capsizings Cosmologies as Common Operational Pictures	Bustamente, Poblete, & … 12/1 Chile Collapses Cosmologies as Guides to Multi-level Interactions	Mannucci, Orazi, & de Walck 11/26 Italy Shootings Cosmologies as Social Struct-ures for Skill Development
Received Organizational Cosmologies are distinct enacted environments (e.g. historical, political, global, economic, volatile, unpredictable, complex, ambiguous, interdependent, leverageable, wicked, or extreme) (Xu, 2020) which serve as inputs into the environment-skill-organization plots (Cleary, 2020) that facilitate the framing of streams of events into bracketed cues (Waldschmidt, 2020).		
Xu 10/23 Japan Collapses Cosmologies as Distinct Enacted Environments	Cleary 11/13 CT Errors Cosmologies as Input-Throughput-Output Plots	Waldschmidt 11/30 Cosmologies as Facilitators of the Framing of Events

Expedition 1: Received National Cosmologies

Received national cosmologies are attitudes of wisdom that maintain a paradoxical balance between belief and doubt (Jha, 2020) that has been built up over thousands of years through deductive, abductive, and inductive reasoning in response to cosmology episodes (Flandin et al., 2020). These cosmologies are leveraged by resilience leadership experts to respond to vicious streams of disruptive shocks (Parrish et al., 2020).

Received national cosmologies are one source of the resilience-creating "attitudes of wisdom" – the maintenance of a paradoxical ambivalence between belief and doubt before, during, and after a catastrophe (Weick, 1993). The other five sources of attitudes of wisdom, discussed later in this chapter, are received community cosmologies, received organizational cosmologies, transmitted organizational cosmologies, transmitted community cosmologies, and transmitted national cosmologies. For example, resilience leadership experts studied how seven aspects of India's received national cosmology shaped the reactions of fifteen Indian start-up companies in the early months of the COVID-19 outbreak: particularism rather than universalism, communitarianism rather than individualism, affective rather than neutral decision-making, diffused rather than specific relationships, ascribed rather than achieved status, short-term rather than long-term time orientation, and external rather than internal direction (Jha, 2020, pp. 106-109). More specifically, Jha documented how India's received national cosmology helped the fifteen start-ups reconcile the improvisational dilemmas of physical interaction versus digital interaction, democratic versus autocratic decision-making, efficiency optimization versus resilience enhancement, exploiting current niches versus exploring better niches, people orientation versus results orientation, continuity versus transformation, and short-term tactics versus long-term strategy (pp. 79-90).

Received national cosmologies provide a starting point for people experiencing cosmology episodes characterized by vicious streams of volatile and complex shocks. Attitudes of wisdom received before a catastrophe begins (received national cosmologies, received industrial cosmologies, received organizational cosmologies, received team cosmologies, and received individual cosmologies) give social units an increased, but not always adequate, capacity to cope with vicious streams of volatile and complex shocks. For example, a U.S. research team studied how a "hotshot crew became trapped after crossing an unburnt hillside, rushing toward a pre-determined safety zone that was just a quarter of a mile further. Blocked by a ridge from seeing the wind-whipped wall of fire approaching, they were soon overrun" (Parrish et al., 2020, p. 78). In their study of the 30 June 2013 Yarnell Hill, Arizona, cosmology episode, Parrish, Clark, and Holloway found that received national cosmologies are not always up to the task of withstanding vicious streams of volatile and complex shocks: "In such cases of simultaneous fire and weather volatility, the conditions within and surrounding an intense fire can change faster than firefighters can understand them" (Parrish et al., 2020, p. 82).

Expedition 2. Received Community Cosmologies

Received community cosmologies are portfolios of common operating pictures built from fragmented sensemaking in arenas in which cosmology episodes take place (Dahlberg et al., 2020; Kruke, 2020). Examples include public shootings, naval capsizings or structure collapses (Bustamente et al., 2020; Mannucci et al., 2020) embedded in social structures that facilitate the development of resilience leadership skills (Mannucci et al., 2020).

Received community cosmologies are composed of numerous common operational pictures -- shared sets of decision-making and problem-solving routines that can be leveraged at the beginning of a cosmology episode, updated throughout the cosmology episode, and revised at the end of a cosmology episode. Norwegian researchers studying naval polar search and rescue operations explained the need for received industrial cosmologies within the context of naval capsizings in the polar region: "This is the initial stage, where people find themselves in an unexpected situation. . . often characterized by a high degree of uncertainty, with some degree of chaos" (Kruke, 2020, p. 4). Danish researchers, studying the same type of cosmology episode, explained the importance of received industrial cosmologies for the creation of common operational pictures (COPs) during Polar Search and Rescue (SAR) operations. "The success of a SAR operation depends on the ability of the participating organizational units to synchronize their ongoing local and distributed sensemaking and thereby to maintain a COP" (Dahlberg et al., p. 159). However, Dahlberg, Vendelø, Sørensen, and Lauta (2020) found COPs are threatened by "the distributed nature of the collaborating organizational units' activities;" the updating and synchronization of COPs is difficult "because diversity in training and experience of their personnel creates a breeding ground for fragmented sensemaking;" and, consequently, "the collaborating organizational units [often] generate more diverse sets of what can be labeled Local Operational Pictures (LOP)" (p. 159).

Received community cosmologies provide examples, explanations, and guidance for the multi-level interactions that occur within cosmology episodes. For example, researchers studied entrepreneurial intentions in Chile in 2008, 2009, 2010, and 2011, with a specific focus on how individual entrepreneurial intentions were disrupted by the societal-level 27 February 2010 Chile earthquakes (Bustamente et al., 2020). Bustamente, Poblete, and Amorós found that "natural disasters trigger unexpected change, ranging from social transformations to change in individual functioning," "survivors of a disaster generally find themselves engulfed in a community in severe shock," and "natural disasters may trigger change in the way people think, feel, and behave" (section 2.1, n. p.). They proposed that the Chilean earthquake affected individual-level entrepreneurial intentions -- positively ("While starting up an informal business may socially unacceptable under normal circumstances, an extreme crisis situation could lead to new subjective norms that allow such businesses," section 2.3.2) or negatively ("[D]ue to the disruptive nature of natural disasters (Weick, 1993), people may choose to protect the limited resources that are left," section 2.3.1, n. p.)

Expedition 3. Received Environmental Cosmologies

Received environmental cosmologies are distinct enacted environments (e.g. historical, political, global, economic, volatile, unpredictable, complex, ambiguous, interdependent, leverageable, wicked, or extreme) (Xu, 2020) which serve as inputs into the environment-skill-organization plots (Cleary, 2020; Waldschmidt, 2020; Xu, 2020) that facilitate the framing of streams of events into bracketed cues.

Table 3. Twelve organizational cosmology plots

Historical environments call forth leadership skills to create well-managed organizations	**Political** environments call forth structure skills to create loosely coupled organizations	**Global** environments call forth institutional skills to create narrative organizations	**Economic** environments call forth strategy skills to create coherent organizations
Volatile environments call forth change skills to create agile organizations	**Unpredictable** environments call forth decision-making skills to create decisive organizations	**Complex** environments call forth learning skills to create learning organizations	**Ambiguous** environments call forth communication skills to create high-reliability organizations
Interdependent environments call forth collaboration skills to create modular organizations	**Leverageable** environments call forth strategizing skills to create strategic organizations	**Wicked** environments call forth improvisation skills to create innovative organizations	**Extreme** environments call forth resilience skills to create resilient organizations

Researchers studying the aftermath of the 2011 complex cosmology episode in Japan of an earthquake (collapses), a tsunami (capsizings), and a nuclear meltdown (accidents) identified some of the characteristics of a *political* received environmental cosmology ("national resources and the social aspect") and a *complex* received environmental cosmology ("the complexity of interactions between social systems" (Xu, 2020, p. 19). Alternatively, Xu's (2020) study of a city's reemergence after the earthquake-tsunami-meltdown as an anime tourist destination can be seen as an example of an *economic* received environmental cosmology: "The external shocks are not always caused by natural disasters but [by] any potential risks to a community such as financial crises, which can also be triggered by natural disasters" (p. 22). Received environmental cosmologies are narratively coupled to transmitted organizational cosmologies. These linkages between environmental cosmologies (e.g., extreme, economic, and complex) and organizational cosmologies (e.g., structures, strategies, and learning) were studied by Xu (2020), who wrote, "Tourism organizations and tourism businesses often have key roles in a community, as they are using local resources and making an economic contribution" (p. 18).

Received environmental cosmologies are the means through which weak signals and disruptive events – through framing processes -- are ignored, noticed, or interpreted. In two of the earliest journal articles on organizational resilience, researchers emphasized the significance of framing in cosmology episodes. Staw, Sandelands, and Dutton (1981) theorized that the initial framing of a weak signal or disruptive event could trigger either a positive, virtuous, "opportunity-flexibility cycle" or a negative, vicious, "threat-rigidity cycle" (Staw, Sandelands, & Dutton, 1981), while Meyer (1982) studied nineteen Bay Area hospitals' different responses to an anesthesiologist strike, finding that different received environmental cosmologies produced different framings of the same event. More recently, Waldschmidt interviewed ten Ottawa, Canada, managers from different organizations on the topic of workplace engagement and discovered three frames -- the idea of success, the idea of care, and the idea of involvement – each of which is a distinct received environmental cosmology likely to lead to distinct subsequent actions.

Sense-Losing Tuesday Hikes: Retentive, Selective, and Enactive

Sense-losing Tuesday begins with a hike from Willow Creek to the upper saddle of Mann Gulch, followed by a reenactment of the Bill Hellman-led hike down the gulch, a reenactment of the Wag Dodge-led hike to Kibbey Ridge near the mouth of Mann Gulch at the Missouri River and a reenactment of the hike from Kibbey Ridge to Tool Drop. The exploration of picnic rock permits an elaboration of Weick's proposed "respectful interaction" concept (which later evolved into Weick and Sutcliffe's high-reliability organizing principle of "deference to expertise") into the evidence-based and updated resilience leadership skill of *sense-losing* (Orton, 1995, 2000; Fukami, 2002, pp. 27-28; O'Grady & Orton, 2016; Orton & O'Grady, 2016). The re-enactment of the Bill Hellman-led crew hike down-gulch, while Dodge was scouting the fire with forest ranger James Harrison, permits an elaboration of three types of sense-losing.

Ever since the *Challenger* space explosion in 1986, some resilience leadership experts have practiced a balanced double-vision reading of Weick's *The Social Psychology of Organizing* (1969, 1979), reading it first as a study of the book's implicit movement from *retentive sense-losing* to *selective sense-losing* to *enactive sense-losing*, and second as a study of the book's explicit movement from enactive sense-remaking to selective sense-remaking to retentive sense-remaking (see Table 3). The re-enactment of Dodge and Harrison's run to overtake the line of thirteen crew members led by Hellman, Hellman's move to the back of the line with Sallee and Rumsey, and Dodge's clamber up Kibbey Ridge to get a view of the fire blocking the crew's escape to the Missouri River permit an elaboration of *enactive sense-losing* as the construction of a brutally honest audit, appraisal, and map of a new socially constructed reality.

Expedition 4. Retentive Sense-Losing

Retentive sense-losing is the noticing of cues, interruptions, violations, and disruptions heralding the arrival of a cosmology episode which is primarily enabled through a palette of simple 19th Century manifestations of twelve core management skills and are partially explained through the biological metaphor of freeze or fright, then flight, then fight (Arif, 2020; Ciuchta et al., 2020; Mithani & Kocoglu, 2020).

Retentive sense-losing is the noticing, by different people at different times, of the emergence of cues, interruptions, violations, or disruptions heralding cosmology episodes, which also vary in intensity from mere perturbations, to substantial disruptions, to frequent crises, to rare disasters, and to incomprehensible catastrophes. For example, a researcher studying organizational responses to the misinformation and disinformation that accompany large-scale disruptive events defined cues as "issues, events, or situations . . . for which the meaning is ambiguous and/or outcomes uncertain" (Arif, 2020, p. 23). Although most cues are not noticed, some cues can "interrupt people's routines, disrupting their understanding of the world and creating uncertainty about how to act" (p. 23). "Cues" and "interruptions" project less intensity than the more emotion-laden "violation[s] of expectations" (p. 23). At the highest level of intensity, "disruptive events" range from an "impact on individual or social identity, and personal goals" to an impact on "larger socioeconomic systems and their ability to cope with disruptive events" (p. 23).

Table 4. An Introduction to Sense-losing Skills during Cosmology Episodes

Retentive Sense-losing is the noticing of cues, interruptions, violations, and disruptions heralding the arrival of a cosmology episode (Arif, 2020); is primarily enabled through a palette of simple 19th Century manifestations of core management skills (Ciuchta et al., 2020); and is partly explained by metaphors of freeze or fright, then flight, then fight (Mithani & Kocoglu, 2020).		
Arif 1/1/21 WA Shootings Sense-losing as Interruptions, Violations, Disruptions	Mithani & Kocoglu 11/23 NJ Shootings Sense-losing as Freeze (or Fright), Flight, and Fight	Ciuchta, O'Toole, & Miner 11/6 WI Fires Sense-losing as 19th, 20th, and 21st Century Manifestations
Selective Sense-losing is the critical period during which resilience leadership decision-making either dampens or accelerates vicious cycles (van Bavel et al., 2020); the general sense of ontological security transitions to a general sense of ontological insecurity (Slade, 2020); and multiple dynamic routines are leveraged to create multiple interpretations of the extreme context (Geiger & Danner-Schröder, 2020).		
van Bavel et al. 10/19 Portugal Collapses Sense-losing as a Component of Temporal Disaster Models	Slade 10/28 Australia Fires Sense-losing as the Rise of Ontological Insecurity	Geiger & Danner-Schröder 11/20 Germany Wrecks Sense-losing as a Portfolio of Dynamic Routines
Enactive Sense-losing is the leveraging of institutional micro-processes to create accurately brutal audits, appraisals, and maps of the extreme context (Creed et al., 2020), primarily enabled through a palette of complex 21st Century manifestations of twelve core management skills (Barlette, 2020), such as the movement from isolated to sequential to complex decision-making skills (Shreeve et al., 2020).		
Barlette 10/28 France Shootings Sense-losing as Rapid Failure Cloud Computing Strategies	Creed, Hudson, Okhuysen ... 10/29 IL Abuses Sense-losing as Brutally Accurate Audits/ Appraisals	Shreeve, Hallett, Edwards ... 11/18 UK Shootings Sense-losing as Complex Team Decision-making

Retentive sense-losing includes three generic strategic responses popularized in the biological metaphor of freeze (or fright), flight, or fight (Mithani & Kocoglu, 2020). *Freeze* is a form of retentive sense-losing characterized by "a heightened state of observation and guardedness where information about the threat is rapidly extracted from the environment, assimilated with preexisting insights about potential implications, and compared to resources and routines available for response" (p. 2082). Freeze "only lasts for a short time during which managers avoid strategic changes in order to calibrate the threat" and is a period when "managers avoid making new strategic choices before they have fully taken into account the threat and organizational preparedness against that threat" (p. 2082). (*Fright* is a related form of retentive sense-losing in which "exposure to a life-threatening even also leads organizations to 'act dead' – a state of dormancy that makes them appear innocuous due to operational inactivity" (p. 2082).) *Flight* is one of many possible responses to a catastrophe: "when confronted by a significant threat, organizations prefer the least risky option: exit or departure from the regions affected by the threat" (p. 2082). *Fight* requires an organization to use materials at hand to improvise an escape path. According to Mithani & Kocoglu, (2020) "It has been observed that some organizations view disruptions as strategic opportunities. Such firms end up with higher assets, larger investments and more visible presence in the affected region that reflects a fight response" (p. 2082). In general, there is a migration from freeze/fright (retentive sense-losing) to flight (selective sense-losing) to fight (enactive sense-losing), a sequence that will be developed in more detail in this chapter.

Expedition 5. Selective Sense-Losing

Selective sense-losing is the leveraging of a portfolio of routines that can be used as diverse lenses to facilitate the movement away from a simple understanding to a more complicated understanding of an emerging extreme situation (Geiger & Danner-Schröder, 2020). Reviewing their research on firefighters and international humanitarian aid organizations, Geiger and Danner-Schröder (2020) found that resilience leadership experts do not simply memorize one routine, but they internalize the logic behind multiple routines by using "intensive training sessions" to build "a shared understanding of action steps" that facilitates "flexible enactment of routines" (p. 3). More specifically, they found that in selective sense-losing, resilience leadership experts begin to reshape the "temporal boundaries between routines (the transition between two distinct routines)" and "adjust the performance of subsequent routines" in order to "flexibly adapt to novel situations" (p. 4).

Selective sense-losing is the erosion of ontological security and the rise of ontological insecurity (Slade, 2020). Slade – in a study of the 2009 Black Saturday bushfires in Australia explained that under normal circumstances (sense-receiving and sense-transmitting) people are likely to benefit from "ontological security" in which "a person … may have a sense of their presence in the world as real, alive, whole, and in a temporal sense, continuous" (p. 58). Under abnormal circumstances (sense-losing, sense-improvising, and sense-remaking) people are likely to be subject to "ontological insecurity" in which "a person . . . may feel more unreal than real, and [perceive] a perpetual threat to his or her existence" (p. 58). Slade found "that the damage caused by the Black Saturday fires was not limited to a mere physical dimension, but also occurred in the form of an attack on ontological security" in which challenged "the mastery people felt they held over the environment" and "the trust structures connected to the assumption that authorities could manage any threats" (p. 61). More specifically, selective sense-losing occurred when "previously reliable wisdom regarding bushfire response was destroyed," "emotional resilience provided by the availability and reliability of that wisdom was simultaneously pierced," and "the fragility of life's structure and order could no longer be ignored" (p. 61).

Expedition 6. Enactive Sense-Losing

Enactive sense-losing leverages a palette of 21st Century manifestations of the twelve core management skills: complexity leadership, open structures, fragmented institutions, networks strategies, evolutionary change, organizational decision-making, exploration learning, enactive sensemaking, cross-functional collaboration, swarming improvisation, and inside-the-boom resilience. For example, resilience leadership experts practicing enactive sense-losing during a cosmology episode leverage a wide variety of swarming improvisation techniques, such as the technology of foolishness, crowdsourcing, artificial intelligence, big data, moneyball, butterfly effects, and rapid failure. For example, information technology experts describe "strategies of rapid failure, based on experimentation and improvisation, at reduced costs due to cloud computing" (translated, by the authors, from Barlette, 2020, p. 74). Barlette found that rapid failure cloud computing "has strategic implications because it permits learning, whether the experiment succeeds or fails;" it "significantly reduces experimentation expenses, because infrastructure and applications can be rented and their implementation is simple and fast;" and it "permits the reduction of implementation cycles from several weeks to several days, which creates a competitive advantage" (p. 74).

Enactive sense-losing is visible in the movement from rational to political to organizational team decision-making during cosmology episodes (Allison & Zelikow, 1999). Organizational decision-making and complex decision-making in teams are illuminated by cosmology episode studies of "decisions made by individuals, teams, and organisations during major disasters" such as the 1949 Mann Gulch cosmology episode, the 1986 *Challenger* explosion, the 2001 terrorist attacks in the United States, and the 2009 H1N1 pandemic (Shreeve et al., 2020, p. 5:15). Resilience leadership experts in the field of cybersecurity risk thinking reanalyzed transcribed data from a "Decisions and Disruptions" tabletop exercise to identify "isolated," "sequential," and "complex" patterns of decision-making (Shreeve et al. 2020). Shreeve, Hallett, Edwards, Anthonysamy, Frey, and Rashid found that complex decision-making is "the most advanced form of discussion, where teams not only develop thoughts sequentially but cross reference prior ideas to explore them in greater depth" (p. 5:16).

For example, Creed, Hudson, Okhuysen, and Smith-Crowe in their analysis of the institutional micro-processes visible in the lived experience of a white supremacist – provide a heart-breakingly, accurately brutal audit, appraisal, or map of "the contemporary conflict over policing as an institution in the United States" (p. 48). People "cannot understand Black Americans' shared world of concern without attending to how sedimented experiences of [police] brutality against themselves and their brothers and sisters, shape their visceral distrust of policing" (p. 48). Furthermore, people "cannot understand White Americans' shared world of concern" without accepting the fact that "few White Americans have a parallel experience of police brutality" and acknowledging the presence of institutional racism, in which White Americans' "sedimented experience is also infused with a manufactured fear of Blackness that is the product of socialization and systemic racism which, for many White people, positions police as protectors" (p. 48).

Sense-Improvising Wednesday Hikes: Temporality, Identity, and Sociality

Sense-improvising Wednesday is grounded in a boat ride to the mouth of Mann Gulch and a hike back to Kibbey Ridge. The Kibbey Ridge to Tool Drop hike permits the elaboration of Weick's proposed "bricolage" concept (which later evolved into Weick and Sutcliffe's high-reliability organizing principle of "commitment to [improvisation]") into the evidence-based and updated resilience leadership skill of sense-improvising. The Tool Drop to Escape Fire hike permits the continuing differentiation among temporal sense-improvising, selective sense-improvising, and sociality sense-improvising (see Table 4). The exploration of the five survival paths created by the crew's escape fire improvisation permits the elaboration of sociality sense-improvising before the hike down from Bill Hellman's death marker to the boat waiting at the mouth of Rescue Gulch.

Expedition 7. Temporality Sense-Improvising

Temporality sense-improvising is the identification of potential escape paths from a cosmology episode through the skillful practice, modification, and resequencing of rolling retrospective rationality communicative hindsight (Fuller et al., 2020; Weick, 2021, p. 91), rolling present-based context-specific mindful insight (Fernandez, 2020), and rolling prospective rationality generative metaphors (LeBoon, 2020).

Table 4. An introduction to sense-losing skills during cosmology episodes

Temporal Sense-improvising is the identification of potential escape paths from a cosmology episode through the skillful practice, elaboration, and resequencing of rolling retrospective rationality communicative hindsight (Fuller et al., 2020), rolling present-based context-specific mindful insight (Fernandez, 2020), and rolling prospective rationality generative metaphors (LeBoon, 2020).		
Fuller, Pyle, Riolli, & Mickel 12/15 CA Outbreaks Sense-improvising as Rolling Hindsight in Communications	Fernandez 12/8 France Wrecks Sense-improvising as Rolling Insight in Industrial Expertise	LeBoon 11/11 CA Fires Sense-improvising as Rolling Foresight in Metaphors
Identity Sense-improvising is the deconstruction and reconstruction of a social unit's perceived role in the universe (Mayfield et al., 2020); the leveraging of individual emotional intelligence, positive emotions, and emotional regulation (Allen et al., 2020); and the fusing of rational and intuitive strategic decision-making processes to create improvisational strategic decision-making (Tabesh & Vera, 2020).		
Mayfield, Mayfield, & Walk. 12/4 CA Abuses Sense-improvising as Cons-tructivist Identity-making	Tabesh & Vera 11/28 NY Crashes Sense-improvising as Fused Rationality and Intuition	Allen, Stevenson, O'Boyle … 11/9 FL Accidents Sense-improvising as Negative/Positive Emotions
Social Sense-improvising is the ability of social units to question operations and generate alternative operations through team reflexivity (Hartmann et al., 2020) when institutional relationships are disrupted, forcing a critical re-evaluation of core beliefs (Rocha et al., 2020) and the generation and screening of numerous possible escape paths from a cosmology episode (Sukhov et al., 2020).		
Hartmann, Weiss, Hoegl … 12/21 Germany Sense-improvising as Team Reflexity Social Processes	Rocha, Pirson, & Suddaby 11/4 Canada Outbreaks Sense-improvising as a Response to Torn Institutions	Sukhov, Sihvonen, Netz … 12/1 Sweden Wrecks Task-related Sensemaking as Sociality Sense-improvising

Temporality sense-improvising is composed of "rolling hindsight," rolling insight, and rolling foresight (Weick, 2021, p. 91). Retrospective rationality is simultaneously an asset (a potentially rich source of interpretations) and a liability (a potentially deadly constraint on the creation of brutally honest appraisals, audits, and maps). For example, in the 2018 California wildfires, communication errors such as "breakdowns, oversights, failures to pass on and receive warning messages, faulty interpretations of messages, and misleading or inaccurate messages" (Fuller et al., 2020, p. 4) may have had larger-than-anticipated negative consequences due to rigid adherence by community members to outdated (non-updated) beliefs about wildfire survivability.

Temporality sense-improvising is manifested in prospective sensemaking, or rolling foresight. Rolling foresight has been elaborated by numerous cosmology episode scholars under the concepts of strategic preoccupation with failure, anticipation, and attention to weak signals of impending disaster. In sense-improvising, quick and deep retrospection are both placed in the service of the present, because "[W]hen a new event is triggered by external uncertainty and ambiguity, it becomes a catalyst for an individual to find internal meaning by extracting a preexisting cue" (LeBoon, p. 28). The broad field of sensemaking has backward-skewed balance of past, present, and future due to its early grounding in retrospective rationality (corrected in a 2005 article balancing retrospective rationality with prospective rationality to create temporal rationality), the more precise concept of sense-improvising has a forward-skewed balance of rolling hindsight, rolling insight, and – especially – rolling foresight: "Sensemaking, therefore, is not about what took place, but the process of discovering and interpreting for action (Weick et al., 2005)" (LeBoon, p. 31).

Expedition 8. Identity Sense-Improvising

Identity sense-improvising is the social deconstruction and reconstruction of a social unit's perceived role in the universe (Mayfield et al., 2020); the leveraging of individual emotional intelligence, positive emotions, and emotional regulation (Allen et al., 2020); and the fusing of rational and intuitive strategic decision-making processes to create improvisational strategic decision-making (Tabesh & Vera, 2020).

Identity sense-improvising does not occur in an individualistic vacuum. Much of an individual's past, present, and future identity is shaped by evolving, received, lived, and received national, industrial, and organizational cosmologies. For example, communication researchers note that meaning-making communication theories "examine how we use communication to shape our understanding of the world" (Mayfield et al., 2020, p. 12). More precisely, resilience leadership experts "shape realities" through an objectivist ontology path (communicating with people in a way that transmits the realities of the cosmology episode), a subjectivist ontology path (communicating with people in a way that "uncovers" realities of the cosmology episode), and a constructivist ontology path (communicating with people in a way that "creates the realities" of a cosmology episode) (p. 120). Of special interest to the topic of identity sense-improvising, meaning-making communication "shapes who we are as people" (p. 120) and helps us "co-create our reality in relationships with others, including among organizational members" (p. 132).

Identity sense-improvising is the primary home of hot, emotional, or affective moods, perceptions, statements, decisions, and actions. A great deal of progress has been made in the last thirty-six years in understanding the role of emotions – negative and positive -- in cosmology episodes (Weick, 1985). A large part of resilience leadership effectiveness is built on the ability to remain calm, hopeful, and generous in the face of catastrophes through emotional intelligence, authentic emotionality, emotional regulation, and positive emotions. This is a difficult undertaking because "Crisis situations are typically characterized by intense negative emotions such as anxiety, fear, panic, and desperation" (Allen et al., 2020, p. 15).

Identity sense-improvising is the conversion of rational strategic decision-making and intuitive strategic decision-making into improvisational strategic decision-making (Tabesh & Vera, 2020). Tabesh and Vera reanalyzed the "January 15, 2009, US Airways Flight 1549 [which] successfully landed in the Hudson River after both engines of the plane were damaged by a bird strike" initiating "a fast and sophisticated decision process that enabled a water landing and rescue mission" (p. 2246). Tabesh and Vera note that improvisation "has been linked to crisis situations in the past," "is referred to by some scholars as a powerful managerial tool in the face of adversity," and is seen "as a source of resilience" (p. 2242). Tabesh and Vera described the landing as improvisational strategic decision-making, or "The extent to which a [Top Management Team] makes important decisions through a process that is spontaneous, novel and action-oriented" (p. 2238).

Expedition 9. Sociality Sense-Improvising

Sociality sense-improvising is the ability of social units to question operations and generate alternative operations through team reflexivity (Hartmann et al., 2021) when institutional relationships are disrupted, forcing a critical re-evaluation of core beliefs (Rocha et al., 2020) and the generation and screening of numerous possible escape paths from a cosmology episode (Sukhov et al., 2020).

Sociality sense-improvising is practiced primarily in groups, teams, and cross-functional teams. Cosmology episode studies within the arena of medical errors demonstrate repeatedly that effective cross-functional teams are able to reduce panic, routinize problem-solving, and surface righteous solutions to wicked problems through socially adept, team-based, and non-frantic attempts to understand, slow, and halt vicious cycles (Brown, 2000). For example, a study of German childcare teams documented the value of "team reflexivity," the ability of a team to question its operations and generate alternative operations, in increasing the impact of a culture of joy on team resilience (Hartmann et al., 2021).

Sociality sense-improvising is the swarming, all-hands-on-deck, largely voluntary crowdsourcing that routinely emerges in response to perturbations, disruptions, crises, disasters, and catastrophes. Although Weick's analysis of the 1999 West Nile Virus outbreak in New York City (Weick, 2005) contains numerous untapped insights for the resolution of disease outbreaks such as the COVID-19 outbreak, researchers have used the Mann Gulch cosmology episode as a starting point for explaining effective sociality improvising in the face of the COVID-19 pandemic (e.g., Sherman & Roberto, 2020). Additionally, diverse studies of the secondary crises from COVID-19 in K-12 education (Schmuhl, 2020), higher education (Miller et al., 2020), and not-for-profit organizations (Gorel et al., 2020) all document the ways in which sociality sense-improvising occurs in organizations. Researchers have also drawn cross-pollinating lines from rebuilding projects after the 2004 Indian Ocean tsunami to the avoidance of inequity-perpetuating mistakes in the post-pandemic recovery (Hamann, 2020). Experts on the role of business schools in creating toxic or non-toxic outcomes in global capitalism have started conversations about how to respond to the COVID-19 opportunity: "As devastating as cosmological episodes can be, they also offer the insight that occurs when the institutional fabric of society is torn open" (Rocha et al., 2020, p. 13). In social sense-improvising, people "have the opportunity to critically re-evaluate the ontological assumptions upon which [their] core institutions have been built" (p. 13). Importantly, though, the social sense-improvising that occurs in the liminal space between sense-losing and sense-remaking only exists "for a brief moment in time" (p. 13).

Sociality sense-improvising is the beginning step in a path -- through enactive sense-remaking, selective sense-remaking, and retentive sense-remaking -- that leads to new product innovations, new process innovations, or new purpose innovations. Swedish researchers found, in the context of idea screening for new product development, a progression from intuition (enactive sense-remaking) to analysis (selective sense-remaking) to sensemaking (retentive sense-remaking) (Sukhov et al., 2020). Sukhov, Sihvonen, Netz, Magnusson, and Olsson found that idea screeners in social organizations employ temporal sense-improvising ("retrospection," "the creation of meaning through interpretation," and "forward-looking creativity"), identity sense-improvising ("justification of actions" in a way that "helps [idea-screening experts] to ground their decisions in their personal values"), and sociality sense-improvising ("task-related sensemaking" which "helps the experts to understand what they are supposed to do when screening ideas") (p. 17). Of special interest to resilience leadership experts seeking to improve their sociality sense-improvising skills, the Swedish research team found that the social task of task-related sensemaking is initiated "when people are given guidelines that orient their actions during new product development," but requires continued social interaction because "these guidelines still need to be understood and made sense of" (p. 14). Social sense-improvising efforts such as task-related sensemaking are important "because failure to understand what the actor is supposed to do can incapacitate them," while "reducing the ambiguity surrounding the task itself can enable the taking of further actions" (p. 14).

Sense-Remaking Thursday Hikes: Enactive, Selective, and Retentive

Sense-remaking Thursday is grounded in a hike from Willow Creek back up the gulch to the site of the ignition point of the escape fire followed by a hike to Stanley Reba's death-marker, a hike to the cluster of the Harrison death-marker, and a hike to the other five early-caught smokejumpers' death-markers. Since the 2010 Haiti earthquake, some resilience leadership experts have used a cosmology episode lens to leverage Weick and Sutcliffe's *Managing the Unexpected* book series as a sequence of pre-occupations with failure (sense-receiving), deference to expertise (sense-losing), commitment to resilience/improvisation (sense-improvising), reluctance to simplify interpretations (sense-remaking), and sensitivity to operations (sense-transmitting). Thursday's hikes help clarify this sequencing of the high-reliability organizing principles.

The first hike permits the elaboration of Weick's proposed "virtual role systems" concept (which later evolved into Weick and Sutcliffe's high-reliability organizing principle, "reluctance to simplify interpretations") as an evidence-based and updated resilience leadership skill of *sense-remaking* (Christianson, 2019). The Harrison hike permits a continuing elaboration of Weick's enactment-selection-retention organizing model, moving from the generative *enactive sense-remaking* period, through the virtuous cycle of *selective sense-remaking*, to the *retentive sense-remaking* hinge between the catastrophe and the post-catastrophe (see Table 5). The Middle Five hike permits the recognition that sense-remaking in cosmology episodes does not happen instantaneously, but is a complex, uphill movement of ideas through the chaotic and improvisational process of enactive sense-remaking, to the multiple points of view of selective sense-remaking, to the elegant simplicity of retentive sense-remaking.

Table 5. An introduction to sense-remaking skills during cosmology episodes

<table>
<tr><td colspan="3">Enactive Sense-remaking is the initial phase of the ontological oscillation among constructivist, subjectivist, and objectivist ontologies (Mueller, 2020) during which numerous story ideas are generated that are later judged to be plausible or implausible (Sherman & Roberto, 2020) by slowly trusted or swiftly trusted frontline responders to the cosmology episode (Kalkman, 2020).</td></tr>
<tr><td>Mueller
12/9 Switzerland Fires
Sense-remaking as Enactive Ontological Oscillation</td><td>Sherman & Roberto
11/2 MT Fires
Sense-remaking as Plausible/ Implausible Story Ideas</td><td>Kalkman
10/26 Netherlands Shootings
Sense-remaking as Swift Frontline Trust/ Discretion</td></tr>
<tr><td colspan="3">Selective Sense-remaking is the winnowing of possible paths forward out of a cosmology episode with caution to biases, interests, and structures (Hamann, 2020), taking place primarily through social organizing processes in the meso domain (Secchi & Cowley, 2020), and facilitated by the distributed presence of team leaders able to generate senses of coherence (Merwe et al., 2020; Wessels, 2020).</td></tr>
<tr><td>Hamann
11/3 Sri Lanka Capsizings
Sense-remaking as Biases, Interests, and Affiliations</td><td>van der Merwe, Koch,...
12/3 South Africa Outbreaks
Sense-remaking as Team Leaders' Sense of Coherence</td><td>Secchi & Cowley
12/25 Denmark Outbreaks
Sense-remaking as Meso Domain Social Organizing</td></tr>
<tr><td colspan="3">Retentive Sense-remaking is the end product of an enactment-selection-retention sequence (Douyon & Paradas, 2020) that serves as a socially constructed temporal hinge between during-crisis sense-remaking and post-crisis sense-transmitting (Vainio, 2020) in which new institutionalized technology, procedures, and purposes are combinations of past traditions and new traditions (Lindén, 2020).</td></tr>
<tr><td>Douyon & Paradas
11/10 France Abuses
Sense-remaking as the End Product of RSE-ESR</td><td>Vainio
11/17 Japan Accidents
Sense-remaking as a Socially Constructed Ending to Crisis</td><td>Lindén
11/16 France Explosions
Sense-remaking as Institu-tionalization of Technologies</td></tr>
</table>

Expedition 10. Enactive Sense-Remaking

Enactive sense-remaking is the initial phase of the ontological oscillation among constructivist, subjectivist, and objectivist ontologies (Mueller, 2020) during which numerous story ideas are generated that are later judged to be plausible or implausible (Sherman & Roberto, 2020) by slowly trusted or swiftly trusted frontline responders to the cosmology episode (Kalkman, 2020). Enactive sense-remaking is primarily accomplished by slowly trusted or swiftly trusted individuals at the bottom of an organization with potentially high degrees of frontline discretion. Because cosmology episodes "are uncertain and disorderly situations," they "temporarily destabilize power relations and impede centralized control over operational crisis responders," creating a situation in which "responders wield considerable autonomy and have room to act on their own initiative" (Kalkman, 2020, n. p.). In cosmology episodes, enactive sense-remaking authority migrates slowly or swiftly to "frontline workers," "frontline responders," "operational crisis responders," or "street-level bureaucrats" such as "firefighters, police officers, paramedics" (n. p.). Slowly trusted frontline responders are "implementers who are considerably constrained by extensive rules, planned routines, and detailed protocols," while swiftly trusted frontline responders are able to "use their discretionary space to shape crisis response efforts" through "independent and proactive behaviors" (n. p.). Slowly trusted responders experience "social and rule-based pressures . . . to explain their discretionary actions as they implement public policy," while swiftly trusted responders leverage "meaning-making attempts" to "enact their discretionary practice" (n. p.). Slowly trusted responders suffer from "legitimacy questions and potentially [burdensome] complex ethical dilemmas," while swiftly trusted responders benefit from "a widespread belief that frontline discretion in crisis response enables much-needed improvisation, creativity, and flexibility" (n. p.).

In sense-remaking, there is constant movement in resilience leadership among constructivist ontologies (we create the environments to which we must then respond), subjectivist ontologies (we interpret, often sloppily, the environment), and objectivist ontologies (we strive to discover and obey the laws of an existing environment). For example, Swiss information technology researchers described Weick's Mann Gulch cosmology episode study as an exemplary product of ontological oscillation: "a surprisingly heavy development of theoretical concepts all the while delivering a gripping narrative" (Mueller, p. 3). In enactive sense-remaking, the constructivist craft ontology is the often-overlooked "messy front-end of the process" (p. 2). The constructivist craft ontology feeds into the subjectivist art ontology characterized by "countless hours of rethinking, refining, rewriting, redeveloping, and revamping" (p. 2). The subjectivist art ontology feeds into the objectivist science ontology in which "few of the papers that end up in print look anything like the initial versions were submitted" (p. 2).

Expedition 11. Selective Sense-Remaking

Selective sense-remaking is a contested terrain of possible paths forward out of a cosmology episode, subject to psychological biases, economic interests, and power structures. For example, international development experts extrapolated from the strategic ambiguity created by the phrase, "build back better," after the 2004 Indian Ocean tsunami to the strategic ambiguity being created by "build back better" advocates after the 2020-2024 COVID-19 outbreak (Hamann, 2020). It is important to be cautious in selective sense-remaking during a cosmology episode because "[w]e are more likely to make judgments and decisions based on preexisting biases when we are under pressure" (p. 44). Some of those biases are the result of economic self-interest, because "disasters provide opportunity for strategic and even sinister efforts by elites in business and government to grab assets" (p. 44). Other biases during selective sense-remaking are the result of political calculations which lead people "to push through national policies that entrench their positions of privilege" (p. 44). People who suffer the most from cosmology episodes are the ones least likely to have a seat at the selective sense-remaking table.

Selective sense-remaking is reluctance-to-simplify reorganizing facilitated by a mastery of micro-, meso-, and macro-level organizational behaviors. Resilience leadership experts are comfortable moving between micro-processes at the individual level; meso-processes at the division, subunit, and team levels; and macro-processes at the organizational level (Secchi & Cowley, 2020). Selective sense-making animates "social organising in the meso domain" between the "micro domain" (in which individuals are "[c]onstrained by brains and bodies") and the "ecological" macro domain (in which organizations are "attune[d] to structural constraints") (n. p.).

Selective sense-remaking is facilitated by the distributed presence of numerous talented team leaders throughout a nation, industry, environment, organization, community, or society. For example, under the leadership of Nelson Mandela and Desmond Tutu, the new 1996 South African constitution enshrined the African cosmology of "ubuntu" into its governing documents (Wessels, 2020). Relatedly, resilience leadership experts van der Merwe, Koch, Correia, and Moganedi explained how, within this received national cosmology, the South African electric company ESKOM institutionalized meso-level resilience teams led by "system stewards" focused on the creation of a plausible "sense of coherence" characterized by *comprehensibility* ("People see the world as comprehensible if they conclude they understand what is happening around them"), *manageability* ("People perceive that the resources required to deal with the demands posed by the world are available through their social connectedness"), and *meaningfulness* ("People see challenges as meaningful if they have the motivation to invest time and effort into it").

Expedition 12. Retentive Sense-Remaking

Retentive sense-remaking is the process through which disruptive new technologies are institutionalized into an escape from the abnormal, a return to normal, a new normal, a next normal, or an entry into a new abnormal. The first iteration of cosmology episode studies was research on the disruptive insertion of personal computers into the managerial workspace in the early 1980s (Weick, 1985). Although this early thread of cosmology episode studies was eclipsed by Weick's subsequent (1993) Mann Gulch cosmology episode study, resilience leadership experts keep the earlier thread alive by associating it with the arena of space exploration cosmology episodes (e.g., Apollo 13, *Challenger*, *Columbia*, and more recently the rise of studies on the inclusion of Artificial Intelligence enabled robots as Mars exploration team members). Retentive sense-remaking is the end product of an enactment-selection-retention sequence (Douyon & Paradas, 2020) that serves as a socially constructed temporal hinge between during-crisis sense-remaking and post-crisis sense-transmitting (Vainio, 2020) in which new institutionalized technology, procedures, and purposes are combinations of past traditions and new traditions (Lindén, 2020).

Retentive sense-losing is the socially constructed hinge between the catastrophe period of sense-remaking and the post-catastrophe period of sense-transmitting. The beginnings and endings of cosmology episode narratives (Maclean, 1992; Weick, 1993), high-risk narratives (Manning, 1999), and disaster narratives (Seeger & Sellnow, 2016) are not fixed events in objective time, but are instead social constructions that are manufactured at different points for different people. The 2011 Great East Japan Earthquake (Xu, 2020), the resulting tsunami, and the Fukushima Daiichi nuclear accident is a cosmology episode that illuminates this socially constructed aspect of retentive sense-making (Vainio, 2020). "Within the landscapes left behind by large scale destructions . . . both beginnings and endings are often seen.

Sense-Transmitting Friday Hikes: Organizational, Community, and Societal

Sense-transmitting Friday is grounded in a hike from the mouth of Mann Gulch back to the Stanley Reba death-marker and up to Harrison's and the Middle Five's death markers. This hike is followed by a hike to the Four Horsemen's death markers. The First Horseman hike permits the elaboration of Weick's proposed "[transmitted] attitudes of wisdom" concept (which later evolved into Weick and Sutcliffe's high-reliability organizing principle, "sensitivity to operations") into the resilience leadership skill of *sense-transmitting*. The Second Horseman hike permits the differentiation among *transmitted organizational cosmologies*, *transmitted industrial cosmologies*, and *transmitted national cosmologies* (see Table 6). The Third/Fourth Horseman hike permits a discussion of several variants of *transmitted national cosmologies*, such as regional cosmologies, societal cosmologies, and global cosmologies – followed by a hike down Rescue Gulch to the boat back to the Gates of the Mountains marina north of Helena, Montana.

Table 6. An introduction to sense-transmitting skills during cosmology episodes

Transmitted Organizational Cosmologies are composed of enacted environment, managerial skill, and organizational characteristic plots yielding well-managed, modular, narrative, and coherent organizations (Roulet, 2020); agile, decisive, learning, and foresightful organizations (Williams et al., 2020); and team-based, strategic, innovative, and resilient organizations (Borjesson, 2020).		
Roulet 11/25 France Abusism Cosmologies as Cognitive/Behavioral Plots	Williams et al. 12/11 Australia Errors Cosmologies as VUCA, CDLA, and ALDF Plots	Borjesson 11/24 Sweden Shootings Cosmologies as Shared Mental Models in Teams
Transmitted Community Cosmologies are built from the improvisation cycles of numerous professional organizations and institutional fields (Eddy-Spicer et al., 2020) and the actions of numerous network organizations and inter-organizational partnerships (Patriotta, 2020).		
Eddy-Spicer et al. 11/12 NC Shootings Cosmologies as Strategic Bricolage in the Professions	Fernandez 12/8 France Cosmologies as High-performance Teams	Patriotta 11/27 Czech Rep. Outbreaks Cosmologies as Inter-organization Partnerships
Transmitted National Cosmologies are regionally shared coherent belief systems shaped by sense-receiving, sense-losing, sense-improvising, sense-remaking, and sense-transmitting processes (Yu & Yu, 2020) composed of lessons learned from cosmology episodes through swarming, recombinant, and disruptive improvisations (Tipaldi et al., 2020), in which national cosmologies serve as components of regional, societal, and global cosmologies (Anholt et al. 2021).		
Yu & Yu 12/7 China Wrecks Cosmologies as Unique Regional-level Perceptions	Tipaldi et al. 11/30 Italy Collapses Cosmologies as Accumulated Social Entrepreneurship	Anholt et al. The Netherlands Cosmologies as Regional, Societal, and Global Belief Systems

Expedition 13. Transmitted Organizational Cosmologies

Transmitted organizational cosmologies are composed of enacted environment, managerial skill, and organizational characteristic plots yielding well-managed, modular, narrative, and coherent organizations (Roulet, 2020); agile, decisive, learning, and foresightful organizations (Williams et al., 2020); and team-based, strategic, innovative, and resilient organizations (Borjesson, 2020).

Transmitted organizational cosmologies are built from the four traditional environment-skill-organization plots of (1) historical environments, leadership skills, and well-managed organizations; (2) political environments, structure skills, and modular organizations; (3) global environments, institutions skills, and narrative organizations; and (4) economic environments, strategy skills, and leveraged organizations. For example, experts in negative social evaluations have advanced understanding of the institutions plot through the study of institutional micro-processes associated with legitimacy, stigma, and illegitimacy (Roulet, 2020). Roulet, building on the work of resilience leadership experts (Williams et al., 2017), identified two institutional micro-processes in stigma cosmology episodes: "Managing a crisis, like managing a negative social evaluation, starts with detecting the adverse signal and is followed by planning and a damage control effort" (n. p.).

Transmitted organizational cosmologies facilitate the "cognitive responding" of planning – even during the chaos of a cosmology episode -- because "the shared values and beliefs provide a common framework to identify the way forward" (n. p.). Transmitted organizational cosmologies facilitate the "behavioral responding" of a damage control effort by providing "consistency: the enacted solutions need to be aligned with the group's overarching ways of thinking" (no page visible). There is an important, recent, and growing alliance between institutional theory experts and resilience leadership experts around the topics of sensemaking and sense-giving – giving rise to the more detailed institutional micro-processes of sense-receiving, sense-losing, sense-improvising, sense-remaking, and sense-transmitting (e.g. Creed et al., 2020; Roulet, 2020).

Expedition 14. Transmitted Community Cosmologies

Transmitted community cosmologies are built from the improvisation cycles of numerous professional organizations, meso-institutions, fields and institutional orders (Eddy-Spicer et al., 2020) and the actions of numerous network organizations and inter-organizational partnerships (Patriotta, 2020). For example, educational administration researchers studied "strategic bricolage" by two U.S. "meso-institutions" (the University Council of Educational Administration and the National Network of Education Research Practice Partnerships) (Eddy-Spicer et al., 2020). Eddy-Spicer, Arce-Trigatti, and Young noted a difference between creativity (aligned with disruptive improvisation) and bricolage (aligned with recombinant improvisation) (p. 33; quoting Weick, 1993, p. 639). "Bricolage . . . encourages the use of available resources, often rooted in the existing institutional order, to generate novel resources that align with the aspirational institutional order" (p. 32). Individual bricolage, team bricolage, and organizational bricolage are conceptual pre-cursors to community-level strategic bricolage – "relational, contingent and opportunistic" leadership practices "that system leaders enact in relation to field building" (p. 30). Resilience leadership experts do not confine themselves to improvisation cycles within their own organizations, but are also participants in improvisation cycles within professional cosmologies.

Transmitted community cosmologies are also built from the actions of a range of network organizations, inter-organizational partnerships, and transdisciplinary collaborations. For example, experts on the future of corporations predict that in the aftermath of the COVID-19 catastrophe the focus on profits at all costs will decline and be complemented by an increased focus on the social purpose of organizations and an increased focus on democratic participation internal and external to corporations (Patriotta, 2020). Patriotta argued that networks of inter-organizational partnerships that "transcend the purpose of individual organizations" will be increasingly necessary "to jointly solve a societal problem and achieve a shared goal" (p. 882). He noted that organizational cosmologies (the "bounded rationality of institutional decision makers") are inadequate in the face of the uncertainty created by global crises characterized by "public controversies" and "politics around meaning" (p. 882), but that inter-organizational partnerships – floating above the organization – can "provide a frame of reference for human action and long-term plans" that "leverage diverse expertise" (p. 882). Like transmitted industrial cosmologies, transmitted network cosmologies can help resilience leadership experts better navigate future global crises, because "[s]olving problems of people and the planet will increasingly require the development of partnerships between corporations and other institutions, based on solidarity and the mutual support of public interests" (p. 882).

Expedition 15. Transmitted Societal Cosmologies

Transmitted national cosmologies are coherent belief systems shaped by sense-receiving, sense-losing, sense-improvising, sense-remaking, and sense-transmitting processes (Yu & Yu, 2020). These belief systems are composed of lessons learned from cosmology episodes through swarming, recombinant, and disruptive improvisations (Tipaldi et al., 2020), in which national cosmologies serve as components of regional, societal, and global cosmologies (Anholt et al. 2021).

Transmitted national cosmologies are visible in cosmology episode studies from all twelve regions of the world (1) South Asia, (2) North Asia; (3) Eastern Europe, (4) Scandinavia/Baltics; (5) South America, (6) Mexico/Caribbean/Central America; (7) West/Central Africa, (8) East/Southern Africa; (9) South Western Europe, (10) North Western Europe, (11) Southern Greater Middle East, and (12) Northern Greater Middle East. Repeated side-by-side comparisons of numerous cosmology episode studies from one of these large regions with numerous cosmology episode studies from one of the other twelve regions surfaces important differences – influenced by different societal cosmologies – in theory, research, education, and practice for all five resilience leadership skills presented in this chapter.

Transmitted national cosmologies incorporate lessons learned from cosmology episodes of all sizes – perturbations, disruptions, crises, disasters, and catastrophes – and the regional, societal, or global responses to those cosmology episodes through swarming, recombinant, and disruptive improvisation. For example, finance experts studied social innovation by social entrepreneurs in Development Impact Bonds in 28 base-of-the-pyramid countries around the world (Tipaldi et al., 2020). Tipaldi, Santulli, and Galluci found that social constructionists – perhaps in countries such as India, Papua New Guinea, and Tajikistan – engage in swarming improvisation when they "identify and exploit market opportunities to create social wealth in those contexts where existing institutions, businesses, nongovernmental organisations and government agencies have failed" (page not visible). Social bricoleurs – perhaps in countries such as Argentina, Brazil, Peru, Colombia, Mexico, Kenya, Uganda, Mozambique, South Africa, Cameroon, Mali, Nigeria, and the two Congos – engage in recombinant improvisation when they "create order out of whatever materials [are] at hand" (Weick, 1993, p. 639). Social engineers – perhaps in places such as Jordan, Lebanon, Turkey, Palestine (the West Bank and Gaza), and Ethiopia – engage in disruptive improvisation when they "identify existing problems within the social system and structures and address them by bringing about a revolutionary change" (n. p.).

FIVE RESILIENCE LEADERSHIP SKILLS FOR MANAGING ORGANIZATIONAL TRAUMA

The primary hoped-for outcome of this chapter was an increase in readers' capacities to reduce human suffering during cosmology episodes through the updating of Weick's (1993) four proposed Mann Gulch resilience leadership skills ("attitudes of wisdom," "respectful interaction," "bricolage," and "virtual role systems") to the present (2020) five evidence-based Mann Gulch resilience leadership skills ("sense-receiving," "sense-losing," "sense-improvising," "sense-remaking," and "sense-transmitting"). Five additional contributions are highlighted below as a review of this chapter and as springboards for the 2021 Mann Gulch executive resilience leadership incubator.

Skill One: Sense-Receiving

Resilience leadership experts should remember that there is nothing new under the sun. So, they should see themselves not as heroic "sense-givers," but as servant leaders who receive attitudes of wisdom from people who have gone before them. They should leverage those attitudes of wisdom to create numerous righteous solutions to the wicked problems that confront them, and transmit attitudes of wisdom to people who follow them. A simple early formulation of resilience leadership was sensemaking followed by sense-giving. However, continuous study of the nearly 6,000 citations to Weick's Mann Gulch cosmology episode study – and the pilot elaborative meta-analysis of the most recent 1% of those scholarly publications presented in this chapter showed that the institutional micro-process of sense-giving (Gioia & Chittipeddi, 1991) is composed of the more precise micro-processes of sense-receiving and sense-transmitting.

Skill Two: Sense-Losing

To address the imbalance of management research on sense-losing and sense-remaking, resilience leadership experts have used Weick's three books to create a more integrated model of cosmology episodes as a movement from order to chaos followed by a movement from chaos to order. A lingering problem for resilience leadership experts is imbalance between the lack of knowledge about sense-losing skills and the overabundance of knowledge about sense-remaking skills. Although there is a near-universal bias in management education to teach best practices in topics such as sense-losing through an order-to-chaos movement from simple (19th Century) to complicated (20th Century) to complex (21st Century) manifestations, there is a corresponding bias in management research to study best practices in topics such as sense-remaking through a chaos-to-order movement from complex (21st Century) to complicated (20th Century) to simple (19th Century).

Skill Three: Sense-Improvising

Initially, Weick (1995) identified three characteristics of sensemaking, which have, 25 years later, been modified by resilience leadership experts after numerous cosmology episode studies. Retrospective sensemaking has been modified by resilience leadership experts as *temporality sense-improvising*, the ability to engage in simultaneous rolling hindsight, rolling insight, and rolling foresight (Weick, 2020). Identity-based sensemaking has been modified as *identity sense-improvising*, the capacity to leverage a portfolio of experiences, emotions, and embodiments to generate righteous solutions to wicked problems. Social sensemaking has been modified as *sociality sense-improvising*, the recombinant juxtaposition of individual cosmologies, roles, and identities within high-performing cross-functional teams to create novel, non-obvious, and effective solutions to complex problems.

Skill Four: Sense-Remaking

Retentive sense-remaking is the revision, simplification, and dissemination of lessons learned through the application of twelve folk theories of resilience leadership: leadership, organizing, institutions, strategy, change, decision-making, learning, sensemaking, collaboration, strategizing, improvisation, and resilience. Enactive sense-remaking is primarily the province of high-expertise professionals at the bottom of organizations -- "increasingly working in transboundary crisis networks" -- closest to the tangible, embodied, emotional, and socio-material details of a cosmology episode (Kalkman, 2020). Selective sense-remaking is the surfacing, expanding, and nurturing of a portfolio of coherent escape paths from the most devastating aspects of a cosmology episode.

Skill Five: Sense-Transmitting

Transmitted Organizational Cosmologies are composed of enacted environment, managerial skill, and organizational characteristic plots yielding well-managed, modular, narrative, and coherent organizations (Roulet, 2020); agile, decisive, learning, and foresightful organizations (Williams et al., 2020); and team-based, strategic, innovative, and resilient organizations (Borjesson, 2020).

IMPLICATIONS FOR RESEARCH AND PRACTICE

The primary practice implication is a reminder that resilience leadership experts who have undergone an extreme executive leadership expedition – even as a thought experiment in a book chapter like this -- carry with them an emplaced, embodied, and emplotted anchor point. This internalized anchor point helps them remember, routinize, and elaborate five resilience leadership skills that they can use to reduce human suffering from organizational trauma in twelve diverse arenas: structure collapses, fatal fires, transportation wrecks, naval capsizings, airplane crashes, nuclear accidents, space explosions, chemical leaks, medical errors, disease outbreaks, public shootings, and institutional abuses.

CONCLUSION

Social units that have survived, and learned from, one cosmology episode are not immune from similar cosmology episodes in the future. For example, the 1986 *Challenger* explosion (Vaughan, 1996) was followed by the 2003 *Columbia* disintegration (Beck & Plowman, 2009) and the 1949 Mann Gulch fire (Weick, 1993) was followed by the 1994 South Canyon fire (Weick, 1996) which was in turn followed by the 2013 Yarnell Hill fire (Parrish et al., 2020). Despite U.S. citizens' deeply desired hope that, from 2021-2024, the new Biden presidential administration will return them to a normal world, the more likely conclusion of the COVID-19 outbreak (based on the previous 58 presidential administrations) will be the socially-constructed, chaotic, and cliff-hanging end of one cosmology episode narrative and the socially-constructed, chaotic, and continuing beginning of a future cosmology episode narrative. The transmitted cosmologies in place at the end of a cosmology episode are the sources of the received cosmologies for beginning of the next cosmology episode. Thus, the task of the 59th U.S. presidential administration in 2020-2024 is not only "to manage the hell out of COVID-19," but to join with international partners to enhance the ability of resilience leadership experts, in the United States and around the world, to manage the hell out of every future global wicked problem, national cosmology episodes, and vexing organizational trauma.

REFERENCES

Allen, J. S., Stevenson, R. M., O'Boyle, E. H., & Seibert, S. (2020). What matters more for entrepreneurship success? A meta-analysis comparing general mental ability and emotional intelligence in entrepreneurial settings. *Strategic Entrepreneurship Journal, 2020,* 1–25. Advance online publication. doi:10.1002ej.1377

Allison, G. T., & Zelikow, P. (1999). *Essence of decision: Explaining the Cuban Missile Crisis* (2nd ed.). Longman.

Anholt, R., van Dullemen, C., de Carvalho, J. S., Rijbroek, J., Sieckelinck, S., & Slootman, M. W. (2020). Understanding societal resilience: The case for engaged scholarship. In M. Ungar (Ed.), *Multisystemic Resilience* (pp. 551–564). Oxford University Press.

Arif, A. (2020). *Troubling matters: Examining the spread of misinformation and disinformation on social media during mass disruption events* [Unpublished dissertation]. University of Washington.

Barlette, Y. (2020). Les comportements des acteurs en matière de sécurité de l'information et leurs determinants: Les théories du 'coping' et leur enrichissement [The behaviors of actors in matters of information security and their determinants: Theories of "coping" and their enrichment]. Report submitted to obtain an advanced certification to supervise dissertations, University of Montpellier.

Beck, T. E., & Plowman, D. A. (2009). Experiencing rare and unusual events richly: The role of middle managers in animating and guiding organizational interpretation. *Organization Science, 20*(5), 909–924.

Bollingtoft, A., & Ulhoi, J. P. (2005). The networked business incubator—Leveraging entrepreneurial agency? *Journal of Business Venturing, 20*(2), 265–290. doi:10.1016/j.jbusvent.2003.12.005

Borjesson, M. (2020). *The psychology of risk and safety in the military: A balancing act* [Doctoral dissertation, Karlstad University, Sweden]. Digitala Vetenskapliga Arkivet id: diva2:1479324.

Brown, A. D. (2000). Making sense of inquiry sensemaking. *Journal of Management Studies, 37*(1), 45–75. doi:10.1111/1467-6486.00172

Bustamente, C., C. Poblete, & J. E. Amorós. (2020). Entrepreneurial intentions in the context of a natural disaster. *International Journal of Emerging Markets.* Advance online publication. doi:10.1108/IJOEM-10-2019-0846

Carlsson-Wall, M., Iredahl, A., Kraus, K., & Wiklund, M. (2020). The role of management controls in managing heterogeneous interests during extreme situations: The Swedish migrant crisis in 2015. *Qualitative Research in Accounting & Management, 18*(1), 1–25. doi:10.1108/QRAM-05-2018-0030

Christianson, M. K. (2019). More and less effective updating: The role of trajectory management in making sense again. *Administrative Science Quarterly, 64*(1), 45–86. doi:10.1177/0001839217750856

Ciuchta, M. P., O'Toole, J., & Miner, A. S. (2021). The organizational improvisation landscape: Taking stock and looking forward. *Journal of Management, 47*(1), 288–316. doi:10.1177/0149206320966987

Cleary, J. (2020). The role of storytelling in a nonhostile takeover. *Qualitative Research in Organizations and Management, 16*(1), 145–169. doi:10.1108/QROM-10-2019-1832

Creed, W. E., Hudson, B. A., Okhuysen, G., & Smith-Crowe, K. (2020, October 30). A place in the world: Vulnerability, wellbeing, and the ubiquitous evaluation that animates participation in institutional processes. *Academy of Management Review*, amr.2018.0367. Advance online publication. doi:10.5465/amr.2018.0367

Cripe, C. C. (2020). *Indiana public school superintendent sensemaking of e-learning* [Doctoral dissertation, Ball State University]. Publication No. 28256327. ProQuest Dissertations Publishing.

Dahlberg, R., Vendelø, M. T., Sørensen, B. R., & Lauta, K. C. (2020). Offshore is onshore: Scalability, synchronization, and speed of decision in Arctic SAR. *Scandinavian Journal of Military Studies, 3*(1), 157–168. doi:10.31374jms.52

Della Lucia, M., Giudici, E., & Secchi, D. (2020). Reshaping tourism. In M. Della Luci & E. Giudici (Eds.), *Humanistic Tourism: Values, Norms and Dignity*. Routledge. doi:10.4324/9781003108993-13

Douyon, R., & A. Paradas. (2020). La sensibilisation des entrepreneurs à la RSE par les structures d'accompagnement au travers de la création de sens [How business incubators use sensemaking to raise awareness of CSR among entrpreneurs]. *Revue internationale de psychosociologie et de gestion des comportements organisationnels, 26*(65), 41-68.

Eddy-Spicer, D., Arce-Trigatti, P., & Young, M. D. (2020). Field building through strategic bricolage: System leadership and the institutionalizing role of intermediary organizations. *Journal of Professional Capital and Community, 6*(1), 29–43. doi:10.1108/JPCC-11-2019-0032

Elbeshausen, H. (2020). *Patient libraries: From the rise and decline of an institutional arrangement.* LBC 83.56 я73: 111.

Fernandez, V. (2020). *L'émergence de la compétence collective en contextes extrêmes: Le cas des équipes de secours en montagne* [The emergence of collective competence in extreme contexts: The case of mountain rescue teams] [Unpublished dissertation]. Université Côte d'Azur.

Flandin, S., Salini, D., Drakos, A., & Poizat, G. (2020). Conceção de formações que facilitem o surgimento de novos significados face a acontecimentos inéditos e críticos [Conception of formations that facilitate the emergence of new meanings in the face of unprecedented and critical events]. *Laboreal (Porto), 16*(2), 1–27. doi:10.4000/laboreal.17042

Fukami, C. V. (2002). 9/11 montage: Professors remember. *Academy of Management Learning & Education, 1*(1), 14–37. doi:10.5465/amle.2002.7373563

Fuller, R. P., Pyle, A., Riolli, L., & Mickel, A. (2020). Creating order out of chaos? Development of a measure of perceived effects of communication on the crisis organizing process. *International Journal of Business Communication.*

Gaille, M., & Terral, P. (Eds.). (2020). Les sciences humaines et sociales face à la première vague de la pandémie de Covid-19: Enjeux et formes de la recherche [Human and social sciences encountering the COVID-19 pandemic: Issues and types of research]. Centre National de la Recherche Scientifique, Université Toulouse III-Paul Sabatier.

Geiger, D., & Danner-Schröder, A. (in press). Unexpected events and routine dynamics. In M. S. Feldman, B. T. Pentland, L. D'Adderio, K. Dittrich, C. Rerup, & D. Seidl (Eds.), Cambridge handbook of routine dynamics. Academic Press.

Gioia, D. A., & Chittipeddi, K. (1991). Sensemaking and sensegiving in strategic change initiation. *Strategic Management Journal, 12*(6), 433–448. doi:10.1002mj.4250120604

Gorel, D. R. (2020). *Evaluating local nonprofit, Terra Birds, using SWOT and 7s* [Doctoral dissertation]. Northern Arizona University.

Hamann, R. (2020). The promise and peril of "building back better". *Environment, 62*(6), 41–50. doi:10.1080/00139157.2020.1820296

Hamdani, D. (2006). Working paper on conceptualizing and measuring business incubation. In *Science, Innovation and Electronic Information.* Division (SIEID) Working Paper.

Hartmann, S., Weiss, M., Hoegl, M., & Carmeli, A. (2021). How does an emotional culture of joy cultivate team resilience? A sociocognitive perspective. *Journal of Organizational Behavior, 42*(3), 313–331. doi:10.1002/job.2496

Jha, C. (2020). *The great disruptive transformation: The impact of COVID-19 crisis on innovative start-ups in India* [Unpublished masters thesis]. University of Gothenburg.

Kalkman, J. P. (2020). Frontline workers in crisis management. In Oxford Research Encyclopedia of Politics. doi:10.1093/acrefore/9780190228637.013.1527

Kruke, B. I. (2020). Survival through coping strategies for resilience following a ship accident in polar waters. *Safety Science, 135*(2021).

LeBoon, R. D. (2020). *How leaders interpret their business challenge through a generative metaphor framing process: A conceptual study* (Publication No. 28151585) [Doctoral dissertation, Fielding Graduate University]. ProQuest Dissertations Publishing.

Lindén, C.-G. (2020). What makes a reporter human? *Questions de communication, 1*, 337-351.

Maclean, N. (1992). *Young men and fire.* The University of Chicago Press. doi:10.7208/chicago/9780226501031.001.0001

Madiot, L. (2020). *Étude de l'improvisation dans le cadre d'une collaboration interprofessionelle selon une perspective de* sensemaking [A study of improvisation in the context of inter-professional collaboration through a *sensemaking* perspective] [Masters thesis]. Université de Montréal. https://papyrus.bib.umontreal.ca/xmlui/ bitstream/handle/1866/24164/Madiot_Laura_2020_memoire.pdf?sequence=2

Maitlis, S., & Christianson, M. (2014). Sensemaking in organizations: Taking stock and moving forward. *The Academy of Management Annals, 8*(1), 57–125. doi:10.5465/19416520.2014.873177

Malinen, A. (2020). *The long-term patterns of organizational risks: Examining the persistence of risks and their impact on management in organizational change* [Unpublished master's thesis]. Aalto University, Finland.

Manning, P. K. (1999). High risk narratives: Textual adventures. *Qualitative Sociology, 22*(4), 285–299. doi:10.1023/A:1022003520356

Mannucci, P. V., Orazi, D. C., & de Valck, K. (2020). Developing improvisation skills: The influence of individual orientations. *Administrative Science Quarterly.*

Mayfield, M., Mayfield, J., & Walker, R. (2020). *Fundamental theories of business Communication.* Palgrave Macmillan. doi:10.1007/978-3-030-57741-4

Meyer, A. D. (1982). Adapting to environmental jolts. *Administrative Science Quarterly, 27*(4), 515–537. doi:10.2307/2392528 PMID:10257768

Miller, A. N., Sellnow, D. D., & Strawser, M. G. (2020). Pandemic pedagogy challenges and opportunities: Instruction communication in remote, HyFlex, and BendFlex courses. *Communication Education, 70*(2), 202–204. doi:10.1080/03634523.2020.1857418

Mithani, M. A., & Kocoglu, I. (2020). Human and organizational responses to extreme threats: A comparative developmental approach. *Management Decision, 58*(10), 2077–2097. doi:10.1108/MD-08-2020-1086

Mueller, B. (2020). The theorizing trifecta. *Journal of Information Technology.*

O'Grady, K. A., & Orton, J. D. (2016). Resilience processes during cosmology episodes: Lessons learned from the Haiti earthquake. *Journal of Psychology and Theology, 44*(2), 109–123. doi:10.1177/009164711604400202

Orton, J. D. (1995). *Reorganizing: An analysis of the 1976 reorganization of U.S. intelligence.* Groupe HEC School of Management.

Orton, J. D. (2000). Enactment, sensemaking and decision making: Redesign processes in the 1976 reorganization of US intelligence. *Journal of Management Studies, 37*(2), 213–234. doi:10.1111/1467-6486.00178

Orton, J. D., & O'Grady, K. A. (2016). Cosmology episodes: A reconceptualization. *Journal of Management, Spirituality & Religion, 13*(3), 226–245. doi:10.1080/14766086.2016.1159975

Park, H., Ritala, P., & Velu, C. (2020). Discovering and managing interdependence with customer-entrepreneurs. *British Journal of Management.*

Parrish, D., Clark, T. S., & Holloway, S. S. (2020). The collapse of sensemaking at Yarnell Hill: The effects of endogenous ecological chaos on enactment. *European Journal of Management Studies*, *25*(2), 77–95. doi:10.1108/EJMS-10-2020-005

Patriotta, G. (2020). The future of the corporation. *Journal of Management Studies*.

Permatasari, P., Putra, F. W. I., & Natasha, V. (2020). Whether or not Indonesia-based companies consider anti-corruption acts important as its countrymen do. *Indonesian Management and Accounting Research*, *16*(1), 35–48.

Perrow, C. (1999). *Normal accidents: Living with high-risk technologies* (2nd ed.). Princeton University Press.

Risberg, A. (2020). *Constantly trying organizations: Ambiguities, contradictions, and paradoxes in diversity work*. Paper presented at NEON 2020, Norway. https://research-api.cbs.dk/ws/files/64201071/annette_risberg_constantly_trying_organizations_konference_paper_NEON_2020.pdf

Rocha, H., Pirson, M., & Suddaby, R. (2020). Business with purpose and the purpose of business schools: Re-imagining capitalism in a post pandemic world: A conversation with Jay Coen Gilbert, Raymond Miles, Christian Felber, Raj Sisodia, Paul Adler, and Charles Wookey. *Journal of Management Inquiry*. Advance online publication. doi:10.1177/1056492620970279

Roulet, T. J. (2020). *The power of being divisive: Understanding negative social evaluations*. Stanford University Press. doi:10.1515/9781503613904

Rudolph, J. W., & Repenning, N. P. (2002). Disaster dynamics: Understanding the role of quantity in organizational collapse. *Administrative Science Quarterly*, *47*(1), 1–30. doi:10.2307/3094889

Schmul, A. T. (2020). *Making sense leading change: A new superintendent's challenge* [Doctoral dissertation]. Vanderbilt University. https://ir.vanderbilt.edu/xmlui/ bitstream/handle/1803/16338/SchmuhlAarynT2020_Aaryn%20Schmuhl.pdf?sequence=1&isAllowed=y

Secchi, Armstrong, Babri, & Kask. (2020). *Call for papers: Track 6.3 – Rethinking behavior in organizations: Reflections on disruption and change*. Paper development workshop, IJOTB special issue. Nordic Academy of Management.

Secchi, D., & Cowley, S. J. (2020). Cognition in organisations: What it is and how it works. *European Management Review*. Advance online publication. doi:10.1111/emre.12442

Seeger, M., & Sellnow, T. L. (2016). *Narratives of crisis: Telling stories of ruin and renewal*. Stanford University Press.

Seijo, G. L., & L. Blugerman. (2020). Buscando al eslabón perdido del desarrollo tecnológico. Entendiendo el desarrollo de simuladores en CITEDEF vis-a-vis su régimen de producción industrial [In search of the technological development missing link. Understanding the development of CITEDEF simulators vis-a-vis its industrial production regime]. *Ciencias Administrativas, 17*(2021), 1-11.

Sherman, W. S., & Roberto, K. J. (2020). Are you talkin' to me? The role of culture in crisis management sensemaking. *Management Decision*, *58*(10), 2105–2221. doi:10.1108/MD-08-2020-1017

Shreeve, Hallett, Edwards, Anthonysamy, Frey, & Rashid. (2020). So if Mr. Blue Head here clicks the link..." Risk thinking in cyber security decision making. *ACM Transactions on Privacy and Security, 24*(1), 5:1-5:29.

Simone, C., Iandolo, F., Fulco, I., & Loia, F. (2020). Rome was not built in a day. Resilience and the eternal city: Insights for urban management. *Cities (London, England), 110*, 103070. doi:10.1016/j.cities.2020.103070

Slade, K. W. J. (2020). *Bushfire risk in late-modernity: An examination of risk perspectives and ontological security structures in Victorian urban-rural interface residents* [Unpublished doctoral dissertation]. La Trobe University, Victoria, Australia.

Staw, B. M., Sandelands, L. E., & Dutton, J. E. (1981). Threat-rigidity effects: A multi-level analysis. *Administrative Science Quarterly, 26*(4), 501–524. doi:10.2307/2392337

Sukhov, A., Sihvonen, A., Netz, J., Magnusson, P., & Olsson, L. E. (2021). How experts screen ideas: The complex interplay of intuition, analysis and sensemaking. *Journal of Product Innovation Management, 38,* 248-270. doi:10.1111/jpim.12559

Tabesh, P., & Vera, D. M. (2020). Top managers' improvisational decision-making in crisis: a paradox perspective. *Management Decision, 58*(10), 2235-2256. doi:10.1108/MD-08-2020-1060

Tipaldi, R., Santulli, R., & Gallucci, C. (2020). Finance for social innovation in emerging economies and developing countries. In M. Ramírez-Pasillas, V. Ratten, & H. Lundberg (Eds.), *Social innovation of new ventures: Achieving social inclusion and sustainability in emerging economies and developing countries* (pp. 14–29). Routledge. doi:10.4324/9781003034933-3

Vainio, A. (2020). *"They don't understand how we feel": An affective approach to improving the 'best practice' of community-based post-disaster recovery* [Unpublished doctoral dissertation]. University of Sheffield, UK.

Valderrama Venegas, E. A. (2020). *Social media platforms as economic organisations: reconstructing the evolution of TripAdvisor's operations* [Doctoral dissertation]. London School of Economics. http://etheses.lse.ac.uk/4215/1/Valderrama__Social-media-platforms.pdf

van Bavel, B., Curtis, D., Dijkman, J., Hannaford, M., de Keyzer, M., van Onacker, E., & Soens, T. (2020). *Disasters and history: The vulnerability and resilience of past societies.* Cambridge University Press. doi:10.1017/9781108569743

van der Merwe, S. E., Koch, R. G., Correia, A. J., & Moganedi, T. S. (2020). Using sense of coherence to cultivate enabling conditions for social resilience. In *Proceeding of the Joint International Resilience Conference 2020, Interconnected: Resilience Innovations for Sustainable Development Goals.* 4TU Centre for Resilience Engineering/Future Resilience Systems – STU.

Vaughan, D. (1996). *The Challenger launch decision: Risky technology, culture, and deviance at NASA.* University of Chicago Press.

Waldschmidt, N. (2020). *Rethinking engagement: How managers frame and make sense of communication strategies, practices, and challenges* [Master's thesis]. University of Ottawa, Canada. https://ruor.uottawa.ca/bitstream/10393/41225/1/Waldschmidt_ Nathalie_2020_Thesis.pdf

Weick, K. E. (1969). *The social psychology of organizing* (1st ed.). Addison Wesley.

Weick, K. E. (1979). *The social psychology of organizing* (2nd ed.). Addison-Wesley.

Weick, K. E. (1985). Cosmos vs. chaos: Sense and nonsense in electronic contexts. *Organizational Dynamics*, *14*(2), 50–64. doi:10.1016/0090-2616(85)90036-1

Weick, K. E. (1988). Enacted sensemaking in crisis situations. *Journal of Management Studies*, *25*(4), 305–317. doi:10.1111/j.1467-6486.1988.tb00039.x

Weick, K. E. (1990). The vulnerable system: An analysis of the Tenerife air disaster. *Journal of Management*, *16*(3), 571–593. doi:10.1177/014920639001600304

Weick, K. E. (1993). The collapse of sensemaking in organizations: The Mann Gulch disaster. *Administrative Science Quarterly*, *38*(4), 628–652. doi:10.2307/2393339

Weick, K. E. (1995). *Sensemaking in organizations*. Sage.

Weick, K. E. (1996, May). *Prepare your organization to fight fires. Harvard Business Review*.

Weick, K. E. (2005). Managing the unexpected: Complexity as distributed sensemaking. In R. R. McDaniels & D. Driebe (Eds.), *Uncertainty and surprise in complex systems: Questions on working with the unexpected* (pp. 51–65). Springer-Verlag. doi:10.1007/10948637_5

Weick, K. E. (2006). Faith, evidence, and action: Better guesses in an unknowable world. *Organization Studies*, *27*(11), 1723–1736. doi:10.1177/0170840606068351

Weick, K. E. (2020). Sensemaking, organizing, and surpassing: A handoff. *Journal of Management Studies*, *57*(7), 1420–1431.

Weick, K. E. (2021). Sensemaking and whistleblowing. In P. J. Svenkerud, J.-O. Sørnes, & L. Browning (Eds.), *Whistleblowing, communication and consequences: Lessons from the Norwegian national lottery* (pp. 81–92). Routledge. doi:10.4324/9780367822033-9

Weick, K. E., & Orton, J. D. (1987). Academic journals in the classroom. *Organizational Behavior Teaching Review*, *11*(2), 27–42.

Weick, K. E., & Sutcliffe, K. M. (2001). *Managing the unexpected: Assuring high performance in an age of complexity*. John Wiley & Sons.

Weick, K. E., & Sutcliffe, K. M. (2007). *Managing the unexpected: Resilient performance in an age of uncertainty* (2nd ed.). John Wiley & Sons.

Weick, K. E., & Sutcliffe, K. M. (2015). *Managing the unexpected: Sustained performance in a complex world* (3rd ed.). Sage Publications. doi:10.1002/9781119175834

Wessels, J. S. (2020). *A policy instrument to access child poverty: The case of the child support grant (CSG) in South Africa*. Academic Press.

Williams, G., Irving, G., Wright, A. L., & Middleton, S. (2020). Managing job-related diversity processes in high-reliability teams in the emergency department. *British Journal of Management, 0*, 1-17. doi:10.1111/1467-8551.12450

Xu, S. (2020). *A changing tourism system in post-disaster recovery: Developing anime tourism in the aftermath of the 2011 great East Japan earthquake in Oarai, Japan* [Unpublished master's thesis]. Lincoln University, New Zealand.

Yu, S., & Yu, J. (2020). Doing while thinking in dynamic environment: A brief review of strategic improvisation. In H. Shioji, D. R. Adhikari, F. Yoshino, & T. Hayashi (Eds.), Management for sustainable and inclusive development in a transforming Asia (pp. 163–177). Academic Press.

KEY TERMS AND DEFINITIONS

Cosmologies: A complex collections of beliefs about the nature of the universe and the role of a social unit, an individual, team, organization, community, or nation in that universe.

Cosmology: Perturbations, disruptions, crises, disasters, and catastrophes that are perceived to be a sudden and deep challenge to national, community, organizational, team, and individual cosmologies (Weick, 1993; O'Grady & Orton, 2016; Orton & O'Grady, 2016).

Cosmology Episode: A sudden loss of meaning that is followed eventually by a transformation, which creates the conditions for revised meaning.

Enacted Environments: Are part of the link between individual cognitive processes and environments. In enacted environments, preconceptions can shape the nature of the environment.

Resilience Leadership Incubator: A peer-to-peer learning experience through which participants work together in a safe, confidential environment, over multiple periods, for leadership development and to solve real-world problems.

Resilient Leaders: These types of leaders have the ability to maintain their energy level under pressure while at the same time coping with disruptive changes and adapting.

Resilient Organizations: These types of organizations anticipate, prepare for, respond, and adapt to incremental change and sudden disruptions in order to survive and thrive (Denver, 2017).

Section 2
Healing and Resilience From Organizational Trauma

The chapters in this section explore the concepts of resilience, trauma, and healing in educational and business settings. In addition, the discussion focuses on why healing and resilience matters, why trauma is problematic, and what to do about it. Some of the chapters also provide practical recommendations to strengthen organizations and to help organizations heal from organizational trauma.

Chapter 7
Healing Comes First:
Creating Trauma-Sensitive Work Environments for Teams to Heal and Produce

Mike Brown
EdRevolution, USA

ABSTRACT

"Job pressure" is the number one cause of stress according to The American Psychological Association. However, there has been no systematic transformation in business practice to intentionally establish stress-reducing psychosocial work environments and to stop the "churn and burn" of employment. Such stress is compounded and becomes a sort of combat stress for employees in high-risk, high-emotion professions. Healing Comes First is an analysis of the critical impact of work stress on the individual employee and organizational productivity. Using the Jobs Demand-Resource Model as a foundational framework, this chapter provides leaders a pathway forward from identifying symptoms of a "stressed out" work environment to enacting mitigating strategies to reduce work stress consequences. Furthermore, the chapter recommends the incorporation of trauma-sensitive practices and the creation of a positive psychosocial work environment to help mitigate the effects of work stress on productivity.

INTRODUCTION

War Stories From the Classroom

What did he get himself into? He was 33 years old running a failing school that could not seem to hold on to students or teachers. He had been in education for 12 years at the time and had traveled the country observing some of the best schools this nation had to offer; but this was not one of them. It was Joe Clark's "Lean on Me" the middle school edition, and now he was the leader hired to turn it around.

His passion for the work called him to an underperforming school in a high poverty district where the Department of Education felt the only remedy was a state takeover. However, day one on the job quickly

DOI: 10.4018/978-1-7998-7016-6.ch007

revealed to him that his students had needs that the schools were never fully prepared to meet. Their trust in school leadership was gone after seeing their fifth principal in three years. More importantly, the teachers who once gave their blood, sweat, and tears for their students were simply spent. It became apparent that before any school turnaround could occur, healing for the staff would have to come first.

While this chapter introduces the struggles and missteps of a stressed-out school leader attempting to lead a stressed-out staff, it is important for every leader to find answers and draw motivation from their own leadership experiences and reflections. No story is more powerful and effective at improving practice than one's own.

Many leaders find themselves facing myriad stress-inducing staffing issues from poor retention to lackluster job performance. They may be worried about meeting the increasing needs of a high-risk population and keeping the team motivated. Some wrestle with trying to overcome company setbacks and finding the right messaging that supports organizational transparency without sending staff running for every available exit. Even more frequently, leaders may simply find themselves in a constant cycle of catch-up where one step forward consistently results in two steps backwards. Whichever scenario most appropriately resembles the organization's current state, the answer for leadership is the same; prioritize healing.

The research is clear that work stress is a risk factor for mental and physical health problems of employees (Steptoe & Kivimäki, 2013), contributes considerably to sickness absence (Henderson, Glozier, & Holland Elliott. 2005), and impedes the efficiency and productivity of daily business (Schonfeld & Chang, 2017). Though tackling work stress seems a massive undertaking and understandably causes trepidation, a leader's stress-mitigating strategies can be a massive undertaking, but attempts at organizational and individual healing can be the solution. The aim of this chapter is to help leaders, supervisors, and managers recognize employee stress and mitigate its effects through the implementation of stress-reducing practices.

BACKGROUND

There is an extensive body of research on poverty's aggressive impact on the student experience in K-12 schooling (Olszewski-Kubilius & Corwith, 2018). Often missing from the conversation is the emotional and physical wear and tear on the teachers who are the front-line workers serving these high-needs communities. K-12 teachers face an array of stressors, yet are provided with few resources with which to alleviate them (Olszewski-Kubilius & Corwith, 2018). Surveys indicate that K-12 teachers report experiencing a moderate to high level of stress, and ample evidence documents the causes and consequences of stress in teaching (Montgomery and Rupp 2005). Surprisingly, despite the professional stressors bearing upon teachers and the distress levels they report, empirical research addressing potential solutions to teachers' work-related stress and burnout is sparse (Poulin et al. 2008).

The job demands on the teachers in this school were immense. As they entered the building each day by 7:15 a.m., the new, passionate, and novice Principal gathered them into the morning huddle. These morning huddles began as a thoughtful organizational strategy to provide staff with brief updates, center the team around the day's priorities, and provide teachers with unfettered access to their leaders and teammates. However, the huddle that was originally intended to mitigate teacher stress through clarity, psychological safety, and team orientation often exacerbated it. For the novice Principal and his staff, such demands included meeting the daily expectation of 10 to 12-hour hands-on support for students and their families, producing on daily, tight deadlines as tasks arise in the moment, and making timely and legally binding decisions multiple times throughout the workday. The Principal also known as the leader throughout this chapter, spent 15 minutes each day unknowingly passing his severe anxiety to his staff.

The demands of the job began noticeably taking a toll on the team. The accumulation of long work hours, problem solving around student needs, and seemingly carrying the load of accountability without care brought about near irreparable damage to the staff. The leader began witnessing first hand the deterioration of his team. Teachers that enthusiastically committed to annual contracts began leaving mid-year while others subtly began inquiring about potential openings at schools across town in not-so-needy neighborhoods. There was a noticeable increase in unpleasant and unprofessional teacher-to-teacher interactions as they turned their student and leader-facing frustrations towards one another. The teachers were starting to exhibit behaviors that signaled they were stressed out.

Among the most visible evidence of teacher stress was the daily call outs or absences. These teacher call outs came with little more explanation than, "I'm sick". The leader disregarded the remaining conversation to immediately begin planning for the absent member. In the life of schools, this entails rescheduling and reworking teacher responsibilities to ensure that all classes are covered. Unfortunately, it was only after stepping out of the role years later that the leader realized "I'm sick" was not a simple diagnosis of a physical illness. It was an abbreviated way of saying, "I can't do this today"; a shorthand for "this place is stressing me out".

Over time, more extreme teacher situations began to occur. The leader reflected on some of the darkest leadership experiences of his career where he rushed multiple times to different parts of the school building to revive coworkers who lost consciousness due to anxiety attacks that turned physical. The young Principal, overwhelmed by his task to lead, found his rock bottom moment when the work environment became so severe that staff members reported increases in blood pressure, the need for anti-depressant medication, and medical leave.

WORK-RELATED STRESS

Researchers and organizational leaders have identified workplace stress as one of the most significant problems facing organizations (Kelloway, Turner, Barling, & Loughlin, 2012). In the last 50 years, scholars have found that workplace stress had harmful outcomes on productivity and employee well-being (Billing et al., 2014). Compared to employees with normal levels of stress, employees with high levels of stress cost organizations more money, are less productive, and are more likely to suffer from conditions such as heart disease, obesity, cancer, diabetes, depression and anxiety (Wolever et al., 2012).

Additionally, numerous other studies have established job stress as a contributor to ill health (Kenisgsberg & Pana-Cryan, 2017). The severe stress this Principal's team was experiencing was originally codified by the Hungarian-Canadian endocrinologist, Hans Selye (1987), who explained it as "the non-specific response of the body to any demand placed upon it" (p.17). Elementary and secondary school educators as frontline employees face many work stressors stemming from economic, political, and social trends. In fact, The National American Federation of Teachers reported significantly higher prevalence of work stressors and poorer physical and mental health compared to U.S. workers overall (Landsbergis et al. 2020).

Work-related stress is an inexorable part of an organization's story. The pressures applied directly by leaders or indirectly by a '*Good to Great*' work environment can be anxiety inducing. Period. Yet, these models combined with high demand, high emotion professions create work environments where stress is the norm rather than the exception. Certain occupations are more likely to involve an emotional element to the work suggesting that employees in these occupations are likely to be more vulnerable to stress than occupations that do not require emotional displays. For example, Kahn (1993) suggested that caregivers (for example, nurses and social workers) are more likely to suffer from emotional exhaustion because they are required to display intense emotions within their jobs. Other stressors are also evident in many occupations, for example, the threat of violence (e.g. social work, police), lack of control over the job (e.g. call centers) or work overload (e.g. teachers). It is therefore, not surprising that much of the research into workplace stress focuses on these "high risk" occupations (Kahn, 1993).

Dana Wilkie's 2018 study revealed that the roles of Firefighters, Police Officers, News Reporters, and Military Personnel were among the most stressful occupations. Each is classified as high demand and high emotion jobs. Working as a frontline employee in the healthcare sector also has been identified as stressful (Galletta et al., 2016). According to the National Foundation for Educational Research, educators are likely to suffer from job-related stress and suffer from increased burnout more than other professions (Pishghadam, Adamson, Sadafian, & Kan, 2013). Other international research has demonstrated that teaching ranks as one of the most stressful jobs globally (Harney, 2008). In fact, in the first five years of their career, teachers exit the profession in droves causing an alarming attrition rate of over 40% (Ingersoll & Smith, 2003). 46% of teachers report daily stress placing them right alongside health care workers as groups experiencing the highest rates of occupational stress (Gallup, 2014). In their most formative years, many educators cave under the stressful conditions of growing state accountability, high stakes testing, and high-consequence evaluations (Kopkowski, 2008).

People are not, however, meant to endure repeated stressors. This is true whether an employee makes their daily contributions from an office building or a school. Those intense demands on a person's emotional and mental capacity continually repeated or prolonged over an extended period of time create a chronic stress that is not only counterproductive to work flow but deadly.

The American Psychological Association (2014) records "job pressure" as the number one cause of stress according to respondents irrespective of profession. Front line workers in high emotion professions are bombarded with risky scenarios that constantly require quick thinking and thick skin. In fact, social workers, EMTs and police officers are often aware of the dramatic scenarios in which they may find themselves. Neither their awareness nor their passion to do good work shields them from the impact of chronic stress. Even the most resilient employees, in the face of work-related stress, gradually lose their positivity, and experience challenges in retaining their commitment and work engagement (van Mol, et al. 2015). As unhealthy as it may be, those altruistically committed to humanitarian works, at best, become emotionally sturdy when confronting the hard realities of their daily work and experience a numbness or "compassion fatigue" (Figley, 1995). At worst they internalize every scenario and wear the pains of their work wherever they go. Whether they hide the stress well or not, their bodies repeatedly endure the stress cycle and are impacted. Front-line health care professionals emotionally connected to their work and experiencing high levels of stress are among the groups suffering in silence as reports show they are less likely to seek help from colleagues in moments of psychological strain (Burgess, Irvine, & Wallymahmed, 2010).

With no intentions of hyperbole and a sincere reverence for all who answer the call of military service, a civilian's stress (like that experienced by teachers and high impact workers) brought on by a single traumatic event or the cumulative impact of daily emotional strain can resemble the effects of soldiers returning from battle. The similarities between the two are the primary reason the American Psychological Association altered its first PTSD diagnosis from purely military designations to terms more representative of the broader society. Classifications such as *shell shock* and *Soldiers Heart,* which first appeared in the original 1952 *Diagnostic and Statistical Manual of Mental Disorders* (DSM-1), were altered by the publication of the 1980 DSM-III and were made more generalizable across the veteran and civilian populations.

In this leader's organization, the staff was experiencing high levels of workplace stress as a reaction to the mental and physical demands being placed on them at work. With the heavy demands for their time, cognition, and compassion coming from both the leader and students, the teachers were well aware that their ability to cope was not simply an aspect of the job, it was the job. This novice leader, like many other leaders, may have had some exposure to individual stress brought on by high-demand work, but what does stress look like when it is organization wide?

Identifying Stressed Out Teams: Signs of a Stressed-Out Organization

Chartered Management Institute (2014) describes the attributes of a stressed-out team. Among the symptoms were:

- Increase in turnover
- Grievances & disputes
- Increased absences due to sickness
- Increased reports of stress
- Poor results
- And inner-team conflicts

It did not take much analysis to recognize that this school's team was a "stressed out" team. They displayed all of the symptoms. Armed with this realization, the leader knew that this team of dedicated, knowledgeable, and capable educators would never be able to operate at their full potential and organizational capacity if healing was not made the first priority of business.

The leader found that attempting to manage stressed out employees was not working well and they were losing teachers at an unsustainable rate. The leader's investment in professional development for the teachers was steadily increasing and had major financial and scheduling implications. However, the investment in teacher development did not produce the desired outcomes due to the lack of focus on a healthy work environment. This lack of a healthy work place fed a vicious cycle that took teachers from onboarding to service to resignation within six months. This is not unique to this organization. Researchers estimate nearly 1 million teachers transition annually, often to other schools (Neason, 2014). The demanding nature of serving marginalized communities places this teacher loss disproportionately at the feet of high-poverty, urban and rural schools. The Consortium of Chicago School Research (CCSR) found that schools serving low-income, minority students turn over half of their staffs every three years (Neason, 2014).

Job Demands-Resources Model and Employee Well-Being

This chapter situates the Job Demand-Resource (JD-R) model as a foundational framework for improving employee well-being and performance. This model was selected because it can be applied to a wide range of occupations (Bakker & Demerouti, 2007). The JD-R model contends that employees that work in demanding roles can experience less stress if the organization provides resources to support them (Bakker & Demerouti, 2007). Practically speaking, heavy job demands contribute to employee emotional strain and stress but, through supportive leadership and the provision of job resources, stress can be mitigated. Examples of job demands include high work pressure, an unfavorable physical environment, and emotionally demanding interactions with colleagues, clients and even students (Bakker & Demerouti, 2007). Although job demands are not necessarily negative, they may turn into job stressors when meeting those demands requires high effort from which the employee has not adequately recovered (Meijman and Mulder, 1998).

On the other hand, job resources refer to those physical, psychological, social, or organizational aspects of the job that are either/or:

- Functional in achieving work goals.
- Reduce job demands and the associated physiological and psychological costs.
- Stimulate personal growth, learning, and development.

Bakker and Demerouti (2007) state that: … job resources are the physical, psychological, social, or organizational aspects of the job that are "functional in achieving work goals", "reduce job demands and the associated physiological and psychological costs", or "stimulate personal growth, learning, and development" (Bakker & Demerouti, 2007). Under the operational definition, not all job demands are negative (Meijman & Mulder, 1998) or unavoidable for leaders trying to be thoughtful about the mental and social health of their teams.

Additionally, the literature has been robust in its acknowledgement of the many job demands that result in employees failing in stressed out work environments. What is less explored are the many job resources that have empirical data showing their ability to emotionally support employees and help them remain productive in high demand occupations (Diener & Fujita,1995). Though work demands may not subside, especially in high demands occupations, findings support that there are many potential job resources that can help leaders sustain employee mental health and organizational production (Diener & Fujita,1995). Among such potential resources are rewards for success, worker autonomy, social support from colleagues, supervisory support, and performance feedback (Halbesleben & Buckley, 2004; Kahn & Byosserie, 1992; Lee & Ashforth, 1996).

Business leaders and their employees often encounter job demands. They surface in the form of extreme work pressure, unfavorable physical environments, and highly emotional interactions with clients. Increased demands on front line workers in the business sector, compounded by persistent work-related stress, reduce job satisfaction, and intensify the risk of stress reactions, long-term absenteeism and overall burnout (Leiter, Bakker, and Maslach, 2014). This, in turn, places a financial burden on organizations (Havermans, et al., 2018).

This chapter also centers its healing and stress mitigating practices on the idea that social and supervisor support can enhance motivation, work engagement, and organizational commitment (Demerouti et al., 2001; Salanova et al., 2005; Taris and Feij, 2004). Bakker et al. (2003c) propose that social and supervisor supports as job resources can effectively work to buffer the emotional impact of stress experienced by employees due to job demands. There is research to show that a number of job resources can be used as a buffer between job demands and the stress-strain sequence (Kahn & Byosserie, 1992). This chapter, in order to speak to high demand leaders in a direct and concise manner, targets social support as it is considered the most familiar situational variable proposed as a potential buffer against job strain (e.g., Haines et al. 1991; Johnson and Hall, 1988). Secondly, supervisor support is targeted as a key mitigating factor of work stress as it is shown to be an effective aid in helping workers cope with work stress and the job demands that contribute to it.

Feeling Stress at Work

During the production of this publication, organizations were frantically responding to the COVID-19 pandemic. One the of the primary safety measures implemented by organizations attempting in-person participation were temperature checks taken at the door. May 2020 CDC guidelines suggested companies hold a strict admittance policy which required a body temperature below 100.4. The basic science says that an abnormally high body temperature is indicative of physical sickness, a numerical measurement of physical health. What a break-through in human science it would be if there were such a direct way to assess an invidual's or an organization's emotional health. With no accurate way to measure the stress level of employees as they enter their buildings, leaders must be extra vigilant and proactive in promoting organization-wide stress-reducing practices if they want to be successful in fighting an enemy that is so difficult to detect.

The overarching stress process represents the daily interactions between an employee and their work environment (Dawson, O'Brien, & Beehr, 2016). Research suggests that job stress is strongly and inversely related to job satisfaction (Coomber & Barriball 2007). Gallup's research in tracking the emotional and mental health of Americans from 2001 to the present shows that their mental health is slightly worse than it has been at any point in the last two decades (2020). There was a 9% decline in the past year alone.

Furthermore, employees are changing jobs more often, and research shows evidence that the rise in work stress is not inconsequential to organization leaders. The Wharton School's journal of business analysis (2015) gathered a series of data to track the relationship between employee stress, health, work engagement, and overall productivity. The data suggested that 8 in 10 people are stressed out by work with more than half reporting that they are "disengaged" from their jobs. Only 10% of their low-stress counterparts, in comparison, said that they are disengaged. Another area covered in the analysis indicated that more than 75% of employees would leave their current employment for another opportunity if given the chance. Also, stressed employees reportedly take twice as many sick days as non-stressed ones. The research demonstrates a dangerous but clear trend that increasing work demands and stress are related to decreasing engagement levels, higher absenteeism, and lower overall employee productivity (Knowledge@Warton, 2015).

The American Psychological Association (2014) reports that "job pressure" is the number one cause of stress according to respondents. Although it is recognized that the onset of mental health concerns such as depression are multifactorial and rarely singular in causation, researchers identify psychosocial working conditions as a critical part of multifactorial causes that result in psychological strain (Schonfeld & Chang, 2017). The health community has been signaling for years that work stress is deadly, and it is critical that leaders as stewards of the working environment fully understand what is happening to their frontline workers.

Research from The Headington Institute plays an integral role in the way society understands the impacts of stress and trauma on the body. The institute explains homeostasis as the body's natural emotional state (Bosch & Jones, 2018). Like the 97.3-degree body temperature, there is a standard emotional level that allows the body to operate at optimal thinking and functioning capacity. Like a body temperature that exceeds the norm, emotional demands surpassing an individual's limit triggers a stress response much like a fever. The fever is not the sickness; it is the body's biological response to sickness as the elevated body temperature causes the body to react by regulating a person's immune system.

Like the young Principal, many leaders hire highly capable, mission-aligned staff to partner with them in carrying out the difficult work of public service. They, then, often unintentionally create more psychological stressors for the team such as an unwelcoming work environment, a frantic work pace, unrealistic time pressures, and unclear or contradictory work expectations (Bencsik et al., 2020). Leaders rarely consider their "try it and let me see what you come up with" directives as stress inducing for high performers, yet ambiguous rules consistently correlate with worker stress and underperformance (Meneze, 2005).

Psychological stressors also tend to be compounded when employee work efforts are not appropriately balanced with organizational rewards. Such work-reward imbalance promotes tension and works in opposition to healthy working conditions (Siegrist et al., 2004). It goes without saying, that any unfair treatment of frontline workers escalates the amount of stress they experience and magnifies the impact on their health. The assumption, for the sake of this chapter, is that all mid to senior level leaders interested enough to study stress reduction in their organizations are reflective enough to limit the appearance of unfair or biased treatment amongst the team.

The novice Principal/leader who found himself leading a *stressed-out* team in a high-demand school, studied and attempted to implement the leadership strategies recommended in *Good to Great, The Five Dysfunctions of a Team,* and *Extreme Ownership: How the U.S. Navy Seals lead and Win.* Like many driven leaders determined to figure it out, the leader analyzed and imitated the signature moves of high-profile leaders in the education field like the recently deceased Joe Clark, depicted in the 1989 movie *Lean on Me* and Geoffrey Canada, founder of the Harlem Children's Zone. The leader simply wanted his amazing team to be their best selves and produce their best work. However, it is the goal of this chapter that leaders like the novice Principal in this chapter understand that the greatest impact on organizational health and productivity is not dependent on the work the employees do, but rather on the environment in which employees are asked to work.

Employee Well-Being

The fact that work-related stress adversely impacts the health of workers and burdens organizations demonstrates that neither workers nor organizations can survive under the constant pressure of high stress work environments (Dewa et al., 2014; Havermans et al., 2018). Companies are losing money but employees are sacrificing much more—their health and sometimes their lives. Public safety employees, healthcare workers, teachers in high poverty districts, and professionals in other high risk service professions have compounded pressures of traumatic daily work experiences and performance mandates from superiors. These repeated negative stressors impair worker performance and perpetuates the effect by making it increasingly difficult to cope with stressful situations (Bernardi, 2019). Employees are burning out as a result. If the workforce is going to survive the demands of employment, it is leaders who must pivot, make drastic changes in the way companies support their employees and prioritize wellbeing and healing.

Work-related wellbeing comprises how employees feel at work (Schaufeli & Salanova, 2014). A greater part of the literature on wellbeing at work asserts that it is an affective state in which positive feelings occur more frequently than negative ones (Diener, 1999; Taris & Schaufeli, 2015). Further, wellbeing is partially a function of helping employees do what is right for them by allowing them to implement behaviors that positively influence engagement and other positive emotions at work (Harter, et al., 2002). Also, wellbeing at work has been widely studied and associated with positive organizational outcomes, such as job satisfaction, organizational commitment and turnover intention (Brunetto et al., 2012; McCarthy et al., 2011; Van De Voorde, et al. 2012).

Thus, there is an established link between health and performance at work. The general hypothesis is that happy and healthy people are more productive (Peiro et al., 2019). According to the happy-productive worker thesis, "happy" workers should have better performance than "less happy" ones (Cropanzano & Wright, 2001). Finally, positive affect has been shown to predict performance quality (Rothbard & Wilk, 2011). All these results support the happy-productive-worker-thesis, which posits that workers with higher levels of wellbeing also tend to show better performance at work, compared to workers with lower levels of wellbeing (Peiro et al., 2019).

However, the leadership literature, has largely neglected research on employee health and wellbeing in favor of employee performance (Grant et al., 2007). Moreover, when included in leadership research, employee wellbeing has either been treated as a secondary outcome or as a mediator that helps explain the leadership-performance relationship (Montano, Reeske, Franke, & Hüffmeier, 2017). That is, employee wellbeing has not been considered in a general sense as an important outcome in and of itself. To make healing a top priority, leaders must prioritize wellbeing.

To make wellbeing and healing a priority, these concepts must be given the same level of importance as constructs, like leadership, satisfaction and performance. The true importance of wellbeing for researchers, leaders and scholars is that it impacts the day-to-day experience of employees. The author hopes that this chapter will foster discussion and research regarding wellbeing and healing.

HEALING IN TRAUMA SENSITIVE WORK ENVIRONMENTS

With seven academic centers across the country, the U.S. Department of Veterans Affairs' National Center for PTSD is profiled as the world's leading research and educational center of excellence on PTSD and stress. There is much to be learned from those who have examined the most extreme cases of stress. Such focused attention on the triggers, behaviors, and long-term impacts of stress have led to the creation of mitigating strategies to support those experiencing emotional strain while reducing the frequency of stressful episodes. Though military facing, the U.S. Department of Veterans Affairs have been successful in codifying practices that are largely generalizable for the broader working community battling daily stressors. What can successfully be translated from military PTSD strategies to stress-reducing work place practices?

All employees, regardless of profession, experience some level of stress in some aspect of their lives, however business leaders have yet to make a large-scale concerted effort to address the traumas of the working population. The cases of work stress are extremely high, and the extended job demands placed on employees without social or supervisor support as job resources to buffer the impact of combat stress make the work unsustainable. However, there is a way forward. Employees spend a majority of their functional day at the workplace (Fujishiro & Heaney, 2007) affording business leaders ample opportunity for organization-wide remedies. The creation of trauma sensitive work environments allows organizations to operationalize the concept of healing as an organizational strategy. The reality is that if the ultimate goal as leaders is to run effective organizations, then the incorporation of social and supervisor supports in a trauma sensitive work environment for the frontline workers should become a part of daily leadership work.

Leaders often become tense when discussions around employee wellbeing arise in meetings. This is a reasonable response given that the vast majority of time spent in leadership development focuses on effective business practices to increase financial solvency and profit rather than on employee wellbeing. In fact, there is research that states that leaders rarely display the ability to accurately identify the presence and source of employee work stress (Gagliardi et al., 2012). Some leaders also shy away from the conversation of mental and emotional health because they feel overwhelmed as they are not necessarily trained to deal with employee stress and burnout. Regardless of the reasons for their hesitation, the price of stress on human life, work productivity, and financial bottom lines is costly. But the good news is that the shift to a more trauma sensitive work environment through social and supervisor support may not be as daunting as previously thought.

Four Practices to Create a Trauma-Sensitive Work Environment

The current realities of work stress demonstrate a clear need to implement systematic and effective prevention strategies (Stefko, 2019; Biron & Karanika-Murray, 2014). It is the hope that the preventative recommendations provided in the remainder of this chapter provide leaders with flexible, low-cost strategies to mitigate work stress, reduce employee absenteeism, and sustain high worker productivity.

Practice One: A Time for Support, Connection, and Decompression

When organizations commit to healing first and implement strategies to heal with commitment and consistency, research studies have shown the positive effects on worker confidence, coping, general health, and job satisfaction (Richardson & Rothstein, 2008). These results are not automatic. Prioritizing healing first requires organizations and their leaders to shift their focus from a product to people-driven practice. The suggestion here is that the implementation of a trauma sensitive work environment demands that leaders establish for employees within their organizations a time for support, connection, and decompression.

Unlike most organizational shifts, moving towards stress reducing work environments does not necessarily increase expenses or increase the budget. When implementing stress prevention practices, leaders will be asked to make trade-offs that appear counterintuitive at first. For example, in this new practice, leaders are encouraged to exchange punitive accountability practices for a more inspiration-driven approach where employee buy-in supersedes fear. This is where leader support trumps leader mandates. Likewise, team solidarity and support will replace dog-eat-dog practices that thrive on individualistic achievement and leave employees feeling isolated. Support and human connectivity should be recurring themes as organizations embark on the journey towards healing.

Practice Two: Time for Support: Reducing Stress Through Supportive Touch Points

Establishing a trauma sensitive work environment includes the simple practice of supporting employees. Because workplace stress has become a national norm with workers reporting high levels of stress, companies are encouraged to find ways to show support and appreciation for employees. Evidence consistently correlates higher levels of support with lower risk of worker stress (Schonfeld & Chang, 2017). Supervisor support, however, is not simply the tangible manager-to-employee guidance on work tasks. For this chapter, support is more accurately defined as "the extent to which employees perceive that their contributions are valued by their organization and that the organization cares about their well-being (Eisenberger et al., 1986, p. 501).

Stress-reducing practices encourage leaders to maintain high work production, attendance, and job satisfaction through supportive touch points that provide workers with daily motivation, positive leader-worker interactions, and recognition of efforts and accomplishments. Businesses have incorporated such practices at varying levels (Hydon et al., 2015). Though many companies opt into the lower impact "employee of the week" practices, the act of recognition does have an effect on those celebrated. Feeling seen and acknowledged by supervisors can feel like "psychological first aid" (Hydon et al., 2015) for hard working employees experiencing the emotional toll of high-demand work, trauma-sensitive work environments. However, leaders should work to create impactful and more robust systems of organizational care through supportive touch points.

Supportive touch points in an organizational setting may resemble the following:

- **Restorative Rounds:** One of the simple yet impactful life-giving strategies a manager can implement to help mitigate employee stress is the restorative round. At risk of being too prescriptive, this chapter implores supervisors to leave the safe surroundings of the corner office to make regular visits to employees on the team or throughout the organization. Whether an employee seems to be suffering from a production slump or experiencing the business quarter of their life, an unstructured visit and conversation from a leader to offer assurance, motivation, or appreciation is always psychologically appropriate. Leaders inhabit a privileged position which grants them the opportunity to actively listen, respond, and immediately provide validation to employee achievements and concerns (Cassedy, 2010). The time a leader spends walking the building to intentionally commune with and check on teammates is often more valuable than the time spent micromanaging tasks placed in the hands of workers too stressed to complete them. The extent to which a supervisor shows support for employees through acknowledgement and encouragement is a strong determinant of workers' perception towards the job and the stresses incurred (Griffin, Patterson, & West, 2001). Thirty-minute walk-throughs filled with supportive touch points with 6 different employees daily provides for 30 workers an organizational hug or embrace which may not lighten the immense work load but may fuel their sense of resilience to continue their high-emotion work another day.
- **Team Huddles:** Some high-support leaders officially begin the workday with daily team huddles in which leaders personally take a moment to highlight the accomplishments of an individual or team within the organization. These are the morning huddles the novice Principal should have implemented rather than his whole group, top down, directive, anxiety inducing check in that more resembled a micro meeting. When healing becomes the goal, every staff interaction matters. Leaders who prioritize organizational healing through supportive touch points also find value in opening the floor for teammates to give each other "shout outs" in the promotion of a celebratory and supportive community. Kind words and recognition pay dividends in employee job satisfaction and stress reduction. Gestures such as these create a work environment that feels more like family.

Whether through restorative rounds, team huddles, or other routine gestures of organizational care, supervisors who thoughtfully build in supportive touch points of motivation and encouragement create nurturing leader-worker relationships and actively promote the reduction of stress (Cassedy, 2010).

Practice Three: Healing Trauma Through Organizational Connectedness

Rather than creating stress, leaders can actually create environments where the opposite is true. Workers thrive when they feel connected to their teammates and rarely call out sick when their workplace feels like home. Connectedness is defined as performing work that is interesting and important, feeling appreciated and respected by the organization/others, and feeling connected to the organization's values (Metzer, 2003). A study researching key levers for positive team climate indicate there is a positive relationship between team-oriented work climates and low levels of work-related stress (Guidet & Gonzalez-Roma, 2011). Any thoughtful moments created by a leader where schedules and tasks become secondary to human connection are priceless and fuel feelings of trust, safety, and comfort. In establishing peer to peer connection opportunities as a key buffer from work stress created by high job demands, leaders are advised to create a more team-based approach to task completion. Social support in the form of team orientation is considered a "straightforward resource" which can help alleviate the impact of work stress (Van der Doef & Maes, 1999) and assist employees in achieving work goals in a functional, stress-mitigating way.

The following are examples of connection-based work strategies:

- **Work Streams in Teams:** Positive perceptions of teamwork are associated with enhanced well-being in the workplace (Budge, Carryer, & Wood, 2003) which shows that effective teamwork is indeed an adequate buffer to work stress for team members. Therefore, leaders working to establish trauma sensitive environments for workers should consider the concept of creating work streams in teams. This strategy not only affords workers the opportunity to pair with partners to shoulder the total responsibility of task completion, but more importantly work streams in teams helps employees build and maintain peer connectedness beneficial for overall work satisfaction and occupational stress reduction. Whether assembled as quick-response ad hoc teams or sustained groupings for long-term assignments, connectedness through teams fosters a collegial and supportive work environment which reduces competition (Kelly et al., 2020) and is critical for interpersonal relationships. The high demands of frontline healthcare workers have led to teamwork being the predominant form of work organization and is becoming increasingly more prevalent across the broader business community. Teaming, like most leadership decisions, must be thoughtful as teams lacking coordination become overly demanding for its members and may contribute rather than reduce workplace stress (Edmondson, 2004).
- **Closing Circles:** Just as leaders are recommended to begin their days convening the staff around common goals and celebration each morning to offer supports as a supervisor, utilizing peer connection and social support as a job resource also offers closing circles as a strategy. Small teams gathering at the close of business to allow employees to share with one another the day's bright spots and struggles reminds workers that they are a part of something bigger than themselves and are not alone in the work. An example of an effective closing circle features team members publicly announcing the daily accomplishments of teammates to the cheers of an entire group. This team activity signals a collective acknowledgment of hard work and a shared responsibility.

Even amidst the longer and more frustrating work days, the closing circle allows an equal shouldering or baring of organizational burdens, hopefully lightening the stress load of the individuals involved. Along with providing a sense of connectedness, closing circles afford individuals an opportunity to officially turn work off which is rarely experienced by dedicated workers in high demand jobs who often carry their cognitive and emotional strains home from work daily. When done well, these closing moments allow teammates to share goals for the next day in recognition that tomorrow presents another opportunity to complete tasks left unfinished today, no stress. Simultaneously, the individual stress response of every teammate in the circle begins decreasing almost as a collective emotional sigh of relief. Yes, company leaders focused on creating a trauma sensitive workplace can have that effect on stress reduction organization-wide.

Practice Four: Time for Decompression—A Flexible Work Schedule as An Opportunity for Healing

It is a major ask for organizations to staff a team of mental health professionals to support employees. It is just as costly to offer sustained outside counseling for workers through extended health care packages. What organizations can, however, effectively do is reduce the work demands on time and provide employees with both adequate time and space for resiliency-building practices during the workday. Findings by Romig, Latif, Gill, Pronovost, and Sapirstein (2012) in a study of health care workers revealed that interventions designed to reduce workload had little effect on burnout while another study showed that shorter work schedules were effective in reducing burnout symptoms (Schonfeld & Chang, 2017).

The myth that increasing hours of work across an organization increases productivity still persists today. At the Ford Motor Company in 1914, at the height of the industrial era, the average American workday was between 10 and 16 hours. However, Ford proved this theory wrong when they shortened their employee workday to eight hours and productivity increased. Furthermore, the Bureau of Labor Statistics shows the average American today spends 8.8 hours doing their job, yet is only productive for approximately three of those hours (Johnson, 2016). Astounding! This statistic may direct some companies to introduce shorter workdays. That can work.

However, a more trauma sensitive approach would be to apply a flexible work schedule for employees. Some leaders seek to reduce work stress by creating a better work-life balance through flexible work arrangements such as increased personal days off (Tetrick & Quick, 2011) compressed workweeks, part-time options, job-sharing, and remote work (Levy, 2013) which has taken centerstage in business operation during COVID-19. These flexible work options were difficult concepts to promote just two years ago, but the pandemic forcibly introduced these innovations in a manner that left no institution untouched.

As a stress mitigating organizational strategy, leaders comfortable with employee flexibility should consider normalizing the practice of two-hour work intervals concluding with 30–60-minute calming activities. Such a practice would indeed be a stretch for many leaders but may lower the stress of their employees. Leader tendencies aside, the benefits of workers having the ability to de-stress in between tasks is important.

Establishing an institutional norm of shorter work intervals is one task. Another task is creating an expectation for what constitutes decompression activities for employees in the work environment. It is important that in this moment, once again, leaders resist the urge to restore a sense of control and overprescribe employee activities. Any mandates from leaders may not feel supportive and now has the potential to become its own stressor. It is important for leaders to remember that the goal is to minimize the frequency of stress responses, not trigger them. Setting the expectations and parameters of the company's calming activities is the leader's best contribution in this decompression model.

For ideas, research shows physical activity as a useful mechanism for improving health conditions associated with stress (Oppizzi & Umberger, 2018). Clinicians themselves encourage activities such as walking programs, aerobics, and yoga. Each was carefully selected to create moments of mindfulness as there is increasing evidence showing the beneficial effects of mindfulness training on various indicators of mental and physical health[1]. Regardless of the activities offered by management to employees, stress management interventions that support employees at the individual level through mindfulness activities show positives effects on workers' mental health (Ebert et al., 2016).

CONCLUSION

When No Healing Could Be Found: Conclusions of a Novice Principal

The aim of this chapter was to help leaders to become more informed about job stress and the mitigating strategies necessary to increase the wellbeing of employees and help sustain them. The novice Principal in this chapter unfortunately did not have access to these strategies and practices. The Principal operated without knowledge of the stress his staff was experiencing. In this case, what the novice Principal did not know absolutely hurt him. His morning rants continued. The students' needs became increasingly more dire. In response, he demanded more time and more effort from the teachers. He began requiring earlier arrivals and later departures. Instead of more flexible schedules, he introduced more rigidity and attached a hierarchy of consequences, because that would surely increase their production and bolster their desire to show up.

Needless to say, the opposite happened and teacher absences increased. The research is clear that when teachers feel the support of their principal, their stress levels at work are significantly reduced (van Dick & Wagner, 2001). This Principal was stuck, and could not provide the support in the form of resources that his staff needed. The leader called on teachers in the building to forfeit their lunchtimes and cover classes which, further exacerbated their stress levels and depleted their efforts. They had nothing left to give. When no organizational healing could be found, the teachers left. Within two years, the leader had lost half of his staff and his own will to lead the school.

Kane-Frieder, Hochwarter, & Ferris (2014) state that a good manager is one who provides workers with desirable assignments, adequate supports, acknowledgement of work overload, and rewards when tremendous effort is extended. The novice Principal, who lost his staff after failing to acknowledge and address the toll that work stress had taken on their lives, vowed to never ignore the signs of a stressed-out staff again. Learning the hard leadership lessons of inaction and paying dearly with his own career, he went on to later become a Principal manager over a network of schools where he now prioritizes support for all teaching staff, teaching in teams as a form of connection, and sacred decompression time for staff leading high emotion work. As a result of his efforts and impact on the network of schools, the concept of trauma sensitive practices made its way through a teacher network of 300 front line workers. Some may find inspiration through this Principal's journey, but remember the key is for every leader to find motivation and guidance in their own story. All leaders have one.

Finding a Path to Success

Leaders cannot hire their way out of a stressful work environment. There is no business model that optimally functions by spending millions of dollars churning and burning through individuals who were once considered top applicants. The truth is, that stress has been killing employees and their productivity, and it is up to organizational leaders to end the cycle. The strategies recommended in this chapter are provided as a potential path to fostering employee wellbeing and as a result, retaining valued staff members. This is especially true for high demand, high emotion professions where workers' sense of service to others drives performance. In these cases, appropriate and thoughtful implementation of work-related stress management interventions can reduce work-related stress (Hoek et al., 2017).

While stress can be contagious, the opposite is also true. When a staff member experiences well-being, the effect seems to spread across the entire team. According to a recent Gallup research report that surveyed 105 teams over six three-month periods, individual team members who reported experiencing well-being were 20% more likely to have other team members who also reported thriving six months later. The takeaway is this: leaders must understand and prioritize activities that promote wellbeing for themselves and their teams. Leaders may be wondering if it is worth their time or even part of their job to focus on employees' resilience and wellbeing. According to recent research published by Gallup, the view that employees should leave their personal lives at home "might sound sensible, but it's totally unrealistic." Gallup analysis shows that wellbeing has an impact on other people at work. Leaders, therefore, really do need to focus on promoting healing and well-being for employees.

The bottom line for leaders is that personal development makes each person, and the entire team, better, enabling higher performance and engagement over time. Doing well at work and encouraging wellbeing is possible. In fact, it is the foundation of a high-performing team. Employee stress is a challenge faced by every organization. The author of this chapter hopes that readers become the leader that steps up to identify and work to mitigate stressful work situations. Employees who manage their stress are mentally healthier. They can do their jobs better. Replacing top-down mandates with signs of care, support, and affirmation calms rather than triggers feelings of trauma, builds resiliency in staff, and fuels increased productivity.

For leaders of industry to produce groundbreaking results and lead sustaining organizations of healthy individuals, a pivot towards the helpful resources of supervisor and social support in a trauma sensitive working environment must become priority. The JD-R model provides an overarching framework through which interventions to promote teachers' wellbeing can be designed (Bakker & Demerouti, 2007). Identification of salient resources and demands, and the implementation of strategies to cultivate resources and reduce demands have yielded promising results in teaching populations across a range of contexts. Although there is considerable evidence to support the implementation of JD-R theory-driven interventions as a means to enhance teachers' wellbeing, such programs must be implemented with caution.

Participating in such interventions may increase teachers' stress, for example, as such interventions may add to teachers' workloads (van Wingerden et al. 2013). Additionally, some teachers may be resistant to participating in these interventions, because they are often organized by the same leaders who may be perceived as the source of high workloads and stress for teachers. Thus, interventions need to be specific to the needs of teachers and implemented in a way that allows them to see the direct benefits to both themselves and their students. It is important to recognize that schools and educational systems have an important role to play in maintaining the wellbeing of teachers. With workplace stress as a primary antagonist to productivity, the overall effectiveness of organizations will ultimately rely on leaders' willingness and ability to counter heavy demands with the job resource of support. The work force, the corporate employees and the high impact front-line workers, are the backbone of society, but they are stressed out. Their healing must come first.

REFERENCES

Aiken, L., Clarke, S., Sloane, D., Sochalski, J. A., Busse, R., Clarke, H., Giovannetti, P., Hunt, J., Rafferty, A. M., & Shamian, J. (2001). Nurses' reports on hospital care in five countries. *Health Affairs (Project Hope)*, *20*(3), 43–54. doi:10.1377/hlthaff.20.3.43 PMID:11585181

American Nurses Association (ANA). (n.d.). *Health and Safety Survey*. ANA.

Bakker, A. B., & Demerouti, E. (2007). The Job Demands-Resources model: State of the art. *Journal of Managerial Psychology*, *22*(3), 309–328.

Bencsik, A., Juhasz, T., & Mura, L. (2020). *Consequences of Workplace Stress*. https://www.researchgate.net/publication/338465922_Consequences_of_Wo

Boles, M., Pelletier, B., & Lynch, W. (2004). The relationship between health risks and work productivity. *Journal of Occupational and Environmental Medicine*, *46*(7), 737–745.

Borland, M. (2011). *Interview. The Oakland Tribune*.

Bosch, D., & Jones, A. (2014). *Allostasis: Why It Matters*. Headington Institute.

Bränström, R., Kvillemo, P., & Moskowitz, J. T. (2012, December). A randomized study of the effects of mindfulness training on psychological well-being and symptoms of stress in patients treated for cancer at 6-month follow-up. *International Journal of Behavioral Medicine*, *19*(4), 535–542. doi:10.100712529-011-9192-3

Campise, R. L., Geller, S. K., & Campise, M. E. (2006). Combat Stress. In C. H. Kennedy & E. A. Zillmer (Eds.), *Military psychology: Clinical and operational applications* (pp. 215–240). The Guilford Press.

Centers for Disease Control and Prevention. (2021). https://usafacts.org/articles/top-causes-death-united-states-heart-disease-cancer-and-covid-19/

Coomber, B., & Barriball, K. L. (2007). Impact of jaob satisfaction components on intent to leave and turnover for hospital-based nurses: A review of the research literature. *International Journal of Nursing Studies*, *44*, 297–314.

Cropanzano, R., & Wright, T. A. (2001). When a "happy" worker is really a "productive" worker: A review and further refinement of the happy-productive worker thesis. *Consult. Psychol. J. Pract. Res.*, *53*, 182–199.

Dewa, C. S. (2014). Incidence rates of sickness absence related to mental disorders: a systematic literature review. *BMC Public Health*, *14*(205). doi:10.1186/1471-2458-14-205

Duvall, J. J., & Andrew, D. R. (2010). Using a structured review of the literature to identify key factors associated with the current nursing shortage. *Journal of Professional Nursing*, *26*(5), 309–317.

Fujishiro & Heaney. (2009). Justice at work, job stress, and employee health. *Health Education & Behavior, 36*(3), 487-504. doi:10.1177/1090198107306435

Gagliardi, D., Marinaccio, A., Valenti, A., & Iavicoli, S. (2012). Occupational Safety and health in Europe: Lessons from the past, challenges and opportunities for the future. *Industrial Health, 50*, 7–11.

Gallup. (2014). *State of American Schools*. Retrieved from https://www.gallup.com/services/178709/state-america-schools-report.aspx

Gallup. (2020). *The 2020 Global Emotions Report*. Gallup_Global_Emotions_2020_Report.pdf

Havermans. (2018). Effectiveness of a Digital Platform-Based Implementation Strategy to Prevent Work Stress in a Healthcare Organization: a 12-Month Follow-up Controlled Trial. *Scandinavian Journal of Work, Environment & Health, 44*(6), 613–21. doi:. doi:10.5271jweh.3758

Hayes, B., Bonner, A., & Pryor, J. (2010). Factors contributing to nurse job satisfaction in the acute hospital setting: Review of recent literature. *Journal of Nursing Management, 18*, 804–814.

Hitt, R., & Massi Lindsey, L. L. (2020). Military Members' Perceptions of Social Norms About Mental Health for Combat Stress. *Military Behavioral Health, 8*(2), 181–190. doi:10.1080/21635781.2019.1630039

Kahn, W. A. (1993). Caring for the caregivers: Patterns of organizational caregiving. *Administrative Science Quarterly, 38*(4), 539–564.

Kane-Frieder, R. E., Hochwarter, W. A., & Ferris, G. R. (2014). Terms of engagement: Political boundaries of work engagement–work outcomes relationships. *Human Relations, 67*(3), 357–382. https://doi.org/10.1177/0018726713495068

Kantor, J. (2017). *High Turnover Costs Way More Than You Think*. Academic Press.

Kelloway, E. K., Turner, N., Barling, J., & Loughlin, C. (2012). Transformational leadership and employee psychological well-being: The mediating role of employee trust in leadership. *Work & Stress, 26*, 39-55. doi:.2012.660774 doi:10.1080/02678373

Knowledge@Wharton. (2015). *Under Pressure: Managing Stress and Engagement on the Job*. Wharton School Press. https://ebookcentral.proquest.com/lib/vand/detail.action?docID=5482541

Kopkowski, C. (2008, February). *Why they leave*. NEA Today. Retrieved July 7, 2008, from https://www.nea.org/neatoday/0804/coverstory1.html

Lu, H., Barriball, L., Zhang, X., & While, A. E. (2012). Job satisfaction among hospital nurses revisited: A systematic review. *International Journal of Nursing Studies, 49*, 1017–1038.

Markovitz, S., & Hullunger, R. (2020). *Six Design Strategies To Reduce Healthcare Worker Stress During The Coronavirus Pandemic*. Academic Press.

Mayzell, G. (2020). *The Resilient Healthcare Organization: How to Reduce Physician and Healthcare Worker Burnout*. Productivity Press. https://ebookcentral.proquest.com/lib/vand/detail.action?docID=6129527

Meijman, T. F., & Mulder, G. (1998). Psychological aspects of workload. In P. J. D. Drenth, H. Thierry, & C. J. de Wolff (Eds.), Handbook of work and organizational psychology (2nd ed.). Handbook of work and organizational: Work psychology (pp. 5–33). Psychology Press/Erlbaum (UK) Taylor & Francis.

Meneze, M. M. (2005). *The Impact of Stress on productivity at Education Training & Development Practices.* Sector Education and Training Authority.

Metzer, J. C. (2003). Volunteering work stress and satisfaction in the service professions. In M. F. Dollard, A. H. Winefield, & H. R. Winefield (Eds.), *Occupational stress in the service professions* (pp. 389–409). Taylor & Francis.

Neason, A. (2014). *Half of teachers leave the job after five years. Here's what to do about it.* The Hechinger Report.

Olszewski-Kubilius, P., & Corwith, S. (2018). Poverty, Academic Achievement, and Giftedness: A Literature Review. *Gifted Child Quarterly, 62*(1), 37–55. https://doi.org/10.1177/0016986217738015

Oppizzi, L. M., & Umberger, R. (2018, February). The Effect of Physical Activity on PTSD. *Issues in Mental Health Nursing, 39*(2), 179–187. doi:10.1080/01612840.2017.1391903

Pew Research Center. (2017). *Gender discrimination comes in many forms for today's working women.* Author.

Picard, J. R., & McEwan, B. (2014). Mitochondrial allostatic load puts the 'gluc' back in glucocorticoids. *Martin Nature Reviews. Endocrinology Picard, 10*, 304–305.

Pierson, E. (2020). A large-scale analysis of racial disparities in police stops across the United States. *Nature Human Behaviour, 4*(7), 736–745. doi:10.103841562-020-0858-1

Poulin, P. A., Mackenzie, C. S., Soloway, G., & Karayolas, E. (2008). Mindfulness training as an evidenced-based approach to reducing stress and promoting well-being among human services professionals. *International Journal of Health Promotion and Education, 46*, 35–43.

Raio, C., Orederu, T., Palazzolo, L., Shurick, A., & Phelps, E. (2013). *Cognitive emotion regulation fails the stress test.* Academic Press.

Report, P. (2006). *The US Department of the Interior.* https://www.doioig.gov/sites/doioig.gov/files/Law_Enforcement_Reform.pdf

Ricciardelli, R. (2020). Canadian Public Safety Personnel and Occupational Stressors: How PSP Interpret Stressors on Duty. *International Journal of Environmental Research and Public Health, 17*(13), 4736. doi:. doi:10.3390/ijerph17134736

Roberts, R. K., & Grubb, P. L. (2014, March-April). The consequences of nursing stress and need for integrated solutions. *Rehabilitation Nursing, 39*(2), 62–69. doi:10.1002/rnj.97

Rosen, & Perrewe. (2017). *Power, Politics, and Political Skill in Job Stress* (1st ed.). Emerald Publishing Limited.

Rothbard, N. P., & Wilk, S. L. (2011). Waking up on the right or wrong side of the bed: Start-of-workday mood, work events, employee affect, and performance. *Academy of Management Journal, 54*, 959–980.

Siegrist, J., Starke, D., Chandola, T., Godin, I., Marmot, M., Niedhammer, I., & Peter, R. (2004). The measurement of effort-reward imbalance at work: European comparisons. *Social Science & Medicine, 58*(8), 1483–1499. doi:10.1016/S0277-9536(03)00351-4

Stefko, M. (2019). Notice for reasons of redundancy as a measure for discrimination on grounds of age. *Central European Journal of Labour Law and Personnel Management, 1*(1), 61–73. doi:10.33382/cejllpm.2019.02.05

The American Institute of Stress. (2019). *The United States of Stress 2019*. The American Institute of Stress Workplace Stress Survey. https://www.stress.org/workplace-stress

Utrainen, K., & Kyanga, S. H. (2009). Hospital nurses' job satisfaction: A literature review. *Journal of Nursing Management, 17*, 1002–1010.

van Dick, R., & Wagner, U. (2001). Stress and strain in teaching: A structural equation approach. *The British Journal of Educational Psychology, 71*, 243–259.

van Wingerden, J., Derks, D., Bakker, A. B., & Dorenbosch, L. (2013). *Job crafting in schools for special education: A qualitative analysis*. Retrieved from https://www.narcis.nl/publication/RecordID/oai:tudelft.nl:uuid:92fb8a18-fc71-4fab-aa4c-b7a96c57115c

Wilkie, D. (2018). *Employees in Stressful Jobs Balance Demands with Helping Others: Airline Pilot, Firefighter, Police Officer among 'most stressful' Jobs of 2018*. HR News.

Wolever, R. Q., Bobinet, K. J., McCabe, K., Mackenzie, E. R., Fekete, E., Kusnick, C. A., & Baime, M. (2012). Effective and viable mind-body stress reduction in the workplace: A randomized controlled trial. *Journal of Occupational Health Psychology, 17*, 246–258. doi:10.1037/a0027278

KEY TERMS AND DEFINITIONS

Burnout: A state of emotional, physical, and mental exhaustion caused by extreme and sustained stress. It occurs when employees feel overwhelmed, emotionally drained, and unable to meet the constant demands of their job.

Educators: A person who provides education or instruction like a teacher.

Employee Well-Being: The state of employees' mental and physical health, resulting from dynamics inside and outside of an organization.

Job Demands: Aspects of the job that include the costs to an individual completing the tasks necessary to do their job.

Job Resources: The physical, psychological, social, or organizational aspects of the job that help individuals achieve work goals; reduce job demands as well as the associated physiological and psychological cost; stimulate personal growth, learning, and development.

Resilience: The individual capacity to thrive in demanding situations.

Stress: The harmful physical and emotional responses that can happen when there is an imbalance between job demands and job resources in which the employee has more demands than resources.

Chapter 8
A Culture of Healing:
Practical Steps to Support Students and Educators in the Face of Collective and Individual Trauma

Aurelia Ortiz
Virginia Department of Education, USA

Maia K. Johnson
Chesterfield County Public Schools, USA

Pascal P. Barreau
Virginia State University, USA

ABSTRACT

The authors of this chapter contextualize terms such as individual trauma, collective trauma, and toxic stress; discuss how trauma impacts school environments; and propose steps to triage traumatic effects among faculty, staff, and students. Based on existing research and studies conducted by the authors of this chapter, strategies are introduced to help school leaders and teachers to overcome the effects of trauma and create a safe culture of healing during and after a traumatic event. While the context surrounding immediate trauma responses may default to macro-level discussions like violence, school shooting incidents, and school closures due to the COVID-19 pandemic, it is noteworthy to underscore less-publicized traumatic events such as adverse childhood experiences, adult workplace trauma, and collective organizational trauma. The authors provide case studies to help practitioners process organizational trauma scenarios.

INTRODUCTION

The research on educator trauma, workplace stress and childhood trauma have become prevalent over the last several decades, suggesting strong correlations between teacher stress and trauma, poor work

DOI: 10.4018/978-1-7998-7016-6.ch008

environment, teacher burnout, teacher attrition, and poor student achievement. The American Federation of Teachers (AFT) *Quality of Work Life Survey* (2017) report acknowledged, "schools still struggle to provide educators and, by extension, students with healthy and productive environments. Districts that fail to recognize the importance of educator well-being may be faced with higher [teacher] turnover … and greater burnout," which directly impacts students. Furthermore, the dual pandemics of COVID-19 and the increasingly clear systemic racial injustices have compounded and intensified existing economic hardships and resource instability of families in need, thereby introducing new layers of trauma and toxic stress. The intersection of these complex and dynamic issues contributing to educator, student, and community trauma warrant examination and the development of strategies to address trauma responses during and well beyond the aforementioned crises.

The daily lives and normalcy of students, teachers, and families were disrupted as schools across the country abruptly shut down in March of 2020, causing a collective level of trauma. A middle school band director in Mississippi somberly described the pandemic events while comparing it to Hurricane Katrina of 2005: "The crisis is different, but the trauma is in many ways the same: the sense of loss, the emotional and economic hardships and the threat of illness [has brought] uncertainty about what the future is going to bring" (Walker, 2020). To compound the effects of the early stages of the 2020 pandemic and national quarantine, media footage of a police arrest of an African-American man surfaced, followed by headlines amplifying the following: "The U.S. has been convulsed by nationwide protests over the death of an African-American man in police custody" (British Broadcasting Corporation [BBC], 2020). The incident itself, while particularly traumatic to African-American populations across the country, was one among several similar incidents that led to a critical mass in the social conscience of the nation. The incident sparked sweeping discussion within the nation's institutions (educational and non-educational alike), creating the need to address how fairly or equitably historically marginalized and underrepresented minorities have been treated.

Wading through the effects of these prevailing national crises, educators have had to work intensively to meet the needs of their students while operationally pivoting from face-to-face learning to online and e-learning platforms and while dealing with personal, familial, and professional stress and trauma themselves. After a crisis event causing a school shutdown, such as the pandemic, "we instinctively think first about the students, then about the educators … delivering online classes for the first time, which comes with its own set of stressors" (Quick, 2020). Quick points out that like the airplane safety briefings that instruct passengers to put on their oxygen masks before helping others, the same should be true in a crisis like the pandemic. Instead, the educators tasked with being a support to students amidst the imposed changes bypassed the time needed to take care of their own physical and social emotional health in order to "effectively and sustainably support students both during and after this crisis" (Quick, 2020).

According to the National Child Traumatic Stress Network (NCTSN), for some children, the pandemic could have compounded "pre-existing trauma, adversity, and disparities … which include increased risk for violence and abuse in the home" (2020). This pre-existing trauma has been labeled in research conducted by Kaiser Permanente and the Centers for Disease Control and Prevention (CDC) as *adverse childhood experiences (ACEs)*. For others, the pandemic has introduced new traumatic stress experiences. The duration of the pandemic has placed many students in a state of having to manage:

- Loss of predictability
- Disrupted sleep - wake patterns
- Disrupted learning

- The switch from face-to-face to virtual instruction
- Lack of access to educational resources
- Heightened awareness of adverse home circumstances
- Loss of an environment that students have viewed as a safe zone

In this chapter, the authors establish some common definitions surrounding the concepts of individual and collective trauma to help the reader develop a foundational understanding of trauma. The authors will subsequently propose steps to triage traumatic effects manifested by faculty, staff, and students. Based on existing research and studies conducted by the authors of this chapter, the authors offer a set of strategies to assist school and teacher leaders to be responsive to trauma experienced by faculty and staff. Subsequently, strategies are provided for faculty and staff primarily in contact with students to be responsive to the effects of trauma experienced by students in an intentional way that helps to create a safe culture of healing during and after a traumatic event. The rationale for this leveled approach to dealing with trauma is the notion of ensuring the social emotional well-being of the adults in order that they may be effective in response to the needs of their own students. The authors provide case studies to help practitioners to identify and process their own positive and effective responses to trauma.

BACKGROUND LITERATURE

At the core of the discussion of being able to respond appropriately to individuals who have experienced trauma is understanding what exactly it is when the authors refer to *trauma*. Trauma has been defined as "the experience of an unpredictable event, which is perceived to be a threat to one's sense of integrity or survival" (Muesser et al., 2002). Trauma can occur as a single event, or it can be a result of a culmination of events. Just as traumatic events differ, so do individuals' responses to them. When people are faced with traumatic experiences, their focus becomes self-protection and survival. To understand the sources of trauma, it can be further categorized into two main types: individual trauma and collective trauma.

Individual trauma results from an event, series of events, or set of circumstances experienced by an individual as physically or emotionally harmful or life-threatening with lasting adverse effects on the individual's functioning and mental, physical, social, emotional, or spiritual well-being (Substance Abuse and Mental Health Services Administration, 2019). Sporleder and Forbes (2016) emphasized that trauma is not specifically about the event but rather the personal reaction to the event. Examples of individual trauma could stem from a car accident, robbery, sexual assault, or the loss of a close relative or friend. Another example is when a child experiences a significant change in his or her life or the loss of an item of high value or material significance. A child being removed from the home might create instability and thus be traumatic for the child.

Collective trauma, in comparison, is a traumatic psychological effect shared by a group of any size, up to and including an entire society. Traumatic events witnessed by an entire society can stir up collective sentiment, often resulting in a shift in that society's culture and mass actions. Based upon organizational systems theory, all parts of any organization are interconnected and interdependent. If one part of the system is affected, all parts are impacted. Applying this notion to schools, when an entire system becomes distressed, teaching then turns to managing behaviors, and learning becomes laborious, if impactful learning is even occurring at all. Examples of collective trauma resulted from violent school shooting incidents across the nation and the national events surrounding the 9/11 tragedies of New York's Twin

Towers and the Pentagon. Arguably, the COVID-19 pandemic has resulted in collective trauma in many of the nation's institutions because it caused widespread fear, the disturbance of normal school, work, home, social, and financial patterns, and ultimately significant loss of health and lives.

Complex trauma addresses the duration of traumatic events. Complex trauma is "the experience of multiple or chronic and prolonged, developmentally adverse traumatic events, most often of a personal nature (e.g., sexual or physical abuse, war, community violence) and early-life onset. These exposures often occur within the child's caregiving system" (Spinazzola et al., 2005, as cited in Sporleder et al., 2016). Spoleder and Forbes (2016) explained *toxic stress*, which is a by-product of prolonged adversity. Children who often endure prolonged adversity without a caring adult in their lives remain in a constant *fight-flight-freeze* mode, and the physiological response is to produce increased levels of stress hormones, which is toxic for the body.

Trauma-informed care is an approach in the human services field that assumes that an individual is more likely than not to have a history of trauma. Trauma-informed care recognizes the presence of trauma symptoms and acknowledges the role trauma may play in an individual's life. Thus, the trauma-informed *culture* is a model for organizational change in human services fields that promote response structures to build resiliency in faculty, staff, and students.

Social and emotional learning has been defined by the Collaborative for Academic, Social, and Emotional Learning (CASEL, 2020) as the process through which all young people and adults acquire and apply the knowledge, skills, and attitudes to develop healthy identities, manage emotions and achieve personal and collective goals, feel and show empathy for others, establish and maintain supportive relationships, and make responsible and caring decisions. This definition speaks directly to the notion of educators developing their own social emotional skills of self-care so that they can then assist students in doing the same.

Childhood Trauma

Adverse childhood experiences (ACEs) is the term ascribed to identified traumatic stressors in children since the age of five. In 1995, the CDC and Kaiser Permanente partnered to conduct what is still considered one of the largest studies into childhood abuse and neglect, giving breath to the term. The study sought to connect traumatic stressors and life events. According to the ACEs study, some experiences are significantly stressful to alter brain development as well as the immune system. Furthermore, the risks of acquiring health and social problems have been known to persist into adulthood.

Essentially, childhood trauma experiences influence health and well-being throughout the lifespan of an individual. The ACE Pyramid model (see Appendix 1) provided by the CDC provides a visualization of the transcendental occurrences that can take place throughout one's lifetime as a result of trauma progressing through the following stages: adverse childhood experiences; social emotional cognitive impairment; adoption of health risk behaviors; impacts on life potential; disease, disability, social problems; and early death. Although there were several more ACEs that emerged from the study, the top ten most frequently identified ACEs disclosed by study participants included: sexual abuse; physical abuse; emotional abuse; physical neglect; emotional neglect; loss of a parent; witnessing family violence; incarceration of a family member; having a mentally ill, depressed, or suicidal family member; and living with a drug-addicted or alcoholic family member (Sporleder & Forbes, 2016).

Trauma can significantly hinder academic success (Delaney-Black et al., 2002). The connection that needs to be made for education leaders and teachers is that learning, remembering, trusting, and managing emotions are all part of a child's daily expectations as a student. However, demanding these everyday tasks of a child who has experienced trauma may lead to unsuccessful outcomes. Learning, remembering, trusting, and managing emotions are the very same tasks that prove to be difficult for a child who has a background of traumatic stressors. Administrators and teachers who are unaware that a child has experienced trauma or ignore this fact may inadvertently lead administrators and teachers to respond in ways that re-traumatize children.

Sporleder and Forbes (2016) discussed trauma, stress studies, and their effects on the brain. They pointed out that, in healthy brain development, the "neocortex keeps the brain in check and can control the limbic system which is the center for our emotions" (Sporleder & Forbes, 2016). They further underscored that in a severely traumatized child, the survival center, which is typically the lower and smaller part of the brain, becomes the part that they tap into the most. A fight or flight response is triggered, and most often, "children coming out of toxic environments will show signs of developmental deficits, which unfortunately can easily be misinterpreted as 'bad' or 'negative' behavior" (Sporleder & Forbes, 2016).

Research indicates that trauma is significantly overlooked and under-documented (Mauritz et al., 2013). The multifaceted demanding roles of the schoolteacher, school building administrator, and school counselor make it unfeasible to know every single student who has experienced traumatic stress. Furthermore, a student or their family members may not be in a position or may not feel comfortable sharing such sensitive information. Realistically, even with the best of intentions, educators must accept that students and families may be experiencing levels of vulnerability, which lessens the possibility of opening up to such scrutiny. Educational professionals should be respectful of this position. However, the authors do not suggest that self-imposed communication barriers make it impossible to provide trauma-sensitive environments. *Trauma-sensitive* environments promote a culture of safety, trust, and collaboration. It is an organizational culture where "everyone - administrators, educators, paraprofessionals, parents, custodians, bus drivers, lunch personnel - must be part of a school-wide change in understanding and response that is supported from the top down and the bottom up" (Cole et al., 2013).

While it would be more convenient to know each individual story that would enable educators to teach and counsel students more effectively, educators must instead be more diligent and intentional in reaching each and every student even if all dimensions of a child's personal story are not shared. The challenge is for educators to implement trauma-sensitive practices as a universal support system for all students. In order to provide an environment where children with backgrounds of trauma can flourish, those responsible for contributing to the culture of such an environment must be cognizant of trauma, the effects it has on children, and how it impacts the ability to perform in a structured setting.

Adult Trauma

Prior to the pandemic, a UCLA national survey showed that 58% of classroom teachers described their mental health as not good (American Federation of Teachers, 2017). Each year, thousands of teachers leave the field of education stressed and disillusioned as a result of teacher burnout (Ingersoll, 2012; Morales, 2011). The exodus of teachers from the field not only affects student success through disrupted continuity; it also places a burden on the school to recruit, induct, and train new staff. Roughly half a million U.S. teachers either move or leave the profession each year (Learning Policy Institute, 2014).

Since the school closings across the nation due to the pandemic, teachers have been faced with added stresses and pressure. These expectations have come amid heightened anxiety, fear, confusion, and depression during the pandemic events. More than 5,000 teachers responded to a survey conducted by the Graide Network in just three days. The survey asked teachers to describe the three most recurrent emotions they felt daily: "The results indicated that teachers felt anxious, fearful, worried, overwhelmed, and sad. Anxiety was the most repeated emotion by a landslide" (Graide Network, 2020, pg. 3). With information changing weekly, if not in some cases, daily, uncertainty has become the order of the day. That alone has created a high level of angst for educators.

In light of these conditions, educational leaders cannot afford to make the mistake of overlooking the mental, physical, and emotional health of teachers and assume that teachers have it all under control. For teachers, the events of the pandemic have perhaps resulted in the most abrupt and immediate changes in how instruction is delivered. Understanding that we have a corps of teachers that research has shown statistically to work regularly under conditions of high stress and are now experiencing additional levels of toxic pandemic stress, a profound question that needs to be asked is: What structures can be put in place to support them?

Schools typically do not have systems in place to support the social emotional well-being of teachers who have experienced stress and trauma. Often, the extent of support for teacher mental health may involve a referral system to professional therapy networks, like the employee assistance programs (EAPs), initiated on the part of the teachers themselves. While few studies have looked at teacher coping mechanisms and self-care practices related to stress, what has been reported is significant data highlighting high rates of teacher stress, burnout, and attrition. Numerous studies have indicated teaching is a stressful job, no matter the makeup of the school, and that individuals working in school settings are particularly vulnerable to work-related stress. According to The Graide Network, "46% of teachers report high daily stress, which ties them with nurses for the most stressful occupation in America today" (2020, pg. 1).

Like with children experiencing ACEs that cause trauma, these traumatic events may affect each adult differently. Trauma responses can vary and be subdued for some, while other responses could be more overt. Therefore, promoting trauma-sensitive organizational cultures and learning environments not only supports students, but the environment is also critically important in allowing teachers to be successful in their roles as nurturers supporting the needs of students. Creating a trauma-sensitive school requires a committed cultural shift on the part of school staff; it also requires the voices of parents, students, educators, community members, and policy-makers. Teachers are expected to be able to access their tool belt of strategies to avoid traumatic triggers in students while maintaining vigilance and preparedness to address the issues of students, particularly when one might begin to escalate in behavior.

It is incumbent upon educational leaders who support trauma-sensitive environments to help shield teachers from becoming frustrated with a lack of specific recommendations for students who have experienced trauma. Teachers may not readily be able to apply theoretical trauma-informed strategies to incidents occurring in their own classrooms. However, it is important to provide avenues to facilitate the self-care of teachers. Teachers need the security of a safe, trusting, and collaborative environment. Otherwise, it may cost school districts to lose quality staff members as teachers begin to feel burnt out and wanting to leave the field of education. While not all educators or students will experience trauma, each teacher will inevitably face other kinds of challenges at some point in his or her career and can benefit from learning skills for managing or coping with adversity. A school with a trauma-sensitive culture that supports a teacher's need to feel safe and supported will help teachers to thrive in the face of difficulties and hardship. In order for teachers to provide effective services and positively affect student achievement, organizations must provide support and resources.

TRAUMA-INFORMED STRATEGIES FOR SCHOOLS

Trauma-Informed Care for Students

One out of every four children attending school in the United States has been exposed to a traumatic event that can affect learning and behavior (NCTSN, 2020). Young children exposed to five or more significant adverse experiences in the first three years of childhood face a 76% likelihood of having one or more delays in their language, emotional, or brain development (Recognize Trauma, n.d.). In today's school environments, educators are highly likely to interact with students who have been through a traumatic occurrence. Students who experience trauma are two-and-a-half times more likely to fail a grade than their peers who have not experienced trauma. They score lower on standardized tests, have higher rates of suspension and expulsion, and are more likely to be placed in special education classrooms (Delaney-Black et al., 2002). Together, personal trauma that many students bring to the educational environment and the collective trauma they are experiencing as a result of the pandemic compounds the negative impact on school performance. The pandemic simply shines a light on the fact that educators need to create safe and welcoming learning environments to overcome the many sources of trauma present in students' lives.

An unintended outcome of the pandemic is that it has illuminated some of the chronically underperforming areas of the educational system, exposing problems of educational practice that have long existed. Specifically, the pandemic magnified many obstacles traditionally faced by vulnerable populations - the same populations who have had a history of underlying traumatic stress - such as a lack of resources and lack of equal access. Collectively and individually, educators have had to navigate the effects of a "dual-pandemic" on their students: both the COVID-19 pandemic and the nationwide unrest as a result of racial and social inequities. Although students have experienced school closures and oft-cited reductions in learning, there have been additional unintended outcomes. Educators and organizations across the country have wrestled with what students have learned in the news and other media, witnessed, or experienced regarding political, civic, and medical landscapes - locally, regionally, and nationally. There has been a consistent and often unsettling barrage of information about the pandemic and other events. Therefore, educators have had to quickly understand how to connect effectively with their students and their respective realities in the midst of closed buildings, remote classrooms, lost social and recreational activities, isolation, and in some extreme cases, the loss of friends or loved ones.

Managing Student Trauma and Stress

The authors suggest that educators engage in four action steps to begin moving schools toward becoming trauma-sensitive for students: (1) conducting training on trauma and trauma recognition, (2) building a culture of empathy, (3) acting through a trauma-informed lens, and (4) focusing on social emotional relationship building with students.

Conducting Training on Trauma and Trauma Recognition

In 2020, one author of the current chapter concluded a small-scaled mixed-methods study that examined teacher perceptions of the effects of trauma-informed care training. The study concluded that the participants who received the treatment (trauma-informed care training) had a strong positive perception of the benefits of receiving the training. Teachers were surveyed and asked, "Do you think the [trauma-informed care] training had an impact on you in the classroom?" All of the participants agreed that they were more aware of the type of support they should be providing for students, were more clear that they needed to support student needs in the classroom academically, socially, and behaviorally, were more cognizant of the importance of relationships and connectedness with students, and simply became more sensitive to the fact that most students might present with background trauma in general.

The findings of this research, along with other larger scaled studies on trauma and its effects on the brain and educational performance, are poignant. The findings inspire consideration for the idea that training for recognizing trauma should be required for all educational faculty and staff. For example, the authors' home state board of education has required child abuse recognition and intervention training for several years as part of state licensing requirements. This is a testament to the importance that has been placed on recognizing the signs of an abused child and the steps required to address the issue. However, child abuse is now part of the spectrum of identified adverse childhood experiences (ACEs). The authors are suggesting that perhaps the scope and training need to be broadened to require recognition of ACEs and intervention steps, which would cover the larger scope of trauma.

As studies further suggest, educators who receive trauma-informed care training feel more confident in their ability to recognize and perhaps support their students. As more teachers gain confidence in their abilities to provide trauma-informed care, the school community can begin to move the needle toward becoming a trauma-sensitive school:

A trauma-sensitive school is one whose culture prioritizes safety, trust, choice and collaboration; one where everyone learns about the prevalence and impact of trauma in the lives of children and families, where trauma-awareness motivates and guides the examination and transformation of the school environment, policies and practices, and where everyone ensures that children impacted by trauma can learn and be successful. (Child Abuse and Neglect Prevention Board, 2020)

Building a Culture of Empathy

Perry and Daniels (2016) outline three important steps for educators to make their educational spaces trauma-sensitive: (1) realizing the impact of adverse childhood experiences on neurobiological development and attachment, (2) recognizing the impact trauma has on learning and behavior, and (3) responding by building resistance and avoiding re-traumatization. Faculty and staff should respond accordingly to prevent re-traumatization by creating a culture of empathy and healing. Triggers should be avoided in ongoing contact and interactions between faculty and students. It is important for educators to recognize the following:

- It is highly likely that educators will interact with students who have been impacted by one or more traumatic events.
- Some of what may be visible at the surface level, such as impulsivity, lack of focus in a structured environment, and defiance, may be a manifestation of traumatic stress.
- All students want to feel safe, valued, heard, and secure, but that may be difficult for a student who has underlying traumatic stress, no matter how many times a teacher or assistant principal may say, "This is a safe space."

- A brain impacted by traumatic or toxic stress remains in a heightened state of survival, in the fight-or-flight response mode.

Simply having an awareness that trauma exists and understanding the impact trauma may have on students within learning environments can help educators temper their initial interactions and avoid re-traumatizing students. Of equal importance is making sure that the culture of empathy permeates the school environment and the thinking and behaviors of all who are a part of it.

Acting Through a Trauma-Informed Lens

The difference between a traditional or punitive structure and that of a trauma-informed approach should be understood throughout a school. Faculty and staff should be careful to reach all students in ways such that they feel safety, security, and genuine care, even when being corrected for an undesired behavior. Examples of responding through traditional and trauma-informed lenses are shown by the language used toward or about students in Table 1.

Table 1. Example responses using traditional and trauma-informed lenses

Traditional	Trauma-Informed
"They have anger management issues."	"Perhaps there is a level of difficulty with emotion management."
"They are defiant."	"There may be underlying trauma, and their trauma response may have been triggered."
"They have ADHD, ODD, or a cognitive deficit."	"Are we doing a good job of meeting their needs [academic, behavioral, social]?"
"This student needs consequences ASAP."	"We should provide supports to teach self-regulation and de-escalation skills."

Considering the prior experiences of trauma endured by students and intentionally structuring educational systems to foster safety and security has the potential to positively impact educational outcomes. Trauma-sensitive practices allow educators to encourage students' strengths to shine through. To be compassionate, educators must first cultivate an understanding of behavior and what survival means for some students. Caring, rigor, and accountability for the student are essential while also promoting positive school environments where relationships, regulation, and ultimately learning can take place. It is important to reiterate that all staff should be trained in how to do this faithfully. Trauma-informed care is a Tier One support: It is universal support that can be used school-wide, not only for a specific group of students. It benefits all students by providing physical, psychological, and emotional safety for all and helps students rebuild a sense of control and empowerment.

Trauma-informed care practices involve an organizational structure and framework that promotes understanding, recognizing, and responding to the effects of all types of trauma. Sporleder and Forbes (2016) detailed an all-inclusive guide designed to give school administrators of any level step-by-step instructions on how to turn a school of any size into a trauma-informed school. In their approach, they vividly emphasized the significance of educators proactively providing support, fostering a sense of security for all students, and potentially diverting situations before they occur. A trauma-informed approach facilitates creating a safe environment and mutually respectful interactions between traumatized individuals and adults within the organization.

Building Relationships Through Social Emotional Connections

Building social emotional connections and relationships should be at the core of the organization's existence and be evident in all situations. The Substance Abuse and Mental Health Services Administration (SAMHSA) has a National Center for Trauma-Informed Care, which delineates the following key principles: safety; trustworthiness and transparency; peer support; collaboration and mutuality; and empowerment, voice, and choice (SAMHSA, 2019). Trauma-sensitive practices include greeting students, offering positive praise, personalizing conversations, fostering relationships, and creating an environment of belonging and community for all students. Most often, behaviors that may come across as attention-seeking are really connection-seeking. Offering activities to help regulate the brain regularly throughout the school day can help those who attend school in a fight-or-flight mode to have moments of relief throughout the demanding school day.

Effective interventions recommended by the NCTSN can be implemented in schools with a trained workforce: teaching students the skills to manage stress and emotions, assisting students in clarifying feelings and perceptions about traumatic events in a manner that does not re-traumatize, and mending inaccurate or unhealthy mindsets. Doing so has the potential to increase student attendance, decrease consequences assigned for student behavior, and foster a collaborative classroom environment. To enhance student perceptions of openness, trust, and interpersonal relationships, educators must understand that how they say something is as important as the words they choose to say (Newberg & Waldman, 2012). It is critical that educators possess communication skills to convey the intended message to traumatized students who may naturally struggle to accurately perceive the intended message.

Trauma-Informed Care for Teachers

As the effects of the pandemic and social justice issues have blanketed the nation and educational system, educators have remained steadfast in effectively working with students in spite of personal, professional, and societal obstacles. Educators often place the demands of teaching and the responsibility of being present for children ahead of their own needs and well-being. In fact, educators extend themselves selflessly for the purpose of meeting the needs of their students first. Similarly, administrators work tirelessly to build teacher capacity and maintain educational momentum in their school communities while supporting the social and emotional needs of their faculty and students. As administrators guide teachers through imposed bouts of collective trauma and pandemic-mandated virtual, hybrid, or face-to-face instructional formats, their tasks remain to continue the process of evaluating and building capacity in teachers while balancing the complex role of being sensitive to the stressors and trauma that teachers face.

Principals must be proactive in supporting the instructional efforts of teachers by communicating directly and frequently with staff about instruction and student needs. While understanding the necessity of meeting the social emotional needs of students, effective school leaders should consistently communicate to teachers that academic gains are still possible with students ... The lesson plan structure is one that remains in order to minimize the understanding gap and increase the opportunities for academic, emotional and social successes. For both teachers and students, the most effective evaluation comes from communication, feedback, and someone alongside who helps build capacity for them to grow. While planning helps to chart the course, evaluations and feedback can be an on-going process of support, development, and capacity building. (Ortiz, 2020b)

The lead author of the present chapter conducted a small-scaled mixed-methods investigation focused on coping strategies of teachers who experienced stress and trauma in high-needs schools. The results of the investigation underscored the need for school principals, school division leaders, university personnel, and policy-makers to "address stress and trauma in teachers to create and to help foster a mentally strong teaching force" (Ortiz, 2020a). This phenomenological study surveyed teacher participants and identified strategies for coping with their own trauma in the school setting. The results of the study suggested that there were three primary ways teachers cope with stress while working in high-needs schools:

1. Time away from work
2. Exercise
3. Prayer or meditation

The study also highlighted that there are negative effects on teachers experiencing stress while working in a high-needs school. Surveyed teachers identified as negative effects of stress, frustration, irritability, and trouble sleeping.

Managing Teacher Trauma and Stress

In a hospital emergency room, *triage* is a process of assessing patients to determine the level of care that patients need. Patients are assigned a degree of urgency, and then the treatment is decided. Throughout the scope of situations administrators must face daily, it should be amongst the prioritized roles of an administrator to maintain an awareness of and to provide support for the types of chronic stress and trauma teachers may be experiencing. Teachers are on the front lines, and as data has shown, failure to address the needs for support may result in chronic and toxic stress, burnout, and attrition. Teachers have evolved from simply being content experts in subjects like reading, writing, arithmetic, and character education to also being vigilant like social workers, watching out for the welfare of their students. Teachers have learned how to monitor their students, identifying gang behaviors and signs, teach fire drills and active shooter safety strategies, and most recently, monitor themselves, as the pandemic has quickly spread through communities, in some instances, causing the loss of life. With all that is demanded of teachers, at what toll does it take on teacher well-being?

Teachers have been active observers of student social emotional well-being for decades. In 2020, the National Health Advisory Service identified teachers as tier one "mental health" professionals. Many teachers, however, feel inadequate to manage student mental health needs in addition to their own feelings of fatigue, irritability, difficulty sleeping or concentrating, or other symptoms associated with chronic stress or trauma. In order to stop the attrition of educators from the field and to begin to address trauma and chronic stress endured by teachers, school divisions must:

- Bring educators' emotional well-being into mainstream everyday discussions
- Create safe avenues for identifying and addressing teacher trauma or stress

- Create frameworks of social emotional support for educators using an approach that employs a necessary multi-tiered system of supports
- Provide opportunities for beneficial, positive stress relief as suggested by the study completed by the author

Bring Educators' Emotional Well-Being Into Mainstream Everyday Discussions

Division leadership, beginning with school boards and Superintendents, sets the tone for the school district, and building administrators set the culture for the building. In order to build support systems that encourage resilience in teachers, a discussion surrounding the emotional well-being of teachers must become front and center. It should no longer be a taboo subject left for teachers to figure out. We value the flexibility and adaptability of teachers and depend on teachers to go above and beyond to meet the needs of students. However, at times, this is at the expense of teachers' social emotional well-being. In order to create a culture of healing and health, there must be balance and boundaries that are both sincere and intentional. Among the benefits teachers are provided should be opportunities to participate in organizational structures and programs that help alleviate the conditions of toxic stress throughout teachers' work lives.

Create Safe Avenues for Identifying and Addressing Teacher Trauma or Stress

This is an essential step to provide an environment conducive to supporting teachers' social emotional well-being. Teachers are attuned to students' social emotional well-being and are trained to monitor and report signs of trauma. How can this expectation be applied to administrators and tailored to teacher well-being?

Perhaps a process for assessing teacher trauma and determining response steps can mirror the steps of a threat assessment protocol. *Threat assessment* is a violence prevention strategy that involves identifying student threats to commit violent acts, determining the seriousness of a threat, and then developing an intervention plan that protects potential victims. The threat assessment process attempts to address the underlying problem or conflict that stimulated the threatening behavior or language. Similarly, by providing clear avenues for teachers to report concerns, the administrative team can perhaps intervene and assess the need for support by pinpointing underlying sources of teacher stress. For example, if teachers find frustration in frequently completing behavior referrals for chronic student behaviors, then the administration can provide appropriate support. The process works when there are clear interventions and team members who support the process from start to finish. In the same way that faculty and staff can keenly identify warning signs and address student situations, the same acuity could be developed for administrators and support teams to create systems to support teachers.

Create Frameworks of Social Emotional Support for Educators

Schools and divisions must ensure that at the tier one level, schools weave trauma sensitivity into the fabric of the school in a multi-tiered system of supports. The next tier would be created based on the support available in the respective school district. When teachers need something beyond the tier one support, due to chronic stress or trauma, school divisions should determine appropriate interventions.

Provide Opportunities for Stress Relief

Time Away From Work

Time spent away from work to recharge and recuperate can foster social emotional well-being among faculty and staff. While time away from work can logistically detract from contractual obligations, the smallest of gestures can go a long way to inspire a sense of appreciation within employees. For example, while serving as an assistant principal, one author of the current chapter worked with a principal who valued the tireless work of her administrative team and wanted to show appreciation. So, the principal provided each of her three assistant principals with a D.E.A.L. voucher, which was an acronym for "Drop Everything and Leave." The principal's thoughtfulness was a testament to her understanding that her assistant principals were inundated with having to resolve many harrowing issues over days and weeks.

The principal also understood that her assistant principals could experience some exhaustion or burnout. One D.E.A.L. voucher could be exchanged for one half-day release from work per semester, amounting to four hours of personal time, whether leaving early or coming in late. The assistant principal's duties would be covered by the remaining administrative team members, and the administrator could then focus on personal matters or simply spend time with family: the individual would not have to disclose the purpose. This variation on personal leave spoke volumes of the principal's ability to build relationships and to display attentiveness to her assistant principals' social emotional well-being and personal needs. Furthermore, the gesture only served to develop tighter bonds of appreciation and loyalty toward seeing that everyone's needs were being met.

Exercise

School division administrators and school improvement teams have been known to develop wellness initiatives within the schools to encourage healthy movement, healthy eating, and other productive outlets to allow faculty and staff to relieve stress. The authors have observed a number of strategies from instituting faculty and staff yoga classes, walking clubs, circuit exercise sessions led by physical education teachers, and faculty basketball pick-up games before or after school.

Prayer or Meditation

Prayer and meditation tend to manifest as personal or independent activities. However, in a few instances, the authors have observed school faculty initiating meditation and optional non-denominational prayer groups, which have served to provide some faculty and staff with sources of rejuvenation and inspiration to continue in the role many teachers see as their calling.

Additional Considerations

The collective trauma and toxic stress as a result of working in a pandemic have been couched among other layers of stress for teachers, including: navigating an abrupt shift to remote instruction, managing student needs and their own family needs while simultaneously working from home, funding personal protective equipment, and learning new technologies to support student learning. In the summer of 2020, the U.S. Department of Homeland Security's Cybersecurity and Infrastructure Security Agency released updated guidance that added teachers and teacher aides to the list of critical infrastructure workers that included doctors, police officers, firefighters, and grocery store workers. Furthermore, teachers were likewise dealing with the effects of the pandemic as professionals, citizens, and perhaps on a personal level. Some teachers who were required to report to work during the pandemic feared the risk of acquiring the illness, leading them to resign.

The immense concerns of balancing educator expectations and risks during a pandemic have been conflated by the notion that teachers are paid to do a job and should rise to the challenges professionally. The expectation however, has not included the benefit of retooling teachers or receiving check-ins to determine whether teachers were professionally or emotionally prepared to rise to the challenges. As a result, school divisions have seen reduced attendance of educators as one data point. It has drawn attention to the need for social emotional, physical, and psychological intervention and support, such as the aforementioned strategies. The return on investment for organizations that focus on overall wellness extends beyond health care costs. Strategically aligning resources and support for all teachers, will pay dividends toward attracting and retaining teachers and ensuring teachers are provided with tools against trauma experiences, stress, and teacher burn-out. School administration and division leaders can play essential roles in building systems of support, addressing challenges, and removing barriers to reduce stress and burnout.

CONCLUSION

When teachers are in crisis due to trauma, the entire system is affected and ultimately, the students at the center of the work are affected. Learning, remembering, trusting, and managing feelings and actions can be a difficult challenge for a student who has been the victim or bystander in individual or collective traumatic experiences. Consequently, teachers whose social and emotional health are left unattended, may find it more challenging to support their students socially, emotionally, or academically. By outlining practical trauma-informed strategies for both teachers and students, the hope is to arm educational practitioners with ways to support teacher efficacy and health while creating learning environments where all students can flourish during and after times of crisis.

A trauma-informed approach facilitates the creation of a safe environment and mutually respectful interactions between traumatized individuals and practitioners within the organization. Educators in today's public schools are charged with the responsibility of instructing the most diverse population of students in American history. Students enter schools with a variety of social, behavioral, and cognitive needs that schools are responsible for meeting. Teachers also bring a variety of needs to the workplace, which are compounded by student needs.

Teachers are still experiencing high levels of stress and trauma themselves, which could cause them to leave the profession. The data highlighted in this chapter suggests the need for school divisions to create and provide ways for teachers to take care of themselves while also creating schools that are trauma-sensitive for all parties, not just students. It is essential that school principals, school division leaders, university personnel, and policy makers continue to support trauma-informed practices for students while also addressing stress and trauma in teachers to create and maintain a mentally strong teaching force.

Trauma-informed care education and training are also supported by the National Education Association, which recognizes the importance of trauma-informed practices and the need to approach student behaviors from a more constructive angle (Phifer & Hull, 2016). As human resources managers and hiring committees seek to recruit and retain teachers, retention efforts should focus on social, emotional, physical, and psychological health, which are essential. By creating and supporting a trauma-informed culture, school divisions are likely to increase both collective and individual capacity to produce and handle the challenges happening in educational settings.

Humans are biologically predisposed to a level of comfort when at homeostasis. Applied to the current social restrictions brought on by the pandemic, this explains the heightened desire for everyone in their respective niches and environments to want to return to a sense of normalcy. The pandemic, however, has had social systems and particularly school systems navigating uncharted territory for students, parents, families, and educators alike. With the high levels of organizational stress and anxiety educators have had to endure, the pandemic has also forced members of society at large to be intentional to reconnect, reimagine, rebrand, rework, and redesign their work, whether in the context of work, family, or social relationships. Educators more specifically have gone to necessary heights to reach students, families, and communities in different ways. They have sought first to understand and then to be understood, being on the giving and sometimes receiving end of grace. Let us remember these times and continue to provide educators and students with appropriate trauma-informed care practices and attention to social emotional well-being that facilitates the education of every child, every day, and in every way.

CASE STUDIES

Consider the following case studies and questions to help with developing trauma-informed responses. Case Study 1 includes reflective questions that will help readers navigate through a scenario involving student individual and complex trauma. Likewise, Case Study 2 includes reflection questions that will help readers to explore an adult trauma scenario. Case Study 3 involves a timely COVID 19 scenario for educators to help process through organizational collective trauma that school stakeholders and/or school divisions might encounter. The Case Study 3 scenario and questions also provide an outline by which other crises and responses may be dissected. Teaching notes for each case study are included in Appendix 2 for use by instructors, facilitators, and trainers. Appendix 3 includes a chart for the reader to organize responses for Case Study 3.

Case Study 1: Student Trauma

Scenario

My name is Maria! One night, when I was nine, my mother's boyfriend came into the room where I slept and began to touch me. I woke up to him rubbing my leg and eventually my private area. He tried to pull my pajama pants down! He also covered my mouth as I yelled for my mom, so that she could not hear me. There I was, lying in my bed, with a grown man on me—I didn't know what was going to happen. All I knew was that I was scared, I was crying and I was calling for my mom, unsuccessfully. My mother's boyfriend almost got my pajama pants down, when I found the strength to kick him (a kick that got him off of me) and run to my mom's room. I woke her up but could not catch my breath or find the words to share what happened. Eventually, I was able to get out the words, "Michael touched my vagina." Frantically, my mom looked for her boyfriend and found him in the living room. When confronted, he denied knowing what my mother spoke of and said that I must have been dreaming. He further stated that he heard noises coming from the room where I slept and only went in there to make sure that I was okay. Again, he said that I must've had a really bad dream. I begged my mom to confront him again, although his story remained steady. The only addition was that he touched me, to wake me up from my dream and let me know that everything was okay.

Fast forward one year later—my grandmother ended up taking the words that I shared with her about this night and acting on it. I have been in and out of court, with my grandmother by my side, testifying about what happened to me. To make a long story short, it was decided that Michael could not be around me. He also had to take some class … he did not even do jail time. But he could not be around me. My mom was so in love with Michael that she decided to stay with him and send me to live with my grandmother. To this day, my mom is in a relationship with Michael and I am living with my grandmother. Oftentimes, I find myself thinking about my mom—I miss her. … Does she miss me? What could I have done differently to make her want to keep me? Perhaps I shouldn't have said anything … then maybe I'd still be with her! When I am in school, I zone out thinking about my mom. My teacher once tapped me on my shoulder, to get my attention, startling me, as I yelled, "Don't touch me!" My little sister … I think about her a lot too. Is Michael doing the same thing to her? I wish she and I could be together. I can't focus on anything but the fact that I miss my mom. Grandma has been very supportive and very nurturing, but I really miss my mom!

Questions

1. What are some of the layers of traumatic experiences Maria experienced in this scenario?
2. How did the trauma manifest itself within this child, in the school building? In other words, what would you identify as traumatic responses that Maria exhibited?
3. What are some of the supports that could be put in place to assist and be able to reach this student?
4. What types of trauma-sensitive approaches might have been helpful to Maria to allow her to navigate through her trauma responses?
5. Understanding that educators may not be aware of a student's background or prior experiences, how can a trauma-sensitive environment be developed to ensure that a student with Maria's background finds safety and trust so that she can be successful?

Case Study 2: Teacher Trauma

Scenario

An eighth-grade student was standing in the main office of Millview Pond Middle School waiting to see the principal, Mrs. Payne. The student reported to the office staff that her teacher, Mrs. Taylor, yelled at the students and told the class to "stop acting like asses!" Upon Mrs. Payne being notified of the incident, she decided to immediately visit Mrs. Taylor's classroom. Mrs. Payne went with the dean, Mr. Nelson, as a precaution to ensure everyone's safety and to be an additional witness present for any potential new occurrences as they arrived to Mrs. Taylor's classroom. The time between the student's report and the arrival of Mrs. Payne and Mr. Nelson included the window of time of the eighth-grade transition to elective classes. Mrs. Taylor was beginning her planning period when Mrs. Payne and Mr. Nelson arrived, and thus the students were no longer in Mrs. Taylor's classroom.

As Mrs. Payne and Mr. Nelson entered the classroom, Mrs. Taylor immediately exclaimed, "I'll flip burgers before I come back and teach these kids! They act just like animals!" Mrs. Payne disclosed to Mrs. Taylor that a student reported the incident of her yelling at the students and telling them to stop acting like "asses." Mrs. Payne then asked for Mrs. Taylor to share details of the events that led to her outburst and name-calling of the students. In a fit of anguish and rage, Mrs. Taylor gave the details while choking back tears.

"They won't do their work, they walk out of the classroom, they curse at each other and at the teachers and nothing is ever done," divulged Mrs. Taylor. "I'm sick of it!!! My family says I'm miserable to be around, but it's because of these kids! They don't care about anything! I can't take it anymore and I'm ready to quit! This is NOT worth it!"

Mrs. Payne and Mr. Nelson sat and listened, occasionally asking follow-up questions to put together a portrait of the situation. Because Mrs. Taylor admitted to the name-calling out of frustration, Mrs. Payne informed her that she would be writing the incident up and placing it in her file. Mrs. Taylor was placed under a probationary period through the end of the year to ensure the incident did not occur again. Mrs. Payne was firm but fair. While she understood that students could "press buttons" and frustrate teachers, she also stood firm that it was never acceptable to berate students and call them names as an adult. Mrs. Payne then asked Mrs. Taylor to take a walk outside or inside but to not leave the campus. During the conversation Mrs. Taylor also mentioned that she often thought of driving off a bridge on the way home because of her frustration and feelings of desperation. Teaching was the only job she knew, and she did not know how she could financially survive without work. The disclosure of Mrs. Taylor's potential for self-harm was alarming and reported to Human Resources along with the school counselor. Mrs. Payne shared resources for counseling services available to employees under the employee benefits package.

To get to the root of addressing why Mrs. Taylor might have been experiencing frustrations in her classroom, Mrs. Payne developed a triangulated approach of support for Mrs. Taylor. First, Mrs. Payne scheduled frequent check-ins with the teacher from an assigned mentor. Second, Mrs. Payne provided opportunities for temporary co-teaching with members of the administrative team who could model some behavioral interventions and instructional strategies to reach some of her non-compliant students. Third, in accordance with the evaluation cycle, the teacher continued receiving walkthroughs and observations with immediate feedback and suggestions for strategies to try in her classroom.

Mrs. Taylor stumbled through the remainder of the school year. There were no further major incidents and, in fact, with the supports and monitoring put in place by Mrs. Payne, very few behavioral referrals were ever written by Mrs. Taylor again. It appeared as though things were on an upward trajectory for Mrs. Taylor. She attended required meetings but did not contribute in any other areas within the building. At the end of the year, Mrs. Taylor submitted her resignation. Mrs. Taylor left the teaching profession, accepting an external position.

Questions

1. What are some of the layers of trauma the teacher, Mrs. Taylor may experience, in this scenario?
2. How did the trauma manifest itself in the school building? In other words, what would you identify as traumatic responses that Mrs. Taylor exhibited?

3. What did the principal, Mrs. Payne, do well? What could she have done differently? Why was it or was it not important for Mrs. Payne to sugget that Mrs. Taylor take a walk but not to leave the campus? What are some additional supports that could be put in place to assist and be able to help this teacher?
4. What types of trauma-sensitive approaches might have been helpful to Mrs. Taylor to allow her to process her trauma response and to help her self-correct for the future?
5. Understanding that school leaders may not be aware of a teacher's background or prior experiences, how can a trauma-sensitive environment be developed to ensure that teachers like Mrs. Taylor find safety, trust, and support so that all teachers can be successful?

Case Study 3: COVID and Collective Trauma

Scenario

Mr. Prescott was recently hired as the new principal of Stoney Glen High School. He was excited to take on the new position because it meant that he had an opportunity to become the principal of the very high school he attended and with which he was quite familiar. He grew up in the community the high school served. Stoney Glen High School is situated in the suburbs of a mid-sized city and is identified as fully accredited with high functioning academic, sports, and extracurricular programs. The school is supported by involved PTSA and athletic booster groups. The school demographics include a mixture of students from highly affluent communities, working-class communities where the family breadwinners were employed by many of the local industries and trades, and low-income families. The breakdown of the demographics was about 50%, 29%, and 21%, respectively. The demographics were not unlike the school in a neighboring school division in which Mr. Prescott formerly served as assistant principal for six years. He was ready and eager to take on the challenges and lead his alma mater.

Mr. Prescott, however, was taking on his new role at a very unusual time, in the middle of a viral pandemic. He was hired during the summer, and his first task was to lead his faculty through a "reopening plan" for the fall session. The local school board, following statewide pandemic protocols, had already decided that instruction would be delivered virtually through the fall, with only certain special needs students being given priority for face-to-face instruction dictated by individualized education plans (IEPs). The school board also determined that sports and all other extracurricular clubs and activities were canceled through the fall. However, the community understood that the governor left room for localities to develop appropriate reopening plans. Upon starting in his new role, Mr. Prescott received emails and requests for several virtual meetings. Some of the concerns included the following:

Student Email

In an email from the president of the Stoney Glen SGA, concern is expressed over the cancellation of school activities. She is reaching out on behalf of many seniors who fear they will be missing out on milestone celebratory activities like homecoming and senior recognition, senior prom, and graduation and would not have a chance to see their classmates again in the school year.

Parent Zoom Meeting

A small group of PTSA and athletic booster parents wanted to voice their concerns over the cancellation of sports. One set of parents expressed that their son would not have the opportunity to be seen by college football scouts. Another parent shared that to the dismay of her son; football is what keeps him focused on school and out of trouble in the neighborhood. Now that there is no football, she sees signs of him getting depressed and acting out.

Teacher Zoom Meeting

In the one-on-one virtual teacher introductory meetings that Mr. Prescott held, many teachers took the liberty to express concerns over their lack of preparation or experience with developing online instructional modules for their students in such a short period of time, which is a cause of great angst. Furthermore, two teachers lamented that because all of the schools are virtual, and their own children are home, they are having to juggle monitoring the school activities of their own young children while having to prepare and engage their own students at Stoney Glen High. How can they do both effectively?

Parent Email

Mr. Prescott is included in an email to the middle school and elementary school principals from a family whose children qualify for free and reduced meals. The parents disclose their concern about a lack of resources and access to the technology their four school-aged children will need to complete the virtual assignments. Also, due to the pandemic restrictions and the closing of businesses through which the parents were employed, the mother has seen reduced hours and hourly wages while the father has been laid off from work. Their main concern is whether they will be able to feed their children and keep the lights and heat on during the pandemic.

Teacher Email

It is now late August, and a special education teacher emails Mr. Prescott, notifying him that he was informed that his mother tested positive for COVID-19 and is on a ventilator in the emergency room, but visitors are not permitted. Furthermore, the teacher has also tested positive for coronavirus because, prior to his mother's diagnosis, he was caring for her over the summer, as she suffered from several pre-existing health conditions. Now he must quarantine, away from his family, and is struggling to focus on planning for the opening and continuing in his role as special education lead.

Questions

1. Identify and explain the layers of trauma present within the scenario?
2. As the new principal, how would you respond to these communications?
3. Revisit your responses to Question 2. As a trauma-informed practitioner, were your responses trauma-sensitive? If not, how would you re-formulate your responses to each of the communications as trauma-sensitive responses?

4. What types of trauma-informed strategies or supports would be beneficial to assist the different stakeholder groups through their various concerns?
5. Understanding that traumatic events may not be readily apparent to an administrator or teacher and also understanding that traumatic events can reoccur, how can a sustainable trauma-sensitive environment be developed to ensure safety, trust, and support of all stakeholders moving forward?

REFERENCES

American Federation of Teachers. (2017). *2017 Educator quality of work life survey*. https://www.aft.org/sites/default/files/2017_eqwl_survey_web.pdf

British Broadcasting Corporation. (2020, July). *George Floyd: What happened in the final moments of his life*. https://www.bbc.com/news/world/-us-canada-52861726

Centers for Disease Control and Prevention. (2019). *Preventing adverse childhood experiences: Leveraging the best available evidence*. National Center for Injury Prevention and Control, Centers for Disease Control and Prevention. https://www.cdc.gov/violenceprevention/pdf/preventingACES.pdf

Child Abuse and Neglect Prevention Board. (2020). *Adverse childhood experiences (ACEs)*. Retrieved from https://preventionboard.wi.gov/Pages/OurWork/ACE.aspx

Cole, S. F., Eisner, A., Gregory, M., & Ristuccia, J. (2013). Helping traumatized children learn 2: Creating and advocating for trauma-sensitive schools. *Trauma and Learning Policy Initiative, Massachusetts Advocates for Children*. https://traumasensitiveschools.org/

Collaborative for Academic, Social, and Emotional Learning. (2020). *What is social and emotional learning (SEL)?* https://casel.org/what-is-sel/

Delaney-Black, V., Covington, C., Ondersma, S. J., Nordstrom-Klee, B., Templin, T., Ager, J., & Sokol, R. J. (2002). Violence exposure, trauma, and IQ and/or reading deficits among urban children. *Archives of Pediatrics & Adolescent Medicine*, *156*(3), 280. doi:10.1001/archpedi.156.3.280 PMID:11876674

Graide Network. (2020, April 13). *The rise of teacher stress: (/blog-all/2018/8/1/crayons-and-cortisol-the-epidemic-of-teacher-stress)*. https://www.thegraidenetwork.com/blog-all/2018/8/1/crayons-and-cortisol-the-epidemic-of-teacher-stress

Ingersoll, R. M. (2012). Beginning teacher induction: What the data tells us. *Phi Delta Kappan*, *93*(8), 47–51. doi:10.1177/003172171209300811

Johnson, M. (2020). *Transforming education via trauma-informed care: Altering perceptions projected onto students with underlying traumatic experiences* [Unpublished doctoral dissertation]. Virginia State University.

Learning Policy Institute. (2014). *Title II data collection*. U.S. Department of Education. https://title2.ed.gov/Public/Home.aspx

Mauritz, M. W., Goosens, P. J. J., Draijer, N., & Van Achterberg, T. (2013). Prevalence of interpersonal trauma exposure and trauma-related disorders in severe mental illness. *European Journal of Psychotraumatology, 4*(1), 1–15. doi:10.3402/ejpt.v4i0.19985 PMID:23577228

Morales, A. I. R. (2011). *Factors that foster Latina English language learners: Nontraditional student resilience in higher education and their persistence in teacher education* [Doctoral dissertation, Kansas City State University]. https://krex.kstate.edu/dspace/bitstream/handle/2097/8567/AmandaMorales201

Muesser, K. T., Rosenberg, S. D., Goodman, L. A., & Trumbetter, S. L. (2002). Trauma, PTSD, and the course of severe mental illness: An interactive model. *Schizophrenia Research, 53*(1-2), 123–143. doi:10.1016/S0920-9964(01)00173-6 PMID:11728845

National Child Traumatic Stress Network. (2020). *Trauma informed school strategies during COVID-19.* https://www.nctsn.org/resources/trauma-informed-schoolstrategies-during-covid-19

Newberg, A., & Waldman, M. R. (2012). *Words can change your brain: 12 conversation strategies to build trust, resolve conflict, and increase intimacy.* Penguin Group.

Ortiz, A. (2020a). *An investigation of coping mechanisms for teachers who experience chronic stress and trauma as a result of working in high-needs schools* [Unpublished doctoral dissertation]. Virginia State University.

Ortiz, A. (2020b, November). *Quality quick takes: Maintaining quality instruction in a COVID era (Issue Brief).* Virginia Department of Education, Office of School Quality.

Perry, D. L., & Daniels, M. L. (2016). Implementing trauma-informed practices in the school setting: A pilot study. *School Mental Health: A Multidisciplinary Research and Practice Journal, 8*(1), 177–188. doi:10.100712310-016-9182-3

Phifer, L. W., & Hull, R. (2016). Helping students heal: Observations of trauma-informed practices in the schools. *School Mental Health, 8*(1), 201–205. doi:10.100712310-016-9183-2

Quick, A. (2020). *Adult trauma in educational settings: How COVID-19 affects educators and operational staff.* Research Triangle Institute International. https://www.rti.org/insights/adult-trauma-educational-settings-covid

Recognize Trauma. (n.d.). *What might have happened?* Retrieved October 16, 2020, from http://recognizetrauma.org/

Sporleder, J., & Forbes, H. T. (2016). *The trauma-informed school: A step by step implementation guide for administrators and school personnel.* Beyond Consequences, LLC.

Substance Abuse and Mental Health Services Administration. (2019). *Trauma and violence.* Retrieved October 16, 2020, from https://www.samhsa.gov/trauma-violence

Walker, T. (2020, August 5). Helping students and educators recover from COVID-19 trauma. *NEA Today.* https://www.nea.org/advocating-for-change/new-from-nea/helping-students-and-educators-recover-covid-19-trauma

ADDITIONAL READING

ACEs Too High News. (2021, April) PACESs science 10. https://acestoohigh.com/aces-101/

ACEs Too High News. (2021, April) PACESs science 10. https://acestoohigh.com/aces-101/

Carver-Thomas, D., & Darling-Hammond, L. (2017). *Teacher turnover: Why it matters and what we can do about it.* Learning Policy Institute. https://learningpolicyinstitute.org/sites/default/files/product-files/Teacher_Turnover_ REPORT.pdf

Carver-Thomas, D., & Darling-Hammond, L. (2017). *Teacher turnover: Why it matters and what we can do about it.* Learning Policy Institute. https://learningpolicyinstitute.org/sites/default/files/product files/Teacher_Turnover_REPORT.pdf

Centers for Disease Control and Prevention. (2019). *Preventing adverse childhood experiences: Leveraging the best available evidence.* National Center for Injury Prevention and Control, Centers for Disease Control and Prevention. https://www.cdc.gov/violenceprevention/pdf/preventingACES.pdf

Centers for Disease Control and Prevention. (2020, April). *About the CDC-Kaiser ACE study.* https://www.cdc.gov/violenceprevention/aces/about.html

Collaborative for Academic, Social, and Emotional Learning. (2020). *What is social and emotional learning (SEL)?* https://casel.org/what-is-sel/

Collaborative for Academic, Social, and Emotional Learning. (2020). *What is social and emotional learning (SEL)?* https://casel.org/what-is-sel/

Collaborative for Academic, Social, and Emotional Learning. (2020). *What is social and emotional learning (SEL)?* https://casel.org/what-is-sel/

Craig, S. E. (2016). *Trauma-sensitive schools: Learning communities transforming children's lives, K–5.* Teachers College Press.

Craig, S. E. (2016). *Trauma-sensitive schools: Learning communities transforming children's lives, K–5.* Teachers College Press.

Forbes, H. T. (2012). *Help for Billy: A beyond consequences approach to helping challenging children in the classroom.* Beyond Consequences, LLC.

Forbes, H. T. (2012). *Help for Billy: A beyond consequences approach to helping challenging children in the classroom.* Beyond Consequences, LLC.

Graide Network. (2020, April 13). *The rise of teacher stress: (/blog-all/2018/8/1/crayons-and-cortisol-the-epidemic-of-teacher-stress).* www.thegraidenetwork.com/blog-all/2018/8/1/crayons-and-cortisol-the-

Hammond, Z. (2015). *Culturally responsive teaching and the brain: Promoting authentic engagement and rigoramong culturally and linguistically diverse students.* Corwin.

Hammond, Z. (2015). *Culturally responsive teaching and the brain: Promoting authentic engagement and rigoramong culturally and linguistically diverse students.* Corwin.

Hart, C., & Nash, F. (2020). *Coaching for teacher resilience during COVID-19: Burnout and trauma (Part 1)*. Research Triangle Institute International. https://www.rti.org/insights/coaching-teacher-resilience-during-covid-19-burnout-and-trauma

Hart, C., & Nash, F. (2020). *Coaching for teacher resilience during COVID-19: Burnout and trauma (Part 1)*. Research Triangle Institute International. https://www.rti.org/insights/coaching-teacher-resilience-during-covid-19-burnout-and-trauma

Masonbrink, A. R., & Hurley, E. (2020). Advocating for children during the COVID-19 school closures. *Pediatrics, 146*(3), 1–4. https://pediatrics.aappublications.org/content/146/3/e20201440. doi:10.1542/peds.2020-1440 PMID:32554517

Masonbrink, A. R., & Hurley, E. (2020). Advocating for children during the COVID-19 school closures. *Pediatrics, 146*(3), 1–4. https://pediatrics.aappublications.org/content/146/3/e20201440

Noddings, N. (2005). Caring in education. *The encyclopedia of informal education.* www.infed.org/biblio/noddings_caring_in_education.htm

Panorama Education. (2020a). *Measure and understand social-emotional learning*. https://www.panoramaed.com/social-emotional-learning-sel

Panorama Education. (2020a). *Measure and understand social-emotional learning*. https://www.panoramaed.com/social-emotional-learning-sel

Panorama Education. (2020b). *Teacher well-being survey*. https://www.panoramaed.com/teacher-

Panorama Education. (2020b). *Teacher well-being survey*. https://www.panoramaed.com/teacher-wellbeing-survey

Park, Y., Nakamura, J., Rush, J., & Fuxman, S. (2020). *Supporting students experiencing Trauma during the COVID-19 pandemic*. Regional Educational Laboratory Appalachia. https://ies.ed.gov/ncee/edlabs/regions/appalachia/blogs/blog30_supporting students-experiencing-trauma-during-COVID-19-pandemic.asp

Sparks, S. D. (2020, September 2). Triaging for trauma during COVID-19. *Education Week*. https://www.edweek.org/ew/articles/2020/09/03/triaging-for-trauma-duringcovid-19.html

Sporleder, J., & Forbes, H. T. (2016). *The trauma-informed school: A step by step Implementation guide for administrators and school personnel*. Beyond Consequences, LLC.

Sporleder, J., & Forbes, H. T. (2016). *The trauma-informed school: A step by step Implementation guide for administrators and school personnel*. Beyond Consequences, LLC.

Sporleder, J., & Forbes, H. T. (2016). *The trauma-informed school: A step by step Implementation guide for administrators and school personnel*. Beyond Consequences, LLC.

Wisconsin Department of Public Instruction. (2020, December). *Wisconsin's trauma sensitive school initiative*. https://dpi.wi.gov/sspw/mental-health/trauma

Wisconsin Department of Public Instruction. (2020, December). *Wisconsin's trauma sensitive school initiative*. https://dpi.wi.gov/sspw/mental-health/trauma

Wisconsin Department of Public Instruction. (2020, December). *Wisconsin's trauma sensitive school initiative*. https://dpi.wi.gov/sspw/mental-health/trauma

KEY TERMS AND DEFINITIONS

Adverse Childhood Experiences (ACEs): A list of several sources of stress identified through a national study known to have long-lasting negative effects on brain development, school performance, and adjustment into adulthood.

Collective Trauma: Similar to the definition of *trauma*, a shared experience or number of experiences that pose a threat to a large number of individuals as part of an organization or self-identified group.

Complex Trauma: A series of threatening occurrences experienced by an individual over an extended period of time, particularly from a young age.

Coping Strategies: Positive and negative activities and behaviors in which an individual will engage to help alleviate a stressful environment.

Individual Trauma: Similar to the definition of *trauma*, an experience or number of experiences that pose a threat to the existence of one person in isolation.

Resilience: The innate ability of an individual to succeed or overcome seemingly insurmountable odds despite adverse life experiences.

Social Emotional Health: Understanding one's need for connection, positive relationships, and belonging that will allow each individual to positively thrive in an environment.

Toxic Stress: A persistent string of adverse threatening experiences over a duration of time imposed on an individual, causing them to be conditioned to respond adversely to stimuli, called the *fight-or-flight response*.

Trauma: An occurrence or set of occurrences experienced by an individual whereby the experience is perceived as a threat against their existence.

Trauma-Informed Care (TIC): Acknowledging that the source of certain behaviors may be from traumatic experiences, trauma-informed care refers to the positive responses aimed at de-escalating an individual's trauma response. TIC is characterized by supportive environments of trust, collaboration, and safety.

APPENDIX 1

Figure 1.
Source: Adverse Childhood Experiences Pyramid (CDC, 2019)

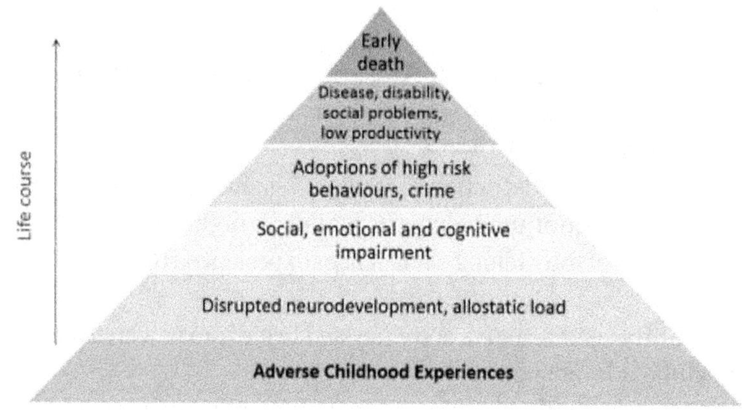

APPENDIX 2

Case Study 1: Student Trauma Teaching Notes

Questions and Answers

1. What are some of the layers of traumatic experiences Maria experienced in this scenario?

Ans.: The instructor can cycle through identifying Maria's experiences of sexual abuse by her mother's boyfriend; feelings of betrayal; not being believed by her mother; the boyfriend lying and still living with Maria's mother; Maria's feelings of loss—unable to see her mom and sister; fear that her sister is being abused.

2. How did the trauma manifest itself in this child, at school? In other words, what would you identify as traumatic responses that Maria exhibited?

Ans.: The instructor should focus on Maria's response to the teacher's tap on the shoulder, which might have been a post-traumatic stress reflex to her mother's boyfriend violating her space and privates. Maria's zoning out may be her preoccupation with thoughts of her being away from her mother and sister.

3. What are some of the supports that could be put in place to assist and be able to reach this student?

Ans.: Focus on strategies to avoid triggers, for example: (a) Teacher and student can develop a non-invasive way to get Maria's attention; (b) Provide an opportunity for a conference with a counselor before referral; (c) Group or individual counseling meetings with a trusted adult in a safe space to help Maria process home issues.

4. What types of trauma-sensitive approaches might have been helpful to Maria to allow her to navigate through her trauma responses?

Ans.: Same as response for Question 3. Focus on de-escalation. Ask Maria if she can help the teacher and administrators understand what her triggers might be. Allow her to build trust and have a voice. Allow Maria's use of headphones at appropriate times for relief.

5. Understanding that educators may not be aware of a student's background or prior experiences, how can a trauma-sensitive environment be developed to ensure that a student with Maria's background finds safety and trust so that she can be successful?

Ans.: The instructor should focus on the idea of supporting a culture of empathy. Understanding that trauma may exist, decide to create an environment of trust, care, belongingness, support. Be mindful of speech, actions, and escalating reactions toward students.

Epilogue

Educators are often conditioned to be tasked-oriented: prepare lesson plans, teach lessons, assess students on what is being taught, reteach if necessary, and make sure homework, skills, and standards are covered. Educators often feel pressure to minimize downtime and remain productive, hindering developing relationships with students. It goes back to the adage, "students don't care what you know until they know that you care." Reaching students for profound learning does not occur until relationships are developed and educators tap into students' social emotional well-being. This helps to establish trust and a sense of belonging with students. While it is possible that some students may be bombarded with negative images, toxic environmental stress, and even adverse childhood experiences, educators should work to make sure that no matter what is happening outside or at home, all students can feel that they always have a trauma-sensitive safe space to go to in the school building.

Lessons Learned

1. Understand the data on trauma and be mindful that there is a high probability that at least one of your students may have experienced trauma, whether individual or collective. Understanding this will impact your own outlook on how you need to engage all students.
2. Provide trauma-sensitive environments for students. Be mindful of the intended and unintended messages you send as an educator. Consistently show empathy, care, and patience while holding students accountable. You may not know the source of a student's trauma response, but it is prudent to recognize that trauma may have played a role. This helps to establish a safe and trusting environment that is required of a trauma-sensitive environment for all students.
3. Develop relationships with students through social-emotional learning. Impactful learning begins when students know that the teacher genuinely cares.

Case Study 2: Teacher Trauma Teaching Notes

Questions and Answers

1. What are some of the sources of trauma the teacher, Mrs. Taylor, may have experienced in this scenario?

Ans.: Identify Mrs. Taylor's experiences of toxic stress with continual unruly behaviors; her lack of classroom management strategies provides for little to no structure, and students behave accordingly. Mrs. Taylor also perceives a lack of support from the administration with her one recourse of disciplinary referrals.

2. How did the trauma manifest itself at school? In other words, what would you identify as traumatic responses that Mrs. Taylor exhibited?

Ans.: The instructor should focus on Mrs. Taylor's uncharacteristic lashing out, name-calling, and berating of students. Mrs. Taylor has reached a tipping point and has aimed her aggression at students. She remains frustrated when administrators arrive.

3. What did the principal, Mrs. Payne, do well? What could she have done differently? Why was it or was it not important for Mrs. Payne to offer that Mrs. Taylor take a walk but not leave the campus? What are some additional supports that could be put in place to assist and be able to help this teacher?

Ans.: Mrs. Payne listened, gathered information, and rendered a fair decision. She showed empathy toward Mrs. Taylor and asked her to take a walk to release stress. Perhaps the probation could have been conditional pending other immediate assistance and demonstrated effort to improve. Supports and strategies were abundant—explore other angles.

4. What types of trauma-sensitive approaches might have been helpful to Mrs. Taylor to allow her to process her trauma response and to help her self-correct for the future?

Ans.: Options might be limited for teachers who are in front of the students daily. Focus on supports and building trust between Mrs. Taylor and the administrator: Provide an open-door opportunity to allow Mrs. Taylor to seek advice from an administrator or mentor prior to behaviors and frustration escalating.

5. Understanding that educators may not be aware of a teacher's background or prior experiences, how can a trauma-sensitive environment be developed to ensure that teachers like Mrs. Taylor find safety, trust, and support so that all teachers can be successful?

Ans.: Focus on elements to support teachers: walkthroughs or check-ins for wellness rather in addition to instruction; stress relief activities for teachers; opportunities to showcase appreciation of teachers; opportunities for teachers to form PLCs to address common issues of stress.

Epilogue

Educators are held to high job performance standards and are expected to push the envelope in terms of providing quality education for students. Often, an altruistic nature pushes teachers to bend over backward to meet the daily student needs. However, data consistently shows that while teachers perform consistently, significant numbers of teachers have also reported through national surveys that teaching is highly stressful and matches the stress level of nurses. Attrition data has reflected that the consistently higher levels of stress cause them to leave. Educator training programs rightfully teach that students are always at the center of educational decision-making, but what is the cost to teachers' mental and social emotional well-being? Research suggests that schools need to culturally shift toward trauma-sensitive environments, for teachers as well as students. Teachers who are stressed and end up leaving the profession provides a great level of instability and has a negative impact on student achievement in the long run due to instability. As such a focus needs to be turned to a culture of empathy for meeting the needs of educators as well, so that they may effectively meet the needs of students.

Lessons Learned

1. The teaching profession involves high and persistent levels of stress. The education profession must take note of this and understand that teachers are human and have basic needs. Teachers whose needs are neglected may end up being detrimental to themselves as well as to the teaching profession.
2. Provide trauma-sensitive environments for teachers. While educators strive to meet student needs, school leaders need to be intentional in showing ensuring teachers empathy, trust, and care. Teachers may be facing stress at home as well as at school, including constant pressure to perform, irate parents, unruly students, and unsupportive administrators. Trauma-sensitive structures should be put in place to ensure teachers do not come to a tipping point of frustration and leave the profession.
3. Celebrate positive teaching results often and in both small and big ways. Provide avenues for positive stress relief, support, and encouragement where necessary. Allow teachers to have a voice and address concerns in positive PLCs. Like students, when teachers know that their leaders care, they will continue to bend over backward to do their jobs well.

Case Study 3: COVID-19 and Collective Trauma Teaching Notes

Questions and Answers

Because this is a multilayered real-time scenario, teaching notes offer a plan for processing the scenario rather than summarizing the many potential combinations of responses. Utilize the scenario to foster trauma-sensitive leaders rather than finding simple answers.

1. Identify and explain the layers of trauma present within the scenario.

Ans.: This case study is meant to represent multiple layers and sources of stress and collective trauma as a result of the COVID-19 pandemic from the many stakeholders: students, parents, and teachers. Take the time to dissect each communication and sources of trauma being reflected. (A chart might be useful consisting of 5 columns. Column 1 begins with this question – See Appendix 3).

2. As the new principal, how would you respond to these communications?

Ans.: Break students into groups and ask them: "Without overthinking, how would you respond as principal?" Respond by completing Column 2 of the response chart by looking at each communication.

3. Revisit your responses to Question 2. As a trauma-informed practitioner, were your responses trauma sensitive? If not, how would you re-formulate your responses to each of the communications as trauma-sensitive responses?

Ans.: Column 3 - The instructor may have students revisit responses in the same or different groups to analyze responses against the trauma-informed care definition. Have them process different trauma-sensitive responses to each communication and share out how it was different from their traditional response. How would the different responses impact the stakeholder?

4. What types of reactive trauma-informed strategies or supports would be beneficial to assist each different stakeholder group through their various concerns?

Ans.: Column 4 - Have students break into trauma-informed care teams, representing different roles, such as administrator, teacher, school counselor, and social worker. Have teams brainstorm trauma-informed reactive responses for each communication here in Column 4.

5. While traumatic events may not be readily apparent to an administrator or teacher, understanding that traumatic events can reoccur, how can a proactive sustainable trauma-sensitive environment be developed to ensure the safety, trust, and support of all stakeholders moving forward?

Ans.: Column 5 - In the same trauma-informed care teams representing the various roles, Column 5 will include team brainstorm ideas of long-term proactive trauma-informed responses that can be systemically instituted to meet the needs of stakeholders during and after the collective crisis or traumatic event.

Epilogue

The pandemic has undoubtedly been the source of ongoing panic, fear, instability, uncertainty, and stress in every aspect of everyone's lives across the globe. Educational systems, built on routines and stability, have been turned upside down. Abrupt change was thrust upon the educational community forcing educators to have to deal with new delivery modes of instruction and loss of physical connectedness giving way to a shift to virtual spaces, superimposed with changed dynamics in the home, family, and parent workspaces, enough to cause major collective stress. The communications in each scenario represent real problems that school and community stakeholders have been facing every day in the pandemic. School systems and school leaders have had to deal with and problem-solve through each of these types of scenarios over the past several months, and the challenges have persisted. As aspiring, newly appointed, or seasoned teachers and administrators, this has been a new daily challenge, literally "building the plane as it flies." A bigger challenge as schools continue to push through is for schools to adjust and provide short-term and long-term systemic trauma-sensitive environments for all stakeholders during and after a traumatic event or organizational crisis. This case study is about working through that challenge.

Lessons Learned

1. Education has been thrust into a new normal, and educators have to embrace the change. It will not be business as usual after the effects of the pandemic. Technological innovations that educators saw as a novel tool prior to the pandemic may stick around as new modes of instructional, informational, and communications delivery.
2. With the many sources of stress and trauma bombarding children, adults, families, and collective organizations, creating trauma-sensitive environments are not a passing fad. Trauma-informed care strategies and support will always be necessary. While it has been true for schools in the past, now more than ever, schools will need to be places of safety, trust, and collaboration in order to get through a crisis.
3. Trauma-sensitive and trauma-informed care, building social-emotional connections and relationships with stakeholders, and the culture of empathy are interrelated parts of the educational environment. In organizations with members who have experienced individual or collective trauma, trauma sensitivity, social-emotional connections, empathy, trust, and safety are key ingredients to breaking through to impactful learning.

APPENDIX 3

Table 2. Sample Chart for Case Study #3

Layers of Trauma	Communication Responses	Responses Trauma Sensitive? Yes/No	Reactive Trauma-Informed Strategies	Proactive Trauma-Informed Strategies

Chapter 9
Organizational Resilience During Times of Trauma

Cynthia Calloway Rhone
University of Phoenix, USA

ABSTRACT

Effective communication and resilience are integral components in an organization's structure, particularly during and after situations of trauma. Trauma includes both internal factors (i.e., layoffs, mergers, unexpected changes in management, lack of positive social support) and external factors (natural disasters, economic insecurity, social violence). An organization's level of resilience to these factors is determined by the event's type, timing, location, rate of recurrence, and duration. In addition, proactive planning impacts organizational resilience. This chapter will focus on the importance of resilience during times of trauma, how resilience relates to leadership, and mental health experiences by employees.

INTRODUCTION

Organizational resilience during times of trauma is an organization's ability to establish an environment that improves employee productivity, positive outcomes, and positive working relationships amid prolonged contact with adverse and challenging events. The literature has established that researchers hold differing viewpoints on the concept of resilience and how it may affect organizational success or failure. Lee et al. (2017) posited that the concept of resilience relates to a period when customary organizational routines are interrupted because of an unexpected catastrophic event. During this author's doctoral journey from 2010 to 2015, she experienced a catastrophic and traumatic event that could have led to an interruption in her own journey. In 2010, the author experienced the death of a niece, who lost her battle with cancer. The author was devastated because this was her favorite niece. The event was so devastating that the author considered taking time away from classes to regroup. Before making a decision, the author contacted a professor at that time to share the situation. The professor offered class modifications so that the author could meet program requirements and complete the coursework.

As time progressed, the author remembered the many talks with her niece about furthering their education, and being advocates for children. As a result of remembering those conversations, the author

DOI: 10.4018/978-1-7998-7016-6.ch009

was motivated to continue and eventually completed the coursework on time without modifications. The author believes that it was resilience and a changed mental state that led her to complete the program and earn her degree. Greene et al. (2020) asserted that the concept of "building resilience" also relates to "professional resilience", which is an individual's ability to succeed during adverse situations. (Greene et al. (2020) explained that resilience is the ability to demonstrate progress through challenges as people develop a strong support system.

Current research also reveals the necessity to develop strategies that will promote organizational resilience, especially regarding healthcare workers during the COVID-19 pandemic. As a result of the COVID-19 pandemic, healthcare workers faced inadequate resources such as Personal Protective Equipment (PPE) shortages while combating the deadly virus. With a lack of proper PPE, healthcare workers experienced emotional stress in their attempts to remain safe, to not get sick and spread the virus to patients and family members.

Arreglado, et al., (2018) indicated that the nursing profession has become a focal point of research to highlight strategies that can be implemented in the workplace to strengthen an individual's resilience. Several studies explore ways to increase and promote resilient strategies to improve work performance during organizational trauma. This chapter on organizational resilience during times of trauma aims to:

- Examine ways to improve organizational resilience.
- Discuss how organizations methodically prepare for and persevere through unexpected trauma.
- Illustrate how organizational resilience impacts leadership during COVID-19.
- Identify leadership structures that preserve organizational resilience in an environment of trust to empower employees to communicate problem-solving ideas to leadership.

BACKGROUND

The author is extremely passionate about the title of this chapter*: Organizational Resilience during Times of Trauma*. This passion is a result of her personal experience as a teacher, building and division administrator. Researching characteristics of resilience, organizational resilience, leadership styles, working with or leading staff in times of trauma, crisis and/or unpleasant situations, provided the author with the opportunity to personally reflect on experiences that she actually witnessed or those in which she had direct involvement. The experience of researching this topic provided the author with new insights when reflecting on whether past administrative decisions were justified.

Were the decisions this author made at the time in the best interest of the staff and students? Did those decisions lead to increased academic achievement? Academic achievement was a focal point in determining the success of the division's strategic plan. Therefore, improved instructional strategies had to be delivered to improve standardized test scores. As the organizational and instructional leader, the author was responsible for ensuring that the faculty had opportunities to participate in professional development programs to address instructional needs. Instructional needs are important for staff and students, but also emotional and social needs should have been addressed to help them become more resilient (Brooks, 2006).

Students need positive relationships with trustworthy adults, who will uphold confidentiality, and who listen to them. Supportive and caring adults in schools should also show empathy, involve students in the decision-making process, and be good role models. To address student's emotional needs, Brooks

(2006) indicated that resilience-building in schools for students can be attained by school personnel taking the following actions:

- recognizing student's strengths,
- rewarding and acknowledging student accomplishments
- encouraging class participation,
- connecting with students by knowing their names,
- getting involved when students are experiencing a crisis,
- and expressing high expectations for their accomplishment.

During times of trauma, the social and emotional needs of the staff should also be addressed in order to help them build resilience and efficiently and productively perform their duties and responsibilities to students. According to Brooks (2006) if teachers experience high anxiety levels, lack adequate instructional training, or are not supported by their school administrators, they may be ineffective in building resilience in their students. Therefore, just as students need support from teachers to ensure success in building resilience, teachers need to be supported by administrators. Teacher's resilience is strengthened when enhanced by encouraging feedback from supervisors and colleagues. Resilience is also enhanced when immediate supervisors demonstrate support for teachers by recognizing their accomplishments. Resilience is also demonstrated through communicating high expectations to teachers and staff by allowing them to participate in the school's decision-making process related to the mission of the school (Brooks, 2006). Therefore, resilience can be considered a process that contributes to positive results in adverse situations (Brooks, 2006).

Transformational Leadership Theory

Transformational leadership is a style of leadership that allows followers to innovate and create change that will help grow and shape the future success of an organization (Bass & Riggio, 2006). Further, transformational leadership theory describes how successful leaders value the beliefs, ideals, and needs of their followers and lead change within their organizations by motivating and inspiring their followers (Burns, 1978). Transformational leaders work with their followers to identify changes within the organization, develop a vision for change to guide the organization through the transformation process, and successfully move through the change process with all members of the group, staying committed to successful outcomes (Bass & Riggio, 2006; Burns, 1978).

At the beginning of each calendar school year, school divisions offer staff development activities for two to three days during the week prior to students' arrival. The activities are typically concurrent sessions that cover topics such as classroom management, developing a strategic plan, increasing student achievement, academic accountability and accommodating outside agencies to work with students in the schools. Building administrators are also in attendance to work with staff from their schools. The author suggests that these activities are examples of transformational leadership.

Additionally, Andrews (2019) stated transformational leadership presents opportunities for both leaders and followers to demonstrate individual professional growth, acquire new skills, and improve their organizational environment. These characteristics are an integral part of leadership's role in supporting the organization's goals and vision. An important aspect of transformational leadership is a leader's ability to mentor staff (Andrews, 2019). Through peer guidance, a mutual bond of trust and confidence develops between leaders and staff. Throughout this leadership process, staff gains skills to enter future leadership positions. Therefore, staff plays a vital role in changing the culture of the organization.

TRAUMA AND RESILIENCE DURING THE GLOBAL PANDEMIC

During times of trauma or dramatic change, organizations must make adjustments to normal business operations (Brown & Sheppard, 2014). An example of this type of trauma is a school's incorporation of technological improvements to address administrative procedures and directives. Some researchers view trauma as having to confront an unfamiliar situation like a technology upgrade to meet new demands of new technological advancements (Brown & Sheppard, 2014). The individual trauma can be seen when staff members are not comfortable with new training on programs to be implemented. Brown and Sheppard (2014) indicated that although teachers may receive a one-day single session or presentation by a technology professional, this upgrade could still present a challenge to them. According to Brown and Sheppard (2014), some teachers may be "technophobic" (p. 89) which means they will possibly avoid interaction with the technological advancements.

The COVID-19 pandemic is another example of how trauma may cause change that can impact routines for healthcare workers. Additionally, the trauma of the pandemic demonstrates how these healthcare workers showed resilience in creating short-term solutions to current problems. In the spring of 2020, hospital admission procedures were disrupted due to the high volume of COVID-19 patients. Montes and Suarez (2020) asserted that doctors and nurses practiced heuristics techniques as a way to make swift triage decisions based upon patient diagnosis. A heuristic technique is any approach to problem solving or self-discovery that employs a practical method that is not guaranteed to be optimal, perfect, or rational, but is still sufficient for reaching an immediate, short-term goal (Myers, 2010). Although hospitals had established admission procedures, the pandemic required them to substitute new routines and procedures to account for the global pandemic. Another example is how health care workers who were not treating COVID-19 patients decided to treat patients who were less ill over the phone or computer instead of in-person visits to practice social distancing.

The resiliency of an organization is determined by how it strategically responds to systematic changes. According to Johnson (2020), a leaders' responsibility in fostering resilience during times of trauma, is to concentrate on prioritizing the physical and emotional well-being of employees. For example, during the COVID-19 pandemic, employees shared concerns of safety, job security, and how to care for family members or themselves in case of sickness. Johnson (2020) also mentioned a leader's role is to establish trust and transparency with employees that would lead toward building positive relationships. In the wake of the COVID-19 pandemic, leadership has become an integral component in building resilience and helping employees to adapt to future challenges.

Warrick (2018) indicated a leader's role and responsibility in fostering resilience during times of change also can be reflected in the leader's leadership style. During change resulting from a crisis, leaders should be candid and forthright with their staff concerning the crisis. Leaders should actively and efficiently involve appropriate staff in the decision-making process related to changes in the organization to improve resilience. Staff should be kept abreast of the organization's progress, and obstacles that may have occurred to impede set goals for establishing resilience. Warrick (2018) continued in fostering resilience leaders should value their staff by demonstrating respect, and listening to their contribution of ideas in problem-solving.

There are underlying methods that benefit resilience for organizations that have been impacted by internal and external factors in the wake of a trauma. External factors, such as economic insecurity, global political instability, and climate change can directly affect employee productivity (Bubb & Daly, 2020). Internal factors, including mergers, layoffs, unexpected changes in management also can cause employees to employ resilient strategies to overcome challenges in the workplace (Winter, 2019).

Research has indicated that healthcare workers were directly impacted by both internal and external factors related to the pandemic. This public health concern challenged leaders to monitor, evaluate, and improve working conditions as staff cared for a high volume of patients in adverse conditions. Regarding frontline workers, Rangachari and Woods (2020) indicated that resilience is described as the ability to manage situations with on-site materials to deliver the best possible patient care in spite of environmental obstacles.

Organizational Resilience Theory

Resilience is the ability to withstand and bounce back from the challenges related to adversity, discontent, and hardship during times of trauma (Ledesma, 2014). Resilience originates from the Latin word 'resiliens', which refers to the pliant or elastic quality of a substance (Greene et al., 2002). Masten (2005) defines resilience as a class of phenomena characterized by good outcomes in spite of threats to adaptation or development. Regarding organizational resilience, Masten (2018) adds that resilience is the capability of an organization to successfully adjust to major challenges that pose a risk to the organization's growth. From conducting studies on individual resilience, Edenborough et al. (2007), concluded that resilience is the ability of individuals to positively overcome adversity which results in improving individual strength through implementing strategies to build positive professional relationships while "developing emotional insight, achieving life balance and spirituality, and becoming more reflective."

In developing organizational resilience during times of trauma, Rangachari and Woods (2020) noted that a key public health concern was sustaining an adequate healthcare workforce during the pandemic. Healthcare workers concerns, included securing the proper PPE for safety at work and protection from spreading the infection to family at home. Additionally, healthcare workers asked leaders to provide training programs to increase knowledge that would encourage teamwork, cohesive efforts, and communication. Healthcare workers also felt it was crucial for leaders to be on the frontlines on a regular basis as the healthcare teams cared for COVID-19 patients. The implementation of these strategies would afford leaders, such as hospital administrators, nurse managers, and department chairs the opportunity to experience the crisis first hand and to in turn provide reassurance and vital resources for emotional support.

Unforeseen events like a global pandemic require a swift and methodical leadership response. Therefore, organizations must know how to reconfigure their structural dynamics to cope with extended times of stress and uncertainty. During times of trauma, an organization's leader must implement strategies to promote resilience in the work environment. Leaders can help to build resilience through a reassuring climate, defining a positive direction as they move forward with employees (Tam, 2020).

Organizational Resilience in the Education Sector

Organizational resilience is linked to the workplace and describes how employees are able to persevere and adapt to unforeseen events. The onset of the COVID-19 pandemic affected almost every organization. The pandemic not only triggered the closing of businesses, but the closing of US schools, which led to alternative means of teaching. In fact, Johnson et al. (2020) conducted a study of organizational resilience in the early weeks of the COVID-19 pandemic. Their study included 897 teachers and administrators in 672 public and private post secondary institutions in the United States. The researchers found that with a few exceptions, the teachers and administrators were able to quickly adapt to new ways of teaching and new learning approaches. The author believes that this ability to quickly adapt is an example of organizational resilience for the study participants. When teachers adjusted to the delivery of new instructional strategies during the pandemic, their resilience was a factor to ensure success for their students.

Rangachari and Woods (2020) stated that resilient organizations reorganize their structure to accomplish agreed upon objectives. Resilient organizations make sure that they include both leaders and staff in decision-making and problem-solving strategies, establishing goals and maintaining a system to provide feedback. To accomplish this, organizational leaders must incorporate resilient learning tools to assist employees through catastrophic events (Bubb & Daly, 2020). Leaders should receive training to support employees through focused healing and renewal processes and the leaders themselves should also have access to supportive social networks from external agencies, trustworthy colleagues, and peers (Ledesma, 2014). Also, leaders should have access to and receive transformational personal development support to avoid seclusion and form partnerships (Ledesma, 2014).

According to Rangachari and Woods (2020), organizational resilience includes the following stages:

1. **Foresight** which references the ability to predict catastrophe.
2. **Coping** is about having the ability to prevent an event from becoming worse.
3. **Recovery** is the ability to heal from a traumatic event through reflection, learning, and growth.

Bubb and Daly (2020) explained that organizational resilience is the capability of an organization to face unexpected adversities, return to the original operational state of the company, and succeed, regardless of different demands, levels of stress, and new opportunities. In reference to the stages of organizational resilience, the United States' education system and businesses did not have the foresight to predict the pandemic. However, in the second stage of coping, regrouping of strategies was used to safely reopen businesses and schools. The author believes that educational institutions and businesses are in the recovery stage and may be in a constant mode of reflection and using external resources to learn strategies to improve their situation during and after the pandemic. Organizational resilience during times of trauma is assessed by the scope of successful change over time, revealing an organization's strengths and ability to endure catastrophic events (Darkow, 2019; Kolay, 2016).

Another example of an environmental transformation was Hurricane Katrina, August 29, 2005, which resulted in the disruption of the education system, businesses, and loss of life and property. Johnson, et al. (2020) reported the Sloan Semester was a project that was made available for students to continue their education who had been affected in that geographic area. Over one hundred institutions provided continuity in online courses for thousands of students to sustain their studies. The project proved to be advantageous because students were able to continue their studies in a virtual environment. The Sloan Semester resulted in student-to-student interface to engage them in class discussions. The virtual environment gave students the opportunity to lend emotional support to each other which was essential for their welfare as they dealt with the trauma of Hurricane Katrina.

However, Johnson and Rainey (2007), share a different perspective on the education system after the trauma of Hurricane Katrina, especially emphasizing the impact on African American Historically Black Colleges and Universities (HBCUs). A high number of students and staff were dislocated from three HBCU's; Dillard University, Xavier University and Southern University at New Orleans to areas all over the United States. As reported by Johnson and Rainey (2007) of displaced students, some were able to evacuate New Orleans prior to the storm spiraling from a category one hurricane to a category five. Students were transported out of Dillard University in New Orleans to Centenary College in Shreveport, Louisiana, that gave housing accommodations for Dillard students. Due to the severity of Hurricane Katrina, students were given three hours to evacuate the campus. As a result, some students were able to find a means to get home by leaving with friends or family.

Students faced the dilemma of continuing their education while experiencing the trauma of Hurricane Katrina. They were welcomed by and enrolled in 67 other HBCU's around the country, who were completely unaware of the students' academic or financial status from their original home school. Southern University in Baton Rouge accepted 960 students; Texas Southern University accepted 600 students; Jackson State University accepted 152 students; and Howard University accepted 12 students. While trying to persevere to complete their education, students received assistance from FEMA, the American Red Cross, and the Katrina Financial Assistance Center. They also received "medical, allied health, public health, social and psychological services, religious support and educational assistance for pre-school, primary and secondary students" (Johnson & Rainey, 2007, p. 7).

The Tom Joyner Foundation initiated an HBCU Scholarship Relief Fund which assisted students from Dillard, Xavier, and Southern University at New Orleans that had been affected by Hurricane Katrina. The HBCU Scholarship Relief Fund contributed $1,000,000.00 to assist students from the three HBCU's who had to relocate because of Hurricane Katrina. The Fund also gave each student from Dillard, Xavier, and Southern University at New Orleans a generous gift of $1,000.00. Greene, et al., (2020) explained that resilience is the ability to demonstrate progress through challenges as people develop a strong support system. The students who were displaced by Hurricane Katrina demonstrated resilience during this period of uncertainty, while developing a strong support system. According to Ledesma (2014) resilience is the ability to withstand the challenges related to adversity, discontent, and hardship during times of trauma. The students who attended the three HBCU's exhibited resilience by continuing their education despite the adversity they faced.

Duchek (2020) stated that resilience can be treated as an outcome of adverse events, determined by how an organization performs during the stages of anticipation, coping, and adaptation. To survive an organization must employ strategies at different stages of the crisis. These strategies must be implemented prior to, for the duration of, and following the catastrophic event. Leaders can prioritize these procedures to determine how they interchange throughout the stages of the crises. Organizational resilience supports the idea that effective leaders must implement various strategies during the different phases of the catastrophic event (Darkow, 2019). Leadership must access resilient resources to cope with unexpected trauma (Duchek et al., 2020). At the same time, organizations must maintain an exceptional level of performance, to realize success and strength. Buzzanell (2018) indicated that resilience is a component of organizational communication, which allows processes to be restored through unification. In addition, it promotes beneficial changes during and after unexpected trauma like natural disasters, career changes, and/or loss of human resources.

TRANSFORMATIONAL LEADERSHIP

Loree (2020) stated that leaders should foster an environment where teams and individuals are essential to the decision-making process through the communication of ideas. Organizational leaders must ensure that employees are aware of their job responsibilities and exhibit determination to persevere in difficult circumstances. However, in certain situations, leaders may not disclose pertinent information with organizational members in an effort to curtail distractions.

Popa (2019) stated that strategic communication is evident through cohesive organizational goals, objectives, values, and mission and vision statements. Strategic communication can directly and positively contribute to an organization's achievements. Popa (2019) mentioned that strategic communication plans should concentrate on supporting communication avenues to involve internal and external stakeholders and company personnel. When leaders establish strategic communication, organizational objectives and leadership actions set an example in implementing objectives (Popa, 2019). Leaders have told staff, "Do as I say, not as I do" (Popa, 2019, p. 175). Unhealthy environments are created when words are not equivalent to actions, leading to distrust and disengagement between leaders and employees.

In connecting communication theory with resilience, Rangachari and Woods (2020) stated the importance of communication between intensive care unit (ICU) nurses during the COVID-19 pandemic. As a result of the high volume of COVID-19 patients, the ICU nurses implemented a "workaround" process to ensure patient safety and accuracy of patient information. The nurses created and used written handoff sheets and supplemental verbal information at the end of their shifts. These sheets were essential in providing the arriving nurses with a medical summary of patients' progress and critical information like medication adjustments.

Healthcare organization leaders provided significant support to healthcare workers who experienced emotional distress during the COVID-19 pandemic (Rangachari & Woods, 2020). This support established employee trust in their organization regarding the prioritization of employee well-being and safety. For example, if the ICU nurses trust their organization, they may feel psychologically secure and empowered to contact their managers with critical concerns on safety and workarounds on the frontlines. Therefore, healthcare leaders should ensure a safe environment for workers to communicate concerns to managers. Employee trust, emotional safety, and empowerment are vital components to encouraging an environment that will result in quality patient care in the face of challenges or trauma. These components are fundamental to preserving organizational resilience and retaining employees, as well as focusing on patient safety during and after a pandemic.

Marsen (2020) indicated that an organizational crisis can interrupt the entire management of an organization, including stakeholders, community leaders, and employees. Organizational leaders should address situations from a communication viewpoint to understand and plan for a crisis (Marsen, 2020). To communicate accurate information to employees, leaders must know that crises will differ depending on the type of catastrophe, degree of damage, number of stakeholders affected, and how much of the crisis was the company's responsibility. All parties involved in a crisis situation should participate in problem-solving strategies, strategic planning, and interpersonal communication. Marsen (2020) also indicated the importance of focusing on resolving problems that occurred during the crisis to establish credibility with the public and stakeholders.

Research shows that organizational trauma has hit the healthcare profession hard due to COVID-19. According to Arreglado, et al. (2018), transformational leaders in the field of professional nursing should establish interventions to encourage employees to identify individual potential to foster a resilient environment. Leaders in nurse management should develop strategies in critical thinking to solve problems and determine solutions for future situations. Nurse leaders can generate work-life balance initiatives for new and veteran nurses. Another strategy is to partner a veteran nurse with a novice nurse to share support and handle unforeseen and/or unfamiliar situations in their medical environment.

According to Rangachari and Woods (2020), healthcare workers stated that they felt it was important to work for leaders who listen to staff needs and who provide emotional and social support. Burnout is a key factor to consider as organizational leaders design programs to address employee satisfaction. The topic of burnout was exacerbated by the exclusion of employees from the decision-making process. In addition, organizations may see an increase in the retention of staff and the well-being of its patients. Rangachari and Woods (2020) noted that resilience training should be implemented in conjunction with other strategies to effectively address employee burnout. Nevertheless, leadership should establish an environment of mutual trust, enabling healthcare workers to voice their safety concerns and become involved in the decision-making process.

According to Tam (2020), other interventions or strategies that effective leaders can use to promote organizational resilience includes problem-solving techniques, especially when established means do not appear beneficial or productive. COVID-19 has forced leaders to be swift, use critical thinking skills, and be responsive and inventive with ideas that will inevitably return the organization to its original state or offer improved outcomes. This strategy will also assist the organization in being prepared for future unforeseen traumas.

At one IBM company, leaders displayed signs of "empathy, solidarity, and understanding" (Bubb & Daly, 2020, p. 22) during a crisis. The organization implemented Slack, a channel where leadership could communicate with employees, share organizational solutions, and provide staff support. Slack was also a means for employees to encourage colleagues, share resources, and send messages. The open communication channel encouraged the implementation of other strategies to assist employees in achieving a work-life balance. The IBM Work from Home Pledge, initiated by the IBM Executive Women's Council, was developed to offer work-from-home opportunities for its employees. The pledge was a set of expectations to help employees have a less stressful work experience during the pandemic.

Transformational Leadership and Resilience

Research shows that transformational leadership is crucial to establishing resilience in an organization (Warrick, 2018). The importance of strong leadership in leading employees through the stages of resilience promotes recovery and advancement. Leaders must understand they can benefit from visibility during a traumatic event. Warrick (2018) described transformational leadership as achieving a new status through significant process changes. Transformational leadership, according to Warrick (2018), is a method whereby leaders create lucrative organizations resulting in notable, positive changes in individuals, teams, and the organization. This author believes leaders can find success implementing the established mission and vision of the organization.

From 1994 to 2007, this author worked as a building administrator. In adhering to the division's mission and vision, the same responsibilities had to be implemented in each school as part of the strategic plan. There were challenges in the later years of the author's administration that resulted in teams working together to achieve the goals of the program. The work team philosophy in an organization can develop strategies to overcome work place adversities. Strategic human resource management (SHRM) strategies can ensure that organizations hire and maintain skilled, dedicated workers (Caliskan, 2010).

SHRM can support an organization by offering human resources initiatives. Efficient human resources solutions can result in better organizational performance.

Transformational leadership has different factors that must be considered for organizational resilience to be successful (Andrews, 2019). Transformational leaders promote opportunities for personal and professional growth among its employees. Staff may receive challenging assignments to enhance their skills. Knowledge and experience of the organization can be shared with staff in an effort to become leaders in the organization. Many factors within transformational leadership must be considered to achieve organizational resilience (Andrews, 2019). Transformational leaders should promote opportunities for personal and professional growth among employees. Staff may receive challenging assignments to enhance their skills. Knowledge and organizational history can be shared with staff to encourage rising leaders in the organization.

To realize individual and/or team resilience, transformational leaders may implement confidence-building strategies. At the onset of the pandemic, Rangachari and Woods (2020) indicated that it was the responsibility of leaders to provide a safe, organized hospital environment for the patients, staff, and community. Without leadership support, emotional stress caused by the pandemic could adversely affect staff safety, morale, and retention. As noted, during the pandemic, healthcare workers felt leaders should be visible on the frontlines when caring for patients. Transformational leadership has different factors that must be considered for organizational resilience to be successful (Andrews, 2019). Transformational leaders promote opportunities for personal and professional growth among its employees. Staff may receive challenging assignments to enhance their skills. Knowledge and experience of the organization can be shared with staff in an effort to become leaders in the organization.

Many factors within transformational leadership must be considered to achieve organizational resilience (Andrews, 2019). Transformational leaders should promote opportunities for personal and professional growth among employees. Staff may receive challenging assignments to enhance their skills. Knowledge and organizational history can be shared with staff to encourage rising leaders in the organization. To realize individual and/or team resilience, transformational leaders may implement confidence-building strategies. At the onset of the pandemic, Rangachari and Woods (2020) indicated that it was the responsibility of leaders to provide a safe, organized hospital environment for the patients, staff, and community. Without leadership support, emotional stress caused by the pandemic could adversely affect staff safety, morale, and retention. As noted, during the pandemic, healthcare workers felt leaders should be visible on the frontlines when caring for patients.

From 1994 to 2007, this author worked as a building administrator where there was shared responsibility among the staff. For instance, instead of scheduling weekly staff meetings during after school hours, grade level meetings were conducted during a block of time that was considered individual and team meeting times. The grade level meetings were conducted once a week to discuss grade level student concerns, along with student achievement, and recommendations for improvement. The grade level meetings replaced after school faculty meetings. The staff found this process to be more advantageous because not all grade levels or departments had the same issues that needed to be addressed. Staff appeared to be very accepting of the idea because meetings were agenda and time driven to address concerns only pertaining to each grade level. Therefore, leaders have the foresight to pursue change to increase morale and motivate staff resulting in improved performance levels. With this example, Collins (2001) indicated that good-to-great (Level 5) organizational leaders require a focus of "getting the right people on the bus" (p. 57). Sometimes leaders must change personnel positions or hire new personnel in organizations to perform at a Level 5 to ensure that decisions are made in the best interest of the organization.

Transformational leadership is valuable in an organization's aim to obtain organizational resilience during traumatic times. An organization's health can be adversely affected by trauma through both individual and group dynamics. Resilience, which is a form of wellness, contributes to the strength and recovery of individuals and the organization (Hormann, 2018). For example, when a school division initiated a new division-wide initiative that affected all staff and administrators in the organization, transformational leadership played a vital role in the success of the program. For the school year 1989-90, a school division changed to the Middle School Program philosophy (Collins, 2001). The original grades levels were Lower Elementary K-3; Upper Elementary grades 4-6; Junior High School grades were seven and eight. The high school consisted of grades 9-12. With the implementation of the Middle School concept, the elementary grades became K-5; Middle School Grades were 6-8; and high school remained the same (Collins, 2001).

Changing to the Middle School concept was an enormous undertaking for the entire school division especially for organizational and transformational leadership at the Central Office and for administrators at the building levels (Collins, 2001). Teachers were reassigned to different schools based on their responses to a survey of their preferences to teach. This process involved the Human Resources Department. There were staff members who had worked together for years that were now going in a different direction based on their choice. For example, two teachers who taught grades four and six in the original school division upper elementary grades, no longer worked together after the middle school concept because grade four was now in the elementary school while grade six was placed in the new middle school. Before the actual middle school concept was implemented in 1989, potential building administrators and staff participated in prior organizational strategies to learn the concept of middle school practices (Collins, 2001).

Building and division administrators visited and observed well-established middle school programs in other cities. The author believes that endorsing the middle school concept, was an example of organizational resilience and transformational leadership. Organizational resilience was demonstrated during the implementation of the middle school concept. For the first couple of years, there were challenges. However, building and division administrators exhibited resilience in their ability and determination to succeed with the middle school concept. It is the author's belief that transformational leadership was demonstrated during the implementation of the middle school concept. This transformational leadership style established long-term networks that provided social, emotional, and cognitive resources necessary for fostering organizational resilience.

SOLUTIONS AND RECOMMENDATIONS

Organizational resilience in the workplace requires the ability of staff to persevere through and adapt to unforeseen events (Ledesma, 2014; Masten, 2018). The traumatic events discussed earlier in this chapter, have affected many organizations, resulting in employees implementing best practices to persevere through workplace adversities. Transformational leadership is vital to the success of an organization experiencing trauma.

Transformational Leadership Best Practices

Transformational leaders must be willing to accept input from employees. Employees should be promoted from within the organization, contributing to positive morale and increased performance during a crisis. Leaders also should actively listen to employees and be mindful of the work environment. To ensure that they are transformational, leaders should rely on and trust experienced employees for their insights. To be effective, leaders should work to stay informed about issues in the external environment that may impact the organization. And should in turn share this information with staff to exhibit a proactive instead of reactive attitude. Additionally, creating an environment of trust fosters resilient leadership. This includes publicly recognizing members in the organization for their contributions.

In establishing an environment of trust, open and honest dialogue between leadership and staff, empowers staff to discuss problem-solving ideas. Organizations need a firm communication policy, as well as both formal and informal communication programs and channels. Leaders should assess their own communication effectiveness on a regular basis. Organizational leaders should update employees prior to any environmental changes, be knowledgeable of the environmental climate, and provide positive affirmations to employees. Leaders must be willing to accept recommendations for change, be accountable, provide opportunities for professional growth, invest in staff, and celebrate small victories. Also, staff should be involved in decision-making processes. Leaders should disclose decisions to employees prior to the release of information to the community.

FUTURE RESEARCH DIRECTIONS

The goal of this chapter is to illustrate how an organization can use both leadership and staff to develop and implement successful resiliency methods using transformational leadership. Future research should focus on how effective transformational leaders respond to staff who oppose resiliency methods. Other studies could also explore if diversity in the workforce influences an organization's resiliency. Finally, future studies could identify relationships between employees' mental well-being and returning to the workplace following a traumatic event.

CONCLUSION

Resilience is influenced by an organization's transformational leadership during times of trauma. Transformational leaders offer employees opportunities for professional and personal growth and recognizes staff performance to help increase morale. Also, staff members should be afforded opportunities to initiate strategies to participate in organizational success.

During traumatic events, employees and leaders must employ effective communication strategies. Leaders must display confidence in setting goals, adhering to the mission and vision of the organization, and empowering staff to work independently or in teams. Resilient leaders who implement these techniques will have a direct impact on their organizations.

ACKNOWLEDGMENT

The work in this chapter received no specific grant from any funding agency in the public, commercial, or not-for-profit sectors.

REFERENCES

Andrews, M. R. (2019). Can transformational leaders improve your organization? *Contract Management, 59*, 38-42, 44-45. Retrieved from https://www.proquest.com/docview/2282756406?accountid=45853

Arreglado, T. M., Garcia-Dia, M. J., & O'Flaherty, D. (2018). Cultivating resilience in the workplace: Relationship between demographic factors and nurses' perception of resilience. *Journal of Nursing Practice Applications & Reviews of Research*, *8*(1), 6–13. doi:10.13178/jnparr.2018.0801.0803

Bass, B. M., & Riggio, R. E. (2006). *Transformational leadership*. Psychology Press. doi:10.4324/9781410617095

Beaulieu, D. (2013). Remembering Boston: Nearly 3 months after the Boston Marathon bombing, physicians say the tragedy taught lessons that will forever influence the care of and response to patients. *Medical Economics*, *90*(13). PMID:25233708

Brooks, J. E. (2006). Strengthening resilience in children and youths: Maximizing opportunities through the schools. *Children & Schools*, *28*(2), 69–76. doi:10.1093/cs/28.2.69

Brown, J., & Sheppard, B. (2014). Leadership for a new vision of public school classrooms: Technology-smart and learner-centered. *Journal of Educational Administration*, *52*(1), 84–96. doi:10.1108/JEA-03-2012-0027

Bubb, D., & Daly, J. (2020). Creating whole-company resilience through emotional health and well-being. *People and Strategy, 43*(3).

Burns, J. M. (1978). *Leadership*. Harper & Row.

Buzzanell, P. M. (2018). Organizing resilience as adaptive-transformational tensions. *Journal of Applied Communication Research*, *46*(1), 14–18. doi:10.1080/00909882.2018.1426711

Caliskan, E. N. (2010). The impact of strategic human resource management on organizational performance. *Journal of Naval Science and Engineering*, *6*(2), 100–116.

Centers for Disease Control and Prevention. (2002). *Rapid assessment of injuries among survivors of the terrorist on the World Trade Center-New York City, September 2001*. Author.

Cho, Y.-S., Choi, B.-H., & Yoon, S. (2016). Tsunami research in Korea. *Natural Hazards*, *84*(S2), 437–454. doi:10.100711069-016-2439-1

Collins, J. (2001). *Good to great. Why some companies make the leap … and others don't*. Harper Collins.

Comer, J. S., Green, J. G., Holt, M. K., Kwong, L., & Xuan, Z. (2016). Teachers report of outreach to school-based providers of mental health services following the 2013 Boston Marathon attack. *Children & Schools*, *38*(4), 227–234. doi:10.1093/cs/cdw035

Darkow, P. M. (2019). Beyond "bouncing back": Towards an integral, capability-based understanding of organizational resilience. *Journal of Contingencies and Crisis Management*, *27*(2), 145–156. doi:10.1111/1468-5973.12246

Duchek, S. (2020). Organizational resilience: A capability-based conceptualization. *Business Research*, *13*(1), 215–246. doi:10.100740685-019-0085-7

Duchek, S., Raetze, S., & Scheuch, I. (2020). The role of diversity in organizational resilience: A theoretical framework. *Business Research*, *13*(2), 387–423. doi:10.100740685-019-0084-8

Essens, P., George, G., van der Vegt, G. S., & Wahlström, M. (2015). Managing risk and resilience. *Academy of Management Journal*, *58*(4), 971–980. doi:10.5465/amj.2015.4004

Greene, K., LeMoine, S., Macasaet, K., & Mulrooney, K. (2020). You matter: Promoting professional resilience during collective crisis. *Zero to Three*, *41*(1), 53–58.

Greene, R. R., Conrad, A. P., Livingstone, N. C., Barton, W. H., Watkins, M. L., Blundo, R., & Riley, J. G. (2002). *An integrated approach to practice, policy, and research*. National Association of Social Workers Press.

Hormann, S. (2018). Exploring resilience: In the face of trauma. *Humanistic Management Journal*, *3*(1), 91–104. doi:10.100741463-018-0035-0

Johnson, G. S., & Rainey, S. A. (2007). Hurricane Katrina impact on three historically black colleges and universities (HBCUs): Voices from displaced student. *Race, Gender & Class, 14*(1), 100-119. Retrieved from https://ww=25853w.proquest.com/scholarly-historically /docview/218845573/se-2?accountid

Johnson, K. (2020). *Building organizational resilience in the face of a ubiquitous challenge*. National Council for Behavioral Health.

Johnson, N., Veletsianos, G., & Seaman, J. (2020). U.S. Faculty and Administrators' Experiences and Approaches in the Early Weeks of the COVID-19 Pandemic. *Online Learning Journal*, *24*(2), 6–21. doi:10.24059/olj.v24i2.2285

King, D. D., Luthans, F., & Newman, A. (2016). Not if, but when we need resilience in the workplace. *Journal of Organizational Behavior*, *37*(5), 782–786. doi:10.1002/job.2063

Kirkman, B. L., Mistry, S., Rosen, B., & Stoverink, A. C. (2020). Bouncing back together: Toward a theoretical model of work team resilience. *Academy of Management Review*, *45*(2), 395–422. doi:10.5465/amr.2017.0005

Kolay, M. K. (2016). Measurement of organizational resilience: An approach. *Productivity*, *57*(3), 300–309.

Ledesma, J. (2014). Conceptual frameworks and research models on resilience in leadership. *Sage (Atlanta, Ga.)*, *4*(3). Advance online publication. doi:10.1177/2158244014545464

Lee, M., Lim, W., & Teo, W. L. (2017). The relational activation of resilience model: How leadership activates resilience in an organizational crisis. *Journal of Contingencies and Crisis Management, 25*(3), 136–147. doi:10.1111/1468-5973.12179

Loree, D. (2020). Building corporate resilience. *Ivey Business Journal*, 2-7. https://search.ebscohost.com/login.aspx?direct=true&AuthType=shib&db=f5h&AN=145640006&site=eds-live&custid=uphoenix

Marsen, S. (2020). Navigating crisis: The role of communication in organizational crisis. *International Journal of Business Communication, 57*(2), 163–175. doi:10.1177/2329488419882981

Montes, J. S., & Suarez, F. F. (2020). Building organizational resilience. *Harvard Business Review.*

Myers, D. G. (2010). *Social psychology* (10th ed.).

Narcikara, E., & Zehir, C. (2016). Effects of resilience on productivity under Authentic Leadership. *Procedia: Social and Behavioral Sciences*, 235.

Popa, B. M. (2019). Strategic communication. *Journal of Defense Resources Management, 10*(2), 174–179.

Rangachari, P., & Woods, J. L. (2020). Preserving organizational resilience, patient safety, and staff retention during COVID-19 requires a holistic consideration of the psychological safety of healthcare workers. *International Journal of Environmental Research and Public Health, 17*(12), 4267. doi:10.3390/ijerph17124267 PMID:32549273

Ross, J. A., & Stoecker, R. (2016). The emotional context of higher education community engagement. *Journal of Community Engagement & Echolarship, 9*(2), 7–18.

Tam, G. (2020). The path forward amid COVID-19. *TD: Talent Development, 74*(6), 38–43.

Warrick, D. D. (2018). The need for transformational leaders that understand organization development fundamentals. *OD Practitioner, 50*(4), 33–40.

Winter, L. (2019). Organizational trauma: A phenomenological study of psychological organizational trauma and its effect on employees and organization. *Management, 14*(2), 117-136. doi:10.26493/1854-4231.14.117-136

KEY TERMS AND DEFINITIONS

Adversity: A situation that results in a misfortune or unfavorable condition, such as hurricanes, flooding, or terrorist attacks. In an organization, adversity may refer to the loss of a team member or company restructuring.

COVID-19: A ubiquitous virus that contributed to long-term health conditions and adjusted to new environments through transformation. COVID-19 is sometimes referred to as Coronavirus.

Crisis: An unexpected event that requires leadership to respond quickly and appropriately to address and solve the issue.

Effective Communication: Information within an organization that ensures all employees understand and implement expectations, goals, and the vision and mission statement.

External Factors: Situations that have a direct impact on the success of a company's production, such as social violence.

Internal Factors: Situations from within an organization that have a direct impact on the success of an organization, such as inconsistent leadership decisions and unexpected management changes.

Mental Health: The stability of a person to process information to make appropriate decisions.

Strategic Human Resource Management: A process by which organizations hire and retain experienced, enthusiastic, and devoted workers.

Chapter 10
From Trauma to Healing:
Leading an Organization's Journey to Restoration

Letizia Gambrell-Boone
New York City Equal Employment Practices Commission, USA

ABSTRACT

Organizational trauma, which results from a singular event or the sum of multiple experiences that occur over time, has an impact on the individuals and the collective that constitute the organization. For an organization to overcome its challenges and function in a new normal, leadership must play an integral role in engaging its individuals in a way that is explicit and intentional. The efforts of the leadership must first effectively describe the culture, as well as define leadership and its role. Undiagnosed and/or unresolved trauma (both crisis and systemic organizational trauma) within an institution may have exponential implications for both the person and the organization as a whole. To restore the organization to a state of wholeness, there must be an acknowledgement of organizational trauma as well as a committed approach to organizational healing. These efforts shift the organization from one that is experiencing organizational trauma to one that is considered to be a restorative community.

INTRODUCTION

While COVID-19 is the most traumatic situation most organizations have faced this century, it is not the first encounter with trauma, and it certainly will not be the last. In any organization, the most important resource to consider is not the brick and mortar the individuals occupy physically or at present, virtually. Rather, it is the human resources that provide the intellectual capital that creates the widget, teaches the classes, paints the picture or sings the song. History documents the evolution of humans from individuals that operated in isolation to the social beings that exist today (Shultz et al., 2011). Humans enjoy interacting with others, sharing common experiences and working together to achieve outcomes. When trauma occurs, people struggle emotionally, physically and financially due to new and unexpected circumstances. And consequently, isolation, despair, sadness, and anger can quickly emerge as the prevailing feelings.

DOI: 10.4018/978-1-7998-7016-6.ch010

Taking away many of the social norms and being left with only a fraction of the human touch points, leaves a lot to be desired and therefore affects one's mental health *and* professional identity (Prescod & Zeligman, 2018; Strauser et al., 2006).

Organizational climate "refers to employees' shared perceptions of policies, practices, and procedures that the organization is likely to reward, support, and expect" (Brawley Newlin & Pury, 2020, p. 540). Research has shown that when the overall general climate is positive, it has a ripple effect on specific areas in the company that bring value, such as safety and customer service (Brawley Newlin & Pury, 2020). Management of human resources is the best resource that an institution has to maintain its competitive advantage in the marketplace. When the diverse talent and contributions of the organization's members are recognized, and the leadership leverages those talents for the betterment of the organization, the organizational environment is healthy and optimizes connectivity for performance and outcomes (Kaya & Baskaya, 2017).

In general leadership practice, leaders have a vested interest in the organization's climate as it impacts outcomes (Nasreen et al., 2019). If the organization is healthy and has a positive general climate, then it is the leader's responsibility to stay attuned to the nuances of the behaviors in the organization to maintain equilibrium. If the organization has less than a positive general climate, then the leaders must take proactive measures to restore the organization's health, which can be impacted by many factors. Whether the negative general climate results from a crisis, individual behaviors have the capacity to quickly shift and modify organizational norms and work efforts (Coelho & Pires, 2020) or a systemic organizational crisis, resulting from organizational imperfections inherent within the organization culture and managerial ignorance which allow the firm's weaknesses to surface and subsequently develop into crisis (Roux-Dufort, 2009, p. 4); leaders must be attuned and establish a way forward.

The crisis, which is a collective occurrence experienced by staff and executives, evolves into organizational trauma, which is a dynamic system of thought shared by members of an organization based on their interactions within the organization (Vivian & Hormann, 2002). This chapter is designed to bridge the gap in literature on best practices for leaders that differentiate leadership in crisis (acute) from leadership in systemic organizational crises and emerge as a restorative organization. Trauma (both crisis and systemic organizational crisis) within an organization left undiagnosed and/or untreated can have exponential consequences for both the individual and the organization as a whole. To return the organization to a place of wholeness, there has to be acknowledgment of the organizational trauma and dedicated commitment to organizational healing. This chapter also provides practical steps for creating a safe and healing culture to restore the organization to function and flourish amid a traumatic state or periods of uncertainty.

LEADERSHIP

This chapter explores the need for leadership to recommit to the organization's values and the role that each individual contributes to the organization's values. In addition, leadership must define or affirm the organization's expectations of professionalism; reinforce the organization's commitment to a culture of worth; set clear expectations for the individual and organization; and explore effective communication to manage both internal and external expectations.

Definition of Leadership

A topic that has been explored for years in organizations is that of leadership (Yuan-Duen et al., 2020; Zaar et. al., 2020; Dugan, 2017). To enhance the understanding of leadership, Schein (2004) considers if leaders are born or made. For the purpose of this chapter, leadership, is defined as the ability to move individuals toward a goal (Prentice, 2004), and will be explored through the consideration of leadership traits. Nwabueze (2011) expands on trait leadership by stating that leadership traits make use of the leader's knowledge of what to do and power to accomplish tasks through the efforts of others. Leadership also considers the notion that the leader embraces the multidimensionality and motivations of those they are charged to lead. The leader is finely attuned to the nuances of each member's behavior and engages accordingly. An understanding of these dynamics and having the capacity to maneuver while continuing to keep the team engaged towards the common goals will typically result in successful outcomes. Over a ten-year review of literature on leadership, Cameron and Green, (2017) curated clusters of qualities in leadership. These clusters are summarized below:

Archetype 1: The Architect-Focusing on design, the architect crafts seemingly disparate ideas and information into a well-thought-out, structured way forward and continually scans the environment for patterns and feedback.

Archetype 2: The Motivator-Focusing on buy-in, the Motivator taps into their own and other people's passions, articulates a compelling picture or vision of the future that motivates and inspires people to engage in the way ahead.

Archetype 3: The Connector-Focusing on connectivity, the Connector reinforces what's important, establishes a few simple rules, connects people and agendas, brings care to process and establishes safety in a measured way.

Archetype 4: The Implementer-Focusing on delivery, the Implementer drives and reviews the plan, holds people to account, leads by delegating and follow-up with tenacity and rigor.

Archetype 5: The Catalyzer-Focusing on discomfort, the Catalyzer asks difficult or probing questions, spots poor performance, dysfunction or resistance and brings any necessary edge which in turn creates the tension for change to happen.

While having an understanding of these leadership traits is beneficial, the application of these traits is not mutually exclusive. There is considerable overlap across the groupings and the development of a trait or traits comes with understanding, application and reflection (Cameron & Green, 2017).

The skills, ability and knowledge of a leader have an impact on organizational results (Bolman & Deal, 1997). Additionally, it is important to recognize the people who bring their own talents, strengths, and aspirations to the organization. When the leader values the unique gifts and talents of its team, the benefits are far reaching. Such a leader creates an environment for what Csikszentmihalyi (1990) describes as flow which is one's "state of mind when consciousness is harmoniously ordered and they want to pursue whatever they are doing for its own sake" (p. 6). In this context, the aim is for the individual to be in this mind state in the pursuit of work. Sigmund Freud further elaborated on this concept by stating that two of the greatest enjoyments in life are simply "work and love" (Csikszentmihalyi, 1990, p. 144). Leaders that focus their efforts on conditions upon which the employee can function in flow, creates an environment in which those individuals benefit optimally as work is not a laborious chore.

While having an autotelic personality, or natural affinity to the intrinsic value of activity, is innate for many, it too can be cultivated when time and effort are dedicated to fostering experiences that are meaningful and have intrinsic value (Csikszentmihalyi, 1990). Contrarily, when the leader marginalizes the individual and devalues their contributions, that is the beginning of a commitment to achieving less than optimal outcomes. If the leader questions how they are perceived by the team, pays attention to the feedback offered by the team, then the leader can get feedback and use it to improve their capacity in service to the team (Shugart, 2013). As a result, the individual grows as a leader and is more effective in service to the organization. This type of leader is also better received by the team.

Listening is a basic and essential act for leaders as it serves as the very foundation for communication (Tenuto, 2018). The leader must assess why communication is important. If the leader's primary desired outcome is to share information, they may effectively do so but miss some of the most important desired outcomes of good communication which are deeply meaningful connections to colleagues, purposeful work, authenticity in expression, establishment of trust and one's commitment to making sacrifices for one another in the name of the work (Shugart, 2013). The skill of listening for good communication, while it is easy for some, it is one that has to be cultivated in others. Good listening skills include (Shugart, 2013):

- Be still and pay attention;
- Don't think about your reply until you have fully heard and processed what the other is saying;
- Never interrupt;
- Reflect back what you think you are hearing from the speaker in paraphrase and confirm that you got it right;
- Use open body posture, hands up and open, no crossed arms;
- Make and sustain eye contact, and for heaven's sake don't be looking at the "bird on my shoulder";
- Ask leading questions and probe more deeply;
- Don't feel the need to respond immediately giving the impression that you've heard all this before and already have a dismissive answer;
- Thank the speaker for what she has shared with you;
- Then, and only then, introduce new information or an alternate view to the conversation, and do so with an attitude and tone of inquiry rather than advocacy;
- If the conversation needs a starter, begin with questions, real questions, that matter and be still long enough for the other to reflect and respond, even if the silence begins to get a little uncomfortable;
- Never flatter, since the act of listening itself, if it is genuine, is enough to reinforce the other to share, and flattery never feels true.

The personal sacrifices associated with the mastery of the listening skill, pales in comparison to value-added in how the leader is received and perceived by the team.

The Role of a Leader

Leadership is the capacity to advance the agenda of the organization by inspiring the actions of others. Block (2009) described the role of leader as being primarily responsible for three things:

1. Shifting the focus of the conversation for which the body gathers;
2. Naming the debate through asking reflective questions and
3. Listening without a desire to influence, judge or answer questions.

Through this lens, the leader must engage in building a common purpose while strategically determining the way forward. Accordingly, the first measure that a leader should take when faced with trauma in an organization is to stop and assess the situation and understand their role. This is a very important step as it allows the leader the opportunity to pause and consider their strategy in leading their team into a safe space through the trauma and into the optimal culture to yield performance. It is during these times that the leader must be confidently self-aware of who they are as a leader. Further, research has shown that in order to gain followers certain characteristics must be present (Rath, 2008):

1. There is an investment in the individual's strengths.
2. The leader focuses on the components of the team to drive maximum team outcomes.
3. The leader is keenly aware of their team members' need for trust, compassion, stability and hope. This establishes the foundation for a healthy relationship between leaders and their teams.

Defining individual leadership styles also has been a widely debated and researched topic over time (Eagly et al., 2003). A pivotal meta-analysis research study was conducted in 2003 that described the nuanced differences in approaches for men and women to leadership (Eagly et al., 2003). The primary approaches are transformational, transactional, and laissez-faire leadership styles. Transformational leaders have characteristics in which they look to serve as models of appropriate behavior and strive to advance the agenda of the organization by inspiring the team (Yukl, 1999). Transactional leaders provide rewards and consequences based upon individual efforts (Bass, 1990). Laissez-faire leaders take a "hands off" approach to providing direction. This is sometimes done at intervals that were later than needed (Pahi & Hamid, 2016). Transformational leadership was found to be most often used by women and was found to be the style that has the most positive outcomes whether used by men or women (Eagly et al., 2003; Jabeen et al., 2020). Understanding one's leadership style and how they show up plays a role in building trust amongst the team. If a leader's style leans towards transactional or laissez-faire, they have the opportunity to be intentional in becoming a transformational leader if they desire. Transformational leadership is the style that can build a community that shares a purpose, resulting in peak efficiency within an organization.

LEADERSHIP AND ORGANIZATIONAL CULTURE

An organization is the sum of the humans in which it serves (Shoup & Studer, 2010). Morgan (2011) emphasizes the importance of acknowledging a fundamental aspect of being human and having confidence in what one knows. Humans make sense of new phenomena through the lens of what they know. The author describes this process of gaining knowledge as being ontological - "showing the relationship between the concepts and categories in a subject area or domain" (Oxford University Press, 2020). To lead in an organization, leaders must see the organization through different lenses in order to comprehend the variables that enable the organization to function.

The culture of an organization is bound by the consciousness of the people that make up the organization. According to Schein (2004), culture is intangible and yet it is strong in its social and organizational impact. The organization's culture is its values, beliefs, and practices. In other words, culture is the organization's personality and it has a life of its own that must be considered. Each organization member brings their own value structure to the organization. The interaction between each member and the organization adds another layer of complexity. If the organization does not understand the operation of these forces, the organization is going to be the target of them.

Complexity leadership could be defined as adaptive mechanisms (unknown problems) developed by complex organizations in new conditions that are required by the information age, rather than technical problems (known problems) entailed by the industrial age (Baltaci & Balci, 2017). In complexity science, outcomes cannot be reduced to a simple cause and effect of stimulus as some organizations have varying levels of complexity (Baltaci & Balci, 2017). Variables such as time, size, location, and input influence outcomes. Shoup and Studer (2010) identify seven principles that describe dynamic organizational interactions to help in understanding how complex structures work amid uncertainty and to offer guidance to those leaders who strive to succeed despite instability. They are as follows:

1. **Homeostasis and change**: Equilibrium is established when the system is in balance, no matter how balance is measured. Change is the twin concept to equilibrium. Equilibrium does not exist unless there is change. Systems are always changing to remain the same.
2. **Strange attractors**: It is a point in the system where the pattern will eventually end up at any point in time, whether from an attraction or repellant in the system.
3. **Fractuals**: Despite the various levels of complexity among comparable organizations, there is an amazing amount of similarity across scales. The patterns that emerge at the macro level because of the strange attractors are mirrored throughout the micro levels of the system. Basically, in dynamic systems, subsets take on the features of the whole in what are known as fractuals. The dominant values will mirror themselves throughout the system to become essential features of the system.
4. **Cybernetics**: Feedback that is heeded or the means in which the system regulates itself (versus feedback that is random or "just noise"). Self-regulating systems have sensors tuned for specific types of feedback in order to make requisite adaptations consistent with the expectations of the strange attractors in the system.
5. **Emergence**: Norms emerge over time as non-negotiables are established. Group norms establish rules of engagement. People do what they do because somehow it is reinforcing, or it works for them, eventually developing routines of behaviors that become ingrained habits,
6. **Sensitive dependence**: The results that emerge are contingent upon the starting points. When the patterns emerge in the direction of the feedback, the impetus for systems to emerge is a function of the interactions between initial variables and existing conditions. It is these initial conditions that imprint the system and give the system its unique essence and characteristics.
7. **Self-organized criticality**: Patterns for performance develop and care constantly interacting with the environment. It is this interaction with the environment that makes the system relatively stable and temperamental at the same time. It acknowledges that complex systems exist at the edge of chaos and could give way to disorder at any point in time under specific conditions (Shoup & Studer, 2010, pp. 22-42).

Bolman and Deal (1997) contend that leaders should look at and approach organizational issues from four perspectives that they call 'Frames'. Frame is a metaphor for perspective and if leaders habitually operate from a single frame, they will not be effective (Bolman & Deal, 1997). In understanding the organization's culture, leaders are faced with varied perceptions of reality or frames. Leaders should approach organizational issues using the four frames if they want to be effective. The four frames as described by Bolman and Deal (1997) are:

1. **Structural** – this frame is mainly task oriented and focuses on strategy, goal setting, role and task clarification, metrics and deadlines.
2. **Human resource** – this frame focuses on empowering employees to do their jobs well while simultaneously addressing their needs for personal growth, community and job satisfaction.
3. **Political** – this frame looks at the organization through the lens of individuals and interest groups having conflicting or hidden agendas during times when resources are scarce.
4. **Symbolic** – This frame addresses an individual's need for a sense of purpose and meaning in their work. Leaders use this lens to inspire and motivate organization members by making the purpose and direction meaningful. as a tool for reframing the organization until the leader has clarity to address issues as they arise (Bolman & Deal, 1997).

Shoup and Studer (2010) affirm, "Leaders do well to vigilantly buffer and nurture the system so that the right patterns emerge consistent with the system's dominant values. As systemic thinkers, leaders also do well to anticipate the intended and unintended consequences of their decisions," (pp. 67-68).

An organization's culture has the power to make or break it. When leadership is in harmony with the organizational culture, the organization can function optimally. Optimal function occurs when the leader has an in-depth understanding of the organizational dynamics and can therefore direct the group to achieve organizational outcomes. When leadership is out of touch with the culture of the organization, it creates the opportunity for systemic conflict and organizational trauma (Schein, 2004).

LEADERSHIP AND ORGANIZATIONAL TRAUMA

Organizations experience trauma like individuals can and the organization's experience of trauma can be just as damaging as it is for individuals (Vivian & Hormann, 2015). When there is trauma in the organization, it can be a barrier to creating a culture of trauma-informed care (Vivian & Hormann, 2015). A culture of trauma-informed care is important because it requires changing the culture to place the emphasis on respect, understanding and responding to the trauma at all levels (Bloom, 2010).

Long (2018) notes that within organizations experiencing trauma, the relationship to the immediate supervisor or leader trumps that of a relationship to the organization as a whole. Each individual in the organization must be committed to understanding the specific responsibility upon which they are charged and understand how their role fits into the desired outcomes of the organization (Karapancheva, 2020). Behaviors demonstrated in traumatized organizations include coercion, attention seeking, and a lack of concern about the impact of actions on the larger society (Karapancheva, 2020).

Leadership has a role in creating a trauma-informed culture. The roles and responsibilities of leaders in traumatized organizations are outlined below (Fallot & Harris, 2001):

- Ensure administrative commitment to integrating a trauma informed culture
- Provide introductory training to all staff
- Establish an internal trauma team
- Include providers and 'providees' in the assessment of services
- Address any re-traumatizing policies and procedures
- Conduct early and respectful trauma screening for all organization members

By implementing these steps, the author believes that leaders can make great strides in helping organization members heal from trauma and gain strength and resilience.

The Crisis and How to Manage It

A crisis or acute trauma occurs as a result of a school shooting, campus hate crime, "product recall, management or employee errors, technical failures, political events, financial debacles, labor strikes, insider trading, sabotage, violation of safety standards, or acts of nature" (Labas, 2017, p. 77). If the organization is stable and has a crisis preparedness model in place, the first step is acknowledging that a trauma crisis exists and then enacts an operational protocol that considers the long-term implication of the crisis on the organization. Nichols et al. (2020) advises that there are certain leadership behaviors that are necessary when in crisis. Leaders should take the following actions:

1. **Understand the importance of decisive intervention** and an admit their limits. This decisive action should occur while maintaining a strong commitment to achieving the best results possible while caring for the organization members in the midst of the crisis. In deciding to choose speed in decision making over precision, leaders will respond to the rapidly changing situation and make the best decisions given the available information (Galetti et al., 2019).
2. **Adapt quickly and boldly**. In the midst of the crisis, leaders should demonstrate vulnerability by admitting that they do not have all of the answers. What should happen next is that leaders should then engage the best minds in the organization to understand the nuances of what is happening in real time from all vantage points in order to make the best decisions possible (Miller & Proctor, 2016).
3. **Deliver reliably** requires that leading happens with ownership and integrity. This calls for the establishment of expectations and regular communication related to newly established priorities and key performance indicators (Nichols et al., 2020).
4. **Engage for impact**. The leader that engages for impact is committed to the care of his or her team and recognizes and acknowledges the challenges experienced yet communicates with transparency (Tenuto, 2018). This is the time to share individual and team successes and the impact of efforts on constituents (Nichols et al., 2020). Leaders will be challenged by leading amid chaos and in areas where they lack strengths.

LEADERSHIP AND STEPS TO RECOVERY

In an organization experiencing trauma, restoring the collective must be emphasized and acted upon at every level. It is through these individual and intentional interactions that leadership can facilitate the organization on its road to recovery and emergence as a resilient, restorative organization. It should be noted that the biggest challenge to implementing restorative practices in an organization is the culture and climate within the organization (McLeod, 2003). Even with much promise for changing an organization's culture to a restorative one, caution must be taken to ensure that the intended results are conveyed and that the people and environment are ready and responsive. An intentional shift in reward for behavior that embraces the new norms in expectations for demonstrated commitment to displaying workplace dignity (Staub & Shoup, 2011); needs resources allocated for tools like a communication plan, training and incentives and may require policy reinforcement (McLeod, 2003).

Restorative Practices

Leadership must take care to rebuild both the individual and the institution in order to ensure that the organization emerges from trauma restored and resilient. The practices outlined below are critical in helping leadership to successfully restore the organization after a trauma.

Step 1: Value Alignment

During periods of uncertainty, familiarity is comforting. Depending upon the organizational culture, familiarity may reinforce the shadow side of the organization that results in increased stressors, group think or over-functioning of the members. The shadow side of organizations are aspects that they do not necessarily know they have (Vivian & Hormann, 2002). The shadow side of an organization undermines consensus and unity within the culture because it may not be apparent. Without addressing issues presented by the organization's shadow side, attempts at unifying the collective are undermined. During an organization's trauma, acknowledging the organization's shadows offers the opportunity to decide how to move forward and heal. This is the time to restate the organization's mission and that for which it stands. However, it is impossible to do so without recognizing, as Theodore Roosevelt stated, "People don't care how much you know, until they know how much you care." This is the time for leadership on all levels to address the collective and individual, while acknowledging these are hard times that are impacting each individual differently. In this context, leadership is to perform as a citizen of its organization.

Block (2009) defines a citizen as "one who is willing to be accountable for and committed to the well-being of the whole" (p. 63). Crises provide leaders the opportunity to act and build confidence in the future of the organization through words and deeds and act as one who values the thoughts and feelings of each member of the community. Organizational leaders should restate the value of the individual contributions of each employee to the organization and that during these trying times, the leader trusts him or her to manage their competing priorities--from their new realities of home and their new reality of work. Organizational citizens must also respect their position as a person who is committed to being responsible for the well-being of the whole, embracing and not delegating responsibility for his or her role in acting in their capacity. In an organization that is respectful of and respects the culture as a restorative one, they embrace the idea of possibility. In addition, the organizational citizen endorses the organization's development by its people's collective wisdom; and supports the collective's unique gifts and abilities by deliberately pursuing those who work on the fray (Block, 2009).

For an organization in trauma that respects the contributions of each member, reinforce to the team that the leader is there to offer support to them as everyone navigates this new normal, acknowledging that the wisdom from the organization's citizens on how best to move the organization forward is sought out and valued. Lencioni (2004) describes the process of engaging members of the community in a discussion centered on the conflict that matters most in the organization as *mining*. This is where the citizens in the organization have passionate and unfiltered discussions on what matters most and after considering the perspective of the collective, the leader makes the decision. This assures the organization's citizens that the leader values team input. Whether it is in the establishment of metrics that best captures the measurement of productivity in meeting desired outcomes or how best to communicate via phone, video call, or email and the frequency of the communication (daily, weekly, bi-weekly, etc.), collectively, everyone works together to determine outcomes in this new reality by valuing the unique thoughts and contributions of the team. Simultaneously aligning with the values of the organization proves to be a win-win for the organization.

Step 2: Establish/Affirm a Paradigm of Professionalism

During periods of uncertainty, it may be necessary to address what was previously unspoken to reaffirm the organization's commitment to the tenets of professionalism. In an organization, culture, beliefs, customs and knowledge held by the collective are what drives how the organization functions (George & Jayan, 2012). What creates shared understanding within the organization also informs what the organization values and how the organization behaves (George & Jayan, 2012). The organization's culture consists of more than just the thoughts and actions of leadership. It contains the behaviors, folklore and beliefs of members of the collective and its system of reward and consequences. Establishing citizenship as a tenet of the culture is important. This exercise of affirming the paradigm of professionalism provides the opportunity to ensure that all team members are operating from the same "play book." This is the time to be clear on expectations like those listed below:

- Arrive on time for meetings
- Meet deadlines
- Uphold dress code
- Maintain virtual etiquette

Why is this important? Theorists have determined a relationship between performance and organizational culture (George & Jayan, 2012). Research has shown that when there is a strong positive organizational culture, positive outcomes related to employee performance occur. Accordingly, once proper decorum is established, by organization leadership, and consequences for lack thereof, there is little room for misinterpretation. Appropriate responses to employee behavior will impact how the individual engages in the organization's culture. If there is misinterpretation, this construct provides a foundation to build upon to address any concerns.

Step 3: Culture of Worth (Workplace Dignity)

Creating a culture that values the worth of team members is a construct that has to be established and consistently reinforced. Organizational behavior shapes this notion and signifies whether the culture of worth is experienced by the staff or is the topic of organizational literature. This culture of worth can be nourishing and positively impact the work environment (Thomas & Lucas, 2019). A culture of worth is highly subjective and is greatly influenced by organizational behavior. It has been found that many employees cannot articulate dignity without describing the impact of the counter feeling which is workplace indignity. Workplace dignity considers variables such as manners in which employees lack confidence, or manners by which their dignity is compromised through threats of retaliation. Under the notion of workplace dignity, there are four main principles. Workplace dignity is:

1. rooted in how one communicates and reacts;
2. acknowledgment of the individual's perception serving as the foundation for qualifying the experience or self-construal;
3. both inherent and earned in that the individual is deserved simply because the employee is human and the individual values respect provided by colleagues; and
4. a means of value or lack is equally felt with similar intense emotions.

Leadership must be intentional in aligning the outcomes of the unit with the talents of the individual. Thomas and Lucas (2019) argued that some corporate leadership finds the organization's performance in preserving and supporting the integrity of workers. There are many assessment tools that can aid in the showcasing of team members' talents. To name a few, Myers-Briggs Type Indicator, Big Five Personality Traits assessment, and DISC (Dominance, Influence, Steadiness, and Conscientiousness) are some of the most cited inventories (Menand, 2018), with the Big Five being referenced as the most scientifically sound (Lim, 2020). It has been proven that in highly effective organizations there is a strong relationship between the personality assessment and performance outcomes. When employees are engaged in accordance with assessment characteristics, there is more "commitment, innovation, and performance" (Carter, 2020). The effort goes into establishing the strategic outcomes for the organizations and determining who is best suited to deliver those outcomes.

In the Big Five Personality Traits assessment, there are characteristics aligned with organizational citizenship behaviors, which describes the individual choices taken outside of employee contracts but are part of the company as a whole (Carter, 2020). The Big Five Personality Traits are openness to experience, conscientiousness, extroversion, agreeableness, and neuroticism. Openness to experience addresses one capacity to consider new ideas that may or may not be outside of the norm; conscientiousness describes one's propensity to seek out order and desirous of outcomes; extraversion is one's tendency to seek outcomes and resist calls to order or conformity; agreeableness tends to focus on balance and kindness and conformity and neuroticism is in opposition to positive traits like efficaciousness and is correlated with negative job performance.

In many instances, organizations look for the hard workers, which results in a select few being overtaxed with opportunities that could produce limited outcomes. Aligning talents and desired outcomes provides a balanced strategic approach that fosters the creativity of visionaries and the practical application of detail-oriented thinkers. It creates a culture where everyone values what the other person brings to the project, and everyone feels valued and can inspire others.

Step 4: Set Clear Expectations

Missed opportunities are centered around unclear expectations, whether it be on behalf of leadership failing to communicate down to staff, or staff not seeking clarity regarding expectations. This is a key concept to consider regardless of the industry, as each department is expected to achieve outcomes. Outcomes at times are based upon ideals with no clear path to delivering the outcomes. Sometimes, outcomes are based upon new trends achieved in one industry seeking to be achieved in another. Outcomes may also be based upon increased demands for accountability. In rare instances are outcomes based upon metrics and with plans to achieve new levels based upon previous performance. Without the latter, productivity levels are left to chance. It is important to note that outcomes in many instances have factors that are beyond the control of an individual that can impact productivity levels. For example, if the desired outcome is an increase in the number of cars produced in a quarter. As part of the quality assurance process, a test drive-in all-weather conditions (i.e., rainy, windy, and snowy) is required. If the plant is located in Las Vegas, Nevada and all other quality assurance metrics are met, the individual will not meet the performance outcomes because the individual is unable to test drive the car in snowy conditions.

While aiming for desired outcomes, one aspect that is tangible, within an individual's realm of control and measurable, is, output. To use the same example related to achieving outcomes, while the individual may be unable to achieve performance outcomes due to something beyond his or her control (i.e., weather), the plant can achieve a measure of outputs. Did the team work for 20 consecutive days? Did the team assemble 3 cars per day? Did the team communicate to management weekly on progress? To maximize productivity and minimize frustration, clear expectations must be set and communicated frequently (Popick, 2014). Mayne (2004) acknowledges that a commitment to excellence is required to develop a result-chain and results expectation chart as it demands a significant investment of time. This chart promises to assist the leader in avoiding the pitfalls associated with focusing only on the final outcomes. It considers the factors as outlined in the example above such as outputs that allow all to agree upon the approach to reaching the outcome. Start at the beginning. Are performance expectations focused on desired targets with adequate resources to achieve the target? Or, are performance expectations centered on the approach one takes to meet the challenges presented (Mayne, 2004)? Targets can be described as predictions that are attainable in the future with adequate resources. This approach is best in articulating outputs as the individual can articulate concrete measures of the outputs. Limitations of using the target approach are as follows:

- Performance reporting can be as much a report on how good a prediction was as on how well a program is performing.
- Readers of a performance report, and many staff, still do not really know what is being reported: are those stretch targets or safe predictions? Are they supposed to be easily met?
- Uncertainty about achieving outcomes, given the various factors not under the program's control, can result in setting targets only or mainly for outputs.
- Predictive targets are met with a view to reporting zero variance. This is not really reporting how well the program is performing: the question remains – could the program have done better? It is also less likely to encourage innovation and learning; a manager may wonder – since the target has been met, why try harder?

Stretch goals or challenges that the individual can achieve offers the organization many opportunities to learn and this can be viewed as an achievement in narrating the organization's success. This affords the organization the opportunity to assess each aspect of the process and outcomes achieved in the process—including learning as it is a valuable process in continuous quality improvement. One can measure year over year accomplishment including time and efficiency. Concentrated time should be spent understanding the difference between outputs and outcomes. Outcomes and measures to achieve them should be set, communicated and used in planning exercises. Just as important is the gathering and understanding of output expectations where the educator can control an activity that can at times take considerable effort with limited outcomes or output. Invest the time in developing expectations that measure outputs, progress and resources needed to implement them. Once expectations are set, communicating up, down and out keeps all parties apprised of progress (Mayne, 2004).

To be explicit, clear expectations do not impede the process of discovery. They are met with resistance as many do not desire their performance to be measured (Mayne, 2004). Clear expectations should be mutually agreed upon between the leader and the subordinate. This should outline the parameters for the desired deliverable that includes the proposal for development–including a communication plan, approval of the proposal, approval of the model, approval of the full implementation, assessment of the deliverable and the final report.

Step 5: Manage Expectations

Once the expectations are set, it is incumbent upon the leader and subordinate to keep open lines of communication regarding the established expectations (i.e., budget, timelines, etc.). Not only should all be aware of the expectations, but the leader must also be clear in articulating how one is to achieve the expected outcomes and outputs and on what basis did one reach in establishing the milestones (Mayne, 2004). Mayne (2004) developed a results-expectations chart to measure and communicate success. This tool is effective in managing performance expectations. Factors to be addressed include similarly situated criteria for calculating the desired outcomes; setting a timetable for measuring the impact; results achieved in the past; defining the direction forward and assessing progress towards determining what is reasonable; expanding the reach of evaluation beyond quantitative methods; and recognizing the needs of the organization's stakeholders as a measure of progress. The aim is to be expansive in setting performance expectations. This affords the leader to be clear in that the staff member understands what is expected and shared in the progress statement. Concrete expectations identify the beneficiaries from the outcomes, specific results to be measured and the timeline.

It is sometimes challenging to be specific at the outset due to new unchartered territory explored in the endeavor. It is possible to present progress towards aims, desired outcomes with the understanding that once sufficient data is obtained that concrete targets will be made. Performance measures should include reliability and validity measures. Reliability is the repeatability of the findings by someone other than the researcher. Validity focuses on the achievement of the specific performance characteristic. One example of this is by trying to assess a car's performance by measuring the time it takes for the car to accelerate. It is a valid measure of time but not a measure of car performance. Performance measures should also be delineated unless the report results are not reflective of what is the aim of the report. The aforementioned expands the organization's ability to understand progress moving beyond having concrete targets. This approach provides a comprehensive means by which all can understand the scope, timeline and expectations of deliverables. The leadership should establish parameters for communication that are confirmed regularly, across multiple mediums if necessary, as to if the team member is ahead of schedule, behind schedule or on track (death by meeting). This alleviates confusion and all parties are in the loop, continuing to add value during periods of vulnerability.

Step 6: Create a Safe, Inclusive Space

Communication is essential in creating safe spaces. Oftentimes, leaders are trained in their disciplines and are not trained in how to lead. Nguyen et al. (2019) postulates that the most important aspect of a leader's capacity to communicate is his or her level of emotional intelligence. This construct considers multiple filters that occur between the sender of the information and how it is received. One's emotional filters drive this transaction. The filters are affected by factors such as the sender's past experience and personal viewpoint (Nguyen et al., 2019). Accordingly, regardless of how well intentioned, conversations go awry. It is expected that the leader has self-awareness regarding how they process information which will inform how they engage with his or her team. There has to be an understanding between the leader's "emotional and rational" ways of thinking (Nguyen et al., 2019, p. 57) as this will inform how the team perceives their leader.

Organizational trauma may result from something that happened recently, such as an unfavorable accreditation report, enrollment decreases, or a campus shooting. It may also result from long-term trauma due to the emotional drain of mission service or reduced support. Regardless, open, and reliable communication is a basic requirement for confidence to be sustained. To address this lack of trust, staff must be taught how to deliver transparent and consistent communication, so that it is delivered in a way that is non-confrontational and builds trust. Leiss (2004) indicated that there is a major discrepancy in the way in which experts communicate traumatic or high-risk assessments and how the citizenry receives risk assessments. The author created guidelines that mandated the essential components of a high-risk communication plan in a previous leadership role. These guidelines stipulate what is tolerable and the risk/benefits associated with the situation:

1. Begin with a statement of commitment to maintaining a communications flow of information pertinent to public concerns about the case at hand.
2. Distinguish clearly between hazard (the types of possible harms) and risk (the likelihood for individuals or populations to suffer those harms).
3. If the type of possible harm has special qualities, eliciting feelings of "dread" or heightened fears, be aware of them and acknowledge them in the communications.
4. Specify what is known about exposures and whether it is likely that sensitive populations (especially children) are likely to be exposed.
5. Indicate the quality of the knowledge base, how it is expected to improve through further research, and who is responsible for improving it.
6. Describe qualitatively the uncertainties in the knowledge base and what further steps might reduce these uncertainties and when.
7. Describe both quantitatively and qualitatively the estimates of probability that have been made, if available, or if not available when they might be expected.
8. Provide a justification for what is thought to be a tolerable or acceptable level of risk in this case, using either risk/risk or risk/benefit tradeoffs, or both.
9. Provide a clear and compelling justification for the type of action response that has been chosen or recommended in this case.
10. Provide contact information where responses to questions may be obtained (Leiss, 2004, p. 403).

Leaders must model how to have conversations with subordinates in a way that seeks to gain valuable insights. Using emotional intelligence (EI) in the work environment offers a strategy that fosters collegiality and promotes productivity in the workplace (Nguyen et al., 2019). This skill is one that has to be cultivated. Scientifically, interactions send signals to the brain by hormones. The heart dictates how the information is processed emotionally, and this is the manifestation of science behind emotional intelligence. These skills should be practiced given every opportunity as it will improve the managers skill set and ultimately positively impact the organizational culture and productivity. To achieve EI mastery for a better, healthier work environment the leader should engage in the following:

- Begin each encounter by considering it as an opportunity for growth and development. This further allows the leader the chance to listen carefully and process the information first through a growth lens.
- Understand that effective communication does not require the leader to compromise his or her authentic identity. It merely provides the leader another tool in his or her tool chest that enhances their ability to communicate. (Nguyen et. al., 2019)

Beginning conversations with an opportunity to learn and grow can be a beneficial approach for leaders that are leading traumatized organizations. Having a growth mindset in which the leader is open to learning from experiences, efforts and collaboration with others is also beneficial. The growth mindset helps the leader create a caring disposition which can result in building trust in the leadership. Crucial conversations (Patterson et al., 2012) are those that occur when there are "strong emotions, opposing opinions and high stakes." Each of these scenarios are present when experiencing organizational trauma. Emotions are strong as individuals are uncertain of outcomes. Opposing opinions are inevitable due to the very nature of an organization having multiple people with multiple perspectives on the optimal way forward. High stakes are present as the nature of trauma in an organization can have an impact on productivity and this impacts the organization's bottom line. Further, it was estimated by Gallup that it costs organizations in the United States between $960 billion and $1.2 trillion per year for managers that lack skills and employees that are not at optimal levels of performance due to dissatisfaction for myriad reasons (Comaford, 2018).

What skills does the organization have to put in place to help the organization meet its objectives? If the leader is aware of the right motives or a commitment to shared purpose, then they begin with the right mindset/perspective to have a crucial conversation. In an institution of higher education where the author served as the senior executive, the author assigned a project to two staff members, John and Jenny, that brought unique and critical skills to bring this project to fruition. Both individuals were very talented and confident in their knowledge base and capacity to achieve the desired outcome. The team was intently working on a project that had a looming deadline. It was a busy time during the academic year so many competing priorities were in motion. The two staff members were in discussion relative to how best to move the project forward. One individual was focused on offering feedback that she thought was helpful. The other was receiving the information as an attack on his intelligence. John was insulted and arose to leave the meeting.

As these interactions unfolded, the author came to recognize that there was a lot occurring that John was experiencing but not sharing. John was silenced. At this moment, the author invited Jenny to leave the room so that she could speak privately with John. John and the author had a crucial conversation. John's emotions were high as he felt humiliated. It was a high-stake matter as there was an impending deadline to meet. Differing opinions were present as the author believed the approach that the team had in place was effective in reaching the overall goal. John felt the approach was ineffective as it was replete with condescension. The conversation centered on the author acknowledging that the approach was ineffective and proposing alternatives to create shared meaning amongst the team that ultimately led to shared purpose. What was the desired outcome? John and the author both wanted to provide the deliverable and meet the deadline. No one desired to discount one another's perspective or be disrespectful. The team avoided what Patterson et al. (2012) call the Fool's Choice, which sacrifices the relationship for the sake of the conversation. As this influenced the team's motives, the alternative approach was received by John. The team now had a mutually beneficial outcome and a way forward.

Recovery in the Organization

If an organization experiences acute or systemic organizational trauma, there is a path to recovery. Understanding organizational culture creates structure in the development of a common mission and tangible deliverables from an operational agenda to a culture in which everybody embraces the concept of shared leadership. McLeod (2003) describes the process to organizational recovery in phases. During the first phase, much focus is placed upon mobilizing the community and the intentional move away from entrenched corporate bureaucracy and into an atmosphere in which managers, individuals and community espouse praise for indicators of the new vision. Momentum is created from the first phase to the definition of standards that operationalize the common vision while still engaging those who put roadblocks in the way of the vision's achievement. In turn, decisions are no longer made because of a commitment to bureaucracy, but rather because of the organization's commitment to its purpose and vision. To achieve sustained commitment to one distinction as a restorative organization, the structure of the organization at every level showcases a confidence and commitment by stakeholders to act in ways that moves the organization forward in the achievement of its goals (McLeod, 2003).

CONCLUSION

Ending with the beginning in mind: there is now an appreciation of the importance of approaching the components of the whole from the initial position of organizational trauma and taking into account the role of the leader and the hearts, minds, skills and experiences of each member of the organization. An organization can now be known as that of a restorative culture if it has done so and done so well. This kind of culture focuses on the potential and how each individual can collectively realize that the organization can build something better together than what was (Block, 2009). This is the beginning of a future that is innovative and better. The restorative organization chooses to concentrate on what can be recovered, and take obstacles into consideration, as well. This involves a commitment to a cultural change in which it is normalized to be brave and understand that it takes heart to care about and behave in the best interests of everyone while evaluating the contributions of the person to the process at the same time. The collective focuses on what is considered a communal possibility in this environment, where the emphasis is on what will emerge from the collective. At the intersection of opportunity and responsibility, this happens. Block (2009) asserts, "Possibility without accountability results in wishful thinking. Accountability without possibility increases despair, for even if we know we are creating the world we exist in, we cannot imagine it being any different from the past that got us here" (p. 48). Through the intentional efforts of the entire community, the organization can flourish.

Whether from acute or systemic organizational trauma, feelings arise during times of uncertainty that are disorienting, unnerving, and scary (Prescod & Zeligman, 2018; Strauser et al., 2006). Yet, through the simple act of acknowledging they exist, leaders have the opportunity to lead the organization from a traumatized state to an organization that is resilient and on the road to healing. This kind of organization values each member's contributions and focuses on moving forward out of trauma. Through the application of the practices in this chapter, organizations can be restored to functioning in a healed state. It is important to note that these practices are to be implemented periodically and revisited often as there is not a scenario where an organizational leader can predict when trauma within the organization will resurface. With demonstrated commitment to understanding the needs of the organization's workforce, the organization will operate in a framework to create an organizational culture that is safe, offers healing and eventually flourishes to its fullest capacity despite uncertainty.

REFERENCES

Bal, P., & De Jong, S. (2016). From human resource management to human dignity development. In *Dignity and Humanistic Management.* Palgrave MacMillan.

Baltaci, A., & Balci, A. (2017). Complexity leadership: A theoretical perspective. *International Journal of Educational Leadership and Management, 5*(1), 30–58. doi:10.17583/ijelm.2017.2435

Bass, B. M. (1990). From transactional to transformational leadership: Learning to share the vision. *Organizational Dynamics, 18*(3), 19–31. https://doi-org.proxygsu-afpl.galileo.usg.edu/10.1016/0090-2616(90)90061-S

Block, P. (2009). *Community: The structure of belonging*. Berrett-Koehler Publisher, Inc.

Bolman, L., & Deal, T. (1997). *Reframing organizations: Artistry, choice, and leadership* (2nd ed.). John Wiley & Sons, Inc.

Bolman, L., & Deal, T. (2017). *Reframing organizations: Artistry, choice, and leadership* (6th ed.). Jossey-Bass. doi:10.1002/9781119281856

Brawley Newlin, A., & Pury, C. (2020). All of the above?: An examination of overlapping organizational climates. *Journal of Business and Psychology, 35*(4), 539–555. doi:10.100710869-019-09639-6

Cameron, E., & Green, M. (2017). *Essential leadership: Develop your leadership qualities through theory and practice*. Kogan Page Limited.

Carter, L. (2020). Most loved workplace research and technical documentation for the most loved workplace validation. *Best Practice Institute Journal of Management and Leadership.* https://www.academia.edu/43619158/Most_Loved_Workplace_Research_and_Technical_Documentation_for_the_Most_Loved_Workplace_Validation

Coelho, D., & Pires, R. (2020). Impact of organizational climate. *Scientific Electronic Archives, 14*(1), 67–73. https://doi-org.proxygsu-afpl.galileo.usg.edu/10.36560/14120211260

Comaford, C. (2018, January 20). Why leaders need to embrace employee motivation? *Forbes*. https://www.forbes.com/sites/christinecomaford/2018/01/20/why-leaders-need-to-embrac e-employee-motivation/?sh=68186a641272

Csikszentmihalyi, C. (1990). *Flow*. HarperCollins Publishers.

Dugan, J. P. (2017). *Leadership theory: Cultivating critical perspectives*. ProQuest Ebook Central. https://ebookcentral.proquest.com

Dweck, C. S. (2016). *Mindset: The new psychology of success*. Ballantine Books.

Eagly, A., Johannesen-Schmidt, M. C., & Engen, M. L. (2003). Transformational, transactional, and laissez-faire leadership styles: A meta-analysis comparing women and men. *Psychological Bulletin, 129*(4), 569–591. doi:10.1037/0033-2909.129.4.569 PMID:12848221

Galetti, B., Golden, J. III, & Brozovich, S. (2019). Inside day 1: How Amazon uses agile team structures and adaptive practices to innovate on behalf of customers. *People & Strategy, 42*(2), 36.

George, J., & Jayan, C. (2012). The impact of organizational culture on personal effectiveness. *Journal of the Indian Academy of Applied Psychology, 39*, 119–129.

Goleman, D., Boyatzis, R., & McKee, A. (2001). Primal leadership: The hidden driver of great performance. *Harvard Business Review, 79*(11), 42–51.

Hopper, E. (2018). *Trauma and organizations* (2nd ed.). Routledge. doi:10.4324/9780429484285

Jabeen, A., Khan, M. A., & Manzoor, M. (2020). Exploring the influence of leadership styles on professional motivation. *Gomal University Journal of Research, 36*(2), 84–92. https://doi-org.proxygsu-afpl.galileo.usg.edu/10.51380/gujr-36-02-08

Karapancheva, M. (2020). The future of organizational culture. *Journal of Sustainable Development, 10*(25), 42–52.

Kaya, C., & Baskaya, R. (2017). The roles of organizational and ethical climate on individual performance of employees. *Business Management Dynamics, 6*(8), 27–38.

Labas, D. (2017). The impact of organizational crisis preparedness on firm business performance. *Market-Trziste, 29*(1), 75-92. http://eds.a.ebscohost.com.proxygsu-afpl.galileo.usg.edu/eds/pdfviewer/pdfviewer?vid=2&sid=9efa0130-aafe-49c5-b55c-f911adfdc4eb%40sdc-v-sessmgr03

Leiss, W. (2004). Effective risk communication practice. *Toxicology Letters, 149*(1-3), 399–404. doi:10.1016/j.toxlet.2003.12.050 PMID:15093287

Lencioni, P. (2004). *Death by meeting: A leadership fable...about solving the most painful problem in business*. Jossey-Bass.

Lim, A. (2020, June 15). The big five personality traits. *Simply Psychology*. https://www.simplypsychology.org/big-five-personality.html

Long, S. (2018). *Trauma as cause and effect of perverse organizational process. In Trauma and organizations* (2nd ed.). Routledge.

Mayne, J. (2004). Reporting on outcomes: Setting performance expectations and telling performance stories. *The Canadian Journal of Program Evaluation*, *19*(1), 31–60. http://citeseerx.ist.psu.edu/viewdoc/download?doi=10.1.1.460.3960&rep=rep1&type=pdf

McLeod, C. (2003). Toward a restorative organization: Transforming police bureaucracies. *Police Practice and Research*, *4*(4), 361–378. doi:10.1080/15614260310001631262

Menand, L. (2018, September 3). What personality tests really deliver? *The New Yorker*. https://www.newyorker.com/magazine/2018/09/10/what-personality-tests-really-deliver

Miller, D., & Proctor, A. (2016). *Enterprise change management: How to prepare your organization for continuous change*. Kogan Page.

Morgan, G. (2011). *Reflections on images* of organization and its implications for organization and environment. *Organization & Environment*, *24*(4), 459–478. doi:10.1177/1086026611434274

Nasreen, A., Varshney, P., & Waseem, C. (2019). Organizational climate in NBFC: Implications on employee engagement. *Amity Global Business Review*, *9*, 7–14.

Nguyen, T., White, S., Hall, K., Bell, R., & Ballentine, W. (2019). Emotional intelligence and managerial communication. *American Journal of Management*, *19*(2). https://doi.org/10.33423/AJM.V19I2.2068

Nichols, C., Hayden, S. C., & Trendler, C. (2020). Four behaviors that help leaders manage a crisis. *Harvard Business Review*. https://hbr.org/2020/04/4-behaviors-that-help-leaders-

Nwabueze, U. (2011). Implementing TQM in healthcare: The critical leadership traits. *Total Quality Management & Business Excellence*, *22*(3), 331–343. doi:10.1080/14783363.2010.532338

Oxford University Press. (2020). Ontological. In *Oxford English and Spanish dictionary*. Retrieved April 8, 2021, from https://en.oxforddictionaries.com/definition/ontological

Pahi, M., & Hamid, K. (2016). The magic of destructive leadership: Laissez-faire leadership and commitment to service quality. *International Journal of Economic Perspectives*, *10*(4), 602–609.

Patterson, K., Grenny, J., McMillian, R., & Switzler, A. (2012). *Crucial conversations: Tools for talking when stakes are high* (2nd ed.). McGraw Hill.

Popick, J. (2014, March 6). *Managing expectations: The most underrated leadership skill*. Academic Press.

Prentice, W. C. H. (2004). Understanding leadership. *Harvard Business Review*.

Prescod, D., & Zeligman, M. (2018). Career adaptability of trauma survivors: The moderating role of posttraumatic growth. *The Career Development Quarterly*, *66*(2), 107–120. https://doi-org.proxygsu-afpl.galileo.usg.edu/10.1002/cdq.12126

Rath, T. (2008). *Strengths based leadership: Great leaders, teams and why people follow*. Gallup Press.

Roux-Dufort, C. (2009). The devil lies in details! How crises build up within organizations. *Journal of Contingencies and Crisis Management*, *17*(1), 4–11.

Schein, E. (2004). *Organizational culture and leadership* (3rd ed.). Jossey-Bass.

Shoup, J., & Studer, S. (2010). *Leveraging chaos: The mysteries of leadership and policy revealed.* Rowman & Littlefield Education.

Shugart, S. (2013). *Leadership in the crucible of work: Discovering the interior life of an authentic leader*. Florida Hospital Publishing.

Shultz, S., Opie, C., & Atkinson, Q. (2011). Stepwise evolution of stable sociality in primates. *Nature, 479*, 219–222. https://doi.org/10.1038/nature10601

Strauser, D. R., Lustig, D. C., Cogdal, P. A., & Uruk, A. Ç. (2006). Trauma symptoms: Relationship with career thoughts, vocational identity, and developmental work personality. *The Career Development Quarterly*, *54*(4), 346–360.

Tenuto, P. (2018). A review of the listening leader: Creating the conditions for equitable school transformation. *Journal of Organizational & Educational Leadership*, *4*(1), 4. https://digitalcommons.gardner-webb.edu/joel/vol4/iss1/4

Thomas, B., & Lucas, K. (2019). Development and validation of the workplace dignity scale. *Group & Organization Management*, *44*(1), 72–111. https://journals.sagepub.com/doi/pdf/10.1177/1059601118807784

Vivian, P., & Hormann, S. (2002). Trauma and healing in organizations. OD Practitioner. *Journal of the National Organization Development Network*, *34*(4), 37–42.

Vivian, P., & Hormann, S. (2015). Persistent traumatization in nonprofit organizations. *OD Practitioner*, *47*(1), 25–30.

Yuan-Duen, L., Pi-Ching, C., & Chin-Lai, S. (2020). The evolution of the leadership theories and the analysis of new research trends. *International Journal of Organizational Innovation*, *12*(3), 88–1.

Yukl, G. (1999). An evaluation of conceptual weaknesses in transformational and charismatic leadership theories. *The Leadership Quarterly*, *10*(2), 285.

Zaar, S., Van Den Bossche, P., & Gijselaers, W. (2020). How business students think about leadership: A qualitative study on leader identity and meaning-making. *Academy of Management Learning & Education*, *2*, 168.

Chapter 11
Proposition MRM:
A Paradigm for Post-Crisis Organizational Healing – The Case of Fishlake Primary School

Ann-Marie Wilmot
Church Teacher's College, Mandeville, Jamaica

Canute S. Thompson
University of the West Indies at Mona, Jamaica

ABSTRACT

This qualitative chapter, which used a case study design, sought to examine whether the leadership theory of proposition modelling, respect, and motivation, MRM, could be used as a framework to guide a primary school through and out of the trauma it was experiencing. Organizational traumas are natural occurrences that affect large and small organizations. They can be triggered by several factors such as mergers, acquisitions, staff retrenchment, interpersonal dysfunctionalities, and drastic change. The research found that by focusing on building trust, pursuing community engagements, managing conflicts, and building capacity, the principal was able to help the school community overcome its trauma. The chapter concludes that an essential ingredient in effective management of organizational trauma is building and maintaining trust, and this strategy is aided by engagement of stakeholders, respecting the collective wisdom, and meaningful power-sharing.

INTRODUCTION

Organizational crises are natural occurrences that reflect the dynamism of human behavior and its impact on organizational functioning, and the impact that external events can have on an organization. There is a strong position within the scientific literature on crisis management and intervention, which suggests that the constructs, crisis, and crisis management remain ill-defined (Bundy et al., 2017; Callahan, 1994; Deverell, 2012). Bundy et al., who propose what they describe as an integrative framework of crisis

DOI: 10.4018/978-1-7998-7016-6.ch011

and crisis management, suggest that there are two primary perspectives in the literature, one focused on the internal dynamics of crisis and the other on external stakeholders. This assessment, by Bundy et al, is consistent with the approach of this study. This chapter seeks to examine how a school in Jamaica, whose relationship with stakeholders was impacted by a set of internal dynamics, applied an effective framework to contend with their reality to protect, preserve, and promote its mission and purpose.

The origins of the concept of *crisis* are in the fields of psychology and psychotherapy. Caplan (1961) is credited with what has become one of the widely accepted definitions of crisis, which states that a crisis occurs when a person is faced with obstacles which, for a time, threaten the attainment of important life goals and thus require extraordinary or unusual means and approaches to cope with or overcome them. Since Caplan's widely accepted definition of crisis in 1961, the scientific literature on the construct has been expanded, with some of the most recent revisions adding the component of organizational healing, as seen in the works of Bhasin (2019) and Fontella (2020). Prior to these scholars, there were Venugopal (2016), Vivian and Hornman (2012), and De Klerk (2007), among others.

Bhasin (2019) defines organizational crises as occurrences that are destabilizing and dangerous to the health and well-being of a community, typically occur at short notice, and can further cause a sequence of unexpected events. Bhasin posits that there are eight types of organizational crises: technological, financial, crises of deception, confrontation, misdeeds, malice, violence, and crises of nature. According to Bhasin, crises of organizational misdeeds occur when the management of organizations makes decisions that are inimical to the interests of stakeholders and are of such a nature that they could cause reputational damage to the organization. Organizational crises, according to Fontella (2020), occur when a company has wronged its customers and damaged mutually beneficial relationships. These actions undermine trust and place the organization at a place of such brokenness that healing of the wounds becomes a condition for restoration, renewal, and advancement. This healing requires acknowledgment of the misdeeds committed and a commitment to repair the damage done. Both acts become preconditions for moving forward.

Fontella (2020) suggests that an organizational or business crisis has three key elements, and the latter is applicable to this study. It must pose an imminent threat, involve an element of shock or surprise, and place the organization under unusual or undue pressure and strain. Fontella identifies the following five types of organizational crises: financial, personnel, organizational, technological, and natural.

Venugopal (2016) offers a specific definition of organizational trauma which carries similar resonances. "Organizational trauma is a situation in which an individual is confronted with actual or threatened death, serious injuries or sexual violation, or exposed to death, injury, or suffering of other people within the same working environment." (p. 65). This study utilizes aspects of the foregoing definitions in addressing the crisis at Fishlake Primary School.

Alongside Bundy's classification of crises, it may be further posited, using Sigmund Freud's and Erik Erikson's categories of human experiences, that crises are developmental and life situational in nature (Cherry, 2019). Developmental crises arise from the normal passages of change which occur in the life of both humans and organizations. On the other hand, life situational crises arise when humans and organizations face unexpected events that exceed their initial coping capacity because their 'weight' is greater than their internal and accumulated resources (Golan, 1978).

One of the arguments of this chapter is that the quality of leadership available to an organization will determine how well the organization is managed in times of crisis and trauma. This assertion is applicable to schools as well as other organizations. Kouzes & Posner (2017) contend that the fortunes of an organization are highly dependent on the quality of its leadership. Their views are supported by

Leithwood & Riehl (2003), who argue that the quality of leadership is second only to the quality of teaching and learning in determining how a school performs. These leadership qualities would be relevant, and perhaps arguably more so, as organizations face and navigate their way through crises.

This chapter examines some crises faced by a primary school in Jamaica, and how it navigated those crises. The researchers assigned both the school and the participants pseudonyms – Fishlake Primary School, Jeanette (Principal), and Mary (Vice Principal) respectively and focused on their leadership approaches in working through those crises. The chapter achieves this by examining some theories of organizational trauma and healing, and by outlining some types, natures and causes of organizational trauma. Consistent with the theme of this book, the chapter advances a model for dealing with organizational crisis. The model known as Proposition MRM (Modeling, Respect, and Motivation) is a leadership theory arguing that organizational performance is largely a function of leadership modeling behaviors expected of others, showing respect to team members, and motivating them (Thompson, 2019).

Proposition MRM was derived from Thompson's research on students' expectations of leadership and represents the three factors that together accounted for the largest variation in the data set. The three factors accounted for over 61% of the variation in the data. This theory was first advanced by Thompson (2009), focusing on leadership behaviors related to power-sharing and collaboration and expanded to exploring sustainable development and ethics, among other constructs, in 2019. In this study, Proposition MRM is examined to determine whether its claims are applicable to, and appear to have been used by, the leadership of Fishlake Primary School in pursuing organizational healing and renewal as the organization seeks to continue recovering from crisis.

Having established the theoretical frame, this chapter provides a description of the methodology, findings and chronicles the evolution of the crisis at Fishlake Primary School. Next, it outlines how both primary power figures responded to the crises. The discussion and analysis capture four main themes: building trust, community engagement, conflict management and resolution, and capacity building. It then recommends Proposition MRM as a paradigm for organizational healing and renewal, as well as illustrates how the current Principal (the former Vice Principal) of the school can apply the related tenets to continue the healing process that the former Principal had begun prior to leaving the school's employment. By making salient connections to the role of the leader in dismantling and mitigating organizational dysfunctions, healing and renewal, the chapter reinforces the importance of trust-building in pursuing organizational achievement. Further, it suggests some trust-building activities, calling for mandatory training for school leaders to help them support their institutions through crisis to healing and for additional interrogation of the usefulness of Proposition MRM as a tool of healing and renewal.

BACKGROUND

Profile of the Fishlake Primary School

Located in a rural community where most of the teachers and administrators are residents who have not worked elsewhere, Fishlake Primary School is over 100 years old. The community has a rich practice of local or traditional folk culture. Parents enter national competitions in dance, dialect and vocals story telling and traditional culinary arts.

At the time the principal joined the staff, Principal Jeanette found that some of the staff members enjoyed a close-knit relationship because about five members of staff were blood relatives. When one of these members had a task, based in the school or the community, the other family members and at least one other staff member would come together to ensure the activity was successful. The disadvantage to this relationship was that it led to the formation of loyalty clusters, within the school. These loyalty clusters had a strong influence on the ethos of the institution, which resulted in the adversarial climate that existed at several levels of the institution, including the general staff, the governance, and community levels. It was an environment of silent intimidation, distrust, and one in which persons think they know what others do not know, according to the findings emanating from the demographic data of the research.

The school's climate was characterized by power plays, mistrust, sabotage, disloyalty, undermining, and general unsupportiveness of those who did not fit into that coterie. As an outlier, the newly appointed Principal, Jeanette, maintained: "Persons got their jobs out of loyalty, were promoted out of loyalty … so they had to know how to play their games. So, [they operated as if] they were always on needles or eggshells." She also explained that the mistrust was so pervasive that "the community felt compromised because they thought certain things were dishonest [and that] there was also a lot of mistrust from the Old School Association, abroad and locally." Documents such as "memos," which she found in the school, did not support the interpersonal display that she observed. In essence, she shared, "you are dealing with the products of years of interpersonal, dysfunctional relationships, and the works."

Theories on Organizational Post-Crisis Trauma / Healing

Trauma induced incidences are pervasive in all spheres of life, on an individual and collective or organizational level. In a study that sought to understand the causes and types of organizational trauma, Venugopal (2016) noted that, though classification of organizational trauma differs, organizational trauma negatively influences both the victims and other staff that are exposed to the victim. According to Venugopal, "vicarious trauma is easily transferable from the victim or materials containing traumatic conditions to people exposed to traumatic conditions" (p. 66).

Despite this, traumatic incidences are likely to occur, and organizations (schools among them) often do not intervene effectively to help their employees address or resolve them. This lack could be because top leaders, in this case school administrators, are insufficiently sensitive to this need in their employees, they lack the will, or they do not possess the requisite skills to do so. However, leaders and their workers should recognize that "the nature of an organization's work directly impacts the culture of the organization. An organization providing services to traumatized individuals, families and/or communities is susceptible to becoming a traumatized system experiencing the cumulative effects of the work itself" (Vivian & Hornman, 2012, p. 37). If the experts are vulnerable, because they remediate the traumatized, leaders should support those with the active experiences to ensure their healing and renewal.

A Campbell Systematic Review (CSR) was conducted to examine the effects of trauma-informed schools on trauma symptoms/mental health, academic performance, behavior, and socio-emotional functioning. The Campbell Collaboration webpage describes itself as "an international social science research network that produces high quality, open and policy-relevant evidence syntheses, plain language summaries and policy briefs" (https://www.campbellcollaboration.org/. para.1). They are among other companies that perform systematic reviews. According to them, "A systematic review is an academic research paper that uses a method called 'evidence synthesis', which can include meta-analysis, to look for answers to a pre-defined question" (https://www.campbellcollaboration.org/. para.2).

In the CRS review, Maynard et al. (2019) cited Overstreet and Chafouleas (2016) in sharing that the promotion and provision of trauma-informed approaches particularly in school settings, is growing at a rapid rate across the United States. This perspective resonates with Venugopal's (2016) observation about vicarious trauma and its transferability. Within this context, it is a fair conclusion that regardless of whoever in the institution experiences trauma, whether students, teachers, or administrators, there is likely to be a collective response. But what are the causes of trauma in schools, whether related to students, faculty, or administrators?

Venugopal (2016) presented the following reasons for trauma in organizations: "downsizing, workload, and complexity of the job, role definition, relationships, career development, organizational culture, or ethical conflict" (pp. 3-5). All of these are applicable to schools, though in varying degrees. Venugopal maintains that the types of relationships employees nurture with supervisors, colleagues, and sub-ordinates are pivotal factors to reducing or increasing the global response to trauma within the same institutions. Venugopal's views is an endorsement for maintaining healthy relationships in schools because of the potential for renewal and healing. Venugopal (2016) links negative interpersonal relationships and lack of social support from other people within the workplace as being significant stressors, with the potential of creating some level of organizational trauma.

Problematic leadership shifts are one of many causes of institutional trauma. In summary of Vivian and Hormann's (2013) theory of the causes and sources of trauma, Vivian et al. (2018) include a single devastating event, ongoing wounding, which can be the internal or external empathetic nature of the work, and the redemptive value of the work. Vivian et al. (2018) resonate with Venugopal (2016) and Cooper et al. (2001), in principle, on the causes of trauma. For example, they describe ongoing wounding as "collective emotional and psychological injury that builds over time and disables an organization with an accumulation of harm" (p. 4). These, they explain, can be either external or internal, with the latter breeding mistrust of leadership and helplessness as fear is enshrined in the organizational culture.

Approaches Organizations Use to Address Organizational Trauma

Researchers have studied the impact of trauma dating back to the immediate Post-World War era (Winter, 2019), but trauma practitioners have expanded its use beyond non-conflict contexts to include business organizations and educational institutions. The impact of trauma and the unresolved hurts that it causes impede peoples' capacity to be effective and their ability to perform, according to De Klerk (2007). While organizational interventions cannot eliminate suffering, some approaches may be instrumental in influencing the healing process. De Klerk outlines a range of factors that can cause trauma in organizations, including mergers, downsizing, restructuring, and terminations due to conflicts and malperformance.

The impacts affect not only those who are victims but also those who observe. These findings are like those Venugopal (2016) shares. De Klerk suggests that among the ways in which organizations can help employees deal with trauma are, firstly, acknowledging that the trauma exists, and secondly, providing a safe space for employees to talk about the effects of the trauma. Within the context of that safe space, employees are to be allowed to discuss the impacts of the experiences on them and draw on the coping strategies of other employees.

Winter (2019) conducted a study of the impact of trauma on an Austrian bank. Many employees exited the organization and findings showed that trauma can affect not just individuals but also entire organizational structures. Winter further posited that the various dimensions of the disruptive effects caused by a single traumatic event can, over time, weigh upon both the organizational structures and hierarchical systems. Winter found that one of the paths used to help employees overcome the impacts of a series of traumatic events at all levels of the organization was to inform and train the remaining staff in the fields of self-awareness, self-compassion, mindfulness, and resilience.

According to Messina (2019), leaders are responsible for managing the culture of an organization and mitigating the traumatic events that can result in mediocre services and organizational peril. He suggests that a transformational leader, "goes beyond managing day-to-day operations and crafts strategies for taking his company, department or work team to the next level of performance and success" (Rowald and Scholtz, 2009, p.29) and is best suited to deal with organizational trauma, as they possess emotional intelligence and the ability to lead in difficult times. Like De Klerk (2007), Messina argues that the starting point for dealing effectively with organizational trauma is to acknowledge the trauma or traumatizing events. Having made acknowledgment, the next step, according to Messina, is to labor in transforming the organizational culture to deal with and mitigate the impact of the trauma through implementing structures and processes, which allow for structured approaches to confronting trauma.

Theoretical Framework: Leadership and Organizational Healing

The review of the literature on organizational trauma has shown that organizations can experience trauma from several factors and that these traumatic events occur quite regularly. The literature also shows that organizations can use the post-crisis experience as a time for renewal and growth.

Alexander et al. (2020) explored the issues of organizational trauma and the phenomenon of organizational posttraumatic growth (OPTG), concluding that an organization can bounce back from trauma and experience growth and renewal. Their study examined the experiences of a company traumatized by a substantial theft, committed by a senior leader. Through the instrumentality of a leadership approach that showed a willingness to confront the issue and facilitate candid conversations with employees, the company was transformed and emerged stronger. This leadership approach was rooted in a commitment to creating a defined organizational culture and a climate of openness.

Organizational culture and climate are the most critical variables shaping the behavior of employees; thus, the starting point for how an organization will manage organizational trauma is rooted in the culture and climate of the organization. A central pillar of the organization's capacity to find healing is the level of trust between organizational leaders. Trauma affects all organizations (Byrd-Poller et al., 2017) and the degree of an organization's trauma is often determined by the level of mistrust in the organization.

The leader, therefore, is tasked with the responsibility to shape the culture of the organization, Thompson (2015) argues, declaring that the leader is the Chief Culture Shaper (C.C.S.). If the leader is the Chief Culture Shaper and culture determines the degree to which an organization will function during and after times of trauma, then a leader's effectiveness, as indeed at all other times but especially at times when faced with trauma, will be dependent on whether they are trusted. A leader can hardly be effective if they are not trusted (Hurley, 2006).

Thompson (2018a) contends that promoting and nurturing trustable relationships is the foundation of a healthy organization. This trust, he suggests, is attained when stakeholders are engaged and their wisdom is considered in making organizational decisions, as well as power shared with them. When there is trust, leaders will be given the benefit of the doubt when tough decisions are made, even in the absence of full information.

On the other hand, even when decisions are justified and justifiable, for example, in traumatic situations such as mergers and downsizing, driven by harsh external realities, leaders are not given the benefit of the doubt if there is a lack of trust, as Thompson (2018a) posits. Notwithstanding the challenges that they may face, if an organization's leadership has not earned credibility through an established history of consultation and power-sharing during a crisis, its best path out of the crisis is still found in engaging the use of those strategies.

This theoretical framework, which guides the analysis of this case and the conclusions of this chapter, is the assertion that a crisis can be a significant learning opportunity (Alexander et al., 2020). But for the organization to experience growth and renewal, it requires a particular kind of leadership (De Klerk, 2007; Messina, 2019). An important element of the kind of leadership that post-crisis organizational healing requires is trust (Byrd-Poller, et al., 2017). The authors contend that the operationalization of these leadership qualities is embedded in Proposition MRM, posited by Thompson (2019). This leadership theory is described in more detail below.

Factor One: Modeling

Modeling shows who a leader is far more precisely than that for which they are known. The expectation is for leaders to model that for which they are known. Others, both inside and outside the organization, can refer to this modeling as a guide towards shaping their conduct and understanding the things for which the organization stands and the values it holds dear. The conduct of the leader, then, sets the tone for others in the organization. Thus, those who seek to serve in and through the organization can rely on what they see in the leadership as a template for what is expected of them.

The areas across which a leader is expected to model appropriate behaviors are many, and a random list of key areas includes, but is not limited to, conflict management, transparency, service beyond the call of duty, managing interpersonal stresses, demonstrating a commitment to the organization's vision and mission, and being held accountable. These issues, collectively, define the nature of organizational trust and are often central to an organization's well-being as Bartsch et al. (2013), Gibbons (2004), Nooteboom (2002), and McAllister (1995) have shown. Modelling then, according to Thompson (2019), is central to building trust for confidence in a leader, and the effectiveness of the leadership of an organization is based on trust, as Thompson (2018a) and Hurley (2006) have argued. Modeling shows who a leader is, which is more compelling than a leader saying who they are. Modeling is, according to Thompson (2009), the surest way for a leader to seek to affect organizational transformation.

Factor Two: Respect

Proposition MRM contends that respect is the chief mode in which leaders relate to others. According to Thompson (2019), the construct 'respect' is tied to the interrogative of how a leader engages others, and the answer given is that the leader relates by showing regard for the skills and abilities, opinions, perspectives, needs, and aspirations of others within the organization or community they lead. In this regard, leadership is seen as an engagement, upliftment, and mutual affirmation in which the leader engages in behaviors that beget that which they give. Thompson (2009) defines respect as an interpersonal facility in which the basic human need for affirmation of a sense of worth and being valued are upheld through the demonstration of deference to the other. This results in the attainment of a climate in which the commitment to serve is stimulated or reinforced.

The construct of respect, as articulated in Proposition MRM, is supported by Wood (1999), who suggests that when one respects another, one is not prone to be oblivious or indifferent to that person or to ignore or quickly dismiss that person, neglecting or disregarding that person. Thompson (2018b) notes that it is instructive that the synonyms for respect are *regard* and *consideration*, which mean, "examine carefully" and "paying close attention." In this construct, 'respect' conveys the idea that a leader will carefully examine the concerns and perspectives of others and pay close attention to the issues which matter to them.

Factor Three: Motivation

Motivation, in Proposition MRM, refers to the skill a leader displays in helping followers or members of the organization (who are themselves leaders) to grasp the purpose of the organization, namely its mission and vision, and to enable them to maintain a commitment to the faithful pursuit of that mission and vision. Thus, while modelling is concerned with 'who' a leader is, and respect with 'how' a leader relates, motivation concerns where the energies of the leader are focused.

In the calculus of Proposition MRM, the energies of the leader are to be focused on keeping the eyes of members of the organization fixed on the larger purpose of the organization, not on some personal preoccupation with the leader or even process. Motivation is about building consciousness and awareness about goals and inspiring the passion needed for the relentless pursuit of the same. An organization that makes the leader its central focus, rather than learning, discovery, and problem-solving, risks becoming both distracted from its goal as well as developing a diminished perspective on its purpose (Senge, 1990). It is for this reason that modelling, as discussed earlier, is not about the leader being a model unto themself, but an example and exemplar of the ideals and standards of the organization, with the intent that the leader promotes organizational learning and continuous renewal.

When members of an organization understand the purpose of the organization, they are better able to negotiate their place in that organization. They are also inoculated from the ills of normlessness (Deflem, 2019) and the sense of alienation that arises from the feeling of uncertainty about one's place. Feelings of uncertainty about place can affect one's worth, which can give rise to demotivation. One of the ways an organization can signal to its members that it values them is by ensuring that it communicates to them where and how they fit into the larger scheme (Thompson, 2019).

Methodology and Description of Findings

This study uses a critical instance case study design. Organizational crises or traumas, while common across organizations, are typically and indeed ideally, not frequent occurrences in organizations. If crises become commonplace, they would logically cease to be crises and be just normal events. Given then the sporadic nature of crises, treating them as critical incidents and studying them as such is logical. According to Creswell (2014), case studies represent an in-depth study of a phenomenon designed to generate insight into how the phenomenon occurs within a given situation. The phenomenon of organizational trauma is widespread, as has been shown earlier, but a case study is used to narrow down a broad field of inquiry into one or a few easily researchable examples. Critical instance case study designs allow for the examination of a situation of unique interest, with little to no interest in generalizability.

The focus on a single institution, a primary school, to study the problem of organizational trauma is consistent with the theory and application of how case study designs are used and, in this case, focusing on the experience of a crisis, which is a critical instance event.

Ultimately, by using this research design, the process of testing whether a specific theory or model applies to phenomena in the real world can be effectuated. Thus, it is the intent of this study to explore whether Proposition MRM can be applied to the experience of an organization experiencing trauma.

Data for the study was gathered using virtual sit-down interviews. These interviews were recorded using the audioNote Voice Recorder, after which the interviewer replayed it and manually transcribed it in the audioNote pad. All data was then transferred and combined in one Microsoft Word document. The typed interview was proofread then shared with the related interviewee to ensure accuracy consistent with the principles of reliability and trustworthiness.

The researchers interviewed former Principal of Fishlake Primary School, Jeanette Brown. She is in her late 30's and her post-graduate level education is inclusive of teacher training and the national principal certification. Mary, the then Vice Principal, is in the early 50's and has only the teaching training diploma, acquired some 30 years prior and no longer the basic requirement for new entrants into the profession. The institution and both former Principal and her then Vice Principal are referenced using pseudonyms. The interview sought to establish and generate an understanding of the school's context, a description of the interpersonal relationships at the time Jeanette joined the staff, the central conflict arising from her assuming the role of Principal, how the conflict evolved, who were the major players and their roles in the conflict, the approaches Jeanette used to address the conflict, and some of the leadership behaviors the current Acting Principal believes are necessary to address similar situations now. The segment below describes the findings of the study.

Crisis and Change: The Evolution of the Conflict at Fishlake School

Jeanette identified three major sets of players in the evolution and perpetuation of the conflict, most of whom were on the school's Board of Governance, namely: The Chairman, Mary (the Vice Principal), one member of the senior teacher's core, and the teacher representative. Interestingly, she remarked, "The chairman was the biggest player," because his position connected to the other major players and, it was common knowledge "…that he had promised the post to the Vice Principal." To this end, he hid the fact that he had gotten the letter from Jamaica Teaching Council regarding Jeanette's provisional appointment. According to Jeanette, the Ministry [of Education Youth & Information] had to inform her about the appointment in November, though the document was available, and it was to be effective beginning in September of the same year.

"So, [when] I eventually took up the post the following January [the chairman having thwarted the realization for the prior September] everybody was surprised because [they] thought Mary would have been the Principal." Jeanette continues: "Additionally, I asked the Chairman to assist me by introducing me to important personnel in the community, but he did not; but I now recognize that it was because he could not go beyond his conscience." In sum, the conflict had touched most areas of the school's organizational structure. These included the general teaching staff, the administrative staff, the Board of Management, and the immediate and diasporic communities. These events created a sense of psychological and emotional dislocation at the school and people began hurting, hence creating a situation to facilitate internal ongoing wounding.

Both Mary and Jeanette were deeply affected by the events, causing a fracture in relationships at the school. Mary was reverted to her role as Vice Principal, though she, along with her supporters, had high hopes of remaining in the position of Principal. Jeanette explained: "Mary and her supporters took several steps, including writing several letters to the Ministry of Education about her work, to boost her chances of being permanently appointed, as the Principal." However, it was not until she took up the position that Jeanette "realized that Mary vied for it and was unsuccessful." Her failure, and consequent disappointment precipitated a crisis. In Jeanette's words, "I came upon some challenges." The fact that Mary's appointment as Principal did not materialize led to her displeasure, which did not set a friendly context in which Jeanette assumed said position. "In her [Mary's] mind she felt mistreated and had an agenda to operate as if she owned the school."

On the other hand, Jeanette's crisis arose from taking up the position to lead a school where the governing body and some teachers were unwelcoming, because they were not prepared for this change in leadership. Like Mary, she had a strong psychological response to the situation. She reportedly felt unsupported in this new leadership role and took the view that "persons on the school's Board of Management felt loyal to Mary." Hence, she concluded, "therein lies my challenge." She further explained: "Because the board chairman believed Mary should have gotten the position, he did not give me the support." This was evidenced by her claim that "he slighted his responsibility" and that very often when she wanted to communicate with him, he would be unavailable unless she used Mary, her rival, as a conduit. She reflected on the conflict: "I would describe the conflict of leadership as one that is typical in most schools where people believe that the person who acts in a position [provisionally] before the vacancy becomes substantive, should get the position." Additionally, "in my case, I was an outsider who got the position over someone who was there internally acting in the position, and who had later simultaneously applied, when the vacancy was advertised."

This sense of entitlement perpetuated the conflict and ill feelings among members of the school community [because] "once Mary felt dissatisfied, her followers would also be dissatisfied, and each family member had a loyalist from the main staff." Therefore, "regardless of what good was being done, I was always perceived as being against her. So even attempts to validate and work with [her] bore no fruit," Jeanette recounts.

Responses to the Leadership Crisis: Mary's Response

The data did not only reveal the nature and evolution of the crisis and its major players. It also provided an opportunity to understand how both leaders responded to the crisis of their leadership realities. Mary's response was combative/defensive and this began showing, even before Jeanette entered the school. She withheld information from Jeanette, which Jeanette requested to prepare for the interview, noting as her reason that she too was applying for the post so that was to be expected. Several other experiences of similar unsupportive attitudes in other interactions were also unearthed. A case in point was when Jeanette suggested that, since she was new, it would be good to understudy Mary, for a few weeks, who had been at the school for several years. Mary showed "scant regard" and indicated that Jeanette "was the principal and needed to be in front." Additionally, another reason Jeanette posited for a feeling of lack of support is the fear of reprisal from Mary and those who support her therefore the staff members "had to know how to play their game. They had to be careful; and, if they didn't have to show me their hands, they didn't do so except if they were outside of the school. [Then], when you get them talking, you get to understand the underbelly of the culture."

In Jeanette's words, Mary engaged "passive resistance," another signal that Mary was hurting. For example, she asserted, "We would have meetings where everything seemed okay but there would be no cooperation, afterward, and because of this, I would have to do most of the leg work myself." Another instance demonstrating a lack of support and a sense of common purpose was when Jeanette organized a Labor Day (a national holiday in Jamaica, characterized by voluntary work) project for the school and invited members of the community to do voluntary work, including renovation and landscaping. Only "two teachers on staff" participated. After the activities picked up, "Mary and her family member, who was also employed to the school, came by, stood and observed, and did not help. Even the security at the school was a challenge because vandals would break [into] the school weekly. I, and even some parents, were able to link that back to malicious efforts to frustrate the current leadership". Mary's response to the trauma of not being appointed school principal involved approaches that included avoidance, negative influence, passive resistance, and an overall attitude of unsupportiveness, all undesirable responses to the crisis, especially from one who is in leadership.

Responses to the Leadership Crisis: Jeanette's Response

On the contrary, the data showed that the Acting Principal's response was diametrically opposed to that of her competitor, though divisive strategies were employed against her; and this revealed a different psychological response to the leadership crisis. She avoided reprisals and, instead, used a wide array of approaches to impact the teachers, students, and surrounding communities. Some of these approaches included empowerment initiatives to build professional and personal efficacies of teachers, such as content workshops and professional development seminars. Others included making the effort to build stronger personal relations with staff members by meeting with them in spaces of comfort outside the school and supporting non-school concerns, such as attending funerals for their loved ones. She also employed the strategy of re-deployment of teachers according to their strengths and their preferences; for example, this was the strategy she employed when she assigned a teacher the responsibility for the first mathematics expo. Additionally, Jeanette immersed herself in the community by doing walk-throughs to meet key community stakeholders, parents (among others), attending funerals, community functions, inviting members into the school and other strategies.

Jeanette explained one of the first approaches she took to the challenges that she experienced with Mary, the Vice Principal of Fishlake Primary School: "In terms of her general operations of the school, I validated her for the work she does in order to secure her cooperation with myself and the rest of the senior management team, though she still held certain things close to her." She initiated empowerment incentives such as a staff of the month award, student of the month, punctuality award, awards for commendable work, and distributed certificates and other tokens at prize-giving ceremonies or graduations. Using an inclusive approach, she sought to build relationship with "even the unsupportive chairman, [and] allowed for some opportunity to recognize his service to the school." In support of her empowerment initiatives, Jeanette "re-examined the strengths and qualifications of the teachers and re-deployed them to areas in which they were comfortable working." She also made extra efforts to integrate them into activities such as sharing responsibilities: "I didn't always do general assembly. I rostered and delegated responsibilities. Then, it became less about me and more about the job." Additionally, "When there was a staff meeting, I assigned different individuals to convene different aspects of the meeting."

As part of her response, Jeanette built personal and communal relationships among stakeholders through in-reach (initiatives within the school) and out-reach (initiatives involving stakeholders external to the school). Of her teachers, she noted: "I had to make it a point of my duty to develop interpersonal relationships with each teacher, empowering them, validating them, and supporting them in the various roles in which I wanted them to function." For example, she delegated her grade six mathematics teacher to host the school's first Math Expo, and invited and involved various stakeholders, inclusive of the print and electronic media. According to her, "It was an excellent day. When the board members, members of the school community and parents saw their children in the papers, it boosted their morale."

Jeanette was very deliberate in the three-pronged approach she took to building relationships with the community. She took an individualistic approach: "I inserted myself in the community. I walked and learnt the community, met the members for myself and showed them who I am and my interest in their children; and, they felt a sense of fairness on my path." The second dimension to her community engagement efforts was that she organized the community to be in service to the school, evidenced by the Labor Day project. This provided an opportunity for them to build appreciation for the school. Not assured of the assistance from her staff, she had shared her contingency: "I brought a core team from my circle, invited corporate interest and the Ministry. We worked by ourselves, but when the community saw our togetherness, they came and really, really got involved."

The final dimension of the three-pronged approach she took involved reciprocating service to the community in a day of voluntarism which she reported was "one of the outstanding activities that the community welcomed." In preparation for the day, "Each grade got to identify a community need, that they would address. Some cleaned community play grounds, visited homes for the elderly, others painted or cleaned preselected areas. People began recognizing that the progress of the school was not about the person at the head but about the advancement of the children." Among the other approaches Jeanette took was the building of external coalitions, inviting experts to provide counseling and mediation for conflict resolution and hosting challenging and even sometimes "explosive conversations" framed by respect, a demonstration of fairness and objectivity, and demonstration of care.

The Staff's Reflection on Jeanette's Leadership Strategies

The staff, including the two antagonists, were more accommodating to Jeanette nearer to the end of her tenure; some even tendered apologies. Even Mary told her, at a send-off function they were attending for her, "Miss, I must acknowledge, I know I have not supported you in the programme, but I am sorry. I hope that you are able to forgive me and we will move on and do what we have to do." There were other similar sentiments from others among the senior core, one of whom expressed, "Miss we are just understanding what you are about and we are sorry that we did not support you but we will carry on the vision." Others, through WhatsApp messages and emails, expressed, "Miss we are really going to miss you." Jeanette substantiated: "Even at graduation, they would not have known that I was leaving but somebody from the School's Foundation was there and awarded me a trophy for volunteer service to the community." The positive attitude was not limited to staff only since even "the Chairman, and even the Vice-Chairman expressed their satisfaction with the way that I had done my job and with the infrastructural changes." Interestingly, others expressed that they "were afraid and were going leave because they said that now I would be gone, there will no longer be any fairness. Others even asked me to write their recommendations before I left." Having probed the reason for this, she responded thus: "they don't believe that the person who would write them would have been fair enough, for them to give them that kind of command over their lives to ask them for one." They also have a concern for confidentiality. So, they believe that if they have me do it, they would feel comfortable asking me to do them so that all would not know they were job hunting."

ANALYSIS AND DISCUSSION

There are four main themes that emerged from the findings, namely: Building Trust, Community Engagement, Conflict Management, and Capacity Building. These themes show that despite the depth of the trauma and, indeed, given that depth, while one leader was focused on thwarting the leadership of the school and deepening the crisis and consequent divisions, the other was focused on finding a way forward to renew and heal the organization.

The Trust Building Factor

The description of Fishlake Primary School as a place where a "climate of silent intimidation exists" and where there was "sabotage, mistrust, powerplays, and disloyalty," suggests that these tensions created an emotional, psychological, and relational void, among the administration, the members of staff, and the community. This environment brings to life Vivian et al's (2018) theory of ongoing wounding and is attributable to the state of inertia that the school was in, resulting from accumulated psychological injury. Trauma affects all areas of an organization, as Byrd-Poller et al. (2017) argue, and the degree of an organization's trauma is often determined by the level of mistrust in the organization.

Lack of trust is one factor that ongoing wounding gives rise to and is injurious for an organization. Covey (2006) supports this notion when he explains that lack of trust in an organization results in a dysfunctional environment and toxic culture, characterized by open warfare, sabotage, grievances, punishing systems and structures, and intense micromanagement, some of which had been nurtured under Mary's stewardship of the institution. Therefore, a lack of trust stymied the growth and development of the organization. The result of this is a set of fractured and decimated relationships, a further impact of demotivation fueled by lack of respect and appropriate models – factors which Thompson (2019) ascribe to effective leadership. As represented by the difficulties at Fishlake School, in institutions where these characteristics are normalized, it also becomes an inordinately huge task for leadership to facilitate renewal and healing.

On the converse, when Jeanette took leadership of the school, she immediately took steps that are attributable to trust-building, a pillar for healing and renewal in institutions. The fact that she did not have a retaliation agenda, intimates that she did not view the leadership challenges as obstacles, but as opportunities to improve the organizational culture. Despite opposition and lack of support, she worked single-handedly to start projects. Her effort to encourage sharing of power and responsibilities was reflected in allowing each staff member their time to lead initiatives such as the math expo. This demonstrates that, for her, the heart of the institution's progress, became not about who was heading the institution but more so about how well the activities of the school were advancing students and staff. "Transformational Leadership inspires followers to go beyond their own self-interests for the good of the group" (Bosman 1997, p. 8).

Transformational Leadership requires trust and emotional intelligence, cited by Messina (2019) as a required characteristic to deal with organizational trauma and the ability to lead in times of crises. She utilized the empowering value of invested trust and its ability to motivate and inspire, as a crucial means of beginning the process of renewal and healing. This is in alignment with Bosman's (1997) views that "when a leader shows concern for others, demonstrates trust and respect, and treats people fairly, people are more likely to want to help and support the leader by doing what he or she asks" (p.19). In other words, trust enables leaders and the people whom they lead to develop a reciprocal relationships. Covey

(2006) corroborates Bosman's (1997) views about trust and supplies additional information, noting that "in a company, high trust materially improves communication, collaboration, execution, innovation, strategy, engagement, partnering, and relationships with all stakeholders" (p.19).

The Community Engagement Factor

Jeanette's three-pronged approach to community engagement, including inserting herself in the community, marshalling the community to serve the school, and having the school reciprocate that action, was a deliberate move to create a common ground, establishing a unified sense of purpose, to initiate the renewal process towards healing. Additionally, it also suggests that she understands that building solid coalitions was one way of increasing the likelihood of success. Though we did not set out to understand if Jeanette applied aspects of Proposition MRM in her community engagement approaches, she displayed aspects of modelling, respect, and motivation in her approach, all appropriate leadership traits for effectively engaging a workplace that is fractured. She modelled the behavior she desired her sub-ordinates to adopt, without any form of confrontation or derision, and modelled respect both for self and others. This behavior aligns well with the position advanced by Thompson (2019), who asserts that modelling reveals the essence of a leader with a force that is more compelling than what the leader says, a statement which we found true of Jeanette when we asked her to describe how she characterized her leadership.

She faced high levels of unsupportiveness, particularly in the initial stages of her initiatives. However, the way she enacted community engagement took grit and courage. This typifies Kouzes and Posner's (2017) belief that "the strongest motivation to deal with challenge and the uncertainty of life and work comes from inside people and not outside" (p.156). They also explain that, whether the times are tumultuous or tranquil, when a leader is implementing an initiative, he or she should create conditions that will allow constituents to readily join in. Jeanette's grit and posture communicate she has a well-defined sense of purpose. "Purpose is a tremendously powerful source of motivation, and people cannot persevere for long without it" (Kouzes & Posner, 2017; p. 155). The inherited emotionally charged ethos of the school did not daunt her drive to accomplish tasks of improving teaching and learning opportunities. She had those tough and "explosive conversations so much so that [she] had to hold herself together, be firm, and love colleagues along", even when they were not receiving it. But the principle she puts to play is Maxwell's (2011) maxim that "care without candor creates dysfunctional relationships. Candor without care creates distant relationships" (p.112). It is safe to extrapolate that dysfunctional and distant relationships are likely to erupt or persist where conflict management and resolution skills are deficient in leaders. The following segment examines how Jeanette utilized these skills.

Conflict Management and Resolution

Conflict management is another strategy that Jeanette used to facilitate renewal and healing in the face of the upheaval resulting from her taking up a leadership post. Conflict management requires the display of respect. Her capacity for this was evident in the peaceful and deliberate ways in which she went about resolving the conflicts. "When stakes are high, opinions vary, and emotions run strong, we are often at our worst" (Patterson et al., 2012, p. 27).

Jeanette's methods of negotiating her way around conflicts defied the prediction of Patterson et al. (2012) regarding what can be the typical response of a leader undergoing crises. One of the conflict management approaches she took was to validate Mary's work, and others, like the Chairman of the school's Board of Governors, who were unprofessional and vindictive in their leadership approaches towards her. These are individuals who were active in the agenda to block Jeanette's access to the job and, having failed at that, erected various bulwarks in her efforts to successfully execute the job, when she got it. Her approach finds favor with Thompson's (2019) interpretation of respect in the corresponding dimension of his Proposition MRM model. In it, he argues that respect is a tool for interpersonal relations, honoring the need for a show of support, a sense of worth and a sense of being valued. The natural result of this, he claims, is that commitment to serve is stimulated or reinforced. She also sought external mediation from specialists to provide counseling and reinforce the value of this professional service. Jeanette's achievement of this goal in an institution where changes were vigorously resisted, and negative counter-narratives normalized is indicative that her leadership played a role in narrowing the gap of the leadership divide.

Jeanette's skill in handling conflict points to, her knowledge of what Northouse (2016) calls supportive behaviors. He attributes these job-related behaviors as useful in helping teams establishing individual and collective comfort with the situation, they are handling. Some of these include asking for input, solving problems, praising, sharing, and listening. Her conflict resolution skills also invite us to reflect on her humility. Though she presents as decisive, strong, and knowledgeable, the leadership crisis at Fishlake could have easily allowed her to make defensive behaviors her priority, given the levels of dysfunctional organizational behavior that were present. Clayton (2010) iterates that an abiding feature of humble people is that their self-esteem levels are high. They are unambiguous about who they are and they have positive self-feelings. One of the ways leaders can bring about renewal and healing is by inspiring others to believe in the change narrative to which they are seeking buy-in. Without being a vessel of positivity, it will prove challenging for a leader to accomplish this, and they will be unable to build the capacity of those they lead. Jeanette demonstrated strong capacity building strategies as outlined in the upcoming segment.

Capacity Building Strategies

In an organization, few things provide greater motivation than when staff feels empowered to do what they need to do. Empowerment is not only about process and space, in terms of freedom, but increased ability to do and to be. Jeanette's approach to building the capacity of the staff at Fishlake Primary School shows that she is highly motivated and dedicated to heal her organization from the divide the leadership tussle caused. For example, she established a Boys in Education Program. Under this program, she invited external stakeholders, over an extended period, to instruct teachers at the school how to use dominoes as a mathematics teaching learning tool. This was a successful venture that merited feature in one of Jamaica's national newspapers and, more importantly, improvements in boys' performance in mathematics was evident. She also reported that "parents were happy and begun to see that the school was for all." She also drew on the resources of experts of the Ministry of Education to conduct mathematics content workshops for her teachers.

Another strategic move she made was to target those "teachers who Mary overlooked who felt marginalized and demotivated." According to Jeanette, she "held their hands to help them reach heights." In explaining, she recounted that through her influence, 2 members enrolled to pursue their bachelor's teaching degree and 1 took the National College for Educational Leadership's (NCEL) flagship Aspiring Principals course.

Jeanette also built teacher's capacity by giving those teachers, and some others, the opportunity to plan a Math Open Day "to plan and demonstrate their best practices." Jeanette assigned tasks to these members and provided guidance to others who were uncomfortable executing, to get them to successfully complete the assigned tasks to take them to new heights. These initiatives not only allowed the members to feel as if they "are a part of the center" but also gave them opportunities, that were otherwise unavailable to them, to build their competencies. In addition, Jeanette assigned tasks liked by supervisees and compatible with professional and personal efficacies. This assisted her leadership efforts because those who she called upon to complete tasks already possessed the skills to do so; and, those who were not as skilled but who made themselves subjects of mentoring all added to the human resource pool of the institution.

Jeanette also organized content workshops, conducted by internal and external personnel, motivational sessions, along with other types of on-the-job training and personal interventions, such as attendance at seminars hosted by expert organizations. She implemented a "Celebration of Success" initiative to recognize "small and big wins." A collaboration was formed with the general staff to develop a transparency criterion for the monthly tokens given throughout the semester and awards given during end of school year Prize Giving Ceremony.

Thompson (2019) opines that demotivation springs from lack of clarity about one's worth. These capacity building and empowerment interventions demonstrate the power of effective leadership to clarify employees' worth, at least in relation to the organization in which they work. Northouse (2016) explains: "empowerment builds followers' confidence in their own capacities to think and act on their own because they are given the freedom to handle difficult situations in the way they feel best" (p. 235).

Jeanette's included parents in her capacity building strategies. These parents benefited from an 8-week Parenting Seminar series and received certificates of completion. The program, according to her, "taught parents how to support their kids in areas of conflict resolution, dealing with the challenges of adolescents, supervising homework and personal hygiene." Serving the needs of the community is a method of galvanizing support and strengthening home school bonds. In turn, the school's students gained a learning advantage and Jeanette won the parents' confidence in her ability to lead.

An organization that suffers trauma, crisis or change is often demoralized. Within the context outlined by Northouse and Thompson, an effective leader's empowerment efforts can suitably function as a gateway to healing and renewal, if they achieve their impact. Additionally, a leader will be unable to get a school to the point of being sustainably functional without a dedicated, highly competent teaching force. Importantly, this achievement requires leaders at all levels guiding and supporting the process (Fullan, 2003). Therefore, the role Jeanette played in creating a work context where she diffused existing tensions, offered new perspectives, and partnered with staff, seems to have been a valuable contribution in establishing the requisite balance the institution needed to move forward to begin the process of healing and renewal.

Proposition M.R.M. as a Paradigm for Organizational Healing and or Renewal: A Model for Application

As outlined earlier, Proposition MRM is a model of leadership, developed by Thompson (2019). The value of this model of leadership is anchored on the philosophy that a leader who models desired behavior, demonstrates respect, and drives motivation will lead successfully. Jeanette took leadership of Fishlake Primary School, a school already operating in trauma; the change her assumption of leadership caused exacerbated the problem of entitlement and cronyism that was present in the school before she arrived, increasing the urgency of the need to renew and heal.

The researchers found that there were many negative activities in the workplace, some of which were emotionally harmful, negative social relationships, lack of social support, and internal on-going wounding, all catalysts of trauma (Cooper et al. al., 2001; Venugopal, 2016; Vivian et al., 2018;). Therefore, the authors make the case that Jeanette reaped some positive behaviors through the process of renewal and healing being initiated and, though she no longer works at Fishlake Primary School, it is still in transition mode. Though classification of organizational trauma differs, a point of similarity is that organizational trauma negatively influences both the victims and other staff that are exposed to the victim, because vicarious trauma is easily transferable.

Among the observable positive outcomes to result from Jeanette's leadership of the school was the attitudinal and dispositional shift of the relationship's antagonists towards being more open to and embracing of Jeanette. For example, during Jeanette's preparation to leave the school, Mary committed to continue the work begun under Jeanette's leadership. This signals that some measure of the resolution of the main conflict had taken place. However, though an optimistic signal that healing and renewal are possible, a resolution of conflict is not synonymous with healing. Now that Jeanette is gone, Mary can build on Jeanette's achievements to continue the process of renewal and change; and Proposition MRM leadership model is an efficient facility to utilize in achieving this, as demonstrated below.

Modeling

The process of healing and renewal at Fishlake School will not thrive under mixed signals. In many ways, Mary, who eventually assumed principalship of Fishlake School, had previously demonstrated individualism, which is grounded in selfishness. This selfishness is evidenced, for example, by her effort to thwart Jeanette's appointment as Principal and then by the lack of support she gave Jeanette, having failed in her effort. One aspect of the tenet of modeling in the Proposition MRM leadership frame is that modeling is the essence of leadership. Thompson (2019) suggests that the qualities attributed to leaders through observation of their behavior must be sufficient to shape their conduct so that others looking on can get an image of what to aspire to and that for which the organization stands. Guided by this tenet, as she picks up from Jeanette, Mary, in her new capacity as Principal, must become more actively involved in school initiatives as a means of moving others to adopt a spirit of cooperation and ownership of the institution in continuing to restore relationships, including those ruptured because of her response to Jeanette's leadership.

The sentiment above is a necessary tool of conviction to influence her staff members to observe a spirit of corporation from Mary, rather than one which suggests individual desires are what drive her actions. Fullan (2003) supports this idea when he advises that "the new school leaders must be fully cognizant of the big picture. She [or he) must understand that the most effective leaders are those who can see and appreciate the larger contexts in which they operate" (pp. 59-60). Once she establishes this display of collective synergy, staff members will eventually begin to see the school as not owned by some (she and her relatives), but by all. Additionally, when Mary models desirable traits and behaviors, her commitment to the vision and mission of the organization will become unquestionable. Modeling a stable commitment will also help her convey the importance of healing, renewal and the urgent need for these to happen.

Another closely related aspect of Proposition MRM is that modeling shows who a leader is and is more compelling than a leader saying who they are. Previously, when Mary was dissatisfied with a decision, she would make it known and withdraw. Modeling this behavior was reflected in the response of other staff members, who would do likewise. As the leader, she must lead in ways that dispel these ambiguities about her integrity, mission and values to reveal her character; therefore clarifying that she will work to support the efforts of collective decisions. Being a model, she must dispense with leveraging negative influence. This incites fear and will not assist her healing agenda for the organization, since fear may bring about compliance, but not commitment.

In an effective leadership model, the leader prioritizes showing consistency in disposition, communicating in words, demeanor and actions to strengthen stakeholder belief that obstacles will be overcome (Kouzes & Posner, 2017). In this way, Mary will be sending a message that she values fairness and objectivity and when all are convinced this exists because the leader models it, the healing and renewal agenda will be prioritized ahead of the organization. Kouzes and Posner (2017) also advised that people get a sense of hope that the future can hold bright prospects, when leaders display positivity and optimism. This, they claim, is crucial, generally. However, in times of great uncertainty, leadership guided by positive emotions "is absolutely essential to moving people upward and forward" (p. 36). Mary must adopt respect as one of the pillars of her leadership, in order to continue expanding on the Jeanette's successes. The authors provide some additional insights in the segment to follow.

Respect

Healing and renewal materialize in an atmosphere of deep-seated respect. Proposition MRM holds the view that respect is the chief conduit leaders use to relate to each other; and that the leader relates by showing regard for the skills, abilities, opinions, perspectives, needs and aspirations of those within their community or organization. Fishlake Primary School is described as a community school, because of the integral role community members play in its development, and the Parent Teacher Association would be the nexus of this effort. However, Jeanette reported that prior to her beginning to regain their support, this community mistrusted the school and consequently, withdrew their support. Bearing in mind Proposition MRM's claim about how respect shapes relationship, Mary can systematically engage the P.T.A. to restore trust and heal the relationship. Mary could achieve this by allowing members to air their concerns and share their suggestions in a non-judgmental manner.

One way of regaining and applying respect is to demonstrate value for and appreciation of the contributions these players make by meaningfully incorporating them in decisions and school activities, to meet some of their needs. When needs are being met, and when one respects another, one is not prone to be oblivious or indifferent to that person, or to ignore or quickly dismiss that person, neglecting or disregarding them (Wood, 1999). Therefore, it becomes vital that Mary "build[s] an organizational culture that aligns with organizational purposes and values, inspires and gives meaning to individual efforts and provides the symbolic glue to coordinate the diverse contributions of many" (Gallos, 2006, p. 349). Mary must send the signal that she values the P.T.A., and they, like members of staff, will begin noticing the difference, hence, paving the way for healing and renewal to begin.

Another tenet of respect in the Proposition MRM model of leadership is that the leader engages behavior which begets that which they give. This implies that if a leader disregards a member of their team, then the expectation is that this behavior is acceptable. In this light, Mary's reputable personal accountability is an essential display of respect. If she wants employees to be true to their words, then she must be respectful enough to honor hers. She can use this to develop trust, which they will reciprocate. In Covey's (2006) aspect of integrity, he affirms congruency can bolster achievement. Congruency, he claims, is when a leader is whole or seamless. That is, they are the same inwardly and outwardly. Unlike compliance, he explains, congruence is what builds trust and develops credibility. Respect will become a corollary when Mary's colleagues, especially those who felt marginalized while she resisted Jeanette, feel comfortable she behaves in a manner to inspire higher levels of trust in her credibility. When leaders show respect in a broken organization, it could very likely spur the healing process. Respect is a catalytic agent for motivation. This concept is featured below.

Motivation

The final element of the Proposition MRM which Mary can apply to heal and renew her school is motivation. One tenet of motivation maintains that leaders should focus their energies on helping followers to remain steadfast on the more significant cause for an organization's existence, and not on some personal preoccupation with the leader or even process. Maxwell (2011) argues similarly, stating that if a leader focuses on themselves, always, and what they desire, instead of maximizing people's potential to learn and grow, then people will be a hindrance in that leader's goals. As a result, he said that such a leader invests much time in nursing disappointment and arising from feeling let down because followers show no support for their self-driven agenda. Unlike Jeanette's motivation to build a positive school culture, Mary's drive to "own" the school placed her in the situation that Maxwell describes. She promoted only those members of staff who were loyal to her. However, motivating staff is necessary to create an equitable field from which to heal the broken relationships and demotivation arising from the divide and rule approach she took to leadership and the privileged family clusters. Motivation is necessary to refocus or focus the attention of the staff to collaborate to improve its services, like Jeanette demonstrated.

Messina (2019) asserts that leaders are responsible for managing the culture of an organization and mitigating the traumatic events that can result in mediocre services and organizational peril. To begin the process of healing and renewal, an excellent way to start restoring or building self-worth and increasing the motivation of members is to treat issues transparently. Mary must advertise job vacancies, rather than hand-picking family members. This will allow the organization's members to view practices and processes through new lenses of fairness and transparency, contributing to them feeling included and secure. Hence, they will be better able to locate their position within the organization and are more likely to commit to it.

Another tenet of motivation that Proposition MRM advances is its aim towards building consciousness and awareness about goals and inspiring the passion needed for a relentless pursuit of them. While Jeanette clearly exhibited this mantra, Mary did not. Moving forward, she needs to urgently understand: With a positive motivation philosophy and practice in place, productivity, quality and service should improve because motivation helps people towards achieving goals, gaining positive perspective, creating the power for change, building self-esteem and capability, managing their development, and helping others (Josephs, 2015). Mary can seize opportunities to collectively construct a celebration frame to celebrate small achievements of the staff members, facilitate change intervention experts, and target those who seem ignored by bringing them to the center.

CONCLUSION AND REFLECTIONS

Given that Proposition MRM can be successfully applied to deal with the crisis of leadership at rural Fishlake Primary School, the conclusion is that it is a viable theory to strategically apply to achieve healing and renewal as an internal intervention. Though Jeanette did not actively apply the theory, the study found that features of it were prominent in her leadership and these features were crucial in addressing some of the school's dysfunctions. The extrapolation from this, then, is that it could be quite applicable in other types of organizations as a single tool or as a means of laying the foundation for successful external interventions, where the complexities are more severe and multi-layered.

From Jeanette's leadership journey, readers can deduce that a leader is foundational not only to treating organizational dysfunctions but also in mitigating them. The researchers' findings underscore that the approach leaders take to leading an institution to a place of healing and renewal must be based on trust. This study highlighted three primary levels, namely the leader's trust in self, trust of others and trust in the process. Leaders of schools and other organizations must possess a high level of trust in themselves as a prerequisite for addressing traumatic situations within their institutions. This is critical because they must trust that they know the strategies they intend to use and that they know how to effectively implement them.

Additionally, trust between leaders and those they lead is always vital but especially in times of crisis. Like Jeanette, in her school Principal role, leaders of other types of organizations are therefore urged to make trust-building a central part of their leadership and management practices (Hurley, 2006). Leaders must not only implement trust-building initiatives for their employees. They must also invest trust in them. But, as the literature and the study's findings show, these exercises require deliberate efforts to create opportunities across the organization for involvement in decision-making, including the utilization of collective wisdom and power-sharing. Jeanette's leadership also demonstrates that support for the creation of organizational structures to make these modes of engagement normal is vital to producing trust. This plants the seeds for better crisis management and resolution. Here also, non-educational institutions have an opportunity to learn, adopt and apply relevant principles from Fishlake Primary School.

Also necessary for managing organizational crisis is the will to acknowledge that the trauma and its antecedents are real, as suggested by De Klerk (2007) and Messina (2019). A leader's acknowledgment of what employees are feeling and fearing as well modeling behavior that validates their feelings and fears, boosts employees' trust in the process for dealing with present and future situations decided or determined crises by the leadership of the organization. Otherwise, employees will undermine the trust and create obstacles to the intended process.

Having acknowledged the existence of the crisis, the leadership of the organization must then implement activities to help employees cope. Among the suggested strategies are those posited by Winter (2019), who discusses the value of activities that build self-awareness, self-compassion, mindfulness, and resilience. This study contributes to capacity building, conflict management, and community engagement, all of which, coupled with Winter's strategies, form complementary roles in an organization's healing and renewal process. Ultimately, all leaders are responsible for managing the culture of their organization and mitigating the traumatic events that can result in mediocre services and reputational harm to the organization as well as imperil the health and well-being of employees (Messina, 2019).

The researchers make the case that, where it does not yet exist, stakeholders should afford school leaders mandatory training that includes strategies to identify and address trauma to enable them to lead their employees to healing and renewal. This training would ensure that they have technical competencies, the ability to nurture required dispositional facilities and the appropriate theoretical underpinning, such as the one this chapter proposes.

Jeanette presents as a leader who is strong, resilient, focused and determined. She seems not only to know what to do but has the grit and courage to make those practices central to her leadership. A consideration in this context is that these traits could be innate or developed over time. Understanding this provides opportunities to further investigate the broader usefulness of Proposition MRM as a leadership tool of healing and renewal.

REFERENCES

Alexander, B. N., Greenbaum, B. E., Shani, A. B., Mitki, Y., & Horesh, A. (2020). Organizational post-traumatic growth: Thriving after adversity show. *The Journal of Applied Behavioural Science, 57*(1), 30–56. https://journals.sagepub.com/doi/pdf/10.1177/0021886320931119

American Psychological Association. (n.d.). *Trauma*. https://www.apa.org/topics/trauma/

Bartsch, V., Ebers, M., & Maurer, I. (2013). Learning in project-based organizations: The role of project teams' social capital for overcoming barriers to learning. *International Journal of Project Management, 31*(2), 239–251. doi:10.1016/j.ijproman.2012.06.009

Bhasin, H. (2019). *8 Different Types of crisis*. https://www.marketing91.com/types-of-crisis/

Bosman, J. P. (1997). *Leadership, power and influence*. Organizational Behaviour. https://www.academia.edu/40931547/Bachelor_of_Commerce_Programme_Organizational_Behaviour

Bundy, J., Pfarrer, M. D., Short, C. E., & Coombs, W. T. (2017). Crises and crisis management: Integration, interpretation, and research development. *Journal of Management, 43*(6), 1661–1692. doi:10.1177/0149206316680030

Byrd-Poller, L., Farmer, J.L., & Ford, V. (2017). The role of leaders in facilitating healing after organizational trauma. In S. Hasa & R. Burnett-Thornton (Eds.), The impact of organizational trauma on workplace behaviour and performance. Information Resources Management Association.

Callahan, J. (1994). Defining crisis and emergency. *The Journal of Crisis Intervention and Suicide Prevention, 15*(4), 164–171. PMID:7729148

Campbell Collaborations. (n.d.). *What are you looking for? Better evidence for the world*. https://www.campbellcollaboration.org/

Caplan, G. (1961). *Approach to community mental health*. Grune and Stratton.

Cherry, K. (n.d.). *How Do Erikson's and Freud's Theories Compare?* Verywell Mind. https://www.verywellmind.com/freud-and-erikson-compared-2795959

Clayton, M. C. (2010). How Will You Measure Your Life? *Harvard Business Review*. https://hbr.org/2010/07/how-will-you-measure-your-life

Covey, S. M. R. (2006). *The speed of trust: The one thing that changes everything*. Free Press.

Creswell, J. (2014). *Educational research: Planning, conducting, and evaluating quantitative and qualitative research* (4th ed.). Pearson Education.

De Klerk, M. (2007). Healing emotional trauma in organizations: An O.D. framework and case study. *Organization Development Journal, 25*(2), 49–55.

Deflem, M. (2019). Anomie. In M. Ryan (Ed.), *Core Concepts in Sociology* (pp. 8–9). Wiley-Blackwell.

Deverell, E. (2012). Investigating the roots of crisis management studies and outlining future trajectories for the field. *Journal of Homeland Security and Emergency Management, 9*(1), 1–21. doi:10.1515/1547-7355.1956

Fontanella, C. (2020). *5 Types of Crisis Your Company Could Face (and Protect Against).* Hubspot. https://blog.hubspot.com/service/types-of-crisis

Fullan, M. (2003). *The moral imperative of school leadership.* Corwin Press.

Gallos, J. V. (2006). Reframing complexity: A four-dimensional approach to organization, diagnosis, development, and change. In J.V. Gallos (Ed.), Organization Development Journal. Jossey-Bass.

Gibbons, D. E. (2004). Friendship and advice networks in the context of changing professional values. *Administrative Science Quarterly, 49*(2), 238–259.

Golan, N. (1978). *Treatment in crisis situations.* Free Press.

Hurley, R. (2006). The decision to trust. *Harvard Business Review.* https://hbr.org/2006/09/the-decision-to-trust

Joseph, O. B. (2015). The effect of employees' motivation on organizational performance. *Journal of Public Administration and Policy Research, 7*(4), 62–75. doi:10.5897/JPAPR2014.0300

Kouzes, J. M., & Posner, B. Z. (2017). *The leadership challenge: How to make extraordinary things happen in organizations* (6th ed.). Wiley & Sons.

Leithwood, K. A., & Riehl, C. (2003). *What we know about successful school leadership.* Academic Press.

Manley, M. (1987). *Up the down escalator: Development and the international economy – A Jamaican case study.* Harvard University Press.

Maxwell, J. C. (2011). *5 Levels of leadership: Proven steps to maximize your potential.* Thomas Nelson.

Maynard, B. M., Farina, A., Dell, N. A., & Kelly, M. S. (2019). Effects of trauma-informed approaches in schools: A systematic review. *Campbell Systematic Reviews, 15*(1-2). Advance online publication. doi:10.1002/cl2.1018

McAllister, D. J. (1995). Affect - and cognition-based trust as foundations for interpersonal cooperation in organizations. *Academy of Management Journal, 38*(1), 24–59.

Messina, M. J. (2019). *Failed dependency: Leadership strategies to prevent, mitigate, and heal organizational trauma in behavioural health systems* (Publication No 13863379) [Doctoral dissertation, Ashford University]. ProQuest Dissertations Publishing.

Nooteboom, B. (2002). *Trust: Forms, foundations, functions, failures and figures*. Edward Elgar Publishing. doi:10.4337/9781781950883

Northouse, P. G. (2016). *Leadership theory and practice* (7th ed.). Sage.

Overstreet, S., & Chafouleas, S. M. (2016). Trauma-informed schools: Introduction to the special issue. *School Mental Health*, *8*(1), 1–6. doi:10.100712310-016-9184-1

Patterson, K., Grenny, J., McMillian, R., & Switzler, A. (2012). *Crucial conversations: Tools for talking when the stakes are high* (2nd ed.). McGraw Hill.

Rivkin, J., & Ryan, M. (2012). Situating colonial and postcolonial studies. In Literary theory: an anthology (pp. 1100–1111). Wiley Blackwell.

Rowold, J., & Schlotz, W. (2009). Transformational and transactional leadership and followers' chronic stress, Kravis Leadership Institute. *Leadership Review*, *9*(2), 35–48.

Senge, P. (1990). *The fifth discipline: The art and practice of learning organizations*. Currency and Doubleday.

Stake, R. E. (1995). The art of case study research. *Sage (Atlanta, Ga.)*.

Thompson, C. S. (2009). *Towards solutions: Fundamentals of transformational leadership in a post-modern era. Mandeville*. Northern Caribbean University Press.

Thompson, C. S. (2015). *Locating the epicentre of effective (educational) leadership in the 21st century*. The Caribbean Leadership Re-Imagination Initiative.

Thompson, C. S. (2018a). Leadership behaviours that nurture organizational trust: Re-Examining the fundamentals. *Journal of Human Resource Management*, *21*(1), 28–42.

Thompson, C. S. (2018b). The construct of 'respect' in teacher-student relationship: Exploring dimensions of ethics of care and sustainable development. *Journal of Leadership Education*, *17*(3), 42–60. doi:10.12806/V17/I3/R3

Thompson, C. S. (2019). *Reimagining educational leadership in the Caribbean*. The University of the West Indies Press.

Tuckman, B. W. (1965). Developmental sequence in small groups. *Psychological Bulletin*, *63*(6), 384–399. doi:10.1037/h0022100 PMID:14314073

Venugopal, V. (2016) Understanding organizational trauma: A background review of types and causes. *IOSR Journal of Business and Management*, *18*(10), 65-69. http://www.iosrjournals.org/iosr-jbm/papers/Vol18-issue10/Version-7/I1810076569.pdf

Vivian, P., Cox, K., Hormann, S., & Murphy-Kangas, S. (2018). Healing traumatized organizations reflections from practitioners. *OD Practitioner*, *49*(4), 45–51. https://static1.squarespace.com/static/515287f7e4b0574a80b7af08/t/5caa4835f4e1fc950f1fb123/1554663479452/Healing+Traumatized+Organizations+2018.pdf

Winter, L. (2019). *Organizational trauma: A phenomenological study of psychological organizational trauma and its effect on employees and organization*. Retrieved: https://www.researchgate.net/publication/339615204_Organizational_Trauma_A_Phenomenological_Study_of_Psychological_Organizational_Trauma_and_Its_Effect_on_Employees_and_Organization

Wood, A. W. (1999). *Kant's ethical thought*. Cambridge University Press. doi:10.1017/CBO9781139173254

KEY TERMS AND DEFINITIONS

Capacity Building: Policies and activities specifically targeted at improving the skills, competencies, leadership efficiency, managerial impact, and overall improvement to an organization's human resources.

Change: Change is a direction or set of decisions translated into actions that influence a difference in organizational operations, identity, and overall ethos.

Conflict Management: Strategies leaders utilize to improve relationships among employees, stakeholders, and their associates to promote actions that drive productivity and mitigate or eliminate those that reduce it—the process of mediating and mitigating fractious differences and disputes among persons.

Engagement: A set of methods/techniques/strategies employers use to reach out to employees to earn their trust, establish their sense of worth that result in employees' commitment to the workplace and improved organizational performance.

Healing: Healing is the process of renewal and recovery where an individual or organization recovers from a state of brokenness resulting from the damaged trust, which occurs because of the misdeeds committed by others. It is also a psychological place of being committed to repair the damage done and move forward.

Modeling: Modeling has to do with leaders displaying behaviors they expect of others, so that others, both inside and outside the organization, can refer to this modeling as a guide towards shaping their conduct and understanding the things for which the organization stands and the values it holds dear.

Motivation: Motivation is a form of energy needed for production and productivity, or a consciousness about the process and expected outcomes and their relationship to a bigger picture or more significant purpose.

Organizational Renewal: Organizational renewal is how an organization alters a downward trajectory and repurposes itself towards refocusing on its existing or new vision and purpose.

Organizational Trauma: Organizational traumas are events that cause significant disruptions in organizations, which can have critical short-term or long-term adverse implications for the organization's stability and effectiveness.

Respect: Respect is an interpersonal facility that supports the creation and maintenance of positive and mutually supportive relationships in which people see each other for whom they are and are enabled to accommodate each other to fulfill their needs and aspirations.

Compilation of References

Aafjes-van Doorn, K., Békés, V., Prout, T. A., & Hoffman, L. (2020). Psychotherapists' vicarious traumatization during the COVID-19 pandemic. *Psychological Trauma: Theory, Research, Practice, and Policy*, *12*(S1), S148–S150. doi:10.1037/tra0000868 PMID:32478559

Adams, T., & Stewart, L. (2015). Chaos Theory and Organizational Crisis: A Theoretical Analysis of the Challenges Faced by the New Orleans Police Department During Hurricane Katrina. *Public Organization Review*, *15*(3), 415–431. doi:10.100711115-014-0284-9

Aiken, L., Clarke, S., Sloane, D., Sochalski, J. A., Busse, R., Clarke, H., Giovannetti, P., Hunt, J., Rafferty, A. M., & Shamian, J. (2001). Nurses' reports on hospital care in five countries. *Health Affairs (Project Hope)*, *20*(3), 43–54. doi:10.1377/hlthaff.20.3.43 PMID:11585181

Alexander, B. N., Greenbaum, B. E., Shani, A. B., Mitki, Y., & Horesh, A. (2020). Organizational posttraumatic growth: Thriving after adversity show. *The Journal of Applied Behavioural Science*, *57*(1), 30–56. https://journals.sagepub.com/doi/pdf/10.1177/0021886320931119

Allen, J. S., Stevenson, R. M., O'Boyle, E. H., & Seibert, S. (2020). What matters more for entrepreneurship success? A meta-analysis comparing general mental ability and emotional intelligence in entrepreneurial settings. *Strategic Entrepreneurship Journal*, *2020*, 1–25. Advance online publication. doi:10.1002ej.1377

Allison, G. T., & Zelikow, P. (1999). *Essence of decision: Explaining the Cuban Missile Crisis* (2nd ed.). Longman.

American Association of School Administrators. (2010). *The American school superintendent decennial study 2010.* https://www.aasa.org/content.aspx?id=458

American Federation of Teachers. (2017). *2017 Educator quality of work life survey.* https://www.aft.org/sites/default/files/2017_eqwl_survey_web.pdf

American Nurses Association (ANA). (n.d.). *Health and Safety Survey.* ANA.

American Psychological Association. (2012). *Building your resilience.* http://www.apa.org/topics/resilience

American Psychological Association. (2015). Retrieved January 23, 2021, from https://www.apa.org/news/press/releases/stress/2015/snapshot

American Psychological Association. (n.d.). *Trauma.* https://www.apa.org/topics/trauma/

American University School of Education Online Programs. (2019, December 5). *Transformational leadership in education.* https://soeonline.american.edu/blog/transformational-leadership-in-education

Andenoro, A. C., Sowcik, M. J., & Balser, T. C. (2017). Addressing Complex Problems: Using Authentic Audiences and Challenges to Develop Adaptive Leadership and Socially Responsible Agency in Leadership Learners. *Journal of Leadership Education, 16*(4), 1–19. doi:10.12806/V16/I4/R1

Anderson, E. C., Carleton, N. R., Diefenbach, M., & Han, P. K. J. (2019). The Relationship Between Uncertainty and Affect. *Frontiers in Psychology*, 10. PMID:31781003

Anderson, M. (2017). Transformational leadership in education: A review of existing literature. *International Social Science Review, 93*(1).

Andrews, M. R. (2019). Can transformational leaders improve your organization? *Contract Management, 59*, 38-42, 44-45. Retrieved from https://www.proquest.com/docview/2282756406?accountid=45853

Anholt, R., van Dullemen, C., de Carvalho, J. S., Rijbroek, J., Sieckelinck, S., & Slootman, M. W. (2020). Understanding societal resilience: The case for engaged scholarship. In M. Ungar (Ed.), *Multisystemic Resilience* (pp. 551–564). Oxford University Press.

Anthony, S. D., & Schwartz, E. I. (2017, May). What the best transformational leaders do. *Harvard Business Review*. https://hbr.org/2017/05/what-the-best-transformational-leaders-do

Arcieri, K. (2020). *Nike levels up digital game in wake of coronavirus hit*. https://www.spglobal.com/marketintelligence/en/news-insights/latest-news-headlines/nike-levels-up-digital-game-in-wake-of-coronavirus-hit-59265634

Arif, A. (2020). *Troubling matters: Examining the spread of misinformation and disinformation on social media during mass disruption events* [Unpublished dissertation]. University of Washington.

Arreglado, T. M., Garcia-Dia, M. J., & O'Flaherty, D. (2018). Cultivating resilience in the workplace: Relationship between demographic factors and nurses' perception of resilience. *Journal of Nursing Practice Applications & Reviews of Research, 8*(1), 6–13. doi:10.13178/jnparr.2018.0801.0803

Austin, D. (1997). The profession of social work: In the second century. In M. Reisch & E. Gambrill (Eds.), *Social work in the 21st century* (pp. 396–401). Pine Forge. doi:10.4135/9781483326405.n36

Avolio, B. J. (2007). Promoting more integrative strategies for leadership theory-building. *The American Psychologist, 62*(1), 25–33. doi:10.1037/0003-066X.62.1.25 PMID:17209677

Bakker, A. B., & Demerouti, E. (2007). The Job Demands-Resources model: State of the art. *Journal of Managerial Psychology, 22*(3), 309–328.

Bal, P., & De Jong, S. (2016). From human resource management to human dignity development. In *Dignity and Humanistic Management*. Palgrave MacMillan.

Baltaci, A., & Balci, A. (2017). Complexity leadership: A theoretical perspective. *International Journal of Educational Leadership and Management, 5*(1), 30–58. doi:10.17583/ijelm.2017.2435

Barlette, Y. (2020). Les comportements des acteurs en matière de sécurité de l'information et leurs determinants: Les théories du 'coping' et leur enrichissement [The behaviors of actors in matters of information security and their determinants: Theories of "coping" and their enrichment]. Report submitted to obtain an advanced certification to supervise dissertations, University of Montpellier.

Barnard, C. I. (1938). *The Functions of the Executive*. Harvard University Press.

Bartsch, V., Ebers, M., & Maurer, I. (2013). Learning in project-based organizations: The role of project teams' social capital for overcoming barriers to learning. *International Journal of Project Management*, *31*(2), 239–251. doi:10.1016/j.ijproman.2012.06.009

Baruth, L., & Manning, L. (2012). *Multicultural counseling and psychotherapy: A lifespan approach* (5th ed.). Pearson College Division.

Bass, B. M. (1990). From transactional to transformational leadership: Learning to share the vision. *Organizational Dynamics*, *18*(3), 19–31. https://doi-org.proxygsu-afpl.galileo.usg.edu/10.1016/0090-2616(90)90061-S

Bass, B. M. (1981). *Handbook of Leadership: Theory, Research, and Managerial Applications* (3rd ed.). The Free Press.

Bass, B. M. (1985). *Leadership and performance beyond expectation*. Free Press.

Bass, B. M. (1990). From transactional to transformational leadership: Learning to share the vision. *Organizational Dynamics*, *18*(3), 19–31. doi:10.1016/0090-2616(90)90061-S

Bass, B. M., & Riggio, R. E. (2006). *Transformational leadership*. Psychology Press. doi:10.4324/9781410617095

Bates, J. (2020). Police Departments, Sheriffs' Offices across the U.S. Grapple with COVID-19's Impact on Public Safety—And Their Own. *TIME*. https://time.com/5812833/coronavirus-police-departments/

Beatty, K., & Quinn, L. (2010). Strategic command: Taking the long view for organizational success. *Leadership in Action*, *30*(1), 3–7. doi:10.1002/lia.1318

Beaulieu, D. (2013). Remembering Boston: Nearly 3 months after the Boston Marathon bombing, physicians say the tragedy taught lessons that will forever influence the care of and response to patients. *Medical Economics*, *90*(13). PMID:25233708

Beck, T. E., & Plowman, D. A. (2009). Experiencing rare and unusual events richly: The role of middle managers in animating and guiding organizational interpretation. *Organization Science*, *20*(5), 909–924.

Beer, M., & Nohria, N. (2005). Cracking the code of change. *Harvard Business Review*, *78*(3), 133–141. PMID:11183975

Beheshti, N. (2020). End Business as Usual—Leaders Must Boldly and Fearlessly Respond to Black Lives Matter. *Forbes*. https://www.forbes.com/sites/nazbeheshti/2020/06/18/end-business-as-usual-leaders-must-boldly-and-fearlessly-respond-to-black-lives-matter/?sh=33c42de24b6a

Bencsik, A., Juhasz, T., & Mura, L. (2020). *Consequences of Workplace Stress*. https://www.researchgate.net/publication/338465922_Consequences_of_Wo

Bennett, N., & Lemoine, G. J. (2014). What VUCA Really Means for You. *Harvard Business Review*.

Bennis, W. G. (2003). *On Becoming a Leader*. Pegasus Publishing.

Bennis, W. G., Benne, K. D., & Chin, R. (1961). *The Planning of Change*. Holt, Rinehart & Winston.

Bhasin, H. (2019). *8 Different Types of crisis*. https://www.marketing91.com/types-of-crisis/

Biggs, D., Hall, C. M., & Stoeckl, N. (2012). The Resilience of Formal and Informal Tourism Enterprises to Disasters: Reef Tourism in Phuket, Thailand. *Journal of Sustainable Tourism*, *20*(5), 645–665. doi:10.1080/09669582.2011.630080

Blanchard, K., & Hodges, P. (2002). *The servant leader: Transforming your heart, head, hands, and habits*. J. Countryman.

Blase, J., & Blase, J. (1999). Effective instructional leadership: Teacher's perspectives on how principals promote teaching and learning in schools. *Journal of Educational Administration*, *38*(2), 130–141. doi:10.1108/09578230010320082

Block, P. (2009). *Community: The structure of belonging*. Berrett-Koehler Publisher, Inc.

Bloom, S., & Sreedhar, S. (2008). The sanctuary model of trauma-informed organizational change. *Reclaiming Children and Youth*, *17*(3), 48–53.

Boles, M., Pelletier, B., & Lynch, W. (2004). The relationship between health risks and work productivity. *Journal of Occupational and Environmental Medicine*, *46*(7), 737–745.

Bollingtoft, A., & Ulhoi, J. P. (2005). The networked business incubator—Leveraging entrepreneurial agency? *Journal of Business Venturing*, *20*(2), 265–290. doi:10.1016/j.jbusvent.2003.12.005

Bolman, L. G., & Deal, T. E. (2015). Think—Or sink. Leading in a VUCA world. *Leader to Leader*, *76*, 35–40. doi:10.1002/ltl.20176

Bolman, L., & Deal, T. (1997). *Reframing organizations: Artistry, choice, and leadership* (2nd ed.). John Wiley & Sons, Inc.

Bonkiewicz, L., & Ruback, R. B. (2012). The role of the police in evacuations: Responding to the social impact of a disaster. *Police (Springfield)*, *15*(2), 137–156. doi:10.1177/1098611112442808

Bordas, J. (2016). Leadership Lessons from Communities of Color: Stewardship and Collective Action. *New Directions for Student Leadership*, *2016*(152), 61–74. doi:10.1002/yd.20209 PMID:27870523

Borden, T., Akhtar, A., Hadden, J., & Bose, D. (2020, October 8). The coronavirus outbreak has triggered unprecedented mass layoffs and furloughs. Here are the major companies that have announced they are downsizing their workforces. *Business Insider*. https://www.businessinsider.com/coronavirus-layoffs-furloughs-hospitality-service-travel-unemployment-2020

Borjesson, M. (2020). *The psychology of risk and safety in the military: A balancing act* [Doctoral dissertation, Karlstad University, Sweden]. Digitala Vetenskapliga Arkivet id: diva2:1479324.

Borland, M. (2011). *Interview. The Oakland Tribune*.

Boscarino, J. A., Figley, C. R., & Adams, R. E. (2004). Compassion fatigue following the September 11 terrorist attacks: A study of secondary trauma among new york city social workers. *International Journal of Emergency Mental Health*, *6*, 57–66. PMID:15298076

Bosch, D., & Jones, A. (2014). *Allostasis: Why It Matters*. Headington Institute.

Bosman, J. P. (1997). *Leadership, power and influence*. Organizational Behaviour. https://www.academia.edu/40931547/Bachelor_of_Commerce_Programme_Organizational_Behaviour

Bränström, R., Kvillemo, P., & Moskowitz, J. T. (2012, December). A randomized study of the effects of mindfulness training on psychological well-being and symptoms of stress in patients treated for cancer at 6-month follow-up. *International Journal of Behavioral Medicine*, *19*(4), 535–542. doi:10.100712529-011-9192-3

Braun, B. (2007). Biopolitics and the molecularization of life. *Cultural Geographies*, *14*(1), 6–28. doi:10.1177/1474474007072817

Brawley Newlin, A., & Pury, C. (2020). All of the above?: An examination of overlapping organizational climates. *Journal of Business and Psychology*, *35*(4), 539–555. doi:10.100710869-019-09639-6

Bridges, W. (2016). *Managing Transitions: Making the Most of Change* (4th ed.). De Capo Lifelong Books.

Bridges, W., & Bridges, S. (2017). *Managing Transitions: Making the most of Change*. Da Capo Lifelong Books.

Brienes, J. (2015). Three Ways Your Beliefs Can Shape Your Reality. *Psychology Today*.https://www.psychologytoday.com/us/blog/in-love-and-war/201508/3-ways-your-beliefs-can-shape-your-reality

British Broadcasting Corporation. (2020, July). *George Floyd: What happened in the final moments of his life*. https://www.bbc.com/news/world/-us-canada-52861726

Brodbeck, F. C., Frese, M., Akerblom, S., Audia, G., Bakacsi, G., Bendova, H., & Castel, P. (2000). Cultural variation of leadership prototypes across 22 European countries. *Journal of Occupational and Organizational Psychology*, *73*(1), 1–29. doi:10.1348/096317900166859

Brooks, J. E. (2006). Strengthening resilience in children and youths: Maximizing opportunities through the schools. *Children & Schools*, *28*(2), 69–76. doi:10.1093/cs/28.2.69

Brown, A. D. (2000). Making sense of inquiry sensemaking. *Journal of Management Studies*, *37*(1), 45–75. doi:10.1111/1467-6486.00172

Brown, E. H. (1997). Improving organizational health by addressing organizational trauma. *Journal of Organizational Change Management*, *10*(2), 175–178. doi:10.1108/09534819710160835

Brown, J., & Sheppard, B. (2014). Leadership for a new vision of public school classrooms: Technology-smart and learner-centered. *Journal of Educational Administration*, *52*(1), 84–96. doi:10.1108/JEA-03-2012-0027

Brown, M. E., & Gioia, D. A. (2002). Making things click: Distributive leadership in an online division of an offline organization. *The Leadership Quarterly*, *13*(4), 397–419. doi:10.1016/S1048-9843(02)00123-6

Bubb, D., & Daly, J. (2020). Creating whole-company resilience through emotional health and well-being. *People and Strategy, 43*(3).

Bueche, R. A. (2018). *Principal perceptions on transformational leadership in Arizona's preparation program* [Doctoral dissertation]. Grand Canyon University.

Bundy, J., Pfarrer, M. D., Short, C. E., & Coombs, W. T. (2017). Crises and crisis management: Integration, interpretation, and research development. *Journal of Management*, *43*(6), 1661–1692. doi:10.1177/0149206316680030

Burgess, A., & Burgess, J. (2011). *Truth*. Princeton University Press. doi:10.23943/princeton/9780691144016.001.0001

Burnes, B. (2004). Emergent change and planned change – competitors or allies? The case of XYZ construction. *International Journal of Operations & Production Management*, *24*(9), 886–902. doi:10.1108/01443570410552108

Burnes, B. (2020). The Origins of Lewin's Three-Step Model of Change. *The Journal of Applied Behavioral Science*, *56*(1), 32–59. doi:10.1177/0021886319892685

Burns, J. M. (1978). *Leadership*. Harper & Row.

Burrows-McCabe, A. (2014). Stepping stones to leadership. *The Learning Forward Journal, 35*(4), 40-43. https://learningforward.org/docs/defaultsource/ jsd-august-2014/stepping-stones-to-leadership.pdf

Bustamente, C., C. Poblete, & J. E. Amorós. (2020). Entrepreneurial intentions in the context of a natural disaster. *International Journal of Emerging Markets*. Advance online publication. doi:10.1108/IJOEM-10-2019-0846

Buzzanell, P. M. (2018). Organizing resilience as adaptive-transformational tensions. *Journal of Applied Communication Research*, *46*(1), 14–18. doi:10.1080/00909882.2018.1426711

Byrd-Poller, L., Farmer, J.L., & Ford, V. (2017). The role of leaders in facilitating healing after organizational trauma. In S. Hasa & R. Burnett-Thornton (Eds.), The impact of organizational trauma on workplace behaviour and performance. Information Resources Management Association.

Byrd-Poller, L., Farmer, J., & Ford, V. (2017). In R. B.-T. S. Háša (Ed.), *Impact of Organizational Trauma on Workplace Behavior and Performance* (pp. 318–340). IGI Global. doi:10.4018/978-1-5225-2021-4.ch014

Byrne, D., & Callaghan, G. (2014). *Complexity Theory and the Social Sciences: The State of the Art.* Routledge.

Caligiuri, P., De Cieri, H., Minbaeva, D., Verbeke, A., & Zimmermann, A. (2020). International HRM insights for navigating the COVID-19 pandemic: Implications for future research and practice. *Journal of International Business Studies, 51*(5), 697–713. doi:10.105741267-020-00335-9 PMID:32836500

Caliskan, E. N. (2010). The impact of strategic human resource management on organizational performance. *Journal of Naval Science and Engineering, 6*(2), 100–116.

Callahan, J. (1994). Defining crisis and emergency. *The Journal of Crisis Intervention and Suicide Prevention, 15*(4), 164–171. PMID:7729148

Cameron, E., & Green, M. (2017). *Essential leadership: Develop your leadership qualities through theory and practice.* Kogan Page Limited.

Cameron, K. S., & Quinn, R. E. (2011). *Diagnosing and Changing Organizational Culture.* Jossey-Bass.

Campbell Collaborations. (n.d.). *What are you looking for? Better evidence for the world.* https://www.campbellcollaboration.org/

Campise, R. L., Geller, S. K., & Campise, M. E. (2006). Combat Stress. In C. H. Kennedy & E. A. Zillmer (Eds.), *Military psychology: Clinical and operational applications* (pp. 215–240). The Guilford Press.

Cao, Y., Gao, J., Lian, D., Rong, Z., Shi, J., Wang, Q., Wu, Y., Yao, H., & Zhou, T. (2018). Orderliness predicts academic performance: Behavioural analysis on campus lifestyle. *Journal of the Royal Society, Interface, 15*(146), 20180210. doi:10.1098/rsif.2018.0210 PMID:30232241

Caplan, G. (1961). *Approach to community mental health.* Grune and Stratton.

Carlsson-Wall, M., Iredahl, A., Kraus, K., & Wiklund, M. (2020). The role of management controls in managing heterogeneous interests during extreme situations: The Swedish migrant crisis in 2015. *Qualitative Research in Accounting & Management, 18*(1), 1–25. doi:10.1108/QRAM-05-2018-0030

Carter, L. (2020). Most loved workplace research and technical documentation for the most loved workplace validation. *Best Practice Institute Journal of Management and Leadership.* https://www.academia.edu/43619158/Most_Loved_Workplace_Research_and_Technical_Documentation_for_the_Most_Loved_Workplace_Validation

Carter, P., & Blanch, A. (2019, Summer). A Trauma Lens for Systems Change. *Stanford Social Innovation Review*, 49–54.

Centers for Disease Control and Prevention. (2002). *Rapid assessment of injuries among survivors of the terrorist on the World Trade Center-New York City, September 2001.* Author.

Centers for Disease Control and Prevention. (2019). *Preventing adverse childhood experiences: Leveraging the best available evidence.* National Center for Injury Prevention and Control, Centers for Disease Control and Prevention. https://www.cdc.gov/violenceprevention/pdf/preventingACES.pdf

Centers for Disease Control and Prevention. (2021). https://usafacts.org/articles/top-causes-death-united-states-heart-disease-cancer-and-covid-19/

Cherry, K. (2020). *Transformational leadership: A closer look at the effects of transformational leadership*. Verywell Mind. https://www.verywellmind.com/what-is-transformational-leadership-2795313

Cherry, K. (n.d.). *How Do Erikson's and Freud's Theories Compare?* Verywell Mind. https://www.verywellmind.com/freud-and-erikson-compared-2795959

Child Abuse and Neglect Prevention Board. (2020). *Adverse childhood experiences (ACEs)*. Retrieved from https://preventionboard.wi.gov/Pages/OurWork/ACE.aspx

Cho, Y.-S., Choi, B.-H., & Yoon, S. (2016). Tsunami research in Korea. *Natural Hazards*, *84*(S2), 437–454. doi:10.100711069-016-2439-1

Christianson, M. K. (2019). More and less effective updating: The role of trajectory management in making sense again. *Administrative Science Quarterly*, *64*(1), 45–86. doi:10.1177/0001839217750856

Ciuchta, M. P., O'Toole, J., & Miner, A. S. (2021). The organizational improvisation landscape: Taking stock and looking forward. *Journal of Management*, *47*(1), 288–316. doi:10.1177/0149206320966987

Clayton, M. C. (2010). How Will You Measure Your Life? *Harvard Business Review*. https://hbr.org/2010/07/how-will-you-measure-your-life

Cleary, J. (2020). The role of storytelling in a nonhostile takeover. *Qualitative Research in Organizations and Management*, *16*(1), 145–169. doi:10.1108/QROM-10-2019-1832

Coelho, D., & Pires, R. (2020). Impact of organizational climate. *Scientific Electronic Archives*, *14*(1), 67–73. https://doi-org.proxygsu-afpl.galileo.usg.edu/10.36560/14120211260

Cole, S. F., Eisner, A., Gregory, M., & Ristuccia, J. (2013). Helping traumatized children learn 2: Creating and advocating for trauma-sensitive schools. *Trauma and Learning Policy Initiative, Massachusetts Advocates for Children*. https://traumasensitiveschools.org/

Collaborative for Academic, Social, and Emotional Learning. (2020). *What is social and emotional learning (SEL)?* https://casel.org/what-is-sel/

Collins, J. (2001). *Good to great. Why some companies make the leap … and others don't*. Harper Collins.

Collins, J. (2001). *Good to great: why some companies make the leap and others don't*. Harper Business.

Comaford, C. (2018, January 20). Why leaders need to embrace employee motivation? *Forbes*. https://www.forbes.com/sites/christinecomaford/2018/01/20/why-leaders-need-to-embrac e-employee-motivation/?sh=68186a641272

Comer, J. S., Green, J. G., Holt, M. K., Kwong, L., & Xuan, Z. (2016). Teachers report of outreach to school-based providers of mental health services following the 2013 Boston Marathon attack. *Children & Schools*, *38*(4), 227–234. doi:10.1093/cs/cdw035

Coomber, B., & Barriball, K. L. (2007). Impact of jaob satisfaction components on intent to leave and turnover for hospital-based nurses: A review of the research literature. *International Journal of Nursing Studies*, *44*, 297–314.

Corkery, M., & Maheshwari, S. (2020). Is There Really a Toilet Paper Shortage? *New York Times*.

Corr, C. A. (2018). Elisabeth Kübler-Ross and the "Five Stages" Model in a Sampling of Recent American Textbooks. *Omega*, *82*(2), 294–322. doi:10.1177/0030222818809766 PMID:30439302

Covey, S. M. R. (2006). *The speed of trust: The one thing that changes everything*. Free Press.

Craine, K. (2008). Managing the cycle of change. *IEEE Engineering Management Review*, *36*(2), 50–54. doi:10.1109/EMR.2008.4534324

Creed, W. E., Hudson, B. A., Okhuysen, G., & Smith-Crowe, K. (2020, October 30). A place in the world: Vulnerability, wellbeing, and the ubiquitous evaluation that animates participation in institutional processes. *Academy of Management Review*, amr.2018.0367. Advance online publication. doi:10.5465/amr.2018.0367

Creswell, J. (2014). *Educational research: Planning, conducting, and evaluating quantitative and qualitative research* (4th ed.). Pearson Education.

Cripe, C. C. (2020). *Indiana public school superintendent sensemaking of e-learning* [Doctoral dissertation, Ball State University]. Publication No. 28256327. ProQuest Dissertations Publishing.

Cropanzano, R., & Wright, T. A. (2001). When a "happy" worker is really a "productive" worker: A review and further refinement of the happy-productive worker thesis. *Consult. Psychol. J. Pract. Res.*, *53*, 182–199.

Csikszentmihalyi, C. (1990). *Flow*. HarperCollins Publishers.

Cuban, L. (1984). Transforming the frog into a prince: Effective school research, policy, and practice at the district level. *Harvard Educational Review*, *54*(2), 129–151. doi:10.17763/haer.54.2.m07133p087795h38

Culver, L. M., McKinney, B. L., & Paradise, L. V. (2011). Mental health professionals' experiences of vicarious traumatization in post-hurricane katrina new orleans. *Journal of Loss and Trauma*, *16*(1), 33–42. doi:10.1080/15325024.2010.519279

Cunningham, M. (2004). Avoiding Vicarious Traumatization: Support, Spirituality, and Self-Care. In N. B. Webb (Ed.), *Social work practice with children and families. Mass trauma and violence: Helping families and children cope* (pp. 327–346). The Guilford Press.

Dahlberg, R., Vendelø, M. T., Sørensen, B. R., & Lauta, K. C. (2020). Offshore is onshore: Scalability, synchronization, and speed of decision in Arctic SAR. *Scandinavian Journal of Military Studies*, *3*(1), 157–168. doi:10.31374jms.52

Darkow, P. M. (2019). Beyond "bouncing back": Towards an integral, capability-based understanding of organizational resilience. *Journal of Contingencies and Crisis Management*, *27*(2), 145–156. doi:10.1111/1468-5973.12246

Davis, S. H., & Darling-Hammond, L. (2012). Innovative principal preparation: What works and how we know. *Planning and Changing*, *43*(1-2), 25–45.

De Klerk, J. (2007). Healing emotional trauma in organizations. *Organization Development Journal*, *25*(2), 35–41.

De Klerk, M. (2007). Healing emotional trauma in organizations: An O.D. framework and case study. *Organization Development Journal*, *25*(2), 49–55.

Deflem, M. (2019). Anomie. In M. Ryan (Ed.), *Core Concepts in Sociology* (pp. 8–9). Wiley-Blackwell.

DeKlerk, M. (2007). Healing emotional trauma in organizations: An o.d framework and case study. *Organization Development Journal*, *25*(2), 35–41.

Delaney-Black, V., Covington, C., Ondersma, S. J., Nordstrom-Klee, B., Templin, T., Ager, J., & Sokol, R. J. (2002). Violence exposure, trauma, and IQ and/or reading deficits among urban children. *Archives of Pediatrics & Adolescent Medicine*, *156*(3), 280. doi:10.1001/archpedi.156.3.280 PMID:11876674

Della Lucia, M., Giudici, E., & Secchi, D. (2020). Reshaping tourism. In M. Della Luci & E. Giudici (Eds.), *Humanistic Tourism: Values, Norms and Dignity*. Routledge. doi:10.4324/9781003108993-13

Deming, W. E. (1986). *Out of the Crisis*. Massachusetts Institute of Technology.

Descza, G., Ingols, C., & Cawsey, T. F. (2019). *Organizational Change: An Action-Oriented Toolkit*. Sage Publications, Inc.

Deverell, E. (2012). Investigating the roots of crisis management studies and outlining future trajectories for the field. *Journal of Homeland Security and Emergency Management*, *9*(1), 1–21. doi:10.1515/1547-7355.1956

Dewa, C. S. (2014). Incidence rates of sickness absence related to mental disorders: a systematic literature review. *BMC Public Health*, *14*(205). doi:10.1186/1471-2458-14-205

DiMaggio, P. J., & Powell, W. W. (1977). The Iron Cage Revisited: Institutional Isomorphism and Collective Rationality in Organizational Fields. *American Sociological Review*, *48*(2), 147–160. doi:10.2307/2095101

Dong, E., Du, H., & Gardner, L. (2020). An interactive web-based dashboard to track COVID-19 in real time. *The Lancet. Infectious Diseases*, *20*(5), 533–534. Advance online publication. doi:10.1016/S1473-3099(20)30120-1 PMID:32087114

Dorociak, K. E., Rupert, P. A., Bryant, F. B., & Zahniser, E. (2017). Development of a Self-Care Assessment for Psychologists. *Journal of Counseling Psychology*, *64*(3), 325–334. doi:10.1037/cou0000206 PMID:28277686

Dosi, G., & Marengo, L. (2007). On the Evolutionary and Behavioral Theories of Organizations: A Tentative Roadmap. *Organization Science*, *18*(3), 491–502. doi:10.1287/orsc.1070.0279

Douyon, R., & A. Paradas. (2020). La sensibilisation des entrepreneurs à la RSE par les structures d'accompagnement au travers de la création de sens [How business incubators use sensemaking to raise awareness of CSR among entrpreneurs]. *Revue internationale de psychosociologie et de gestion des comportements organisationnels, 26*(65), 41-68.

Drucker, P. (1995). *Managing in a Time of the Great Change*. Truman Talley Books.

Drucker, P. (2012). *Managing in the Next Society*. Routledge.

Duchek, S. (2020). Organizational resilience: A capability-based conceptualization. *Business Research*, *13*(1), 215–246. doi:10.100740685-019-0085-7

Duchek, S., Raetze, S., & Scheuch, I. (2020). The role of diversity in organizational resilience: A theoretical framework. *Business Research*, *13*(2), 387–423. doi:10.100740685-019-0084-8

Dugan, J. P. (2017). *Leadership theory: Cultivating critical perspectives*. ProQuest Ebook Central. https://ebookcentral.proquest.com

Duvall, J. J., & Andrew, D. R. (2010). Using a structured review of the literature to identify key factors associated with the current nursing shortage. *Journal of Professional Nursing*, *26*(5), 309–317.

Dweck, C. S. (2016). *Mindset: The new psychology of success*. Ballantine Books.

Eagly, A., Johannesen-Schmidt, M. C., & Engen, M. L. (2003). Transformational, transactional, and laissez-faire leadership styles: A meta-analysis comparing women and men. *Psychological Bulletin*, *129*(4), 569–591. doi:10.1037/0033-2909.129.4.569 PMID:12848221

Eddy-Spicer, D., Arce-Trigatti, P., & Young, M. D. (2020). Field building through strategic bricolage: System leadership and the institutionalizing role of intermediary organizations. *Journal of Professional Capital and Community*, *6*(1), 29–43. doi:10.1108/JPCC-11-2019-0032

Edmonstone, J. (2016). Complex adaptive leadership: Embracing paradox and uncertainty. *Action Learning Research and Practice*, *13*(1), 86–89. doi:10.1080/14767333.2015.1130353

Einhorn, C. S. (2020, August). How to Make Rational Decisions in the Face of Uncertainty. *Harvard Business Review*.

Ejimabo, N. (2015). The influence of decision making in organizational leadership and management activities. *Journal of Entrepreneurship & Organization Management, 04*(02). Advance online publication. doi:10.4172/2169-026X.1000138

Eklund, U., Olsson, H., & Strøm, N. (2014). *Industrial challenges of scaling agile in mass-produced embedded systems. Agile Methods. Large-Scale Development, Refactoring, Testing, and Estimation*. Springer International Publishing.

Elbeshausen, H. (2020). *Patient libraries: From the rise and decline of an institutional arrangement*. LBC 83.56 я73: 111.

Emmett, J., Schrah, G., Schrimper, M., & Wood, A. (2020). *Covid-19 and the employee experience: How leaders can seize the moment*. https://www.mckinsey.com/business-functions/organization/our-insights/covid-19-and-the-employee-experience-how-leaders-can-seize-the-moment#

Esaki, N., Benamati, J., Yanosy, S., Middleton, J. S., Hopson, L. M., Hummer, V. L., & Bloom, S. L. (2018). The sanctuary model: Theoretical framework. *Families in Society, 94*(2), 87–95. doi:10.1606/1044-3894.4287

Essens, P., George, G., van der Vegt, G. S., & Wahlström, M. (2015). Managing risk and resilience. *Academy of Management Journal, 58*(4), 971–980. doi:10.5465/amj.2015.4004

Everington, K. (2020). Taiwan president ranked in Bloomberg 50 for crushing Covid. *Taiwan News*. https://www.taiwannews.com.tw/en/news/4069341

Farnsworth, D., Clark, J. L., Hall, J., Johnson, S., Wysocki, A., & Kepner, K. (2019). *Transformational leadership: The transformation of managers and associates*. EDIS. https://edis.ifas.ufl.edu

Fayol, H. (1929). *Industrial and General Administration*. Management Institute.

Feinstein, O. (2020, May). Development and Radical Uncertainty. *Development in Practice, 30*(8), 1105–1113. doi:10.1080/09614524.2020.1763258

Fernandez, V. (2020). *L'émergence de la compétence collective en contextes extrêmes: Le cas des équipes de secours en montagne* [The emergence of collective competence in extreme contexts: The case of mountain rescue teams] [Unpublished dissertation]. Université Côte d'Azur.

Ferrari, B. T. (2012). *Power listening: Mastering the most critical business skill of all*. Portfolio/Penguin.

Fiedler, F. E. (1974). The Contingency Model—New Directions for Leadership Utilization. *Journal of Contemporary Business, 3*(4), 65–80.

Flandin, S., Salini, D., Drakos, A., & Poizat, G. (2020). Conceção de formações que facilitem o surgimento de novos significados face a acontecimentos inéditos e críticos [Conception of formations that facilitate the emergence of new meanings in the face of unprecedented and critical events]. *Laboreal (Porto), 16*(2), 1–27. doi:10.4000/laboreal.17042

Fontanella, C. (2020). *5 Types of Crisis Your Company Could Face (and Protect Against)*. Hubspot. https://blog.hubspot.com/service/types-of-crisis

Frontiera, J. (2010). Leadership and organizational culture transformation in professional sport. *Journal of Leadership & Organizational Studies, 17*(1), 71–86. doi:10.1177/1548051809345253

Fujishiro & Heaney. (2009). Justice at work, job stress, and employee health. *Health Education & Behavior, 36*(3), 487-504. doi:10.1177/1090198107306435

Fukami, C. V. (2002). 9/11 montage: Professors remember. *Academy of Management Learning & Education, 1*(1), 14–37. doi:10.5465/amle.2002.7373563

Fullan, M. (2003). *The moral imperative of school leadership*. Corwin Press.

Fuller, R. P., Pyle, A., Riolli, L., & Mickel, A. (2020). Creating order out of chaos? Development of a measure of perceived effects of communication on the crisis organizing process. *International Journal of Business Communication.*

Gagliardi, D., Marinaccio, A., Valenti, A., & Iavicoli, S. (2012). Occupational Safety and health in Europe: Lessons from the past, challenges and opportunities for the future. *Industrial Health, 50*, 7–11.

Gaille, M., & Terral, P. (Eds.). (2020). Les sciences humaines et sociales face à la première vague de la pandémie de Covid-19: Enjeux et formes de la recherche [Human and social sciences encountering the COVID-19 pandemic: Issues and types of research]. Centre National de la Recherche Scientifique, Université Toulouse III-Paul Sabatier.

Galetti, B., Golden, J. III, & Brozovich, S. (2019). Inside day 1: How Amazon uses agile team structures and adaptive practices to innovate on behalf of customers. *People & Strategy, 42*(2), 36.

Gallos, J. V. (2006). Reframing complexity: A four-dimensional approach to organization, diagnosis, development, and change. In J.V. Gallos (Ed.), Organization Development Journal. Jossey-Bass.

Gallucci, J., & Seetharaman, M. (2020). How Fortune 500 companies are utilizing their resources and expertise during the coronavirus pandemic. *Fortune*. https://fortune.com/2020/04/13/fortune-500-companies-coronavirus-response-covid-19-pandemic/

Gallup. (2014). *State of American Schools*. Retrieved from https://www.gallup.com/services/178709/state-america-schools-report.aspx

Gallup. (2020). *The 2020 Global Emotions Report*. Gallup_Global_Emotions_2020_Report.pdf

Galton, F. (1869). *Hereditary Genius*. doi:10.1037/13474-000

Garcia, E., & Weiss, E. (2019). *U.S. schools struggle to hire and retain teachers*. Economic Policy Institute. https://www.epi.org/publication/u-s-schools-struggle-to-hire-and-retain-teachers-the-second-report-in-the-perfect-storm-in-the-teacher-labor-market-series/

Geiger, D., & Danner-Schröder, A. (in press). Unexpected events and routine dynamics. In M. S. Feldman, B. T. Pentland, L. D'Adderio, K. Dittrich, C. Rerup, & D. Seidl (Eds.), Cambridge handbook of routine dynamics. Academic Press.

George, J., & Jayan, C. (2012). The impact of organizational culture on personal effectiveness. *Journal of the Indian Academy of Applied Psychology, 39*, 119–129.

Gibbons, D. E. (2004). Friendship and advice networks in the context of changing professional values. *Administrative Science Quarterly, 49*(2), 238–259.

Gibson, D., Dollarhide, C., Moss, J., Aras, Y., & Mitchell, T. (2018). Examining leadership with American counseling association presidents: A grounded theory of leadership identity development. *Journal of Counseling and Development, 96*(4), 361–371. doi:10.1002/jcad.12219

Gioia, D. A., & Chittipeddi, K. (1991). Sensemaking and sensegiving in strategic change initiation. *Strategic Management Journal, 12*(6), 433–448. doi:10.1002mj.4250120604

Gioia, D. A., & Thomas, J. B. (1996). Institutional identity, image, and issue interpretation: Sensemaking during strategic change in academia. *Administrative Science Quarterly, 41*(3), 370–403. doi:10.2307/2393936

Gioia, D., Thomas, J. S. C., & Chittipeddi, K. (1994). Symbolism and Strategic Change in Academia: The Dynamics of Sensemaking and Influence. *Organization Science, 5*(3), 363–383. doi:10.1287/orsc.5.3.363

Gleeson, B. (2018). The critical role of leadership development during organizational change. *Forbes*. https://www.forbes.com/

Golan, N. (1978). *Treatment in crisis situations*. Free Press.

Goleman, D., Boyatzis, R., & McKee, A. (2001). Primal leadership: The hidden driver of great performance. *Harvard Business Review*, *79*(11), 42–51.

Gorel, D. R. (2020). *Evaluating local nonprofit, Terra Birds, using SWOT and 7s* [Doctoral dissertation]. Northern Arizona University.

Gorman, J. (2003). *Rights and Reason: An Introduction to the Philosophy of Rights*. Acumen Publishing. doi:10.1017/UPO9781844653461

Graide Network. (2020, April 13). *The rise of teacher stress: (/blog-all/2018/8/1/crayons-and-cortisol-the-epidemic-of-teacher-stress)*. https://www.thegraidenetwork.com/blog-all/2018/8/1/crayons-and-cortisol-the-epidemic-of-teacher-stress

Greene, K., LeMoine, S., Macasaet, K., & Mulrooney, K. (2020). You matter: Promoting professional resilience during collective crisis. *Zero to Three*, *41*(1), 53–58.

Greene, R. R., Conrad, A. P., Livingstone, N. C., Barton, W. H., Watkins, M. L., Blundo, R., & Riley, J. G. (2002). *An integrated approach to practice, policy, and research*. National Association of Social Workers Press.

Greenleaf, R. K. (2002). Servant leadership: A journey into the nature of legitimate power and greatness. Paulist Press.

Griffith, E. (2020). Airbnb Tops $100 Billion on First Day of Trading, Reviving Talk of a Bubble. *New York Times*. https://www.nytimes.com/2020/12/10/technology/airbnb-tops-100-billion-on-first-day-of-trading-reviving-talk-of-a-bubble.html?auth=login-email&login=email

Gronn, P. (2002). Distributed leadership as a unit of analysis. *The Leadership Quarterly*, *13*(4), 423–451. doi:10.1016/S1048-9843(02)00120-0

Groysberg, B., & Abrahams, R. (2020, August 17). *What the Stockdale paradox tells us about crisis leadership*. Harvard Business School.

Hallinger, P. (2007). *Research on the practice of instructional and transformational leadership:Retrospect and prospect*. Australian Council for Educational Research. https://research.acer.edu.au/research_conference_2007/7

Hallinger, P. (2010). Developing instructional leadership. Studies in Educational Leadership, 11(10). doi:10.1007/978-90-481-9106-2_5

Hamann, R. (2020). The promise and peril of "building back better". *Environment*, *62*(6), 41–50. doi:10.1080/00139157.2020.1820296

Hamdani, D. (2006). Working paper on conceptualizing and measuring business incubation. In *Science, Innovation and Electronic Information*. Division (SIEID) Working Paper.

Handy, C. (1989). *The Age of Unreason*. Harvard Business School Press.

Handy, C. (1996). *Beyond Certainty*. Arrow Business Books.

Hartmann, S., Weiss, M., Hoegl, M., & Carmeli, A. (2021). How does an emotional culture of joy cultivate team resilience? A sociocognitive perspective. *Journal of Organizational Behavior*, *42*(3), 313–331. doi:10.1002/job.2496

Havermans. (2018). Effectiveness of a Digital Platform-Based Implementation Strategy to Prevent Work Stress in a Healthcare Organization: a 12-Month Follow-up Controlled Trial. *Scandinavian Journal of Work, Environment & Health*, *44*(6), 613–21. doi:. doi:10.5271jweh.3758

Hayes, B., Bonner, A., & Pryor, J. (2010). Factors contributing to nurse job satisfaction in the acute hospital setting: Review of recent literature. *Journal of Nursing Management*, *18*, 804–814.

Hazy, J. K. (2006). Measuring leadership effectiveness in complex socio-technical systems. *Emergence*, *8*(3), 58–77.

Heifetz, R. (1994). *Leadership without easy answers*. Belknap Press.

Heifetz, R., Grashow, A., & Linsky, M. (2009). *The Practice of Adaptive Leadership: Tools and Tactics for Changing Your Organization and the World*. Harvard Business Press.

Hersey, P., & Blanchard, K. H. (1988). *Management of organizational behavior* (5th ed.). Prentice Hall.

Hirschberger, G. (2018). Collective Trauma and the Social Construction of Meaning. *Frontiers in Psychology*, *9*, 9. doi:10.3389/fpsyg.2018.01441 PMID:30147669

Hitt, R., & Massi Lindsey, L. L. (2020). Military Members' Perceptions of Social Norms About Mental Health for Combat Stress. *Military Behavioral Health*, *8*(2), 181–190. doi:10.1080/21635781.2019.1630039

Holland, J. (1992). Complex Adaptive Systems. *Daedalus*, *121*(1), 17–30.

Hopper, E. (2012). *Trauma and Organizations*. Routledge.

Hopper, E. (2018). *Trauma and organizations* (2nd ed.). Routledge. doi:10.4324/9780429484285

Hopper, E., Bassuk, E., & Olivet, J. (2010). Shelter from the storm: Trauma-informed care in homelessness services settings. *The Open Health Services and Policy Journal*, *3*(2), 80–100. doi:10.2174/1874924001003020080

Hormann, S. (2007). *Organizational trauma: A phenomenological study of leaders in traumatized organizations* [Doctoral Thesis, Antioch University]. https://aura.antioch.edu/etds/184

Hormann, S., & Vivian, P. (2013). *Organizational Trauma and Healing*. Academic Press.

Hormann, S. (2018). Exploring Resilience: In the Face of Trauma. *Humanist Management Journal*, *3*(3), 91–104. doi:10.100741463-018-0035-0

Hormann, S., & Vivian, P. (2005). Toward An Understanding of Traumatized Organizations and How to Intervene in Them. *Traumatology*, *11*(3), 159–169. doi:10.1177/153476560501100302

Hormann, S., & Vivian, P. (2017). Intervening in Organizational Trauma: A Tale of Three Organizations. In S. A. Tirmizi & J. D. Vogelsang (Eds.), *Leading and Managing in the Social Sector: Strategies for Advancing Human Dignity and Social Justice* (pp. 175–189). Springer International Publishing. doi:10.1007/978-3-319-47045-0_11

Horwitz, M. (1998). Social worker trauma: Building resilience in child protection social workers. *Smith College Studies in Social Work*, *68*(3), 363–377. doi:10.1080/00377319809517536

Hurley, R. (2006). The decision to trust. *Harvard Business Review*. https://hbr.org/2006/09/the-decision-to-trust

Ingersoll, R. M. (2012). Beginning teacher induction: What the data tells us. *Phi Delta Kappan*, *93*(8), 47–51. doi:10.1177/003172171209300811

Iordanoglou, D. (2018). Future Trends in Leadership Development Practices and the Crucial Leadership Skills. *Journal of Leadership, Accountability and Ethics*, *15*(2).

Izard, C. E. (2009). Emotion theory and research: Highlights, unanswered questions, and emerging issues. *Annual Review of Psychology*, *60*(1), 1–25. doi:10.1146/annurev.psych.60.110707.163539 PMID:18729725

Jabeen, A., Khan, M. A., & Manzoor, M. (2020). Exploring the influence of leadership styles on professional motivation. *Gomal University Journal of Research, 36*(2), 84–92. https://doi-org.proxygsu-afpl.galileo.usg.edu/10.51380/gujr-36-02-08

Jacobs, D., Pfaff, H., Lehner, B., Driller, E., Nitzsche, A., Stieler-Lorenz, B., Wasem, J., & Jung, J. (2013). The influence of transformational leadership on employee well-being: Results from a survey of companies in the information and communication technology sector in Germany. *Journal of Occupational and Environmental Medicine, 55*(7), 772–778. doi:10.1097/JOM.0b013e3182972ee5 PMID:23836019

Jacobsen, D. (2021). Protecting Employees from Organizational Trauma. *Workhuman.*

Jennings, D. B. (2002). Those who would lead must first serve: The praxis of servant leadership by public school principals. *Dissertations Abstracts International, 63*(04), 1207.

Jha, C. (2020). *The great disruptive transformation: The impact of COVID-19 crisis on innovative startups in India* [Unpublished masters thesis]. University of Gothenburg.

Johnson, G. S., & Rainey, S. A. (2007). Hurricane Katrina impact on three historically black colleges and universities (HBCUs): Voices from displaced student. *Race, Gender & Class, 14*(1), 100-119. Retrieved from https://ww=25853w.proquest.com/scholarly-historically /docview/218845573/se-2?accountid

Johnson, M. (2020). *Transforming education via trauma-informed care: Altering perceptions projected onto students with underlying traumatic experiences* [Unpublished doctoral dissertation]. Virginia State University.

Johnson, K. (2020). *Building organizational resilience in the face of a ubiquitous challenge.* National Council for Behavioral Health.

Johnson, N., Veletsianos, G., & Seaman, J. (2020). U.S. Faculty and Administrators' Experiences and Approaches in the Early Weeks of the COVID-19 Pandemic. *Online Learning Journal, 24*(2), 6–21. doi:10.24059/olj.v24i2.2285

Jones, R., & Gottfried, M. (2020). Abu Dhabi's $230 Billion Man Bet the World Would Overcome Covid-19. *The Wall Street Journal.*

Jones-Smith, E. (2019). *Culturally diverse counseling: theory and practice.* Sage Publications. doi:10.4135/9781071800744

Jordan, J., Wade, M., & Teracino, E. (2020). Every leader needs to navigate these 7 tensions. *Harvard Business Review.* https://hbrorg.cdn.ampproject.org/c/s/hbr.org/amp/2020/02

Joseph, O. B. (2015). The effect of employees' motivation on organizational performance. *Journal of Public Administration and Policy Research, 7*(4), 62–75. doi:10.5897/JPAPR2014.0300

Kahn, W. A. (1993). Caring for the caregivers: Patterns of organizational caregiving. *Administrative Science Quarterly, 38*(4), 539–564.

Kahn, W. A. (2003). The Revelation of Organizational Trauma. *The Journal of Applied Behavioral Science, 39*(4), 364–381. doi:10.1177/0021886303261954

Kahn, W. A., Barton, M. A., & Fellows, S. (2013). Organizational Crises and the Disturbance of Relational Systems. *Academy of Management Review, 38*(3), 38. doi:10.5465/amr.2011.0363

Kail, R., & Cavanaugh, J. (2016). *Human development: a life-span view* (7th ed.). Cengage Learning.

Kalkman, J. P. (2020). Frontline workers in crisis management. In Oxford Research Encyclopedia of Politics. doi:10.1093/acrefore/9780190228637.013.1527

Kane-Frieder, R. E., Hochwarter, W. A., & Ferris, G. R. (2014). Terms of engagement: Political boundaries of work engagement–work outcomes relationships. *Human Relations*, *67*(3), 357–382. https://doi.org/10.1177/0018726713495068

Kanter, R. M. (1997). *The Change Masters*. International Thomson Press.

Kanter, R. M., A., S. B., & Jick, T. D. (1992). How effective leaders achieve success in critical change initiatives, part 2: Why change leadership must transcend project management for complex change initiatives to be successful. *Healthcare Quarterly*, *10*(2), 70–75. PMID:17491570

Kanter, R. M., Stein, B. A., & Jick, T. D. (1992). *The Challenge of Organisational Change*. Free Press.

Kantor, J. (2017). *High Turnover Costs Way More Than You Think*. Academic Press.

Kaplan, A., & Garner, J. (2017). A complex dynamic systems perspective on identity and its development: The dynamic systems model of role identity. *Developmental Psychology*, *53*(11), 2036–2051. doi:10.1037/dev0000339 PMID:29094968

Karapancheva, M. (2020). The future of organizational culture. *Journal of Sustainable Development, 10*(25), 42–52.

Kaya, C., & Baskaya, R. (2017). The roles of organizational and ethical climate on individual performance of employees. *Business Management Dynamics*, *6*(8), 27–38.

Kaye, B., Bentley, C., & Rogers, L. (2020). Leveraging pandemic "ahas": Just getting it isn't doing it. *Leadership Excellence*, *37*(11), 16–19.

Kelloway, E. K., Turner, N., Barling, J., & Loughlin, C. (2012). Transformational leadership and employee psychological well-being: The mediating role of employee trust in leadership. *Work & Stress, 26*, 39-55. doi:.2012.660774 doi:10.1080/02678373

King, D. D., Luthans, F., & Newman, A. (2016). Not if, but when we need resilience in the workplace. *Journal of Organizational Behavior*, *37*(5), 782–786. doi:10.1002/job.2063

Kinicki, A. J., McKee, F. M., & Wade, K. J. (1996). Annual Review, 1991–1995: Occupational Health. *Journal of Vocational Behavior*, *49*(2), 190–220. doi:10.1006/jvbe.1996.0040

Kirkman, B. L., Mistry, S., Rosen, B., & Stoverink, A. C. (2020). Bouncing back together: Toward a theoretical model of work team resilience. *Academy of Management Review*, *45*(2), 395–422. doi:10.5465/amr.2017.0005

Knowledge@Wharton. (2015). *Under Pressure: Managing Stress and Engagement on the Job*. Wharton School Press. https://ebookcentral.proquest.com/lib/vand/detail.action?docID=5482541

Koenig, H. G. (2015). Religion, spirituality, and health: A review and update. *Advances in Mind-Body Medicine*, *29*(3), 19–26. PMID:26026153

Kolay, M. K. (2016). Measurement of organizational resilience: An approach. *Productivity*, *57*(3), 300–309.

Kopkowski, C. (2008, February). *Why they leave*. NEA Today. Retrieved July 7, 2008, from https://www.nea.org/neatoday/0804/coverstory1.html

Kotter, J. P. (1996). *Leading Change*. Harvard Business School Press.

Kotter, J. P., & Heskett, J. L. (1992). *Corporate culture and performance*. The Free Press.

Kotter, J. P., & Schlesinger, L. A. (2008). Choosing Strategies for Change. *Harvard Business Review*, 1–11. PMID:10240501

Kouzes, J. M., & Posner, B. Z. (2012). *The leadership challenge* (5th ed.). Jossey-Bass.

Kouzes, J. M., & Posner, B. Z. (2017). *The leadership challenge: How to make extraordinary things happen in organizations* (6th ed.). Wiley & Sons.

Kruke, B. I. (2020). Survival through coping strategies for resilience following a ship accident in polar waters. *Safety Science, 135*(2021).

Kübler-Ross, E. (1969). *On Death and Dying*. Routledge.

Labas, D. (2017). The impact of organizational crisis preparedness on firm business performance. *Market-Trziste, 29*(1), 75-92. http://eds.a.ebscohost.com.proxygsu-afpl.galileo.usg.edu/eds/pdfviewer/pdfviewer?vid=2&sid=9efa0130-aafe-49c5-b55c-f911adfdc4eb%40sdc-v-sessmgr03

Lansing, J. S. (2003). Complex Adaptive Systems. *Annual Review of Anthropology, 32*(1), 183–204. doi:10.1146/annurev.anthro.32.061002.093440

Laufs, J., Bowers, K., Birks, D., & Johnson, S. D. (2020). Understanding the concept of 'demand' in policing: A scoping review and resulting implications for demand management. *Policing and Society, 20*, 1–24. doi:10.1080/10439463.2020.1791862

Leach, J. (2011). Survival psychology: They won't live. *The British Psychological Society, 24*, 26–29.

Learning Policy Institute. (2014). *Title II data collection*. U.S. Department of Education. https://title2.ed.gov/Public/Home.aspx

LeBoon, R. D. (2020). *How leaders interpret their business challenge through a generative metaphor framing process: A conceptual study* (Publication No. 28151585) [Doctoral dissertation, Fielding Graduate University]. ProQuest Dissertations Publishing.

Ledesma, J. (2014). Conceptual frameworks and research models on resilience in leadership. *Sage (Atlanta, Ga.), 4*(3). Advance online publication. doi:10.1177/2158244014545464

Lee, M., Lim, W., & Teo, W. L. (2017). The relational activation of resilience model: How leadership activates resilience in an organizational crisis. *Journal of Contingencies and Crisis Management, 25*(3), 136–147. doi:10.1111/1468-5973.12179

Leiss, W. (2004). Effective risk communication practice. *Toxicology Letters, 149*(1-3), 399–404. doi:10.1016/j.toxlet.2003.12.050 PMID:15093287

Leithwood, K. A., & Riehl, C. (2003). *What we know about successful school leadership*. Academic Press.

Lemieux, P. (2020). Toilet Paper: Increasing Marginal Cost. *The Library of Economics and Liberty*. https://www.econlib.org/toilet-paper-increasing-marginal-cost/

Lencioni, P. (2004). *Death by meeting: A leadership fable...about solving the most painful problem in business*. Jossey-Bass.

Levin, S., & Bradley, K. (2019, March 19). *Understanding and addressing principal turnover: A review of the research*. Learning Policy Institute. https://learningpolicyinstitute.org/product/nassp-understanding-addressing-principal-turnover-review-research-report

Lewin, K. (1935). *A Dynamic Theory of Personality*. McGraw-Hill.

Lewin, K. (1947). *Field Theory in Social Science*. Harper & Row.

Lewin, K. (1947). Frontiers in group dynamics: Concept, method and reality in social science equilibrium and social change. *Human Relations, 1*(1), 5–41. doi:10.1177/001872674700100103

Lichtenstein, B. B. (2014). *Generative emergence*. Oxford University Press. doi:10.1093/acprof:oso/9780199933594.001.0001

Lichtenstein, B. B., Uhl-Bien, M., Russ, M., Seers, A., Orton, J. D., & Schreiber, C. (2006). Complexity leadership theory: An interactive perspective on leading in complex adaptive systems. *Emergence*, *8*(4), 2–12.

Likert, R. (1955). *Developing patterns in management.* American Management Association.

Lim, A. (2020, June 15). The big five personality traits. *Simply Psychology.* https://www.simplypsychology.org/big-five-personality.html

Lindén, C.-G. (2020). What makes a reporter human? *Questions de communication, 1*, 337-351.

Long, D. (2019). *An E.R. doctor on triaging your "crazy busy" life.* https://www.ted.com/talks/darria_long_an_er_doctor_on_triaging_your_crazy_busy_life

Long, S. (2018). *Trauma as cause and effect of perverse organizational process. In Trauma and organizations* (2nd ed.). Routledge.

Loree, D. (2020). Building corporate resilience. *Ivey Business Journal*, 2-7. https://search.ebscohost.com/login.aspx?direct=true&AuthType=shib&db=f5h&AN=145640006&site=eds-live&custid=uphoenix

Lovelace, K. J., Manz, C. C., & Alves, J. C. (2007). Work stress and leadership development: The role of self-leadership, shared leadership, physical fitness and flow in managing demands and increasing job control. *Human Resource Management Review*, *17*(4), 374–387. doi:10.1016/j.hrmr.2007.08.001

Lu, H., Barriball, L., Zhang, X., & While, A. E. (2012). Job satisfaction among hospital nurses revisited: A systematic review. *International Journal of Nursing Studies*, *49*, 1017–1038.

Lynch, M. (2015). *The four attributes of transformational leadership.* The EdVocate. https://www.theedvocate.org/the-4-attributes-of-transformational-leadership/

Macias, O. (2020). Social emotional competence, emotional intelligence, and the prosocial school leader:how the pandemic, school closures and distance learning can guide leaders. *Leadership*, *50*(1), 12–14.

Mack, O., Khare, A., Krämer, A., & Burgartz, T. (2016). *Managing in a VUCA world.* Springer. doi:10.1007/978-3-319-16889-0

Maclean, N. (1992). *Young men and fire.* The University of Chicago Press. doi:10.7208/chicago/9780226501031.001.0001

MacMillan, D., Whoriskey, P., & O'Connell, J. (2020, December 16). America's biggest companies are flourishing during the pandemic and putting thousands of people out of work. *The Washington Post.* https://www.washingtonpost.com/graphics/2020/business/50-biggest-companies-coronavirus-layoffs/

Madiot, L. (2020). *Étude de l'improvisation dans le cadre d'une collaboration interprofessionelle selon une perspective de* sensemaking [A study of improvisation in the context of inter-professional collaboration through a *sensemaking* perspective] [Masters thesis]. Université de Montréal. https://papyrus.bib.umontreal.ca/xmlui/bitstream/handle/1866/24164/Madiot_Laura_2020_memoire.pdf?sequence=2

Maitlis, S., & Christianson, M. (2014). Sensemaking in organizations: Taking stock and moving forward. *The Academy of Management Annals*, *8*(1), 57–125. doi:10.5465/19416520.2014.873177

Maitlis, S., & Sonenshein, S. (2010). Sensemaking in Crisis and Change: Inspiration and Insights from Weick. *Journal of Management Studies*, *47*(3), 551–580. doi:10.1111/j.1467-6486.2010.00908.x

Malinen, A. (2020). *The long-term patterns of organizational risks: Examining the persistence of risks and their impact on management in organizational change* [Unpublished master's thesis]. Aalto University, Finland.

Manley, M. (1987). *Up the down escalator: Development and the international economy – A Jamaican case study.* Harvard University Press.

Manning, P. K. (1999). High risk narratives: Textual adventures. *Qualitative Sociology, 22*(4), 285–299. doi:10.1023/A:1022003520356

Mannucci, P. V., Orazi, D. C., & de Valck, K. (2020). Developing improvisation skills: The influence of individual orientations. *Administrative Science Quarterly.*

Marion, R. (1999). *The edge of organization: Chaos and complexity theories of formal social organizations.* Sage Publications.

Markovitz, S., & Hullunger, R. (2020). *Six Design Strategies To Reduce Healthcare Worker Stress During The Coronavirus Pandemic.* Academic Press.

Marsen, S. (2020). Navigating crisis: The role of communication in organizational crisis. *International Journal of Business Communication, 57*(2), 163–175. doi:10.1177/2329488419882981

Martin, H. J., de Lope, J., & Maravall, D. (2009). Adaptation, Anticipation and Rationality in Natural and Artificial Systems: Computational Paradigms Mimicking Nature. *Natural Computing, 8*(4), 757–775. doi:10.100711047-008-9096-6

Mauritz, M. W., Goosens, P. J. J., Draijer, N., & Van Achterberg, T. (2013). Prevalence of interpersonal trauma exposure and trauma-related disorders in severe mental illness. *European Journal of Psychotraumatology, 4*(1), 1–15. doi:10.3402/ejpt.v4i0.19985 PMID:23577228

Maxwell, J. C. (2011). *5 Levels of leadership: Proven steps to maximize your potential.* Thomas Nelson.

Mayfield, M., Mayfield, J., & Walker, R. (2020). *Fundamental theories of business Communication.* Palgrave Macmillan. doi:10.1007/978-3-030-57741-4

Maynard, B. M., Farina, A., Dell, N. A., & Kelly, M. S. (2019). Effects of trauma-informed approaches in schools: A systematic review. *Campbell Systematic Reviews, 15*(1-2). Advance online publication. doi:10.1002/cl2.1018

Mayne, J. (2004). Reporting on outcomes: Setting performance expectations and telling performance stories. *The Canadian Journal of Program Evaluation, 19*(1), 31–60. http://citeseerx.ist.psu.edu/viewdoc/download?doi=10.1.1.460.3960&rep=rep1&type=pdf

Mayzell, G. (2020). *The Resilient Healthcare Organization: How to Reduce Physician and Healthcare Worker Burnout.* Productivity Press. https://ebookcentral.proquest.com/lib/vand/detail.action?docID=6129527

McAllister, D. J. (1995). Affect - and cognition-based trust as foundations for interpersonal cooperation in organizations. *Academy of Management Journal, 38*(1), 24–59.

McCann, L., & Pearlman, L. A. (1990). *Constructivist self-development theory as a framework for assessing and treating victims of family violence.* Springer.

McLeod, C. (2003). Toward a restorative organization: Transforming police bureaucracies. *Police Practice and Research, 4*(4), 361–378. doi:10.1080/15614260310001631262

McManus, S., Seville, E., Vargo, J., & Brunsdon, D. (2008). Facilitated Process for Improving Organizational Resilience. *Natural Hazards Review, 9*(2), 81–90. doi:10.1061/(ASCE)1527-6988(2008)9:2(81)

McMaster, T., Wastell, D., & Henriksen, H. Z. (2005). Fooling Around: The Corporate Jester as an Effective Change Agent for Technological Innovation. In R. Baskerville, L. Mathiasen, J. Pres-Heje, & J. DeGross (Eds.), *Business Agility and Information Technology Diffusion.* Springer. doi:10.1007/0-387-25590-7_8

Meijman, T. F., & Mulder, G. (1998). Psychological aspects of workload. In P. J. D. Drenth, H. Thierry, & C. J. de Wolff (Eds.), Handbook of work and organizational psychology (2nd ed.). Handbook of work and organizational: Work psychology (pp. 5–33). Psychology Press/Erlbaum (UK) Taylor & Francis.

Menand, L. (2018, September 3). What personality tests really deliver? *The New Yorker.* https://www.newyorker.com/magazine/2018/09/10/what-personality-tests-really-deliver

Mendes, M., Gomes, C., Marques-Quintiero, P., Lind, P., & Curral, L. (2016). Promoting learning and innovation in organizations through complexity leadership theory. *Team Performance Management, 22*(5/6), 301–309. doi:10.1108/TPM-02-2016-0004

Meneze, M. M. (2005). *The Impact of Stress on productivity at Education Training & Development Practices.* Sector Education and Training Authority.

Messina, M. J. (2019). *Failed dependency: Leadership strategies to prevent, mitigate, and heal organizational trauma in behavioural health systems* (Publication No 13863379) [Doctoral dissertation, Ashford University]. ProQuest Dissertations Publishing.

Metzer, J. C. (2003). Volunteering work stress and satisfaction in the service professions. In M. F. Dollard, A. H. Winefield, & H. R. Winefield (Eds.), *Occupational stress in the service professions* (pp. 389–409). Taylor & Francis.

Meyer, A. D. (1982). Adapting to environmental jolts. *Administrative Science Quarterly, 27*(4), 515–537. doi:10.2307/2392528 PMID:10257768

Miller, A. N., Sellnow, D. D., & Strawser, M. G. (2020). Pandemic pedagogy challenges and opportunities: Instruction communication in remote, HyFlex, and BendFlex courses. *Communication Education, 70*(2), 202–204. doi:10.1080/03634523.2020.1857418

Miller, D., & Proctor, A. (2016). *Enterprise change management: How to prepare your organization for continuous change.* Kogan Page.

Mineo, D. L. (2014). The importance of trust in leadership. *Research Management Review, 20*(1).

Mithani, M. A., & Kocoglu, I. (2020). Human and organizational responses to extreme threats: A comparative developmental approach. *Management Decision, 58*(10), 2077–2097. doi:10.1108/MD-08-2020-1086

Montes, J. S., & Suarez, F. F. (2020). Building organizational resilience. *Harvard Business Review.*

Morales, A. I. R. (2011). *Factors that foster Latina English language learners: Nontraditional student resilience in higher education and their persistence in teacher education* [Doctoral dissertation, Kansas City State University]. https://krex.kstate.edu/dspace/bitstream/handle/2097/8567/AmandaMorales201

Morgan, G. (2011). *Reflections on images* of organization and its implications for organization and environment. *Organization & Environment, 24*(4), 459–478. doi:10.1177/1086026611434274

Muchiri, P., Pintelon, L., Gelders, L., & Martin, H. (2011). Development of maintenance function performance measurement framework and indicators. *International Journal of Production Economics, 131*(1), 295–302. doi:10.1016/j.ijpe.2010.04.039

Mueller, B. (2020). The theorizing trifecta. *Journal of Information Technology.*

Muesser, K. T., Rosenberg, S. D., Goodman, L. A., & Trumbetter, S. L. (2002). Trauma, PTSD, and the course of severe mental illness: An interactive model. *Schizophrenia Research, 53*(1-2), 123–143. doi:10.1016/S0920-9964(01)00173-6 PMID:11728845

Murphy, J. (2002). Reculturing the Profession of Educational Leadership: New Blueprints. *Educational Administration Quarterly*, *38*(2), 176–191. doi:10.1177/0013161X02382004

Myers, D. G. (2010). *Social psychology* (10th ed.).

Narcikara, E., & Zehir, C. (2016). Effects of resilience on productivity under Authentic Leadership. *Procedia: Social and Behavioral Sciences*, 235.

Nasreen, A., Varshney, P., & Waseem, C. (2019). Organizational climate in NBFC: Implications on employee engagement. *Amity Global Business Review*, *9*, 7–14.

National Child Traumatic Stress Network. (2020). *Trauma informed school strategies during COVID-19*. https://www.nctsn.org/resources/trauma-informed-schoolstrategies-during-covid-19

National Policy Board for Educational Administration. (2015). *Professional standards for educational leaders 2015*. Author.

Neason, A. (2014). *Half of teachers leave the job after five years. Here's what to do about it.* The Hechinger Report.

Neerman, P. (2020). Aldi to employ redundant McDonald's staff. *Food*. https://www.retaildetail.eu/en/news/food/aldi-employ-redundant-mcdonald's-staff

Newberg, A., & Waldman, M. R. (2012). *Words can change your brain: 12 conversation strategies to build trust, resolve conflict, and increase intimacy*. Penguin Group.

Nguyen, T., White, S., Hall, K., Bell, R., & Ballentine, W. (2019). Emotional intelligence and managerial communication. *American Journal of Management*, *19*(2). https://doi.org/10.33423/AJM.V19I2.2068

Nichols, C., Hayden, S. C., & Trendler, C. (2020). Four behaviors that help leaders manage a crisis. *Harvard Business Review*. https://hbr.org/2020/04/4-behaviors-that-help-leaders-

Niu, C., Liang, F., Meng, X., & Liu, Y. O. (2020). The inverted U-shaped relationship between authentic leadership and unethical pro-organizational behavior. *Social Behavior and Personality*, *48*(11), 9416. doi:10.2224bp.9416

Nooteboom, B. (2002). *Trust: Forms, foundations, functions, failures and figures*. Edward Elgar Publishing. doi:10.4337/9781781950883

Northouse, P. G. (2016). *Leadership theory and practice* (7th ed.). Sage.

Nwabueze, U. (2011). Implementing TQM in healthcare: The critical leadership traits. *Total Quality Management & Business Excellence*, *22*(3), 331–343. doi:10.1080/14783363.2010.532338

O'Grady, K. A., & Orton, J. D. (2016). Resilience processes during cosmology episodes: Lessons learned from the Haiti earthquake. *Journal of Psychology and Theology*, *44*(2), 109–123. doi:10.1177/009164711604400202

O'Reilly, N. (2019). *In this together: how successful women support each other in work and life*. Adams Media.

Olszewski-Kubilius, P., & Corwith, S. (2018). Poverty, Academic Achievement, and Giftedness: A Literature Review. *Gifted Child Quarterly*, *62*(1), 37–55. https://doi.org/10.1177/0016986217738015

Onorato, M. (2013). Transformational leadership theory style in the education sector: An empirical study of corporation managers and educational leaders. *Academy of Educational Leadership Journal*, *17*(1), 33–47.

Oppizzi, L. M., & Umberger, R. (2018, February). The Effect of Physical Activity on PTSD. *Issues in Mental Health Nursing*, *39*(2), 179–187. doi:10.1080/01612840.2017.1391903

Ortiz, A. (2020a). *An investigation of coping mechanisms for teachers who experience chronic stress and trauma as a result of working in high-needs schools* [Unpublished doctoral dissertation]. Virginia State University.

Ortiz, A. (2020b, November). *Quality quick takes: Maintaining quality instruction in a COVID era (Issue Brief)*. Virginia Department of Education, Office of School Quality.

Orton, J. D. (1995). *Reorganizing: An analysis of the 1976 reorganization of U.S. intelligence*. Groupe HEC School of Management.

Orton, J. D. (2000). Enactment, sensemaking and decision making: Redesign processes in the 1976 reorganization of US intelligence. *Journal of Management Studies, 37*(2), 213–234. doi:10.1111/1467-6486.00178

Orton, J. D., & O'Grady, K. A. (2016). Cosmology episodes: A reconceptualization. *Journal of Management, Spirituality & Religion, 13*(3), 226–245. doi:10.1080/14766086.2016.1159975

Overstreet, S., & Chafouleas, S. M. (2016). Trauma-informed schools: Introduction to the special issue. *School Mental Health, 8*(1), 1–6. doi:10.100712310-016-9184-1

Oxford University Press. (2020). Ontological. In *Oxford English and Spanish dictionary*. Retrieved April 8, 2021, from https://en.oxforddictionaries.com/definition/ontological

Pahi, M., & Hamid, K. (2016). The magic of destructive leadership: Laissez-faire leadership and commitment to service quality. *International Journal of Economic Perspectives, 10*(4), 602–609.

Pandey, G. (2020). Covid-19: The woman who has become India's 'corona voice. *BBC News*. https://www.bbc.com/news/world-asia-india-53047296

Park, H., Ritala, P., & Velu, C. (2020). Discovering and managing interdependence with customer-entrepreneurs. *British Journal of Management*.

Parrish, D., Clark, T. S., & Holloway, S. S. (2020). The collapse of sensemaking at Yarnell Hill: The effects of endogenous ecological chaos on enactment. *European Journal of Management Studies, 25*(2), 77–95. doi:10.1108/EJMS-10-2020-005

Patriotta, G. (2020). The future of the corporation. *Journal of Management Studies*.

Patterson, K., Grenny, J., McMillian, R., & Switzler, A. (2012). *Crucial conversations: Tools for talking when stakes are high* (2nd ed.). McGraw Hill.

Patterson, K., Grenny, J., McMillian, R., & Switzler, A. (2012). *Crucial conversations: Tools for talking when the stakes are high* (2nd ed.). McGraw Hill.

Pearlman, L. A., & Saakvitne, K. W. (1995). *Trauma and the therapist: Countertransference and vicarious traumatization in psychotherapy with incest survivors*. New York: W.W. Norton.

Pearlman, L. A., & Mac Ian, P. S. (1995). Vicarious traumatization: An empirical study of the effects of trauma work on trauma therapists. *Professional Psychology, 26*(6), 558–565. doi:10.1037/0735-7028.26.6.558

Permatasari, P., Putra, F. W. I., & Natasha, V. (2020). Whether or not Indonesia-based companies consider anti-corruption acts important as its countrymen do. *Indonesian Management and Accounting Research, 16*(1), 35–48.

Perrow, C. (1999). *Normal accidents: Living with high-risk technologies* (2nd ed.). Princeton University Press.

Perry, D. L., & Daniels, M. L. (2016). Implementing trauma-informed practices in the school setting: A pilot study. *School Mental Health: A Multidisciplinary Research and Practice Journal, 8*(1), 177–188. doi:10.100712310-016-9182-3

Pew Research Center. (2017). *Gender discrimination comes in many forms for today's working women*. Author.

Phifer, L. W., & Hull, R. (2016). Helping students heal: Observations of trauma-informed practices in the schools. *School Mental Health, 8*(1), 201–205. doi:10.100712310-016-9183-2

Picard, J. R., & McEwan, B. (2014). Mitochondrial allostatic load puts the 'gluc' back in glucocorticoids. *Martin Nature Reviews. Endocrinology Picard, 10*, 304–305.

Pierson, E. (2020). A large-scale analysis of racial disparities in police stops across the United States. *Nature Human Behaviour, 4*(7), 736–745. doi:10.103841562-020-0858-1

Pillai, J. A., Hall, C. B., Dickson, D. W., Buschke, H., Lipton, R. B., & Verghese, J. (2011). Association of crossword puzzle participation with memory decline in persons who develop dementia. *Journal of the International Neuropsychological Society, 17*(6), 1006–1013. doi:10.1017/S1355617711001111 PMID:22040899

Plowman, D. A., Baker, L. T., Beck, T. E., Kulkarni, M., Solansky, S. T., & Travis, D. V. (2007). Radical change accidentally: The emergence and amplification of small change. *Academy of Management Journal, 50*(3), 513–541. doi:10.5465/amj.2007.25525647

Poller, L., & Wallace, D. (2008, March 15-17). *Types of reluctant educators* [Conference Presentation]. Association for Supervision and Curriculum Development's (ASCD) 63rd Annual Conference and Exhibit Show, New Orleans, LA, United States.

Popa, B. M. (2019). Strategic communication. *Journal of Defense Resources Management, 10*(2), 174–179.

Popick, J. (2014, March 6). *Managing expectations: The most underrated leadership skill.* Academic Press.

Poulin, P. A., Mackenzie, C. S., Soloway, G., & Karayolas, E. (2008). Mindfulness training as an evidenced-based approach to reducing stress and promoting well-being among human services professionals. *International Journal of Health Promotion and Education, 46*, 35–43.

Prentice, W. C. H. (2004). Understanding leadership. *Harvard Business Review.*

Prescod, D., & Zeligman, M. (2018). Career adaptability of trauma survivors: The moderating role of posttraumatic growth. *The Career Development Quarterly, 66*(2), 107–120. https://doi-org.proxygsu-afpl.galileo.usg.edu/10.1002/cdq.12126

Pressman, A. (2020). *The holidays used to be UPS's busiest time. Then came COVID-19.* https://www.google.com/amp/s/fortune.com/longform/ups-ceo-carol-tome-shipping-coronavirus-covid-19-pandemic-home-depot-cfo/amp/

Priest, K., & Middleton, E. (2016). Exploring leader identity and development. *New Directions for Student Leadership, 49*(149), 37–47. doi:10.1002/yd.20160 PMID:26895262

Quick, A. (2020). *Adult trauma in educational settings: How COVID-19 affects educators and operational staff.* Research Triangle Institute International. https://www.rti.org/insights/adult-trauma-educational-settings-covid

Raio, C., Orederu, T., Palazzolo, L., Shurick, A., & Phelps, E. (2013). *Cognitive emotion regulation fails the stress test.* Academic Press.

Rangachari, P., & Woods, J. L. (2020). Preserving organizational resilience, patient safety, and staff retention during COVID-19 requires a holistic consideration of the psychological safety of healthcare workers. *International Journal of Environmental Research and Public Health, 17*(12), 4267. doi:10.3390/ijerph17124267 PMID:32549273

Rank, M. G., & Hutchison, W. S. (2000). An Analysis of Leadership Within the Social Work Profession. *Journal of Social Work Education, 36*(3), 487–502. doi:10.1080/10437797.2000.10779024

Rath, T. (2008). *Strengths based leadership: Great leaders, teams and why people follow.* Gallup Press.

Recognize Trauma. (n.d.). *What might have happened?* Retrieved October 16, 2020, from http://recognizetrauma.org/

Report, P. (2006). *The US Department of the Interior.* https://www.doioig.gov/sites/doioig.gov/files/Law_Enforcement_Reform.pdf

Ricciardelli, R. (2020). Canadian Public Safety Personnel and Occupational Stressors: How PSP Interpret Stressors on Duty. *International Journal of Environmental Research and Public Health, 17*(13), 4736. doi:. doi:10.3390/ijerph17134736

Rigby, D., Berez, S., & Elk, S. (2020). *Doing Agile Right.* Harvard Business Review Press.

Riggio, R. (2009, March 24). Are you a transformational leader? *Psychology Today.*

Riolli, L., & Savicki, V. (2003). Optimism and Coping as Moderators of the Relation Between Work Resources and Burnout in Information Service Workers. *International Journal of Stress Management, 10*(3), 235–252. doi:10.1037/1072-5245.10.3.235

Risberg, A. (2020). *Constantly trying organizations: Ambiguities, contradictions, and paradoxes in diversity work.* Paper presented at NEON 2020, Norway. https://research-api.cbs.dk/ws/files/64201071/annette_risberg_constantly_trying_organizations_konference_paper_NEON_2020.pdf

Rivkin, J., & Ryan, M. (2012). Situating colonial and postcolonial studies. In Literary theory: an anthology (pp. 1100–1111). Wiley Blackwell.

Roberts, R. K., & Grubb, P. L. (2014, March-April). The consequences of nursing stress and need for integrated solutions. *Rehabilitation Nursing, 39*(2), 62–69. doi:10.1002/rnj.97

Robinson, B. (2020, Nov.). 6 Ways To Cope With More Uncertainty. *Forbes Magazine.*

Rocha, H., Pirson, M., & Suddaby, R. (2020). Business with purpose and the purpose of business schools: Re-imagining capitalism in a post pandemic world: A conversation with Jay Coen Gilbert, Raymond Miles, Christian Felber, Raj Sisodia, Paul Adler, and Charles Wookey. *Journal of Management Inquiry.* Advance online publication. doi:10.1177/1056492620970279

Rock, D. (2021). *Dr. David Rock.* https://davidrock.net/publications/

Rogers, E. M., Medina, U. E., & Wiley, C. H. (2005). Complex adaptive systems and the diffusion of innovations. *The Innovation Journal, 30,* 1–26.

Rosen, & Perrewe. (2017). *Power, Politics, and Political Skill in Job Stress* (1st ed.). Emerald Publishing Limited.

Ross, J. A., & Stoecker, R. (2016). The emotional context of higher education community engagement. *Journal of Community Engagement & Echolarship, 9*(2), 7–18.

Rothbard, N. P., & Wilk, S. L. (2011). Waking up on the right or wrong side of the bed: Start-of-workday mood, work events, employee affect, and performance. *Academy of Management Journal, 54,* 959–980.

Roulet, T. J. (2020). *The power of being divisive: Understanding negative social evaluations.* Stanford University Press. doi:10.1515/9781503613904

Roux-Dufort, C. (2009). The devil lies in details! How crises build up within organizations. *Journal of Contingencies and Crisis Management, 17*(1), 4–11.

Rowold, J., & Schlotz, W. (2009). Transformational and transactional leadership and followers' chronic stress, Kravis Leadership Institute. *Leadership Review, 9*(2), 35–48.

Rubel, B. (2019). *Loss, grief, and bereavement: Helping individuals cope.* Western Schools.

Rudolph, J. W., & Repenning, N. P. (2002). Disaster dynamics: Understanding the role of quantity in organizational collapse. *Administrative Science Quarterly*, *47*(1), 1–30. doi:10.2307/3094889

Ruiz-Martin, C., Lopez-Paredes, A., & Wainer, G. (2018). What we know and do not know about organizational resilience. *International Journal of Production Management and Engineering*, *6*(1), 11–28. doi:10.4995/ijpme.2018.7898

Russ, M., & Uhl-Bien, M. (2001). Leadership in Complex Organizations. Management Department Faculty Publications, 11.

Samad, A., Reaburn, P., Davis, H., & Ahmed, E. (2015). An empirical study on the effect of leadership styles on employee wellbeing and organizational outcomes within an Australian regional university. *Proceedings Of The Australasian Conference On Business And Social Sciences*.

Schein, E. (1980). *Organizational psychology*. Prentice-Hall.

Schein, E. (2004). *Organizational culture and leadership* (3rd ed.). Jossey-Bass.

Schmul, A. T. (2020). *Making sense leading change: A new superintendent's challenge* [Doctoral dissertation]. Vanderbilt University. https://ir.vanderbilt.edu/xmlui/ bitstream/handle/1803/16338/SchmuhlAarynT2020_Aaryn%20Schmuhl.pdf?sequence=1&isAllowed=y

Schneider, M., & Somers, M. (2006). Organizations as complex adaptive systems: Implications of Complexity Theory for leadership research. *The Leadership Quarterly*, *17*(4), 351–365. doi:10.1016/j.leaqua.2006.04.006

Scoblic, J. P. (2020). Learning from the future: How to Make Robust Strategy in Times of Deep Uncertainty. *Harvard Business Review*, *98*(4), 37–47.

Secchi, Armstrong, Babri, & Kask. (2020). *Call for papers: Track 6.3 – Rethinking behavior in organizations: Reflections on disruption and change*. Paper development workshop, IJOTB special issue. Nordic Academy of Management.

Secchi, D., & Cowley, S. J. (2020). Cognition in organisations: What it is and how it works. *European Management Review*. Advance online publication. doi:10.1111/emre.12442

Seeger, M., & Sellnow, T. L. (2016). *Narratives of crisis: Telling stories of ruin and renewal*. Stanford University Press.

Seijo, G. L., & L. Blugerman. (2020). Buscando al eslabón perdido del desarrollo tecnológico. Entendiendo el desarrollo de simuladores en CITEDEF vis-a-vis su régimen de producción industrial [In search of the technological development missing link. Understanding the development of CITEDEF simulators vis-a-vis its industrial production regime]. *Ciencias Administrativas, 17*(2021), 1-11.

Senge, P. (1990). *The fifth discipline: The art and practice of learning organizations*. Currency and Doubleday.

Shaukat, N., Ali, D. M., & Razzak, J. (2020). Physical and mental health impacts of COVID-19 on healthcare workers: A scoping review. *International Journal of Emergency Medicine*, *13*(1), 40. doi:10.118612245-020-00299-5 PMID:32689925

Sherman, W. S., & Roberto, K. J. (2020). Are you talkin' to me? The role of culture in crisis management sensemaking. *Management Decision*, *58*(10), 2105–2221. doi:10.1108/MD-08-2020-1017

Shoup, J., & Studer, S. (2010). *Leveraging chaos: The mysteries of leadership and policy revealed*. Rowman & Littlefield Education.

Shreeve, Hallett, Edwards, Anthonysamy, Frey, & Rashid. (2020). So if Mr. Blue Head here clicks the link..." Risk thinking in cyber security decision making. *ACM Transactions on Privacy and Security, 24*(1), 5:1-5:29.

Shrivastava, P. (1987). Bhopal: Anatomy of a Crisis. Ballinger.

Shugart, S. (2013). *Leadership in the crucible of work: Discovering the interior life of an authentic leader*. Florida Hospital Publishing.

Shultz, S., Opie, C., & Atkinson, Q. (2011). Stepwise evolution of stable sociality in primates. *Nature*, *479*, 219–222. https://doi.org/10.1038/nature10601

Siegrist, J., Starke, D., Chandola, T., Godin, I., Marmot, M., Niedhammer, I., & Peter, R. (2004). The measurement of effort-reward imbalance at work: European comparisons. *Social Science & Medicine*, *58*(8), 1483–1499. doi:10.1016/S0277-9536(03)00351-4

Simone, C., Iandolo, F., Fulco, I., & Loia, F. (2020). Rome was not built in a day. Resilience and the eternal city: Insights for urban management. *Cities (London, England)*, *110*, 103070. doi:10.1016/j.cities.2020.103070

Sipe, J., & Frick, D. (2009). *Seven pillars of servant leadership: Practicing the wisdom of leading by serving*. Paulist Press.

Slade, K. W. J. (2020). *Bushfire risk in late-modernity: An examination of risk perspectives and ontological security structures in Victorian urban-rural interface residents* [Unpublished doctoral dissertation]. La Trobe University, Victoria, Australia.

Sparks, D. (2002). *Designing powerful professional development for teachers and principals*. National Staff Development Council.

Spears, L. (2010). Character and servant leadership: Ten characteristics of effective, caring leaders. *The Journal of Virtues & Leadership*, *1*(1), 25–30.

Sporleder, J., & Forbes, H. T. (2016). *The trauma-informed school: A step by step implementation guide for administrators and school personnel*. Beyond Consequences, LLC.

St. Thomas University. (2018). *What is transformational leadership? How new ideas produce impressive results*. STU Online. https://online.stu.edu/articles/education/what-is-transformational-leadership.aspx

Stacey, R. D. (2011). *Strategic Management and Organisational Dynamics: The Challenge of Complexity to Ways of Thinking about Organisations*. Pearson Education.

Stake, R. E. (1995). The art of case study research. *Sage (Atlanta, Ga.)*.

Staw, B. M., Sandelands, L. E., & Dutton, J. E. (1981). Threat-rigidity effects: A multi-level analysis. *Administrative Science Quarterly*, *26*(4), 501–524. doi:10.2307/2392337

Stefko, M. (2019). Notice for reasons of redundancy as a measure for discrimination on grounds of age. *Central European Journal of Labour Law and Personnel Management*, *1*(1), 61–73. doi:10.33382/cejllpm.2019.02.05

Stein, H. F. (2009). Understanding and Consulting with Inconsolable Organizations. *Illness, Crisis & Loss*, *17*(3), 243–259. doi:10.2190/IL.17.3.e

Stewart, G. L., Courtright, S. H., & Barrick, M. M. (2012). Peer-Based Control in Self-Managing Teams: Linking Rational and Normative Influence With Individual and Group Performance. *The Journal of Applied Psychology*, *97*(2), 435–447. doi:10.1037/a0025303 PMID:21895352

Stogdill, R. M. (1948). Personal factors associated with leadership: A survey of the literature. *The Journal of Psychology*, (25), 35–71.

Stogner, J., Miller, B. L., & McLean, K. (2020). Police stress, mental health, and resiliency during the COVID-19 pandemic. *American Journal of Criminal Justice*, *1*, 1–13. PMID:32837167

Strauser, D. R., Lustig, D. C., Cogdal, P. A., & Uruk, A. Ç. (2006). Trauma symptoms: Relationship with career thoughts, vocational identity, and developmental work personality. *The Career Development Quarterly*, *54*(4), 346–360.

Substance Abuse and Mental Health Services Administration. (2019). *Trauma and violence*. Retrieved October 16, 2020, from https://www.samhsa.gov/trauma-violence

Substance Abuse and Mental Health Services Administration. (2020, September 17). *Infographic: 6 guiding principles to a trauma informed approach*. https://www.cdc.gov/cpr/infographics/6_principles_trauma_info.htm

Sukhov, A., Sihvonen, A., Netz, J., Magnusson, P., & Olsson, L. E. (2021). How experts screen ideas: The complex interplay of intuition, analysis and sensemaking. *Journal of Product Innovation Management, 38*, 248-270. doi:10.1111/jpim.12559

Tabesh, P., & Vera, D. M. (2020). Top managers' improvisational decision-making in crisis: a paradox perspective. *Management Decision, 58*(10), 2235-2256. doi:10.1108/MD-08-2020-1060

Tafvelin, S., Hyvönen, U., & Westerberg, K. (2014). Transformational leadership in the social work context: The importance of leader continuity and co-worker support. *British Journal of Social Work*, *44*(4), 886–904. doi:10.1093/bjsw/bcs174

Tam, G. (2020). The path forward amid COVID-19. *TD: Talent Development*, *74*(6), 38–43.

Tapscott, D., & Ticoll, D. (2003). *The naked corporation: How the age of transparency will revolutionize business*. Free Press.

Taylor, F. W. (1911). *Shop Management*. Harper & Brothers.

Temperley, A. J. (2016). *Servant Leadership as Defined by K-12 ACSI Christian School Administrators in Arizona, USA* [Doctoral Dissertation]. Temple University.

Tenuto, P. (2018). A review of the listening leader: Creating the conditions for equitable school transformation. *Journal of Organizational & Educational Leadership*, *4*(1), 4. https://digitalcommons.gardner-webb.edu/joel/vol4/iss1/4

The American Institute of Stress. (2019). *The United States of Stress 2019*. The American Institute of Stress Workplace Stress Survey. https://www.stress.org/workplace-stress

Thomas, L. (2020). Nike shakes up its executive team to bolster its digital business, announces job cuts. *CNBC*. https://www.cnbc.com/2020/07/22/nike-shakes-up-its-executive-team-announces-job-cuts.html

Thomas, B., & Lucas, K. (2019). Development and validation of the workplace dignity scale. *Group & Organization Management*, *44*(1), 72–111. https://journals.sagepub.com/doi/pdf/10.1177/1059601118807784

Thompson, C. S. (2009). *Towards solutions: Fundamentals of transformational leadership in a postmodern era. Mandeville*. Northern Caribbean University Press.

Thompson, C. S. (2015). *Locating the epicentre of effective (educational) leadership in the 21st century*. The Caribbean Leadership Re-Imagination Initiative.

Thompson, C. S. (2018a). Leadership behaviours that nurture organizational trust: Re-Examining the fundamentals. *Journal of Human Resource Management*, *21*(1), 28–42.

Thompson, C. S. (2018b). The construct of 'respect' in teacher-student relationship: Exploring dimensions of ethics of care and sustainable development. *Journal of Leadership Education*, *17*(3), 42–60. doi:10.12806/V17/I3/R3

Thompson, C. S. (2019). *Reimagining educational leadership in the Caribbean*. The University of the West Indies Press.

Thygeson, M., Morrissey, L., & Ulstad, V. (2010). Adaptive leadership and the practice of medicine: A complexity-based approach to reframing the doctor-patient relationship. *Journal of Evaluation in Clinical Practice, 16*(5), 1009–1015. doi:10.1111/j.1365-2753.2010.01533.x PMID:20846289

Tipaldi, R., Santulli, R., & Gallucci, C. (2020). Finance for social innovation in emerging economies and developing countries. In M. Ramírez-Pasillas, V. Ratten, & H. Lundberg (Eds.), *Social innovation of new ventures: Achieving social inclusion and sustainability in emerging economies and developing countries* (pp. 14–29). Routledge. doi:10.4324/9781003034933-3

Torres, R., & Reeves, M. (2011). Adaptive Leadership: How many of these practices do you employ? *Leadership Excellence, 28*(7).

Tuckman, B. W. (1965). Developmental sequence in small groups. *Psychological Bulletin, 63*(6), 384–399. doi:10.1037/h0022100 PMID:14314073

Turner, J. R., & Baker, R. M. (2019). Complexity Theory: An Overview with Potential Applications for the Social Sciences. *Systems, 7*(1), 22. doi:10.3390ystems7010004

Uhl-Bien, M. (2006). Relational Leadership Theory: Exploring the social processes of leadership and organizing. *The Leadership Quarterly Yearly Review of Leadership, 17*(6), 654–676. doi:10.1016/j.leaqua.2006.10.007

Uhl-Bien, M., & Arena, M. (2018). Leadership for organizational adaptability: A theoretical synthesis and integrative framework. *The Leadership Quarterly, 29*(1), 89–104. doi:10.1016/j.leaqua.2017.12.009

Uhl-Bien, M., Marion, R., & McKelvey, B. (2007). Complexity Leadership Theory: Shifting leadership from the industrial age to the knowledge era. *The Leadership Quarterly, 18*(4), 298–318. doi:10.1016/j.leaqua.2007.04.002

Umberson, D., & Montez, J. K. (2010). Social relationships and health: A flashpoint for health policy. *Journal of Health and Social Behavior, 51*(1_suppl), 54–66. doi:10.1177/0022146510383501 PMID:20943583

Utrainen, K., & Kyanga, S. H. (2009). Hospital nurses' job satisfaction: A literature review. *Journal of Nursing Management, 17*, 1002–1010.

Vainio, A. (2020). *"They don't understand how we feel": An affective approach to improving the 'best practice' of community-based post-disaster recovery* [Unpublished doctoral dissertation]. University of Sheffield, UK.

Valderrama Venegas, E. A. (2020). *Social media platforms as economic organisations: reconstructing the evolution of TripAdvisor's operations* [Doctoral dissertation]. London School of Economics. http://etheses.lse.ac.uk/4215/1/Valderrama__Social-media-platforms.pdf

van Bavel, B., Curtis, D., Dijkman, J., Hannaford, M., de Keyzer, M., van Onacker, E., & Soens, T. (2020). *Disasters and history: The vulnerability and resilience of past societies.* Cambridge University Press. doi:10.1017/9781108569743

Van der Kolk, B. A. (2014). *The body keeps the score: Brain, mind, and body in the healing of trauma.* Penguin Group, LLC.

van der Merwe, S. E., Koch, R. G., Correia, A. J., & Moganedi, T. S. (2020). Using sense of coherence to cultivate enabling conditions for social resilience. In *Proceeding of the Joint International Resilience Conference 2020, Interconnected: Resilience Innovations for Sustainable Development Goals.* 4TU Centre for Resilience Engineering/Future Resilience Systems – STU.

van Dick, R., & Wagner, U. (2001). Stress and strain in teaching: A structural equation approach. *The British Journal of Educational Psychology, 71*, 243–259.

van Wingerden, J., Derks, D., Bakker, A. B., & Dorenbosch, L. (2013). *Job crafting in schools for special education: A qualitative analysis*. Retrieved from https://www.narcis.nl/publication/RecordID/oai:tudelft.nl:uuid:92fb8a18-fc71-4fab-aa4c-b7a96c57115c

VanGronigen, B. A., Cunningham, K. M. W., Young, M., & Tucker, P. D. (2021). *Exploring Principal Development and Teacher Outcomes*. Routledge.

Vaughan, D. (1996). *The Challenger launch decision: Risky technology, culture, and deviance at NASA*. University of Chicago Press.

Venugopal, V. (2016) Understanding organizational trauma: A background review of types and causes. *IOSR Journal of Business and Management, 18*(10), 65-69. http://www.iosrjournals.org/iosr-jbm/papers/Vol18-issue10/Version-7/I1810076569.pdf

Venugopal, V. (2016). Understanding Organizational Trauma: A Background Review of Types and Causes. *IOSR Journal of Business and Management, 18*(10), 65–69.

Vivian, P., Cox, K., Hormann, S., & Murphy-Kangas, S. (2018). Healing traumatized organizations reflections from practitioners. *OD Practitioner, 49*(4), 45–51. https://static1.squarespace.com/static/515287f7e4b0574a80b7af08/t/5caa4835f4e1fc950f1fb123/1554663479452/Healing+Traumatized+Organizations+2018.pdf

Vivian, P., & Hormann, S. (2002). Trauma and Healing in Organizations. *OD Practitioner, 34*(4), 37–42.

Vivian, P., & Hormann, S. (2002). Trauma and healing in organizations. OD Practitioner. *Journal of the National Organization Development Network, 34*(4), 37–42.

Vivian, P., & Hormann, S. (2015). Persistent traumatization in nonprofit organizations. *OD Practitioner, 47*(1), 25–30.

Vogus, T. J., & Sutcliffe, K. M. (2007). Organizational resilience: Towards a theory and research agenda. In *2007 IEEE International Conference on Systems, Man and Cybernetics*, Montreal, QC, Canada. 10.1109/ICSMC.2007.4414160

Vrklevski, L. P., & Franklin, J. (2008). Vicarious trauma: The impact on solicitors of exposure to traumatic material. *Traumatology, 14*(1), 106–118. doi:10.1177/1534765607309961

Wagner, T. (2006). *Change Leadership*. Jossey-Bass.

Waldschmidt, N. (2020). *Rethinking engagement: How managers frame and make sense of communication strategies, practices, and challenges* [Master's thesis]. University of Ottawa, Canada. https://ruor.uottawa.ca/bitstream/10393/41225/1/Waldschmidt_ Nathalie_2020_Thesis.pdf

Walker, T. (2018). *How many teachers are highly stressed? Maybe more than people think*. NEA Today. https://www.nea.org/advocating-for-change/new-from-nea/how-many-teacher-are-highly-stressed-maybe-more-people-think

Walker, T. (2020). *Helping students and educators recover from COVID-19 trauma*. NEA Today. https://www.nea-org/advocating-for-change/new-from-nea/helping-Students-and-educators-recover-covid-19-trauma

Walker, T. (2020, August 5). Helping students and educators recover from COVID-19 trauma. *NEA Today*. https://www.nea.org/advocating-for-change/new-from-nea/helping-students-and-educators-recover-covid-19-trauma

Walker, T. (2020). Healing from COVID-19 trauma in our schools. *NEA Today, 39*(1), 28–31.

Wang, X., Zhang, X., & He, J. (2020). Challenges to the system of reserve medical supplies for public health emergencies: Reflections on the outbreak of the severe acute respiratory syndrome coronavirus 2 (SARS-CoV-2) epidemic in China. *Bioscience Trends, 14*(1), 3–8. doi:10.5582/bst.2020.01043 PMID:32062645

Warrick, D. D. (2018). The need for transformational leaders that understand organization development fundamentals. *OD Practitioner*, *50*(4), 33–40.

Watson, J. (2015). *Strategy: An Introduction to Game Theory*. WW Norton.

Watzlawik, P., Weakland, J. H., & Fisch, R. (1974). *Change: Principles of problem formation and problem resolution*. Norton.

Weick, K. E. (1969). *The social psychology of organizing* (1st ed.). Addison Wesley.

Weick, K. E. (1985). Cosmos vs. chaos: Sense and nonsense in electronic contexts. *Organizational Dynamics*, *14*(2), 50–64. doi:10.1016/0090-2616(85)90036-1

Weick, K. E. (1988). Enacted sensemaking in crisis situations. *Journal of Management Studies*, *25*(4), 305–317. doi:10.1111/j.1467-6486.1988.tb00039.x

Weick, K. E. (1990). The vulnerable system: An analysis of the Tenerife air disaster. *Journal of Management*, *16*(3), 571–593. doi:10.1177/014920639001600304

Weick, K. E. (1993). The collapse of sensemaking in organizations: The Mann Gulch disaster. *Administrative Science Quarterly*, *38*(4), 628–652. doi:10.2307/2393339

Weick, K. E. (1993). The collapse of sensemaking: The Mann Gulch disaster. *Administrative Science Quarterly*, *38*, 628–652.

Weick, K. E. (1995). *Sensemaking in organizations*. Sage.

Weick, K. E. (1996, May). *Prepare your organization to fight fires. Harvard Business Review*.

Weick, K. E. (2005). Managing the unexpected: Complexity as distributed sensemaking. In R. R. McDaniels & D. Driebe (Eds.), *Uncertainty and surprise in complex systems: Questions on working with the unexpected* (pp. 51–65). Springer-Verlag. doi:10.1007/10948637_5

Weick, K. E. (2006). Faith, evidence, and action: Better guesses in an unknowable world. *Organization Studies*, *27*(11), 1723–1736. doi:10.1177/0170840606068351

Weick, K. E. (2020). Sensemaking, organizing, and surpassing: A handoff. *Journal of Management Studies*, *57*(7), 1420–1431.

Weick, K. E. (2021). Sensemaking and whistleblowing. In P. J. Svenkerud, J.-O. Sørnes, & L. Browning (Eds.), *Whistleblowing, communication and consequences: Lessons from the Norwegian national lottery* (pp. 81–92). Routledge. doi:10.4324/9780367822033-9

Weick, K. E., & Orton, J. D. (1987). Academic journals in the classroom. *Organizational Behavior Teaching Review*, *11*(2), 27–42.

Weick, K. E., & Roberts, K. H. (1993). Collective Mind in Organizations: Heedful Interrelating on Flight Decks. *Administrative Science Quarterly*, *38*(3), 357–381.

Weick, K. E., & Sutcliffe, K. M. (2001). *Managing the unexpected: Assuring high performance in an age of complexity*. John Wiley & Sons.

Weick, K. E., & Sutcliffe, K. M. (2007). *Managing the unexpected: Resilient performance in an age of uncertainty* (2nd ed.). John Wiley & Sons.

Weick, K. E., & Sutcliffe, K. M. (2015). *Managing the unexpected: Sustained performance in a complex world* (3rd ed.). Sage Publications. doi:10.1002/9781119175834

Wessels, J. S. (2020). *A policy instrument to access child poverty: The case of the child support grant (CSG) in South Africa*. Academic Press.

White, S. K. (2018). *What is transformational leadership? A model for motivating innovation.* CIO. https://www.cio.com/article/3257184/what-is-transformational-leadership-a-model-for-motivating-innovation.html

Wilkie, D. (2018). *Employees in Stressful Jobs Balance Demands with Helping Others: Airline Pilot, Firefighter, Police Officer among 'most stressful' Jobs of 2018*. HR News.

Williams, G., Irving, G., Wright, A. L., & Middleton, S. (2020). Managing job-related diversity processes in high-reliability teams in the emergency department. *British Journal of Management, 0*, 1-17. doi:10.1111/1467-8551.12450

Winter, L. (2019). Organizational trauma: A phenomenological study of psychological organizational trauma and its effect on employees and organization. *Management, 14*(2), 117-136. doi:10.26493/1854-4231.14.117-136

Winter, L. (2019). *Organizational trauma: A phenomenological study of psychological organizational trauma and its effect on employees and organization.* Retrieved: https://www.researchgate.net/publication/339615204_Organizational_Trauma_A_Phenomenological_Study_of_Psychological_Organizational_Trauma_and_Its_Effect_on_Employees_and_Organization

Wirthman, L. (2014). Is flat better? Zappos ditches hierarchy to improve company performance. *Forbes*.

Wolever, R. Q., Bobinet, K. J., McCabe, K., Mackenzie, E. R., Fekete, E., Kusnick, C. A., & Baime, M. (2012). Effective and viable mind-body stress reduction in the workplace: A randomized controlled trial. *Journal of Occupational Health Psychology, 17*, 246–258. doi:10.1037/a0027278

Wong, P., & Page, D. (2003). *Servant leadership: An Opponent-Process Model and the Revised Servant Leadership Profile*. Servant Leadership Roundtable.

Wood, A. W. (1999). *Kant's ethical thought*. Cambridge University Press. doi:10.1017/CBO9781139173254

Wright, B. E., Moynihan, D. P., & Pandey, S. K. (2012). Pulling the levers: Transformational leadership, public service motivation, and mission valence. *Public Administration Review, 72*(2), 206–215. doi:10.1111/j.1540-6210.2011.02496.x

Xu, S. (2020). *A changing tourism system in post-disaster recovery: Developing anime tourism in the aftermath of the 2011 great East Japan earthquake in Oarai, Japan* [Unpublished master's thesis]. Lincoln University, New Zealand.

Yeung, A., & Ulrich, D. (2019). *Reinventing the Organization*. Harvard Business Review Press.

Yu, S., & Yu, J. (2020). Doing while thinking in dynamic environment: A brief review of strategic improvisation. In H. Shioji, D. R. Adhikari, F. Yoshino, & T. Hayashi (Eds.), Management for sustainable and inclusive development in a transforming Asia (pp. 163–177). Academic Press.

Yuan-Duen, L., Pi-Ching, C., & Chin-Lai, S. (2020). The evolution of the leadership theories and the analysis of new research trends. *International Journal of Organizational Innovation, 12*(3), 88–1.

Yukl, G. (1999). An evaluation of conceptual weaknesses in transformational and charismatic leadership theories. *The Leadership Quarterly, 10*(2), 285.

Zaar, S., Van Den Bossche, P., & Gijselaers, W. (2020). How business students think about leadership: A qualitative study on leader identity and meaning-making. *Academy of Management Learning & Education, 2*, 168.

Related References

To continue our tradition of advancing information science and technology research, we have compiled a list of recommended IGI Global readings. These references will provide additional information and guidance to further enrich your knowledge and assist you with your own research and future publications.

Abtahi, M. S., Behboudi, L., & Hasanabad, H. M. (2017). Factors Affecting Internet Advertising Adoption in Ad Agencies. *International Journal of Innovation in the Digital Economy*, *8*(4), 18–29. doi:10.4018/IJIDE.2017100102

Agrawal, S. (2017). The Impact of Emerging Technologies and Social Media on Different Business(es): Marketing and Management. In O. Rishi & A. Sharma (Eds.), *Maximizing Business Performance and Efficiency Through Intelligent Systems* (pp. 37–49). Hershey, PA: IGI Global. doi:10.4018/978-1-5225-2234-8.ch002

Alnoukari, M., Razouk, R., & Hanano, A. (2016). BSC-SI: A Framework for Integrating Strategic Intelligence in Corporate Strategic Management. *International Journal of Social and Organizational Dynamics in IT*, *5*(2), 1–14. doi:10.4018/IJSODIT.2016070101

Alnoukari, M., Razouk, R., & Hanano, A. (2016). BSC-SI, A Framework for Integrating Strategic Intelligence in Corporate Strategic Management. *International Journal of Strategic Information Technology and Applications*, *7*(1), 32–44. doi:10.4018/IJSITA.2016010103

Altındağ, E. (2016). Current Approaches in Change Management. In A. Goksoy (Ed.), *Organizational Change Management Strategies in Modern Business* (pp. 24–51). Hershey, PA: IGI Global. doi:10.4018/978-1-4666-9533-7.ch002

Alvarez-Dionisi, L. E., Turner, R., & Mittra, M. (2016). Global Project Management Trends. *International Journal of Information Technology Project Management*, *7*(3), 54–73. doi:10.4018/IJITPM.2016070104

Anantharaman, R. N., Rajeswari, K. S., Angusamy, A., & Kuppusamy, J. (2017). Role of Self-Efficacy and Collective Efficacy as Moderators of Occupational Stress Among Software Development Professionals. *International Journal of Human Capital and Information Technology Professionals*, *8*(2), 45–58. doi:10.4018/IJHCITP.2017040103

Aninze, F., El-Gohary, H., & Hussain, J. (2018). The Role of Microfinance to Empower Women: The Case of Developing Countries. *International Journal of Customer Relationship Marketing and Management, 9*(1), 54–78. doi:10.4018/IJCRMM.2018010104

Arsenijević, O. M., Orčić, D., & Kastratović, E. (2017). Development of an Optimization Tool for Intangibles in SMEs: A Case Study from Serbia with a Pilot Research in the Prestige by Milka Company. In M. Vemić (Ed.), *Optimal Management Strategies in Small and Medium Enterprises* (pp. 320–347). Hershey, PA: IGI Global. doi:10.4018/978-1-5225-1949-2.ch015

Aryanto, V. D., Wismantoro, Y., & Widyatmoko, K. (2018). Implementing Eco-Innovation by Utilizing the Internet to Enhance Firm's Marketing Performance: Study of Green Batik Small and Medium Enterprises in Indonesia. *International Journal of E-Business Research, 14*(1), 21–36. doi:10.4018/IJEBR.2018010102

Atiku, S. O., & Fields, Z. (2017). Multicultural Orientations for 21st Century Global Leadership. In N. Baporikar (Ed.), *Management Education for Global Leadership* (pp. 28–51). Hershey, PA: IGI Global. doi:10.4018/978 1 5225 1013-0.ch002

Atiku, S. O., & Fields, Z. (2018). Organisational Learning Dimensions and Talent Retention Strategies for the Service Industries. In N. Baporikar (Ed.), *Global Practices in Knowledge Management for Societal and Organizational Development* (pp. 358–381). Hershey, PA: IGI Global. doi:10.4018/978-1-5225-3009-1.ch017

Ávila, L., & Teixeira, L. (2018). The Main Concepts Behind the Dematerialization of Business Processes. In M. Khosrow-Pour, D.B.A. (Ed.), Encyclopedia of Information Science and Technology, Fourth Edition (pp. 888-898). Hershey, PA: IGI Global. doi:10.4018/978-1-5225-2255-3.ch076

Bartens, Y., Chunpir, H. I., Schulte, F., & Voß, S. (2017). Business/IT Alignment in Two-Sided Markets: A COBIT 5 Analysis for Media Streaming Business Models. In S. De Haes & W. Van Grembergen (Eds.), *Strategic IT Governance and Alignment in Business Settings* (pp. 82–111). Hershey, PA: IGI Global. doi:10.4018/978-1-5225-0861-8.ch004

Bashayreh, A. M. (2018). Organizational Culture and Organizational Performance. In W. Lee & F. Sabetzadeh (Eds.), *Contemporary Knowledge and Systems Science* (pp. 50–69). Hershey, PA: IGI Global. doi:10.4018/978-1-5225-5655-8.ch003

Bedford, D. A. (2018). Sustainable Knowledge Management Strategies: Aligning Business Capabilities and Knowledge Management Goals. In N. Baporikar (Ed.), *Global Practices in Knowledge Management for Societal and Organizational Development* (pp. 46–73). Hershey, PA: IGI Global. doi:10.4018/978-1-5225-3009-1.ch003

Benmoussa, F., Nakara, W. A., & Jaouen, A. (2016). The Use of Social Media by SMEs in the Tourism Industry. In I. Lee (Ed.), *Encyclopedia of E-Commerce Development, Implementation, and Management* (pp. 2159–2170). Hershey, PA: IGI Global. doi:10.4018/978-1-4666-9787-4.ch155

Berger, R. (2016). Indigenous Management and Bottom of Pyramid Countries: The Role of National Institutions. In U. Aung & P. Ordoñez de Pablos (Eds.), *Managerial Strategies and Practice in the Asian Business Sector* (pp. 107–123). Hershey, PA: IGI Global. doi:10.4018/978-1-4666-9758-4.ch007

Bharwani, S., & Musunuri, D. (2018). Reflection as a Process From Theory to Practice. In M. Khosrow-Pour, D.B.A. (Ed.), Encyclopedia of Information Science and Technology, Fourth Edition (pp. 1529-1539). Hershey, PA: IGI Global. doi:10.4018/978-1-5225-2255-3.ch132

Bhatt, G. D., Wang, Z., & Rodger, J. A. (2017). Information Systems Capabilities and Their Effects on Competitive Advantages: A Study of Chinese Companies. *Information Resources Management Journal, 30*(3), 41–57. doi:10.4018/IRMJ.2017070103

Bhushan, M., & Yadav, A. (2017). Concept of Cloud Computing in ESB. In R. Bhadoria, N. Chaudhari, G. Tomar, & S. Singh (Eds.), *Exploring Enterprise Service Bus in the Service-Oriented Architecture Paradigm* (pp. 116–127). Hershey, PA: IGI Global. doi:10.4018/978-1-5225-2157-0.ch008

Bhushan, S. (2017). System Dynamics Base-Model of Humanitarian Supply Chain (HSCM) in Disaster Prone Eco-Communities of India: A Discussion on Simulation and Scenario Results. *International Journal of System Dynamics Applications, 6*(3), 20–37. doi:10.4018/IJSDA.2017070102

Biswas, A., & De, A. K. (2017). On Development of a Fuzzy Stochastic Programming Model with Its Application to Business Management. In S. Trivedi, S. Dey, A. Kumar, & T. Panda (Eds.), *Handbook of Research on Advanced Data Mining Techniques and Applications for Business Intelligence* (pp. 353–378). Hershey, PA: IGI Global. doi:10.4018/978-1-5225-2031-3.ch021

Bücker, J., & Ernste, K. (2018). Use of Brand Heroes in Strategic Reputation Management: The Case of Bacardi, Adidas, and Daimler. In A. Erdemir (Ed.), *Reputation Management Techniques in Public Relations* (pp. 126–150). Hershey, PA: IGI Global. doi:10.4018/978-1-5225-3619-2.ch007

Bureš, V. (2018). Industry 4.0 From the Systems Engineering Perspective: Alternative Holistic Framework Development. In R. Brunet-Thornton & F. Martinez (Eds.), *Analyzing the Impacts of Industry 4.0 in Modern Business Environments* (pp. 199–223). Hershey, PA: IGI Global. doi:10.4018/978-1-5225-3468-6.ch011

Buzady, Z. (2017). Resolving the Magic Cube of Effective Case Teaching: Benchmarking Case Teaching Practices in Emerging Markets – Insights from the Central European University Business School, Hungary. In D. Latusek (Ed.), *Case Studies as a Teaching Tool in Management Education* (pp. 79–103). Hershey, PA: IGI Global. doi:10.4018/978-1-5225-0770-3.ch005

Campatelli, G., Richter, A., & Stocker, A. (2016). Participative Knowledge Management to Empower Manufacturing Workers. *International Journal of Knowledge Management, 12*(4), 37–50. doi:10.4018/IJKM.2016100103

Căpusneanu, S., & Topor, D. I. (2018). Business Ethics and Cost Management in SMEs: Theories of Business Ethics and Cost Management Ethos. In I. Oncioiu (Ed.), *Ethics and Decision-Making for Sustainable Business Practices* (pp. 109–127). Hershey, PA: IGI Global. doi:10.4018/978-1-5225-3773-1.ch007

Carneiro, A. (2016). Maturity in Health Organization Information Systems: Metrics and Privacy Perspectives. *International Journal of Privacy and Health Information Management, 4*(2), 1–18. doi:10.4018/IJPHIM.2016070101

Chan, R. L., Mo, P. L., & Moon, K. K. (2018). Strategic and Tactical Measures in Managing Enterprise Risks: A Study of the Textile and Apparel Industry. In K. Strang, M. Korstanje, & N. Vajjhala (Eds.), *Research, Practices, and Innovations in Global Risk and Contingency Management* (pp. 1–19). Hershey, PA: IGI Global. doi:10.4018/978-1-5225-4754-9.ch001

Chandan, H. C. (2016). Motivations and Challenges of Female Entrepreneurship in Developed and Developing Economies. In N. Baporikar (Ed.), *Handbook of Research on Entrepreneurship in the Contemporary Knowledge-Based Global Economy* (pp. 260–286). Hershey, PA: IGI Global. doi:10.4018/978-1-4666-8798-1.ch012

Charlier, S. D., Burke-Smalley, L. A., & Fisher, S. L. (2018). Undergraduate Programs in the U.S: A Contextual and Content-Based Analysis. In J. Mendy (Ed.), *Teaching Human Resources and Organizational Behavior at the College Level* (pp. 26–57). Hershey, PA: IGI Global. doi:10.4018/978-1-5225-2820-3.ch002

Chaudhuri, S. (2016). Application of Web-Based Geographical Information System (GIS) in E-Business. In U. Panwar, R. Kumar, & N. Ray (Eds.), *Handbook of Research on Promotional Strategies and Consumer Influence in the Service Sector* (pp. 389–405). Hershey, PA: IGI Global. doi:10.4018/978-1-5225-0143-5.ch023

Choudhuri, P. S. (2016). An Empirical Study on the Quality of Services Offered by the Private Life Insurers in Burdwan. In U. Panwar, R. Kumar, & N. Ray (Eds.), *Handbook of Research on Promotional Strategies and Consumer Influence in the Service Sector* (pp. 31–55). Hershey, PA: IGI Global. doi:10.4018/978-1-5225-0143-5.ch002

Dahlberg, T., Kivijärvi, H., & Saarinen, T. (2017). IT Investment Consistency and Other Factors Influencing the Success of IT Performance. In S. De Haes & W. Van Grembergen (Eds.), *Strategic IT Governance and Alignment in Business Settings* (pp. 176–208). Hershey, PA: IGI Global. doi:10.4018/978-1-5225-0861-8.ch007

Damnjanović, A. M. (2017). Knowledge Management Optimization through IT and E-Business Utilization: A Qualitative Study on Serbian SMEs. In M. Vemić (Ed.), *Optimal Management Strategies in Small and Medium Enterprises* (pp. 249–267). Hershey, PA: IGI Global. doi:10.4018/978-1-5225-1949-2.ch012

Daneshpour, H. (2017). Integrating Sustainable Development into Project Portfolio Management through Application of Open Innovation. In M. Vemić (Ed.), *Optimal Management Strategies in Small and Medium Enterprises* (pp. 370–387). Hershey, PA: IGI Global. doi:10.4018/978-1-5225-1949-2.ch017

Daniel, A. D., & Reis de Castro, V. (2018). Entrepreneurship Education: How to Measure the Impact on Nascent Entrepreneurs. In A. Carrizo Moreira, J. Guilherme Leitão Dantas, & F. Manuel Valente (Eds.), *Nascent Entrepreneurship and Successful New Venture Creation* (pp. 85–110). Hershey, PA: IGI Global. doi:10.4018/978-1-5225-2936-1.ch004

David, F., van der Sijde, P., & van den Besselaar, P. (2016). Enterpreneurial Incentives, Obstacles, and Management in University-Business Co-Operation: The Case of Indonesia. In J. Saiz-Álvarez (Ed.), *Handbook of Research on Social Entrepreneurship and Solidarity Economics* (pp. 499–518). Hershey, PA: IGI Global. doi:10.4018/978-1-5225-0097-1.ch024

David, R., Swami, B. N., & Tangirala, S. (2018). Ethics Impact on Knowledge Management in Organizational Development: A Case Study. In N. Baporikar (Ed.), *Global Practices in Knowledge Management for Societal and Organizational Development* (pp. 19–45). Hershey, PA: IGI Global. doi:10.4018/978-1-5225-3009-1.ch002

Delias, P., & Lakiotaki, K. (2018). Discovering Process Horizontal Boundaries to Facilitate Process Comprehension. *International Journal of Operations Research and Information Systems*, *9*(2), 1–31. doi:10.4018/IJORIS.2018040101

Denholm, J., & Lee-Davies, L. (2018). Success Factors for Games in Business and Project Management. In *Enhancing Education and Training Initiatives Through Serious Games* (pp. 34–68). Hershey, PA: IGI Global. doi:10.4018/978-1-5225-3689-5.ch002

Deshpande, M. (2017). Best Practices in Management Institutions for Global Leadership: Policy Aspects. In N. Baporikar (Ed.), *Management Education for Global Leadership* (pp. 1–27). Hershey, PA: IGI Global. doi:10.4018/978-1-5225-1013-0.ch001

Deshpande, M. (2018). Policy Perspectives for SMEs Knowledge Management. In N. Baporikar (Ed.), *Knowledge Integration Strategies for Entrepreneurship and Sustainability* (pp. 23–46). Hershey, PA: IGI Global. doi:10.4018/978-1-5225-5115-7.ch002

Dezdar, S. (2017). ERP Implementation Projects in Asian Countries: A Comparative Study on Iran and China. *International Journal of Information Technology Project Management*, *8*(3), 52–68. doi:10.4018/IJITPM.2017070104

Domingos, D., Martinho, R., & Varajão, J. (2016). Controlled Flexibility in Healthcare Processes: A BPMN-Extension Approach. In M. Cruz-Cunha, I. Miranda, R. Martinho, & R. Rijo (Eds.), *Encyclopedia of E-Health and Telemedicine* (pp. 521–535). Hershey, PA: IGI Global. doi:10.4018/978-1-4666-9978-6.ch040

Domingos, D., Respício, A., & Martinho, R. (2017). Reliability of IoT-Aware BPMN Healthcare Processes. In C. Reis & M. Maximiano (Eds.), *Internet of Things and Advanced Application in Healthcare* (pp. 214–248). Hershey, PA: IGI Global. doi:10.4018/978-1-5225-1820-4.ch008

Dosumu, O., Hussain, J., & El-Gohary, H. (2017). An Exploratory Study of the Impact of Government Policies on the Development of Small and Medium Enterprises in Developing Countries: The Case of Nigeria. *International Journal of Customer Relationship Marketing and Management*, *8*(4), 51–62. doi:10.4018/IJCRMM.2017100104

Durst, S., Bruns, G., & Edvardsson, I. R. (2017). Retaining Knowledge in Smaller Building and Construction Firms. *International Journal of Knowledge and Systems Science*, *8*(3), 1–12. doi:10.4018/IJKSS.2017070101

Edvardsson, I. R., & Durst, S. (2017). Outsourcing, Knowledge, and Learning: A Critical Review. *International Journal of Knowledge-Based Organizations*, *7*(2), 13–26. doi:10.4018/IJKBO.2017040102

Edwards, J. S. (2018). Integrating Knowledge Management and Business Processes. In M. Khosrow-Pour, D.B.A. (Ed.), Encyclopedia of Information Science and Technology, Fourth Edition (pp. 5046-5055). Hershey, PA: IGI Global. doi:10.4018/978-1-5225-2255-3.ch437

Ejiogu, A. O. (2018). Economics of Farm Management. In *Agricultural Finance and Opportunities for Investment and Expansion* (pp. 56–72). Hershey, PA: IGI Global. doi:10.4018/978-1-5225-3059-6.ch003

Ekanem, I., & Abiade, G. E. (2018). Factors Influencing the Use of E-Commerce by Small Enterprises in Nigeria. *International Journal of ICT Research in Africa and the Middle East*, *7*(1), 37–53. doi:10.4018/IJICTRAME.2018010103

Ekanem, I., & Alrossais, L. A. (2017). Succession Challenges Facing Family Businesses in Saudi Arabia. In P. Zgheib (Ed.), *Entrepreneurship and Business Innovation in the Middle East* (pp. 122–146). Hershey, PA: IGI Global. doi:10.4018/978-1-5225-2066-5.ch007

El Faquih, L., & Fredj, M. (2017). Ontology-Based Framework for Quality in Configurable Process Models. *Journal of Electronic Commerce in Organizations*, *15*(2), 48–60. doi:10.4018/JECO.2017040104

El-Gohary, H., & El-Gohary, Z. (2016). An Attempt to Explore Electronic Marketing Adoption and Implementation Aspects in Developing Countries: The Case of Egypt. *International Journal of Customer Relationship Marketing and Management*, *7*(4), 1–26. doi:10.4018/IJCRMM.2016100101

Entico, G. J. (2016). Knowledge Management and the Medical Health Librarians: A Perception Study. In J. Yap, M. Perez, M. Ayson, & G. Entico (Eds.), *Special Library Administration, Standardization and Technological Integration* (pp. 52–77). Hershey, PA: IGI Global. doi:10.4018/978-1-4666-9542-9.ch003

Faisal, M. N., & Talib, F. (2017). Building Ambidextrous Supply Chains in SMEs: How to Tackle the Barriers? *International Journal of Information Systems and Supply Chain Management*, *10*(4), 80–100. doi:10.4018/IJISSCM.2017100105

Fernandes, T. M., Gomes, J., & Romão, M. (2017). Investments in E-Government: A Benefit Management Case Study. *International Journal of Electronic Government Research*, *13*(3), 1–17. doi:10.4018/IJEGR.2017070101

Fouda, F. A. (2016). A Suggested Curriculum in Career Education to Develop Business Secondary Schools Students' Career Knowledge Management Domains and Professional Thinking. *International Journal of Technology Diffusion*, *7*(2), 42–62. doi:10.4018/IJTD.2016040103

Gallardo-Vázquez, D., & Pajuelo-Moreno, M. L. (2016). How Spanish Universities are Promoting Entrepreneurship through Your Own Lines of Teaching and Research? In L. Carvalho (Ed.), *Handbook of Research on Entrepreneurial Success and its Impact on Regional Development* (pp. 431–454). Hershey, PA: IGI Global. doi:10.4018/978-1-4666-9567-2.ch019

Gao, S. S., Oreal, S., & Zhang, J. (2018). Contemporary Financial Risk Management Perceptions and Practices of Small-Sized Chinese Businesses. In I. Management Association (Ed.), Global Business Expansion: Concepts, Methodologies, Tools, and Applications (pp. 917-931). Hershey, PA: IGI Global. doi:10.4018/978-1-5225-5481-3.ch041

Garg, R., & Berning, S. C. (2017). Indigenous Chinese Management Philosophies: Key Concepts and Relevance for Modern Chinese Firms. In B. Christiansen & G. Koc (Eds.), *Transcontinental Strategies for Industrial Development and Economic Growth* (pp. 43–57). Hershey, PA: IGI Global. doi:10.4018/978-1-5225-2160-0.ch003

Gencer, Y. G. (2017). Supply Chain Management in Retailing Business. In U. Akkucuk (Ed.), *Ethics and Sustainability in Global Supply Chain Management* (pp. 197–210). Hershey, PA: IGI Global. doi:10.4018/978-1-5225-2036-8.ch011

Giacosa, E. (2016). Innovation in Luxury Fashion Businesses as a Means for the Regional Development. In L. Carvalho (Ed.), *Handbook of Research on Entrepreneurial Success and its Impact on Regional Development* (pp. 206–222). Hershey, PA: IGI Global. doi:10.4018/978-1-4666-9567-2.ch010

Giacosa, E. (2018). The Increasing of the Regional Development Thanks to the Luxury Business Innovation. In L. Carvalho (Ed.), *Handbook of Research on Entrepreneurial Ecosystems and Social Dynamics in a Globalized World* (pp. 260–273). Hershey, PA: IGI Global. doi:10.4018/978-1-5225-3525-6.ch011

Gianni, M., & Gotzamani, K. (2016). Integrated Management Systems and Information Management Systems: Common Threads. In P. Papajorgji, F. Pinet, A. Guimarães, & J. Papathanasiou (Eds.), *Automated Enterprise Systems for Maximizing Business Performance* (pp. 195–214). Hershey, PA: IGI Global. doi:10.4018/978-1-4666-8841-4.ch011

Gianni, M., Gotzamani, K., & Linden, I. (2016). How a BI-wise Responsible Integrated Management System May Support Food Traceability. *International Journal of Decision Support System Technology, 8*(2), 1–17. doi:10.4018/IJDSST.2016040101

Glykas, M., & George, J. (2017). Quality and Process Management Systems in the UAE Maritime Industry. *International Journal of Productivity Management and Assessment Technologies, 5*(1), 20–39. doi:10.4018/IJPMAT.2017010102

Glykas, M., Valiris, G., Kokkinaki, A., & Koutsoukou, Z. (2018). Banking Business Process Management Implementation. *International Journal of Productivity Management and Assessment Technologies, 6*(1), 50–69. doi:10.4018/IJPMAT.2018010104

Gomes, J., & Romão, M. (2017). The Balanced Scorecard: Keeping Updated and Aligned with Today's Business Trends. *International Journal of Productivity Management and Assessment Technologies, 5*(2), 1–15. doi:10.4018/IJPMAT.2017070101

Gomes, J., & Romão, M. (2017). Aligning Information Systems and Technology with Benefit Management and Balanced Scorecard. In S. De Haes & W. Van Grembergen (Eds.), *Strategic IT Governance and Alignment in Business Settings* (pp. 112–131). Hershey, PA: IGI Global. doi:10.4018/978-1-5225-0861-8.ch005

Grefen, P., & Turetken, O. (2017). Advanced Business Process Management in Networked E-Business Scenarios. *International Journal of E-Business Research, 13*(4), 70–104. doi:10.4018/IJEBR.2017100105

Haider, A., & Saetang, S. (2017). Strategic IT Alignment in Service Sector. In S. Rozenes & Y. Cohen (Eds.), *Handbook of Research on Strategic Alliances and Value Co-Creation in the Service Industry* (pp. 231–258). Hershey, PA: IGI Global. doi:10.4018/978-1-5225-2084-9.ch012

Haider, A., & Tang, S. S. (2016). Maximising Value Through IT and Business Alignment: A Case of IT Governance Institutionalisation at a Thai Bank. *International Journal of Technology Diffusion, 7*(3), 33–58. doi:10.4018/IJTD.2016070104

Hajilari, A. B., Ghadaksaz, M., & Fasghandis, G. S. (2017). Assessing Organizational Readiness for Implementing ERP System Using Fuzzy Expert System Approach. *International Journal of Enterprise Information Systems*, *13*(1), 67–85. doi:10.4018/IJEIS.2017010105

Haldorai, A., Ramu, A., & Murugan, S. (2018). Social Aware Cognitive Radio Networks: Effectiveness of Social Networks as a Strategic Tool for Organizational Business Management. In H. Bansal, G. Shrivastava, G. Nguyen, & L. Stanciu (Eds.), *Social Network Analytics for Contemporary Business Organizations* (pp. 188–202). Hershey, PA: IGI Global. doi:10.4018/978-1-5225-5097-6.ch010

Hall, O. P. Jr. (2017). Social Media Driven Management Education. *International Journal of Knowledge-Based Organizations*, *7*(2), 43–59. doi:10.4018/IJKBO.2017040104

Hanifah, H., Halim, H. A., Ahmad, N. H., & Vafaei-Zadeh, A. (2017). Innovation Culture as a Mediator Between Specific Human Capital and Innovation Performance Among Bumiputera SMEs in Malaysia. In N. Ahmad, T. Ramayah, H. Halim, & S. Rahman (Eds.), *Handbook of Research on Small and Medium Enterprises in Developing Countries* (pp. 261–279). Hershey, PA: IGI Global. doi:10.4018/978-1-5225-2165-5.ch012

Hartlieb, S., & Silvius, G. (2017). Handling Uncertainty in Project Management and Business Development: Similarities and Differences. In Y. Raydugin (Ed.), *Handbook of Research on Leveraging Risk and Uncertainties for Effective Project Management* (pp. 337–362). Hershey, PA: IGI Global. doi:10.4018/978-1-5225-1790-0.ch016

Hass, K. B. (2017). Living on the Edge: Managing Project Complexity. In Y. Raydugin (Ed.), *Handbook of Research on Leveraging Risk and Uncertainties for Effective Project Management* (pp. 177–201). Hershey, PA: IGI Global. doi:10.4018/978-1-5225-1790-0.ch009

Hassan, A., & Privitera, D. S. (2016). Google AdSense as a Mobile Technology in Education. In J. Holland (Ed.), *Wearable Technology and Mobile Innovations for Next-Generation Education* (pp. 200–223). Hershey, PA: IGI Global. doi:10.4018/978-1-5225-0069-8.ch011

Hassan, A., & Rahimi, R. (2016). Consuming "Innovation" in Tourism: Augmented Reality as an Innovation Tool in Digital Tourism Marketing. In N. Pappas & I. Bregoli (Eds.), *Global Dynamics in Travel, Tourism, and Hospitality* (pp. 130–147). Hershey, PA: IGI Global. doi:10.4018/978-1-5225-0201-2.ch008

Hawking, P., & Carmine Sellitto, C. (2017). Developing an Effective Strategy for Organizational Business Intelligence. In M. Tavana (Ed.), *Enterprise Information Systems and the Digitalization of Business Functions* (pp. 222–237). Hershey, PA: IGI Global. doi:10.4018/978-1-5225-2382-6.ch010

Hawking, P., & Sellitto, C. (2017). A Fast-Moving Consumer Goods Company and Business Intelligence Strategy Development. *International Journal of Enterprise Information Systems*, *13*(2), 22–33. doi:10.4018/IJEIS.2017040102

Hawking, P., & Sellitto, C. (2017). Business Intelligence Strategy: Two Case Studies. *International Journal of Business Intelligence Research*, *8*(2), 17–30. doi:10.4018/IJBIR.2017070102

Haynes, J. D., Arockiasamy, S., Al Rashdi, M., & Al Rashdi, S. (2016). Business and E Business Strategies for Coopetition and Thematic Management as a Sustained Basis for Ethics and Social Responsibility in Emerging Markets. In M. Al-Shammari & H. Masri (Eds.), *Ethical and Social Perspectives on Global Business Interaction in Emerging Markets* (pp. 25–39). Hershey, PA: IGI Global. doi:10.4018/978-1-4666-9864-2.ch002

Hee, W. J., Jalleh, G., Lai, H., & Lin, C. (2017). E-Commerce and IT Projects: Evaluation and Management Issues in Australian and Taiwanese Hospitals. *International Journal of Public Health Management and Ethics*, *2*(1), 69–90. doi:10.4018/IJPHME.2017010104

Hernandez, A. A. (2018). Exploring the Factors to Green IT Adoption of SMEs in the Philippines. *Journal of Cases on Information Technology*, *20*(2), 49–66. doi:10.4018/JCIT.2018040104

Hernandez, A. A., & Ona, S. E. (2016). Green IT Adoption: Lessons from the Philippines Business Process Outsourcing Industry. *International Journal of Social Ecology and Sustainable Development*, *7*(1), 1–34. doi:10.4018/IJSESD.2016010101

Hollman, A., Bickford, S., & Hollman, T. (2017). Cyber InSecurity: A Post-Mortem Attempt to Assess Cyber Problems from IT and Business Management Perspectives. *Journal of Cases on Information Technology*, *19*(3), 42–70. doi:10.4018/JCIT.2017070104

Igbinakhase, I. (2017). Responsible and Sustainable Management Practices in Developing and Developed Business Environments. In Z. Fields (Ed.), *Collective Creativity for Responsible and Sustainable Business Practice* (pp. 180–207). Hershey, PA: IGI Global. doi:10.4018/978-1-5225-1823-5.ch010

Ilahi, L., Ghannouchi, S. A., & Martinho, R. (2016). A Business Process Management Approach to Home Healthcare Processes: On the Gap between Intention and Reality. In M. Cruz-Cunha, I. Miranda, R. Martinho, & R. Rijo (Eds.), *Encyclopedia of E-Health and Telemedicine* (pp. 439–457). Hershey, PA: IGI Global. doi:10.4018/978-1-4666-9978-6.ch035

Iwata, J. J., & Hoskins, R. G. (2017). Managing Indigenous Knowledge in Tanzania: A Business Perspective. In P. Jain & N. Mnjama (Eds.), *Managing Knowledge Resources and Records in Modern Organizations* (pp. 198–214). Hershey, PA: IGI Global. doi:10.4018/978-1-5225-1965-2.ch012

Jabeen, F., Ahmad, S. Z., & Alkaabi, S. (2016). The Internationalization Decision-Making of United Arab Emirates Family Businesses. In N. Zakaria, A. Abdul-Talib, & N. Osman (Eds.), *Handbook of Research on Impacts of International Business and Political Affairs on the Global Economy* (pp. 1–22). Hershey, PA: IGI Global. doi:10.4018/978-1-4666-9806-2.ch001

Jain, P. (2017). Ethical and Legal Issues in Knowledge Management Life-Cycle in Business. In P. Jain & N. Mnjama (Eds.), *Managing Knowledge Resources and Records in Modern Organizations* (pp. 82–101). Hershey, PA: IGI Global. doi:10.4018/978-1-5225-1965-2.ch006

Jamali, D., Abdallah, H., & Matar, F. (2016). Opportunities and Challenges for CSR Mainstreaming in Business Schools. *International Journal of Technology and Educational Marketing*, *6*(2), 1–29. doi:10.4018/IJTEM.2016070101

James, S., & Hauli, E. (2017). Holistic Management Education at Tanzanian Rural Development Planning Institute. In N. Baporikar (Ed.), *Management Education for Global Leadership* (pp. 112–136). Hershey, PA: IGI Global. doi:10.4018/978-1-5225-1013-0.ch006

Janošková, M., Csikósová, A., & Čulková, K. (2018). Measurement of Company Performance as Part of Its Strategic Management. In R. Leon (Ed.), *Managerial Strategies for Business Sustainability During Turbulent Times* (pp. 309–335). Hershey, PA: IGI Global. doi:10.4018/978-1-5225-2716-9.ch017

Jean-Vasile, A., & Alecu, A. (2017). Theoretical and Practical Approaches in Understanding the Influences of Cost-Productivity-Profit Trinomial in Contemporary Enterprises. In A. Jean Vasile & D. Nicolò (Eds.), *Sustainable Entrepreneurship and Investments in the Green Economy* (pp. 28–62). Hershey, PA: IGI Global. doi:10.4018/978-1-5225-2075-7.ch002

Jha, D. G. (2016). Preparing for Information Technology Driven Changes. In S. Tiwari & L. Nafees (Eds.), *Innovative Management Education Pedagogies for Preparing Next-Generation Leaders* (pp. 258–274). Hershey, PA: IGI Global. doi:10.4018/978-1-4666-9691-4.ch015

Joia, L. A., & Correia, J. C. (2018). CIO Competencies From the IT Professional Perspective: Insights From Brazil. *Journal of Global Information Management, 26*(2), 74–103. doi:10.4018/JGIM.2018040104

Juma, A., & Mzera, N. (2017). Knowledge Management and Records Management and Competitive Advantage in Business. In P. Jain & N. Mnjama (Eds.), *Managing Knowledge Resources and Records in Modern Organizations* (pp. 15–28). Hershey, PA: IGI Global. doi:10.4018/978-1-5225-1965-2.ch002

K., I., & A, V. (2018). Monitoring and Auditing in the Cloud. In K. Munir (Ed.), *Cloud Computing Technologies for Green Enterprises* (pp. 318-350). Hershey, PA: IGI Global. doi:10.4018/978-1-5225-3038-1.ch013

Kabra, G., Ghosh, V., & Ramesh, A. (2018). Enterprise Integrated Business Process Management and Business Intelligence Framework for Business Process Sustainability. In A. Paul, D. Bhattacharyya, & S. Anand (Eds.), *Green Initiatives for Business Sustainability and Value Creation* (pp. 228–238). Hershey, PA: IGI Global. doi:10.4018/978-1-5225-2662-9.ch010

Kaoud, M. (2017). Investigation of Customer Knowledge Management: A Case Study Research. *International Journal of Service Science, Management, Engineering, and Technology, 8*(2), 12–22. doi:10.4018/IJSSMET.2017040102

Kara, M. E., & Fırat, S. Ü. (2016). Sustainability, Risk, and Business Intelligence in Supply Chains. In M. Erdoğdu, T. Arun, & I. Ahmad (Eds.), *Handbook of Research on Green Economic Development Initiatives and Strategies* (pp. 501–538). Hershey, PA: IGI Global. doi:10.4018/978-1-5225-0440-5.ch022

Katuu, S. (2018). A Comparative Assessment of Enterprise Content Management Maturity Models. In N. Gwangwava & M. Mutingi (Eds.), *E-Manufacturing and E-Service Strategies in Contemporary Organizations* (pp. 93–118). Hershey, PA: IGI Global. doi:10.4018/978-1-5225-3628-4.ch005

Khan, M. A. (2016). MNEs Management Strategies in Developing Countries: Establishing the Context. In M. Khan (Ed.), *Multinational Enterprise Management Strategies in Developing Countries* (pp. 1–33). Hershey, PA: IGI Global. doi:10.4018/978-1-5225-0276-0.ch001

Khan, M. A. (2016). Operational Approaches in Organizational Structure: A Case for MNEs in Developing Countries. In M. Khan (Ed.), *Multinational Enterprise Management Strategies in Developing Countries* (pp. 129–151). Hershey, PA: IGI Global. doi:10.4018/978-1-5225-0276-0.ch007

Kinnunen, S., Ylä-Kujala, A., Marttonen-Arola, S., Kärri, T., & Baglee, D. (2018). Internet of Things in Asset Management: Insights from Industrial Professionals and Academia. *International Journal of Service Science, Management, Engineering, and Technology*, *9*(2), 104–119. doi:10.4018/IJSSMET.2018040105

Klein, A. Z., Sabino de Freitas, A., Machado, L., Freitas, J. C. Jr, Graziola, P. G. Jr, & Schlemmer, E. (2017). Virtual Worlds Applications for Management Education. In L. Tomei (Ed.), *Exploring the New Era of Technology-Infused Education* (pp. 279–299). Hershey, PA: IGI Global. doi:10.4018/978-1-5225-1709-2.ch017

Kożuch, B., & Jabłoński, A. (2017). Adopting the Concept of Business Models in Public Management. In M. Lewandowski & B. Kożuch (Eds.), *Public Sector Entrepreneurship and the Integration of Innovative Business Models* (pp. 10–46). Hershey, PA: IGI Global. doi:10.4018/978-1-5225-2215-7.ch002

Kumar, J., Adhikary, A., & Jha, A. (2017). Small Active Investors' Perceptions and Preferences Towards Tax Saving Mutual Fund Schemes in Eastern India: An Empirical Note. *International Journal of Asian Business and Information Management*, *8*(2), 35–45. doi:10.4018/IJABIM.2017040103

Lassoued, Y., Bouzguenda, L., & Mahmoud, T. (2016). Context-Aware Business Process Versions Management. *International Journal of e-Collaboration*, *12*(3), 7–33. doi:10.4018/IJeC.2016070102

Lavassani, K. M., & Movahedi, B. (2017). Applications Driven Information Systems: Beyond Networks toward Business Ecosystems. *International Journal of Innovation in the Digital Economy*, *8*(1), 61–75. doi:10.4018/IJIDE.2017010104

Lazzareschi, V. H., & Brito, M. S. (2017). Strategic Information Management: Proposal of Business Project Model. In G. Jamil, A. Soares, & C. Pessoa (Eds.), *Handbook of Research on Information Management for Effective Logistics and Supply Chains* (pp. 59–88). Hershey, PA: IGI Global. doi:10.4018/978-1-5225-0973-8.ch004

Lederer, M., Kurz, M., & Lazarov, P. (2017). Usage and Suitability of Methods for Strategic Business Process Initiatives: A Multi Case Study Research. *International Journal of Productivity Management and Assessment Technologies*, *5*(1), 40–51. doi:10.4018/IJPMAT.2017010103

Lee, I. (2017). A Social Enterprise Business Model and a Case Study of Pacific Community Ventures (PCV). In V. Potocan, M. Üngan, & Z. Nedelko (Eds.), *Handbook of Research on Managerial Solutions in Non-Profit Organizations* (pp. 182–204). Hershey, PA: IGI Global. doi:10.4018/978-1-5225-0731-4.ch009

Lee, L. J., & Leu, J. (2016). Exploring the Effectiveness of IT Application and Value Method in the Innovation Performance of Enterprise. *International Journal of Enterprise Information Systems*, *12*(2), 47–65. doi:10.4018/IJEIS.2016040104

Lee, Y. (2016). Alignment Effect of Entrepreneurial Orientation and Marketing Orientation on Firm Performance. *International Journal of Customer Relationship Marketing and Management*, *7*(4), 58–69. doi:10.4018/IJCRMM.2016100104

Leon, L. A., Seal, K. C., Przasnyski, Z. H., & Wiedenman, I. (2017). Skills and Competencies Required for Jobs in Business Analytics: A Content Analysis of Job Advertisements Using Text Mining. *International Journal of Business Intelligence Research*, *8*(1), 1–25. doi:10.4018/IJBIR.2017010101

Leu, J., Lee, L. J., & Krischke, A. (2016). Value Engineering-Based Method for Implementing the ISO14001 System in the Green Supply Chains. *International Journal of Strategic Decision Sciences*, *7*(4), 1–20. doi:10.4018/IJSDS.2016100101

Levy, C. L., & Elias, N. I. (2017). SOHO Users' Perceptions of Reliability and Continuity of Cloud-Based Services. In M. Moore (Ed.), *Cybersecurity Breaches and Issues Surrounding Online Threat Protection* (pp. 248–287). Hershey, PA: IGI Global. doi:10.4018/978-1-5225-1941-6.ch011

Levy, M. (2018). Change Management Serving Knowledge Management and Organizational Development: Reflections and Review. In N. Baporikar (Ed.), *Global Practices in Knowledge Management for Societal and Organizational Development* (pp. 256–270). Hershey, PA: IGI Global. doi:10.4018/978-1-5225-3009-1.ch012

Lewandowski, M. (2017). Public Organizations and Business Model Innovation: The Role of Public Service Design. In M. Lewandowski & B. Kożuch (Eds.), *Public Sector Entrepreneurship and the Integration of Innovative Business Models* (pp. 47–72). Hershey, PA: IGI Global. doi:10.4018/978-1-5225-2215-7.ch003

Lhannaoui, H., Kabbaj, M. I., & Bakkoury, Z. (2017). A Survey of Risk-Aware Business Process Modelling. *International Journal of Risk and Contingency Management*, *6*(3), 14–26. doi:10.4018/IJRCM.2017070102

Li, J., Sun, W., Jiang, W., Yang, H., & Zhang, L. (2017). How the Nature of Exogenous Shocks and Crises Impact Company Performance?: The Effects of Industry Characteristics. *International Journal of Risk and Contingency Management*, *6*(4), 40–55. doi:10.4018/IJRCM.2017100103

Lu, C., & Liu, S. (2016). Cultural Tourism O2O Business Model Innovation-A Case Study of CTrip. *Journal of Electronic Commerce in Organizations*, *14*(2), 16–31. doi:10.4018/JECO.2016040102

Machen, B., Hosseini, M. R., Wood, A., & Bakhshi, J. (2016). An Investigation into using SAP-PS as a Multidimensional Project Control System (MPCS). *International Journal of Enterprise Information Systems*, *12*(2), 66–81. doi:10.4018/IJEIS.2016040105

Malega, P. (2017). Small and Medium Enterprises in the Slovak Republic: Status and Competitiveness of SMEs in the Global Markets and Possibilities of Optimization. In M. Vemić (Ed.), *Optimal Management Strategies in Small and Medium Enterprises* (pp. 102–124). Hershey, PA: IGI Global. doi:10.4018/978-1-5225-1949-2.ch006

Malewska, K. M. (2017). Intuition in Decision-Making on the Example of a Non-Profit Organization. In V. Potocan, M. Üngan, & Z. Nedelko (Eds.), *Handbook of Research on Managerial Solutions in Non-Profit Organizations* (pp. 378–399). Hershey, PA: IGI Global. doi:10.4018/978-1-5225-0731-4.ch018

Maroofi, F. (2017). Entrepreneurial Orientation and Organizational Learning Ability Analysis for Innovation and Firm Performance. In N. Baporikar (Ed.), *Innovation and Shifting Perspectives in Management Education* (pp. 144–165). Hershey, PA: IGI Global. doi:10.4018/978-1-5225-1019-2.ch007

Martins, P. V., & Zacarias, M. (2017). A Web-based Tool for Business Process Improvement. *International Journal of Web Portals*, *9*(2), 68–84. doi:10.4018/IJWP.2017070104

Matthies, B., & Coners, A. (2017). Exploring the Conceptual Nature of e-Business Projects. *Journal of Electronic Commerce in Organizations*, *15*(3), 33–63. doi:10.4018/JECO.2017070103

McKee, J. (2018). Architecture as a Tool to Solve Business Planning Problems. In M. Khosrow-Pour, D.B.A. (Ed.), Encyclopedia of Information Science and Technology, Fourth Edition (pp. 573-586). Hershey, PA: IGI Global. doi:10.4018/978-1-5225-2255-3.ch050

McMurray, A. J., Cross, J., & Caponecchia, C. (2018). The Risk Management Profession in Australia: Business Continuity Plan Practices. In N. Bajgoric (Ed.), *Always-On Enterprise Information Systems for Modern Organizations* (pp. 112–129). Hershey, PA: IGI Global. doi:10.4018/978-1-5225-3704-5.ch006

Meddah, I. H., & Belkadi, K. (2018). Mining Patterns Using Business Process Management. In R. Hamou (Ed.), *Handbook of Research on Biomimicry in Information Retrieval and Knowledge Management* (pp. 78–89). Hershey, PA: IGI Global. doi:10.4018/978-1-5225-3004-6.ch005

Mendes, L. (2017). TQM and Knowledge Management: An Integrated Approach Towards Tacit Knowledge Management. In D. Jaziri-Bouagina & G. Jamil (Eds.), *Handbook of Research on Tacit Knowledge Management for Organizational Success* (pp. 236–263). Hershey, PA: IGI Global. doi:10.4018/978-1-5225-2394-9.ch009

Mnjama, N. M. (2017). Preservation of Recorded Information in Public and Private Sector Organizations. In P. Jain & N. Mnjama (Eds.), *Managing Knowledge Resources and Records in Modern Organizations* (pp. 149–167). Hershey, PA: IGI Global. doi:10.4018/978-1-5225-1965-2.ch009

Mokoqama, M., & Fields, Z. (2017). Principles of Responsible Management Education (PRME): Call for Responsible Management Education. In Z. Fields (Ed.), *Collective Creativity for Responsible and Sustainable Business Practice* (pp. 229–241). Hershey, PA: IGI Global. doi:10.4018/978-1-5225-1823-5.ch012

Muniapan, B. (2017). Philosophy and Management: The Relevance of Vedanta in Management. In P. Ordóñez de Pablos (Ed.), *Managerial Strategies and Solutions for Business Success in Asia* (pp. 124–139). Hershey, PA: IGI Global. doi:10.4018/978-1-5225-1886-0.ch007

Muniapan, B., Gregory, M. L., & Ling, L. A. (2016). Marketing Education in Sarawak: Looking at It from the Employers' Viewpoint. In B. Smith & A. Porath (Eds.), *Global Perspectives on Contemporary Marketing Education* (pp. 112–130). Hershey, PA: IGI Global. doi:10.4018/978-1-4666-9784-3.ch008

Murad, S. E., & Dowaji, S. (2017). Using Value-Based Approach for Managing Cloud-Based Services. In A. Turuk, B. Sahoo, & S. Addya (Eds.), *Resource Management and Efficiency in Cloud Computing Environments* (pp. 33–60). Hershey, PA: IGI Global. doi:10.4018/978-1-5225-1721-4.ch002

Mutahar, A. M., Daud, N. M., Thurasamy, R., Isaac, O., & Abdulsalam, R. (2018). The Mediating of Perceived Usefulness and Perceived Ease of Use: The Case of Mobile Banking in Yemen. *International Journal of Technology Diffusion*, *9*(2), 21–40. doi:10.4018/IJTD.2018040102

Naidoo, V. (2017). E-Learning and Management Education at African Universities. In N. Baporikar (Ed.), *Management Education for Global Leadership* (pp. 181–201). Hershey, PA: IGI Global. doi:10.4018/978-1-5225-1013-0.ch009

Naidoo, V., & Igbinakhase, I. (2018). Opportunities and Challenges of Knowledge Retention in SMEs. In N. Baporikar (Ed.), *Knowledge Integration Strategies for Entrepreneurship and Sustainability* (pp. 70–94). Hershey, PA: IGI Global. doi:10.4018/978-1-5225-5115-7.ch004

Nayak, S., & Prabhu, N. (2017). Paradigm Shift in Management Education: Need for a Cross Functional Perspective. In N. Baporikar (Ed.), *Management Education for Global Leadership* (pp. 241–255). Hershey, PA: IGI Global. doi:10.4018/978-1-5225-1013-0.ch012

Ndede-Amadi, A. A. (2016). Student Interest in the IS Specialization as Predictor of the Success Potential of New Information Systems Programmes within the Schools of Business in Kenyan Public Universities. *International Journal of Information Systems and Social Change*, *7*(2), 63–79. doi:10.4018/IJISSC.2016040104

Nedelko, Z., & Potocan, V. (2016). Management Practices for Processes Optimization: Case of Slovenia. In G. Alor-Hernández, C. Sánchez-Ramírez, & J. García-Alcaraz (Eds.), *Handbook of Research on Managerial Strategies for Achieving Optimal Performance in Industrial Processes* (pp. 545–561). Hershey, PA: IGI Global. doi:10.4018/978-1-5225-0130-5.ch025

Nedelko, Z., & Potocan, V. (2017). Management Solutions in Non-Profit Organizations: Case of Slovenia. In V. Potocan, M. Üngan, & Z. Nedelko (Eds.), *Handbook of Research on Managerial Solutions in Non-Profit Organizations* (pp. 1–22). Hershey, PA: IGI Global. doi:10.4018/978-1-5225-0731-4.ch001

Nedelko, Z., & Potocan, V. (2017). Priority of Management Tools Utilization among Managers: International Comparison. In V. Wang (Ed.), *Encyclopedia of Strategic Leadership and Management* (pp. 1083–1094). Hershey, PA: IGI Global. doi:10.4018/978-1-5225-1049-9.ch075

Nedelko, Z., Raudeliūnienė, J., & Črešnar, R. (2018). Knowledge Dynamics in Supply Chain Management. In N. Baporikar (Ed.), *Knowledge Integration Strategies for Entrepreneurship and Sustainability* (pp. 150–166). Hershey, PA: IGI Global. doi:10.4018/978-1-5225-5115-7.ch008

Nguyen, H. T., & Hipsher, S. A. (2018). Innovation and Creativity Used by Private Sector Firms in a Resources-Constrained Environment. In S. Hipsher (Ed.), *Examining the Private Sector's Role in Wealth Creation and Poverty Reduction* (pp. 219–238). Hershey, PA: IGI Global. doi:10.4018/978-1-5225-3117-3.ch010

Nycz, M., & Pólkowski, Z. (2016). Business Intelligence as a Modern IT Supporting Management of Local Government Units in Poland. *International Journal of Knowledge and Systems Science*, *7*(4), 1–18. doi:10.4018/IJKSS.2016100101

Obaji, N. O., Senin, A. A., & Olugu, M. U. (2016). Supportive Government Policy as a Mechanism for Business Incubation Performance in Nigeria. *International Journal of Information Systems and Social Change*, *7*(4), 52–66. doi:10.4018/IJISSC.2016100103

Obicci, P. A. (2017). Risk Sharing in a Partnership. In *Risk Management Strategies in Public-Private Partnerships* (pp. 115–152). Hershey, PA: IGI Global. doi:10.4018/978-1-5225-2503-5.ch004

Obidallah, W. J., & Raahemi, B. (2017). Managing Changes in Service Oriented Virtual Organizations: A Structural and Procedural Framework to Facilitate the Process of Change. *Journal of Electronic Commerce in Organizations*, *15*(1), 59–83. doi:10.4018/JECO.2017010104

Ojasalo, J., & Ojasalo, K. (2016). Service Logic Business Model Canvas for Lean Development of SMEs and Start-Ups. In N. Baporikar (Ed.), *Handbook of Research on Entrepreneurship in the Contemporary Knowledge-Based Global Economy* (pp. 217–243). Hershey, PA: IGI Global. doi:10.4018/978-1-4666-8798-1.ch010

Ojo, O. (2017). Impact of Innovation on the Entrepreneurial Success in Selected Business Enterprises in South-West Nigeria. *International Journal of Innovation in the Digital Economy*, *8*(2), 29–38. doi:10.4018/IJIDE.2017040103

Okdinawati, L., Simatupang, T. M., & Sunitiyoso, Y. (2017). Multi-Agent Reinforcement Learning for Value Co-Creation of Collaborative Transportation Management (CTM). *International Journal of Information Systems and Supply Chain Management*, *10*(3), 84–95. doi:10.4018/IJISSCM.2017070105

Ortner, E., Mevius, M., Wiedmann, P., & Kurz, F. (2016). Design of Interactional Decision Support Applications for E-Participation in Smart Cities. *International Journal of Electronic Government Research*, *12*(2), 18–38. doi:10.4018/IJEGR.2016040102

Pal, K. (2018). Building High Quality Big Data-Based Applications in Supply Chains. In A. Kumar & S. Saurav (Eds.), *Supply Chain Management Strategies and Risk Assessment in Retail Environments* (pp. 1–24). Hershey, PA: IGI Global. doi:10.4018/978-1-5225-3056-5.ch001

Palos-Sanchez, P. R., & Correia, M. B. (2018). Perspectives of the Adoption of Cloud Computing in the Tourism Sector. In J. Rodrigues, C. Ramos, P. Cardoso, & C. Henriques (Eds.), *Handbook of Research on Technological Developments for Cultural Heritage and eTourism Applications* (pp. 377–400). Hershey, PA: IGI Global. doi:10.4018/978-1-5225-2927-9.ch018

Parry, V. K., & Lind, M. L. (2016). Alignment of Business Strategy and Information Technology Considering Information Technology Governance, Project Portfolio Control, and Risk Management. *International Journal of Information Technology Project Management*, *7*(4), 21–37. doi:10.4018/IJITPM.2016100102

Pashkova, N., Trujillo-Barrera, A., Apostolakis, G., Van Dijk, G., Drakos, P. D., & Baourakis, G. (2016). Business Management Models of Microfinance Institutions (MFIs) in Africa: A Study into Their Enabling Environments. *International Journal of Food and Beverage Manufacturing and Business Models*, *1*(2), 63–82. doi:10.4018/IJFBMBM.2016070105

Patiño, B. E. (2017). New Generation Management by Convergence and Individual Identity: A Systemic and Human-Oriented Approach. In N. Baporikar (Ed.), *Innovation and Shifting Perspectives in Management Education* (pp. 119–143). Hershey, PA: IGI Global. doi:10.4018/978-1-5225-1019-2.ch006

Pawliczek, A., & Rössler, M. (2017). Knowledge of Management Tools and Systems in SMEs: Knowledge Transfer in Management. In A. Bencsik (Ed.), *Knowledge Management Initiatives and Strategies in Small and Medium Enterprises* (pp. 180–203). Hershey, PA: IGI Global. doi:10.4018/978-1-5225-1642-2.ch009

Pejic-Bach, M., Omazic, M. A., Aleksic, A., & Zoroja, J. (2018). Knowledge-Based Decision Making: A Multi-Case Analysis. In R. Leon (Ed.), *Managerial Strategies for Business Sustainability During Turbulent Times* (pp. 160–184). Hershey, PA: IGI Global. doi:10.4018/978-1-5225-2716-9.ch009

Perano, M., Hysa, X., & Calabrese, M. (2018). Strategic Planning, Cultural Context, and Business Continuity Management: Business Cases in the City of Shkoder. In A. Presenza & L. Sheehan (Eds.), *Geopolitics and Strategic Management in the Global Economy* (pp. 57–77). Hershey, PA: IGI Global. doi:10.4018/978-1-5225-2673-5.ch004

Pereira, R., Mira da Silva, M., & Lapão, L. V. (2017). IT Governance Maturity Patterns in Portuguese Healthcare. In S. De Haes & W. Van Grembergen (Eds.), *Strategic IT Governance and Alignment in Business Settings* (pp. 24–52). Hershey, PA: IGI Global. doi:10.4018/978-1-5225-0861-8.ch002

Perez-Uribe, R., & Ocampo-Guzman, D. (2016). Conflict within Colombian Family Owned SMEs: An Explosive Blend between Feelings and Business. In J. Saiz-Álvarez (Ed.), *Handbook of Research on Social Entrepreneurship and Solidarity Economics* (pp. 329–354). Hershey, PA: IGI Global. doi:10.4018/978-1-5225-0097-1.ch017

Pérez-Uribe, R. I., Torres, D. A., Jurado, S. P., & Prada, D. M. (2018). Cloud Tools for the Development of Project Management in SMEs. In R. Perez-Uribe, C. Salcedo-Perez, & D. Ocampo-Guzman (Eds.), *Handbook of Research on Intrapreneurship and Organizational Sustainability in SMEs* (pp. 95–120). Hershey, PA: IGI Global. doi:10.4018/978-1-5225-3543-0.ch005

Petrisor, I., & Cozmiuc, D. (2017). Global Supply Chain Management Organization at Siemens in the Advent of Industry 4.0. In L. Saglietto & C. Cezanne (Eds.), *Global Intermediation and Logistics Service Providers* (pp. 123–142). Hershey, PA: IGI Global. doi:10.4018/978-1-5225-2133-4.ch007

Pierce, J. M., Velliaris, D. M., & Edwards, J. (2017). A Living Case Study: A Journey Not a Destination. In N. Silton (Ed.), *Exploring the Benefits of Creativity in Education, Media, and the Arts* (pp. 158–178). Hershey, PA: IGI Global. doi:10.4018/978-1-5225-0504-4.ch008

Radosavljevic, M., & Andjelkovic, A. (2017). Multi-Criteria Decision Making Approach for Choosing Business Process for the Improvement: Upgrading of the Six Sigma Methodology. In J. Stanković, P. Delias, S. Marinković, & S. Rochhia (Eds.), *Tools and Techniques for Economic Decision Analysis* (pp. 225–247). Hershey, PA: IGI Global. doi:10.4018/978-1-5225-0959-2.ch011

Radovic, V. M. (2017). Corporate Sustainability and Responsibility and Disaster Risk Reduction: A Serbian Overview. In M. Camilleri (Ed.), *CSR 2.0 and the New Era of Corporate Citizenship* (pp. 147–164). Hershey, PA: IGI Global. doi:10.4018/978-1-5225-1842-6.ch008

Raghunath, K. M., Devi, S. L., & Patro, C. S. (2018). Impact of Risk Assessment Models on Risk Factors: A Holistic Outlook. In K. Strang, M. Korstanje, & N. Vajjhala (Eds.), *Research, Practices, and Innovations in Global Risk and Contingency Management* (pp. 134–153). Hershey, PA: IGI Global. doi:10.4018/978-1-5225-4754-9.ch008

Raman, A., & Goyal, D. P. (2017). Extending IMPLEMENT Framework for Enterprise Information Systems Implementation to Information System Innovation. In M. Tavana (Ed.), *Enterprise Information Systems and the Digitalization of Business Functions* (pp. 137–177). Hershey, PA: IGI Global. doi:10.4018/978-1-5225-2382-6.ch007

Rao, Y., & Zhang, Y. (2017). The Construction and Development of Academic Library Digital Special Subject Databases. In L. Ruan, Q. Zhu, & Y. Ye (Eds.), *Academic Library Development and Administration in China* (pp. 163–183). Hershey, PA: IGI Global. doi:10.4018/978-1-5225-0550-1.ch010

Ravasan, A. Z., Mohammadi, M. M., & Hamidi, H. (2018). An Investigation Into the Critical Success Factors of Implementing Information Technology Service Management Frameworks. In K. Jakobs (Ed.), *Corporate and Global Standardization Initiatives in Contemporary Society* (pp. 200–218). Hershey, PA: IGI Global. doi:10.4018/978-1-5225-5320-5.ch009

Renna, P., Izzo, C., & Romaniello, T. (2016). The Business Process Management Systems to Support Continuous Improvements. In W. Nuninger & J. Châtelet (Eds.), *Handbook of Research on Quality Assurance and Value Management in Higher Education* (pp. 237–256). Hershey, PA: IGI Global. doi:10.4018/978-1-5225-0024-7.ch009

Rezaie, S., Mirabedini, S. J., & Abtahi, A. (2018). Designing a Model for Implementation of Business Intelligence in the Banking Industry. *International Journal of Enterprise Information Systems, 14*(1), 77–103. doi:10.4018/IJEIS.2018010105

Riccò, R. (2016). Diversity Management: Bringing Equality, Equity, and Inclusion in the Workplace. In J. Prescott (Ed.), *Handbook of Research on Race, Gender, and the Fight for Equality* (pp. 335–359). Hershey, PA: IGI Global. doi:10.4018/978-1-5225-0047-6.ch015

Romano, L., Grimaldi, R., & Colasuonno, F. S. (2017). Demand Management as a Success Factor in Project Portfolio Management. In L. Romano (Ed.), *Project Portfolio Management Strategies for Effective Organizational Operations* (pp. 202–219). Hershey, PA: IGI Global. doi:10.4018/978-1-5225-2151-8.ch008

Rostek, K. B. (2016). Risk Management: Role and Importance in Business Organization. In D. Jakóbczak (Ed.), *Analyzing Risk through Probabilistic Modeling in Operations Research* (pp. 149–178). Hershey, PA: IGI Global. doi:10.4018/978-1-4666-9458-3.ch007

Rouhani, S., & Savoji, S. R. (2016). A Success Assessment Model for BI Tools Implementation: An Empirical Study of Banking Industry. *International Journal of Business Intelligence Research, 7*(1), 25–44. doi:10.4018/IJBIR.2016010103

Ruan, Z. (2016). A Corpus-Based Functional Analysis of Complex Nominal Groups in Written Business Discourse: The Case of "Business". *International Journal of Computer-Assisted Language Learning and Teaching, 6*(2), 74–90. doi:10.4018/IJCALLT.2016040105

Ruhi, U. (2018). Towards an Interdisciplinary Socio-Technical Definition of Virtual Communities. In M. Khosrow-Pour, D.B.A. (Ed.), Encyclopedia of Information Science and Technology, Fourth Edition (pp. 4278-4295). Hershey, PA: IGI Global. doi:10.4018/978-1-5225-2255-3.ch371

Ryan, J., Doster, B., Daily, S., & Lewis, C. (2016). A Case Study Perspective for Balanced Perioperative Workflow Achievement through Data-Driven Process Improvement. *International Journal of Healthcare Information Systems and Informatics, 11*(3), 19–41. doi:10.4018/IJHISI.2016070102

Safari, M. R., & Jiang, Q. (2018). The Theory and Practice of IT Governance Maturity and Strategies Alignment: Evidence From Banking Industry. *Journal of Global Information Management, 26*(2), 127–146. doi:10.4018/JGIM.2018040106

Sahoo, J., Pati, B., & Mohanty, B. (2017). Knowledge Management as an Academic Discipline: An Assessment. In B. Gunjal (Ed.), *Managing Knowledge and Scholarly Assets in Academic Libraries* (pp. 99–126). Hershey, PA: IGI Global. doi:10.4018/978-1-5225-1741-2.ch005

Saini, D. (2017). Relevance of Teaching Values and Ethics in Management Education. In N. Baporikar (Ed.), *Management Education for Global Leadership* (pp. 90–111). Hershey, PA: IGI Global. doi:10.4018/978-1-5225-1013-0.ch005

Sambhanthan, A. (2017). Assessing and Benchmarking Sustainability in Organisations: An Integrated Conceptual Model. *International Journal of Systems and Service-Oriented Engineering*, *7*(4), 22–43. doi:10.4018/IJSSOE.2017100102

Sambhanthan, A., & Potdar, V. (2017). A Study of the Parameters Impacting Sustainability in Information Technology Organizations. *International Journal of Knowledge-Based Organizations*, *7*(3), 27–39. doi:10.4018/IJKBO.2017070103

Sánchez-Fernández, M. D., & Manríquez, M. R. (2018). The Entrepreneurial Spirit Based on Social Values: The Digital Generation. In P. Isaias & L. Carvalho (Eds.), *User Innovation and the Entrepreneurship Phenomenon in the Digital Economy* (pp. 173–193). Hershey, PA: IGI Global. doi:10.4018/978-1-5225-2826-5.ch009

Sanchez-Ruiz, L., & Blanco, B. (2017). Process Management for SMEs: Barriers, Enablers, and Benefits. In M. Vemić (Ed.), *Optimal Management Strategies in Small and Medium Enterprises* (pp. 293–319). Hershey, PA: IGI Global. doi:10.4018/978-1-5225-1949-2.ch014

Sanz, L. F., Gómez-Pérez, J., & Castillo-Martinez, A. (2018). Analysis of the European ICT Competence Frameworks. In V. Ahuja & S. Rathore (Eds.), *Multidisciplinary Perspectives on Human Capital and Information Technology Professionals* (pp. 225–245). Hershey, PA: IGI Global. doi:10.4018/978-1-5225-5297-0.ch012

Sarvepalli, A., & Godin, J. (2017). Business Process Management in the Classroom. *Journal of Cases on Information Technology*, *19*(2), 17–28. doi:10.4018/JCIT.2017040102

Satpathy, B., & Muniapan, B. (2016). Ancient Wisdom for Transformational Leadership and Its Insights from the Bhagavad-Gita. In U. Aung & P. Ordoñez de Pablos (Eds.), *Managerial Strategies and Practice in the Asian Business Sector* (pp. 1–10). Hershey, PA: IGI Global. doi:10.4018/978-1-4666-9758-4.ch001

Saygili, E. E., Ozturkoglu, Y., & Kocakulah, M. C. (2017). End Users' Perceptions of Critical Success Factors in ERP Applications. *International Journal of Enterprise Information Systems*, *13*(4), 58–75. doi:10.4018/IJEIS.2017100104

Saygili, E. E., & Saygili, A. T. (2017). Contemporary Issues in Enterprise Information Systems: A Critical Review of CSFs in ERP Implementations. In M. Tavana (Ed.), *Enterprise Information Systems and the Digitalization of Business Functions* (pp. 120–136). Hershey, PA: IGI Global. doi:10.4018/978-1-5225-2382-6.ch006

Seidenstricker, S., & Antonino, A. (2018). Business Model Innovation-Oriented Technology Management for Emergent Technologies. In M. Khosrow-Pour, D.B.A. (Ed.), Encyclopedia of Information Science and Technology, Fourth Edition (pp. 4560-4569). Hershey, PA: IGI Global. doi:10.4018/978-1-5225-2255-3.ch396

Senaratne, S., & Gunarathne, A. D. (2017). Excellence Perspective for Management Education from a Global Accountants' Hub in Asia. In N. Baporikar (Ed.), *Management Education for Global Leadership* (pp. 158–180). Hershey, PA: IGI Global. doi:10.4018/978-1-5225-1013-0.ch008

Sensuse, D. I., & Cahyaningsih, E. (2018). Knowledge Management Models: A Summative Review. *International Journal of Information Systems in the Service Sector, 10*(1), 71–100. doi:10.4018/IJISSS.2018010105

Sensuse, D. I., Wibowo, W. C., & Cahyaningsih, E. (2016). Indonesian Government Knowledge Management Model: A Theoretical Model. *Information Resources Management Journal, 29*(1), 91–108. doi:10.4018/irmj.2016010106

Seth, M., Goyal, D., & Kiran, R. (2017). Diminution of Impediments in Implementation of Supply Chain Management Information System for Enhancing its Effectiveness in Indian Automobile Industry. *Journal of Global Information Management, 25*(3), 1–20. doi:10.4018/JGIM.2017070101

Seyal, A. H., & Rahman, M. N. (2017). Investigating Impact of Inter-Organizational Factors in Measuring ERP Systems Success: Bruneian Perspectives. In M. Tavana (Ed.), *Enterprise Information Systems and the Digitalization of Business Functions* (pp. 178–204). Hershey, PA: IGI Global. doi:10.4018/978-1-5225-2382-6.ch008

Shaikh, A. A., & Karjaluoto, H. (2016). On Some Misconceptions Concerning Digital Banking and Alternative Delivery Channels. *International Journal of E-Business Research, 12*(3), 1–16. doi:10.4018/IJEBR.2016070101

Shams, S. M. (2016). Stakeholder Relationship Management in Online Business and Competitive Value Propositions: Evidence from the Sports Industry. *International Journal of Online Marketing, 6*(2), 1–17. doi:10.4018/IJOM.2016040101

Shamsuzzoha, A. (2016). Management of Risk and Resilience within Collaborative Business Network. In R. Addo-Tenkorang, J. Kantola, P. Helo, & A. Shamsuzzoha (Eds.), *Supply Chain Strategies and the Engineer-to-Order Approach* (pp. 143–159). Hershey, PA: IGI Global. doi:10.4018/978-1-5225-0021-6.ch008

Shaqrah, A. A. (2018). Analyzing Business Intelligence Systems Based on 7s Model of McKinsey. *International Journal of Business Intelligence Research, 9*(1), 53–63. doi:10.4018/IJBIR.2018010104

Sharma, A. J. (2017). Enhancing Sustainability through Experiential Learning in Management Education. In N. Baporikar (Ed.), *Management Education for Global Leadership* (pp. 256–274). Hershey, PA: IGI Global. doi:10.4018/978-1-5225-1013-0.ch013

Shetty, K. P. (2017). Responsible Global Leadership: Ethical Challenges in Management Education. In N. Baporikar (Ed.), *Innovation and Shifting Perspectives in Management Education* (pp. 194–223). Hershey, PA: IGI Global. doi:10.4018/978-1-5225-1019-2.ch009

Sinthupundaja, J., & Kohda, Y. (2017). Effects of Corporate Social Responsibility and Creating Shared Value on Sustainability. *International Journal of Sustainable Entrepreneurship and Corporate Social Responsibility*, *2*(1), 27–38. doi:10.4018/IJSECSR.2017010103

Škarica, I., & Hrgović, A. V. (2018). Implementation of Total Quality Management Principles in Public Health Institutes in the Republic of Croatia. *International Journal of Productivity Management and Assessment Technologies*, *6*(1), 1–16. doi:10.4018/IJPMAT.2018010101

Smuts, H., Kotzé, P., Van der Merwe, A., & Loock, M. (2017). Framework for Managing Shared Knowledge in an Information Systems Outsourcing Context. *International Journal of Knowledge Management*, *13*(4), 1–30. doi:10.4018/IJKM.2017100101

Soares, E. R., & Zaidan, F. H. (2016). Information Architecture and Business Modeling in Modern Organizations of Information Technology: Professional Career Plan in Organizations IT. In G. Jamil, J. Poças Rascão, F. Ribeiro, & A. Malheiro da Silva (Eds.), *Handbook of Research on Information Architecture and Management in Modern Organizations* (pp. 439–457). Hershey, PA: IGI Global. doi:10.4018/978-1-4666-8637-3.ch020

Sousa, M. J., Cruz, R., Dias, I., & Caracol, C. (2017). Information Management Systems in the Supply Chain. In G. Jamil, A. Soares, & C. Pessoa (Eds.), *Handbook of Research on Information Management for Effective Logistics and Supply Chains* (pp. 469–485). Hershey, PA: IGI Global. doi:10.4018/978-1-5225-0973-8.ch025

Spremic, M., Turulja, L., & Bajgoric, N. (2018). Two Approaches in Assessing Business Continuity Management Attitudes in the Organizational Context. In N. Bajgoric (Ed.), *Always-On Enterprise Information Systems for Modern Organizations* (pp. 159–183). Hershey, PA: IGI Global. doi:10.4018/978-1-5225-3704-5.ch008

Steenkamp, A. L. (2018). Some Insights in Computer Science and Information Technology. In *Examining the Changing Role of Supervision in Doctoral Research Projects: Emerging Research and Opportunities* (pp. 113–133). Hershey, PA: IGI Global. doi:10.4018/978-1-5225-2610-0.ch005

Studdard, N., Dawson, M., Burton, S. L., Jackson, N., Leonard, B., Quisenberry, W., & Rahim, E. (2016). Nurturing Social Entrepreneurship and Building Social Entrepreneurial Self-Efficacy: Focusing on Primary and Secondary Schooling to Develop Future Social Entrepreneurs. In Z. Fields (Ed.), *Incorporating Business Models and Strategies into Social Entrepreneurship* (pp. 154–175). Hershey, PA: IGI Global. doi:10.4018/978-1-4666-8748-6.ch010

Sun, Z. (2016). A Framework for Developing Management Intelligent Systems. *International Journal of Systems and Service-Oriented Engineering*, *6*(1), 37–53. doi:10.4018/IJSSOE.2016010103

Swami, B., & Mphele, G. T. (2016). Problems Preventing Growth of Small Entrepreneurs: A Case Study of a Few Small Entrepreneurs in Botswana Sub-Urban Areas. In N. Baporikar (Ed.), *Handbook of Research on Entrepreneurship in the Contemporary Knowledge-Based Global Economy* (pp. 479–508). Hershey, PA: IGI Global. doi:10.4018/978-1-4666-8798-1.ch020

Tabach, A., & Croteau, A. (2017). Configurations of Information Technology Governance Practices and Business Unit Performance. *International Journal of IT/Business Alignment and Governance, 8*(2), 1–27. doi:10.4018/IJITBAG.2017070101

Talaue, G. M., & Iqbal, T. (2017). Assessment of e-Business Mode of Selected Private Universities in the Philippines and Pakistan. *International Journal of Online Marketing, 7*(4), 63–77. doi:10.4018/IJOM.2017100105

Tam, G. C. (2017). Project Manager Sustainability Competence. In *Managerial Strategies and Green Solutions for Project Sustainability* (pp. 178–207). Hershey, PA: IGI Global. doi:10.4018/978-1-5225-2371-0.ch008

Tambo, T. (2018). Fashion Retail Innovation: About Context, Antecedents, and Outcome in Technological Change Projects. In I. Management Association (Ed.), Fashion and Textiles: Breakthroughs in Research and Practice (pp. 233-260). Hershey, PA: IGI Global. doi:10.4018/978-1-5225-3432-7.ch010

Tambo, T., & Mikkelsen, O. E. (2016). Fashion Supply Chain Optimization: Linking Make-to-Order Purchasing and B2B E-Commerce. In S. Joshi & R. Joshi (Eds.), *Designing and Implementing Global Supply Chain Management* (pp. 1–21). Hershey, PA: IGI Global. doi:10.4018/978-1-4666-9720-1.ch001

Tandon, K. (2016). Innovative Andragogy: The Paradigm Shift to Heutagogy. In S. Tiwari & L. Nafees (Eds.), *Innovative Management Education Pedagogies for Preparing Next-Generation Leaders* (pp. 238–257). Hershey, PA: IGI Global. doi:10.4018/978-1-4666-9691-4.ch014

Tantau, A. D., & Frăţilă, L. C. (2018). Information and Management System for Renewable Energy Business. In *Entrepreneurship and Business Development in the Renewable Energy Sector* (pp. 200–244). Hershey, PA: IGI Global. doi:10.4018/978-1-5225-3625-3.ch006

Teixeira, N., Pardal, P. N., & Rafael, B. G. (2018). Internationalization, Financial Performance, and Organizational Challenges: A Success Case in Portugal. In L. Carvalho (Ed.), *Handbook of Research on Entrepreneurial Ecosystems and Social Dynamics in a Globalized World* (pp. 379–423). Hershey, PA: IGI Global. doi:10.4018/978-1-5225-3525-6.ch017

Trad, A., & Kalpić, D. (2016). The E-Business Transformation Framework for E-Commerce Architecture-Modeling Projects. In I. Lee (Ed.), *Encyclopedia of E-Commerce Development, Implementation, and Management* (pp. 733–753). Hershey, PA: IGI Global. doi:10.4018/978-1-4666-9787-4.ch052

Trad, A., & Kalpić, D. (2016). The E-Business Transformation Framework for E-Commerce Control and Monitoring Pattern. In I. Lee (Ed.), *Encyclopedia of E-Commerce Development, Implementation, and Management* (pp. 754–777). Hershey, PA: IGI Global. doi:10.4018/978-1-4666-9787-4.ch053

Trad, A., & Kalpić, D. (2018). The Business Transformation Framework, Agile Project and Change Management. In M. Khosrow-Pour, D.B.A. (Ed.), Encyclopedia of Information Science and Technology, Fourth Edition (pp. 620-635). Hershey, PA: IGI Global. doi:10.4018/978-1-5225-2255-3.ch054

Trad, A., & Kalpić, D. (2018). The Business Transformation and Enterprise Architecture Framework: The Financial Engineering E-Risk Management and E-Law Integration. In B. Sergi, F. Fidanoski, M. Ziolo, & V. Naumovski (Eds.), *Regaining Global Stability After the Financial Crisis* (pp. 46–65). Hershey, PA: IGI Global. doi:10.4018/978-1-5225-4026-7.ch003

Turulja, L., & Bajgoric, N. (2018). Business Continuity and Information Systems: A Systematic Literature Review. In N. Bajgoric (Ed.), *Always-On Enterprise Information Systems for Modern Organizations* (pp. 60–87). Hershey, PA: IGI Global. doi:10.4018/978-1-5225-3704-5.ch004

van Wessel, R. M., de Vries, H. J., & Ribbers, P. M. (2016). Business Benefits through Company IT Standardization. In K. Jakobs (Ed.), *Effective Standardization Management in Corporate Settings* (pp. 34–53). Hershey, PA: IGI Global. doi:10.4018/978-1-4666-9737-9.ch003

Vargas-Hernández, J. G. (2017). Professional Integrity in Business Management Education. In N. Baporikar (Ed.), *Management Education for Global Leadership* (pp. 70–89). Hershey, PA: IGI Global. doi:10.4018/978-1-5225-1013-0.ch004

Vasista, T. G., & AlAbdullatif, A. M. (2017). Role of Electronic Customer Relationship Management in Demand Chain Management: A Predictive Analytic Approach. *International Journal of Information Systems and Supply Chain Management, 10*(1), 53–67. doi:10.4018/IJISSCM.2017010104

Vergidis, K. (2016). Rediscovering Business Processes: Definitions, Patterns, and Modelling Approaches. In P. Papajorgji, F. Pinet, A. Guimarães, & J. Papathanasiou (Eds.), *Automated Enterprise Systems for Maximizing Business Performance* (pp. 97–122). Hershey, PA: IGI Global. doi:10.4018/978-1-4666-8841-4.ch007

Vieru, D., & Bourdeau, S. (2017). Survival in the Digital Era: A Digital Competence-Based Multi-Case Study in the Canadian SME Clothing Industry. *International Journal of Social and Organizational Dynamics in IT*, *6*(1), 17–34. doi:10.4018/IJSODIT.2017010102

Vijayan, G., & Kamarulzaman, N. H. (2017). An Introduction to Sustainable Supply Chain Management and Business Implications. In M. Khan, M. Hussain, & M. Ajmal (Eds.), *Green Supply Chain Management for Sustainable Business Practice* (pp. 27–50). Hershey, PA: IGI Global. doi:10.4018/978-1-5225-0635-5.ch002

Vlachvei, A., & Notta, O. (2017). Firm Competitiveness: Theories, Evidence, and Measurement. In A. Vlachvei, O. Notta, K. Karantininis, & N. Tsounis (Eds.), *Factors Affecting Firm Competitiveness and Performance in the Modern Business World* (pp. 1–42). Hershey, PA: IGI Global. doi:10.4018/978-1-5225-0843-4.ch001

von Rosing, M., Fullington, N., & Walker, J. (2016). Using the Business Ontology and Enterprise Standards to Transform Three Leading Organizations. *International Journal of Conceptual Structures and Smart Applications*, *4*(1), 71–99. doi:10.4018/IJCSSA.2016010104

von Rosing, M., & von Scheel, H. (2016). Using the Business Ontology to Develop Enterprise Standards. *International Journal of Conceptual Structures and Smart Applications*, *4*(1), 48–70. doi:10.4018/IJCSSA.2016010103

Walczak, S. (2016). Artificial Neural Networks and other AI Applications for Business Management Decision Support. *International Journal of Sociotechnology and Knowledge Development*, *8*(4), 1–20. doi:10.4018/IJSKD.2016100101

Wamba, S. F., Akter, S., Kang, H., Bhattacharya, M., & Upal, M. (2016). The Primer of Social Media Analytics. *Journal of Organizational and End User Computing*, *28*(2), 1–12. doi:10.4018/JOEUC.2016040101

Wang, C., Schofield, M., Li, X., & Ou, X. (2017). Do Chinese Students in Public and Private Higher Education Institutes Perform at Different Level in One of the Leadership Skills: Critical Thinking?: An Exploratory Comparison. In V. Wang (Ed.), *Encyclopedia of Strategic Leadership and Management* (pp. 160–181). Hershey, PA: IGI Global. doi:10.4018/978-1-5225-1049-9.ch013

Wang, F., Raisinghani, M. S., Mora, M., & Wang, X. (2016). Strategic E-Business Management through a Balanced Scored Card Approach. In I. Lee (Ed.), *Encyclopedia of E-Commerce Development, Implementation, and Management* (pp. 361–386). Hershey, PA: IGI Global. doi:10.4018/978-1-4666-9787-4.ch027

Wang, J. (2017). Multi-Agent based Production Management Decision System Modelling for the Textile Enterprise. *Journal of Global Information Management, 25*(4), 1–15. doi:10.4018/JGIM.2017100101

Wiedemann, A., & Gewald, H. (2017). Examining Cross-Domain Alignment: The Correlation of Business Strategy, IT Management, and IT Business Value. *International Journal of IT/Business Alignment and Governance, 8*(1), 17–31. doi:10.4018/IJITBAG.2017010102

Wolf, R., & Thiel, M. (2018). Advancing Global Business Ethics in China: Reducing Poverty Through Human and Social Welfare. In S. Hipsher (Ed.), *Examining the Private Sector's Role in Wealth Creation and Poverty Reduction* (pp. 67–84). Hershey, PA: IGI Global. doi:10.4018/978-1-5225-3117-3.ch004

Wu, J., Ding, F., Xu, M., Mo, Z., & Jin, A. (2016). Investigating the Determinants of Decision-Making on Adoption of Public Cloud Computing in E-government. *Journal of Global Information Management, 24*(3), 71–89. doi:10.4018/JGIM.2016070104

Xu, L., & de Vrieze, P. (2016). Building Situational Applications for Virtual Enterprises. In I. Lee (Ed.), *Encyclopedia of E-Commerce Development, Implementation, and Management* (pp. 715–724). Hershey, PA: IGI Global. doi:10.4018/978-1-4666-9787-4.ch050

Yablonsky, S. (2018). Innovation Platforms: Data and Analytics Platforms. In *Multi-Sided Platforms (MSPs) and Sharing Strategies in the Digital Economy: Emerging Research and Opportunities* (pp. 72–95). Hershey, PA: IGI Global. doi:10.4018/978-1-5225-5457-8.ch003

Yusoff, A., Ahmad, N. H., & Halim, H. A. (2017). Agropreneurship among Gen Y in Malaysia: The Role of Academic Institutions. In N. Ahmad, T. Ramayah, H. Halim, & S. Rahman (Eds.), *Handbook of Research on Small and Medium Enterprises in Developing Countries* (pp. 23–47). Hershey, PA: IGI Global. doi:10.4018/978-1-5225-2165-5.ch002

Zanin, F., Comuzzi, E., & Costantini, A. (2018). The Effect of Business Strategy and Stock Market Listing on the Use of Risk Assessment Tools. In *Management Control Systems in Complex Settings: Emerging Research and Opportunities* (pp. 145–168). Hershey, PA: IGI Global. doi:10.4018/978-1-5225-3987-2.ch007

Zgheib, P. W. (2017). Corporate Innovation and Intrapreneurship in the Middle East. In P. Zgheib (Ed.), *Entrepreneurship and Business Innovation in the Middle East* (pp. 37–56). Hershey, PA: IGI Global. doi:10.4018/978-1-5225-2066-5.ch003

About the Contributors

Lynda Byrd-Poller earned her doctorate in Human and Organizational Learning from The George Washington University. She currently serves as the director of Human Resources, Strategic Planning & Professional Learning for Charles City County Public Schools and serves as an adjunct professor in GWU Organizational Leadership & Learning graduate studies. She has experience in education, leadership, organization sciences, and human resources development. Her research interests include organizational and adult learning, leadership, diversity and cultural studies as well as other areas of social science.

Valerie Ford earned her doctorate in human and organizational learning from The George Washington University in Washington, DC. Her research interests comprise a broad range of topics, including how data and information technology change behaviors and processes in organizations, understanding the changing nature of organizations, teams, crowds and markets in the 21st century, effectively using decision analytics and 'big data' to build collective intelligence, and fostering organizational creativity and innovation to generate new processes and products. Her experience in MIS has given her a keen awareness of the technology issues in corporate environments and she feels fortunate to experience and investigate technology in organizations as both a scholar and a practitioner.

Jennifer Farmer is Vice President, Global Diversity and Inclusion for Thermo Fisher Scientific. Jennifer leads Thermo Fisher's global diversity and inclusion strategy, working closely with company leaders and key stakeholders to advance the company's strategy and help embed diversity and inclusion into the business and organizational culture. She is focused on driving sustainable change, helping remove barriers to inclusion throughout the colleague lifecycle. Prior to joining Thermo Fisher, Jennifer was with Northrop Grumman Corporation, where she led global diversity and inclusion strategy for the Defense Systems and Space Systems businesses. Prior to that, Jennifer held roles in diversity and inclusion, talent strategy and finance at Pfizer; and finance and customer support roles at Bristol-Meyers Squibb. As an academic practitioner, Dr. Farmer's key research interests include: Diversity, Inclusion, Equity and Belonging, Leadership, Change Management, Organizational Culture and Organizational Trauma. Jennifer, a Florida native, has a Doctorate in Human and Organizational Learning from The George Washington University and a joint B.S.-M.B.A. degree from Florida Agricultural and Mechanical University (FAMU).

* * *

Pascal P. Barreau is a career educator who serves in his current role as Assistant Professor of Educational Leadership and Program Coordinator of Master of Education programs in the Department of Educational Leadership at Virginia State University. He brings to VSU over 25 years of educational and administrative experience at all levels of education between elementary, middle, high, postsecondary, and graduate level programs. Dr. Barreau's experiences have spanned across K-12 building administration, classroom teaching, higher education faculty-administration, and various roles within community non-profit agencies. His interested areas of study are Organizational Leadership, Structure, & Behavior; K-12 Administrative Preparation; K-12 to Higher Education student transition; and he is currently researching and writing about topics in K-12 and higher education leadership and diversity, equity and inclusion, (D.E.I.) in education. During his tenure at Virginia State University, he has presented at local, regional, and national conferences at Virginia State University, Virginia Education Association (VEA), University Council for Educational Administration (UCEA) and American Educational Studies Association (AESA). He has authored publications in the SAGE Journal of Cases in Educational Leadership (JCEL), SAGE Encyclopedia of Higher Education, and NASSP's Principal Leadership magazine. He aims to continue developing culturally responsive and equity-minded leaders in his work with VSU's aspiring and practicing leaders. Dr. Barreau earned a B.A. in Communications from the University of Virginia; an M.A. in Teaching, Early Childhood Education from Norfolk State University; and both his Licensure Certification in Pre-K12 Administration and Supervision and Ed.D. in Educational Policy, Planning & Leadership from the College of William and Mary. He currently resides with his family in Virginia.

Mike Brown, a native of New Jersey, has spent the last 20 years fighting for high quality education for students and families in urban settings. He earned his BA from Hampton University, Master's from Boston College, and his Doctorate from Vanderbilt in Educational Leadership & Policy. Mike's education journey began as a middle school teacher and eventually led him to the principalship. He served as a turnaround Principal, Chief Schools Officer managing a network of Principals, and currently helps high-impact education leaders launch innovative schools in underserved communities around the country as the Founder of EdRevolution.

Erin Burns is a principal with RBL and a member of the global management team. Her client work includes consulting in leadership development, organization design and transformation, and executive coaching. In her consulting, she partners with companies from a broad range of industries to find the best approaches to identify and develop tomorrow's leaders and to create organizations that are designed to effectively and efficiently get the right work done. In her executive coaching, she helps C-suite and senior executives achieve their goals and improve their leadership effectiveness. She brings subtle and powerful insights, empathy, and a pragmatic approach to help her clients grow personally and professionally. She is also Co-Faculty/Coach with Dave Ulrich at HR Learning Partnership and has worked closely with many of RBL's research initiatives, including the Top Companies for Leaders (with AonHewitt and Fortune) and the Human Resource Competency Study (with the University of Michigan). She has been responsible for the development of new products and methodologies at RBL and is the author of several articles and book chapters.

Camilla Ellehave is a principal with the RBL Group and partner in RBL Nordics. Her consulting work for clients and her research focuses on leading organizational and cultural transformations, as well as leadership, organizational and functional HR development that measurably impact company performance and market value. Before joining the RBL Group, Camilla spent almost 20 years in international leadership roles within HR and Organizational Transformation working for companies like A. P. Moller-Maersk and Novo Nordisk where she has worked in Denmark, Russia, Singapore, India, Japan, the Netherlands, and the Philippines. Camilla holds a Ph.D. in Organizational studies from Copenhagen Business School and was a Fulbright Scholar at the University of Massachusetts at Amherst. She is the author and editor of several articles, book chapters and books covering a range of themes within leadership and HR practices.

Letizia Gambrell-Boone earned her doctorate in Higher Education Administration from The George Washington University in 2002. A proud two-time alumna of Hampton University, she also began her career in higher education at her alma mater in 1992 and continued her career in a variety of student success and administrative positions. Her leadership experience has been largely in historically black colleges and universities, but also encompasses a public liberal arts college, private universities, and a university system. Before joining the senior leadership team at the Equal Employment Practices Commission in New York City, Dr. Gambrell-Boone was the vice president of student success and engagement at Virginia State University. She writes and presents on diversity and inclusion, authenticity, organizational culture, leadership, data analytics and student achievement.

David W. Gaston is the President and Chief Executive Officer of Gaston Educational Consulting, LLC, a Virginia-based educational consulting firm specializing in organizational dynamics and leadership training, strategic planning, curriculum and instruction support and private-public sector partnerships. Dr. Gaston's educational career allowed him to serve as a classroom teacher, elementary, middle, and high school assistant principal and principal and central office administrator with the York County School Division, Hampton City Schools, and Williamsburg-James City (WJCC) County Public Schools in Virginia for 24 years. He was named the Division Superintendent for Charles City Public Schools in Charles City, VA in 2014 and served the Charles City County community in this capacity until 2020, when he retired after 30 years of public service. Prior to assuming the Superintendency, Dr. Gaston served WJCC Public Schools as the Principal of James River Elementary School (2004-2007) and Berkeley Middle School (2004-2011). His leadership in WJCC Public Schools in their Central Office Administration saw him devote four years serving as the Senior Director for Student Services and the Senior Director for Accountability, Quality and Innovation. Prior to WJCC, he was as an elementary principal in Hampton City Schools. He began his educational career in York County, where he served as an elementary and high school assistant principal, an International Baccalaureate Diploma Programme Coordinator, central office administrator and history and social studies teacher. Dr. Gaston is an adjunct professor at the Darden School of Education at Old Dominion University, where he has facilitated undergraduate, graduate and doctoral level courses in Educational Leadership Studies and Teaching and Learning for the past 14 years. His work in education also extended to training and consulting with the International Baccalaureate of the Americas (IBA) for 18 years. As an IB-trained educator, he established the first and fifth elementary school Primary Years Programme (PYP) sites in Virginia. He has also worked with schools across the United States, Canada, the Caribbean, and Europe as an independent education consultant. He holds B.A, M.A.Ed., and Ed.D. degrees from The College of William and Mary in Williamsburg, VA and lives in Williamsburg, VA with his wife, Susan, and their two yellow labs, Mary and Morgan. Their oldest son, John, is a 1st Lieutenant in the United States Marine Corps and their youngest son, Henry, is a Project Manager with Guidehouse Consulting in Washington, DC.

Tamara Hawkins is a licensed Therapist and Researcher with the US Department of Veterans Affairs. She received a Doctorate in Counseling Psychology from the Florida School of Professional Psychology and earned a Master of Social Work Degree from the Florida State University. She has 21 years of mental health training and experience with specialties in the areas of Epidemiology, Trauma, Cyberpsychology, Telehealth, Psychiatry, University Teaching and Counseling, Children and Family Services, Domestic and Sexual Violence Advocacy, Corrections, Military Families and Diversity and Inclusion.

Maia K. Johnson is a student-centered educator who has worked as an Exceptional Education Teacher, School Counselor, School Counseling Coordinator and currently serves as the Coordinator of Equity, Diversity and Inclusion for Chesterfield County Public Schools, in Chesterfield County, Virginia. Having started her career in education teaching in an alternative setting that served many students who experienced traumatic stress, Dr. Johnson devotes much of her practice to raising awareness about adverse childhood experiences, the impact it has on the brain and how trauma-sensitive practices can be implemented as a universal support for students. Dr. Johnson's doctoral research examined teacher-perceptions of the effects of Trauma-Informed Care training. Dr. Johnson is an ACE-Interface Master Trainer and Certified Child and Adolescent Trauma Professional. She is also an active member of the Virginia Education Association's Community of Practice for Trauma-Informed Care. Dr. Johnson has presented at the local, state and national level, to raise awareness about the importance of connecting students with trauma-informed educators to promote educational outcomes and ramping-up schools to be trauma informed. She holds her degrees; B.A. in Communications, M.Ed. in Counselor Education with a concentration in School Counseling and Ed.D. in Educational Administration and Supervision, all from Virginia State University in Petersburg, Virginia. Dr. Johnson was recognized as the 2019 Middle School Counselor of the Year for Chesterfield County Public Schools. She and her husband reside in Chesterfield County, Virginia with their three young children.

Andrew Moffitt is a senior at Brigham Young University, majoring in psychology and minoring in statistics. He takes part in diversity-related issues as a member of the psychology department's Diversity and Inclusion Committee, where he focuses on improving the university's environment by educating others on sensitive issues of diversity. He also takes part in research as the lab manager of the Organizational Psychology and Societal Resilience Lab. He is interested in large-scale traumas and the corresponding sensemaking processes that either preclude or promote resilience and growth.

Kari O'Grady is a visiting associate professor and co-chair of diversity and inclusion in the psychology department at BYU. She is on the advisory board of BYU's Healthcare Leadership Collaborative. Dr. O'Grady is the President of the American Psychological Association Division 36, Psychology of Religion and Spirituality. She has served on the Council of Representatives on the Diversity and Inclusion Committee for the American Psychological Association. Dr. O'Grady is the founding director of the Center for Resilience Leadership which focuses on the reduction of human suffering through the study of resilience processes at the individual, team, organizational and societal levels. She has written several books, articles and book chapters and presented at national and international professional conferences on the topics of resilience leadership processes and multiculturalism. Dr. O'Grady and her doctoral students have researched the psychological, social, and spiritual processes involved in resilience following extreme trauma throughout the world including DR Congo, Haiti, Liberia, Mexico, The Netherlands, Afghanistan, China, and the United States.

Aurelia Ortiz has been described as a courageous and intentional servant leader; one who has led school transformation work for nearly two decades. Prior to joining the Virginia Department of Education as Director of School Quality, Dr. Ortiz served in rural and suburban educational settings at all levels between elementary and high school. Her touted professional experiences combined with her dissertation research focused on the coping mechanisms of teachers who have experienced trauma in high needs schools have positioned her as an educator and expert deeply grounded in trauma-informed care practice. Dr. Ortiz has delivered and facilitated professional development at the school building, school division, regional and national levels. Key highlights of her school transformation work include publishing with the Virginia Journal of Education on the topic of student motivation; and presentations with the Virginia Department of Education (VDOE); Association for Middle Level Educators (AMLE); Virginia State University Summer Institute on Innovation; and National Association of Secondary School Principals (NASSP), as a panelist for a session specifically titled: Ramping Up Your School to Respond to Mass Trauma. She was recognized and lauded for her turnaround work as a Principal with Chesterfield County School Division in Virginia and was featured in the 2020 NASSP article titled: A Success Story, Effective School Turnaround. Dr. Ortiz holds an Ed.D. in Educational Leadership from Virginia State University, VA; an M.Ed. in School Administration and Secondary English from Columbus State University, GA; and a B.A. in Communications from the University of Texas – Arlington, TX. She currently resides in Virginia with her family.

J. Douglas Orton is the co-founder, research director, and professor of management for the Center for Resilience Leadership – an internationally focused, doctoral-level, nature-grounded, and extreme-context research organization striving to reduce human suffering through executive resilience leadership expeditions on the U.S. Great Western Trail between Yarnell Hill, Arizona, and Mann Gulch, Montana. Before crafting his current position in 2006, Dr. Orton pursued a traditional academic path through Brigham Young University, University of Texas at Austin, University of Michigan, Boston College, HEC Paris, MIT, University of Nevada Las Vegas, University of California Irvine, and Michigan Technological University -- always focused on the elaboration of Dr. Karl E. Weick's cosmology episode studies into a coherent theory of resilience leadership skills. In Washington, DC, from 2006-2016, Dr. Orton worked with Dr. Kari A. O'Grady on the identification of righteous resilience leadership solutions to numerous cosmology episode wicked problems: Human Terrain Teams deployed to Afghanistan in 2007, U.S. national security reform in 2008, the Haiti earthquake in 2010, diverse catastrophes in China in 2014, the killing of Michael Brown in Ferguson, Missouri, in 2014, women experiencing extreme sexual violence in the eastern D. R. Congo in 2015, sexual abuse at U.S. faith-based universities in 2017, and vaccine hesitancy in faith communities of color in 2020.

Cynthia C. Rhone is a retired school division administrator after serving 32 years within two divisions. She taught fifth and sixth grades for 17 years. She has held positions such as Middle School Coordinator, Middle School Assistant Principal and Middle School Principal. She also was principal at The Center for Educational Opportunities, an alternative educational program for students in the division. Before retiring, Dr. Rhone was the division's Disciplinary School Hearing Officer. After leaving the school division, Dr. Rhone became a teacher for five years in a Day and Evening Supervision Program in a local city, which serviced students who had been long-term suspended or expelled from their regular school and some were associated with the judicial system. Therefore, Dr. Rhone has served a total of 37 years in education. Dr. Rhone received her Doctorate of Educational Leadership Degree with an emphasis in Curriculum and Instruction from the University of Phoenix in 2015. As a result of her passion for children, her dissertation was entitled Scholastic Success after Attending a Disciplinary Alternative Education Program: A Qualitative Phenomenological Hermeneutic Study. Dr. Rhone has also presented at workshops and conferences.

Canute Thompson, PhD; CMC Canute Thompson is Senior Lecturer in Educational Policy, Planning, and Leadership and Head of the Caribbean Centre for Educational Planning at the University of the West Indies, Mona Campus. A social activist, he is a co-founder of the Caribbean Leadership Re-Imagination Initiative and the author of six books, the most recent of which are: Education and Development: Policy Priorities for Jamaica and the Caribbean (2020); Reimagining Educational Leadership in the Caribbean (2019); Reflections on Leadership and Governance in Jamaica: Towards a Better Society (2018); and Locating the Epicentre of Effective Educational Leadership in the 21st Century (2015).

Dave Ulrich is the Rensis Likert Professor at the Ross School of Business, University of Michigan and a partner at the RBL Group (http://www.rbl.net) a consulting firm focused on helping organizations and leaders deliver value. He has published over 200 articles and book chapters and over 30 books. He edited Human Resource Management 1990-1999, served on editorial board of 4 Journal and on the Board of Directors for Herman Miller (16 years), has spoken to large audiences in 90 countries; performed workshops for over half of the Fortune 200; coached successful business leaders, and is a Distinguished Fellow in the National Academy of Human Resources. He is known for continually learning, turning complex ideas into simple solutions, and creating real value to those he works with in three fields: organization, leadership, and HR.

Denelle Wallace received a Ph.D. in Urban Services with a concentration in Academic Leadership from Old Dominion University, a M.Ed. in School Counseling from Georgia State University, and a B.S. in Elementary Education from Old Dominion University. Her current research focus involves diversifying the school counseling and teaching populations, culturally competent school environments, academic equity and access, culturally relevant instructional delivery and classroom management methods, effective leadership in public school reform and program assessment for positive change. For the last 5 years, she has focused on diversifying the teacher population and providing the support needed for candidate success on teacher licensure examinations as the Future Teacher Academy Director. She has served as a member of a number of program and school accreditation teams over the last 17 years at the school district, university, and state level. Currently, she is the Interim Dean and CAEP Coordinator for the School of Education at Norfolk State University.

Ann-Marie Wilmot, EdD, is currently a Principal Lecturer and Head of the School of Languages and Literatures at Church Teachers' College, Jamaica. She is a graduate of Mico Teachers' College with a diploma in English and History, The University of the West Indies, Mona – with a first-class honours Bachelor of Education in English Language Education, a Master of Arts in English (literature), and Temple University with a Doctorate in Educational Leadership, K-13. Dr. Wilmot has 25 years of teaching experience, 15 of which were gained at her current institution, specializing in teacher training. She has extensive experience in teaching several genres of literature and English language and developed expertise in teaching grammar and communication-related courses as well as various types of writing. She also has teaching experience in educational leadership up to the doctoral level, has developed and presented leadership interventions for staff and students and in community high and primary schools. Her main research interests are in leading collaboration for learning, heads of department leadership for teacher development and improved student outcomes, education for sustainable development, strategic planning, and instructional leadership. She is a spoken word poet and author of several other publications in the areas of leadership and English Literature.

Index

M

N

O

P

Q

R

S

T

V

W

www.ingramcontent.com/pod-product-compliance
Lightning Source LLC
LaVergne TN
LVHW080525300926
849162LV00007B/1534